MONITORING BIRD POPULATIONS USING MIST NETS

C. John Ralph and Erica H. Dunn, Editors

Studies in Avian Biology No. 29

A PUBLICATION OF THE COOPER ORNITHOLOGICAL SOCIETY

Cover illustration: the life cycle of a Western Tanager (*Piranga ludoviciana*) shown through capture
and banding. Original by Keith Hanson, redrawn by Gary Bloomfield.

STUDIES IN AVIAN BIOLOGY

Edited by

John T. Rotenberry
Department of Biology
University of California
Riverside, CA 92521

Studies in Avian Biology is a series of works too long for *The Condor*, published at irregular intervals by the Cooper Ornithological Society. Manuscripts for consideration should be submitted to the editor. Style and format should follow those of previous issues.

Price $23.00 including postage and handling. All orders cash in advance; make checks payable to Cooper Ornithological Society. Send orders to Cooper Ornithological Society, *c/o* Western Foundation of Vertebrate Zoology, 439 Calle San Pablo, Camarillo, CA 93010.

ISBN: 0-943610-61-3

Library of Congress Control Number: 2004111015
Printed at Cadmus Professional Communications, Ephrata, Pennsylvania 17522
Issued: 8 December 2004

CONTENTS

LIST OF AUTHORS

RAYMOND J. ADAMS
Kalamazoo Nature Center
7000 N. Westnedge Avenue
Kalamazoo, MI 49004

WAYNE J. ARENDT
International Institute of Tropical Forestry
U.S.D.A. Forest Service
P.O. Box 490
Palmer, PR 00721

STEPHEN R BAILLIE
British Trust for Ornithology
The Nunnery
Thetford, Norfolk, IP24 2PU, UK

GRANT BALLARD
PRBO Conservation Science
4990 Shoreline Highway
Stinson Beach, CA 94970

PETER BERTHOLD
Max Planck Research Center for Ornithology
Vogelwarte Radolfzell, Schlossallee 2
78315 Radolfzell-Möggingen, Germany

NICHOLAS BROKAW
Institute for Tropical Ecosystem Studies
University of Puerto Rico
P.O. Box 23341
San Juan, PR 00931-3341

STEPHEN T. BUCKLAND
Mathematical Institute
University of St. Andrews
North Haugh, St. Andrews
Fife, KY16 9SS, UK

KENNETH M. BURTON
The Institute for Bird Populations
P.O. Box 1346
Point Reyes Station, CA 94956-1346
(Current address: P.O. Box 716, Inverness, CA 94937)

BRENDA C. DALE
Canadian Wildlife Service
200 - 4999 98th Avenue
Edmonton, Alberta, T6B 2X3

DAVID F. DESANTE
The Institute for Bird Populations
P.O. Box 1346
Point Reyes Station, CA 94956-1346

CHRIS R. DU FEU
66 High Street
Beckingham, Nottinghamshire, DN10 4PF, UK

KATIE M. DUGGER
Oregon Cooperative Fish & Wildlife Research Unit
Oregon State University
104 Nash Hall
Corvallis, OR 97331-3803

ERICA H. DUNN
Canadian Wildlife Service
National Wildlife Research Centre
Carleton University
Ottawa, Ontario K1A 0H3

JOHN FAABORG
Division of Biological Sciences
University of Missouri-Columbia
Columbia, MO 65211-7400

STEVEN D. FACCIO
Vermont Institute of Natural Science
27023 Church Hill Road
Woodstock, VT 05091

CHARLES M. FRANCIS
Bird Studies Canada
P.O. Box 160
Port Rowan, Ontario, N0E 1M0
(Current address: Canadian Wildlife Service
  National Wildlife Research Centre, Carleton University
  Ottawa, Ontario K1A 0H3)

SIDNEY A. GAUTHREAUX
Department of Biological Sciences
Clemson University
Clemson, SC 29634

GEOFFREY R. GEUPEL
PRBO Conservation Science
4990 Shoreline Highway
Stinson Beach, CA 94970

JOHN M. HAGAN, III
Manomet Center for Conservation Sciences
14 Maine Street, Suite 404
Brunswick, ME 04011

COLLEEN M. HANDEL
U.S.G.S. Alaska Science Center
1011 E. Tudor Road
Anchorage, AK 99503-6119

STEVEN C. HESS
U.S.G.S. Pacific Islands Ecosystems Research Center
Kilauea Field Station
P. O. Box 44
Hawai`i National Park, HI 96718

JAMES E. HINES
U.S.G.S. Patuxent Wildlife Research Center
12100 Beech Forest Road
Laurel, MD 20708-4039

KIMBERLY HOLLINGER
U.S.D.A. Forest Service
Redwood Sciences Laboratory
1700 Bayview Drive
Arcata, CA 95521

DAVID J. T. HUSSELL
Wildlife Research and Development Section
Ontario Ministry of Natural Resources
300 Water Street
Peterborough, Ontario K9J 8M5

ANDREAS KAISER
Max Planck Research Center for Ornithology
Vogelwarte Radolfzell, Schlossallee 2
78315 Radolfzell-Möggingen, Germany

WILLIAM L. KENDALL
U.S.G.S. Patuxent Wildlife Research Center
12100 Beech Forest Road
Laurel, MD 20708-4039

WILLIAM A. LINK
U.S.G.S. Patuxent Wildlife Research Center
12100 Beech Forest Road
Laurel, MD 20708-4039

TREVOR L. LLOYD-EVANS
Manomet Center for Conservation Sciences
P.O. Box 1770
Manomet, MA 02345

ELIZABETH P. MALLORY
Manomet Center for Conservation Sciences
P.O. Box 1770
Manomet, MA 02345

JON D. MCCRACKEN
Bird Studies Canada
P.O. Box 160
Port Rowan, Ontario, N0E 1M0

JOHN M. MCMEEKING
The Whimbrels, Goverton
Bleasby, Nottingham, NG14 7FN, UK

SHERRI L. MILLER
U.S.D.A. Forest Service
Redwood Sciences Laboratory
1700 Bayview Drive
Arcata, CA 95521

FRANK R. MOORE
Department of Biological Sciences
University of Southern Mississippi
Hattiesburg, MS 39406

NADAV NUR
PRBO Conservation Science
4990 Shoreline Highway
Stinson Beach, CA 94970

JAMES D. NICHOLS
U.S.G.S. Patuxent Wildlife Research Center
12100 Beech Forest Road
Laurel, MD 20708-4039

DANIELLE R. O'GRADY
The Institute for Bird Populations

P.O. Box 1346
Point Reyes Station, CA 94956-1346

WILL J. PEACH
British Trust for Ornithology
The Nunnery
Thetford, Norfolk, IP24 2PU, UK
(Current address: Royal Society for the Protection of Birds
The Lodge, Sandy, Bedfordshire, SG19 2DL, UK)

ROGER PRADEL
CEFE CNRS
1919 Route de Mende
34 293 Montpellier cedex 5, France

C. JOHN RALPH
U.S.D.A. Forest Service
Redwood Sciences Laboratory
1700 Bayview Drive
Arcata, CA 95521

CHRISTOPHER C. RIMMER
Vermont Institute of Natural Science
27023 Church Hill Road
Woodstock, VT 05091

JAMES F. SARACCO
The Institute for Bird Populations
P.O. Box 1346
Point Reyes Station, CA 94956-1346

JOHN R. SAUER
U.S.G.S. Patuxent Wildlife Research Center
12100 Beech Forest Road
Laurel, MD 20708-4039

THEODORE R. SIMONS
U.S.G.S. North Carolina Cooperative Research Unit
Department of Zoology
North Carolina State University
Raleigh, NC 27695

LEN THOMAS
Centre for Applied Conservation Biology
Faculty of Forestry
University of British Columbia
Vancouver, British Columbia, V6T 1Z4
(Current address: Centre for Research into Ecological
and Environmental Modelling, The Observatory
University of St Andrews, Scotland KY16 9LZ)

BRETT L. WALKER
The Institute for Bird Populations
P.O. Box 1346
Point Reyes Station, CA 94956-1346
(Current address: Department of Ecosystem
Conservation Science, University of Montana,
Missoula, MT 59812)

ANDREW A. WHITMAN
Manomet Center for Conservation Sciences
14 Maine Street, Suite 404
Brunswick, ME 04011

PREFACE

Mist nets were introduced to North America about mid-way through the 20th century. In the decades since then, they have become a widely adopted and indispensable bird-capturing tool for the scientific study of birds. At first, mist nets were an inventory tool, allowing in-hand comparison of species previously scrutinized only over the barrel of a shotgun, but in the early 1970s, netting began to be used for monitoring population trends and demographic composition. Early users had to develop protocols for mist netting based on their own experience. Some 30 years later, there has still been relatively little evaluation to determine the effect of different mist netting methods (or of extrinsic factors) on the numbers and kinds of birds that are captured, and the degree to which demography of captured birds represents true population characteristics.

Recognizing the need for greater evaluation of mist-netting and the need for standards on the use of this technique, a workshop was held in October 1993 entitled "The use of mist nets to monitor bird populations." The workshop took place at the Marconi Conference Center on the shores of Tomales Bay, California, and was sponsored by the Point Reyes Bird Observatory, U.S. Forest Service, U.S. Fish and Wildlife Service, Canadian Wildlife Service, and the Institute for Bird Populations.

The objectives of the workshop were to examine the strengths and weaknesses of mist-netting for a variety of population monitoring purposes, with a primary focus on passerines, and to develop recommendations on the best methods for using mist nets as a population monitoring tool. The conference attracted 40 participants from Canada, Costa Rica, Germany, Great Britain, and France, as well as from all across the United States. The majority of papers presented at the workshop are included in this volume, as well as several prepared as follow-up. During intensive breakout sessions, all participants reached consensus on recommended standards, reflected in the final chapter of this volume, "Recommendations for the use of mist nets for inventory and monitoring of bird populations." All manuscripts underwent extensive peer review as well as review by editors. During this process, delays made it possible for a reevaluation of all the manuscripts. All the authors enthusiastically participated in this process, and as a result many new data were brought forward, and updated analyses were incorporated into manuscripts during 2001–2003. As well, several new manuscripts were submitted that were not presented at the workshop. The co-editors completed the final editing in late 2003.

Both the manuscripts and the recommended standards for mist netting were greatly improved by comments from authors of all the papers in this volume, as well as from Bob Altman, Doug Barnum, Jeffrey Brawn, Deanna Dawson, Sam Droege, Joseph Engler, Denise Hardesty, Daniel Hernandez, Jane Hicks, Stephanie Jones, Joe Kaplan, James Karr, Martin McNicholl, Bill McShea, Rhonda Millikin, Nicolle Mode, Bert Murray, Glenn Olsen, Peter Pyle, John Rappole, Dan Reinking, W. John Richardson, Christian Vansteenwegen, Dennis Vroman, George Wallace, and Richard Weisbrod. The editors are also indebted to Linda Long for her dedicated and extensive work as editorial assistant, to John Rotenberry for his help in finalizing this volume, and to Keith Hanson for the very topical artwork that appears on its cover (redrawn by Gary Bloomfield). Finally, we thank the Canadian Wildlife Service, Institute for Bird Populations, Point Reyes Bird Observatory, U.S. Fish and Wildlife Service, and U.S. Forest Service for their contributions to the costs of the workshop and publication.

C. John Ralph
Erica H. Dunn

Studies in Avian Biology No. 29:1–6

USE OF MIST NETS AS A TOOL FOR BIRD POPULATION MONITORING

ERICA H. DUNN AND C. JOHN RALPH

Abstract. Mist nets are an important tool for population monitoring, here defined as assessment of species composition, relative abundance, population size, and demography. We review the strengths and limitations of mist netting for monitoring purposes, based on papers in this volume and other literature. Advantages of using mist nets over aural or visual count methods include ease of standardized sampling, low observer bias, ability to detect species that are often missed using other count methods, and opportunity to examine birds in the hand (providing information on condition, age, sex, and capture history). The primary limitation of mist netting, in common with most other survey methods, is from potential bias in sampling. However, there are many approaches to reducing or adjusting for bias, including standardization of netting methods, combining mist-net sampling with other survey types, and using mark–recapture techniques. Mist netting is an essential tool for species inventory, provides useful indices of relative abundance, and can be used to track temporal trends in abundance. It is also one of the most efficient methods of capture for mark–recapture studies.

Key Words: mark–recapture, mist net, population monitoring, sampling bias.

Mist netting is an important technique for population monitoring, helping to assess species composition, relative abundance, population size, and demography (productivity and survival). Whereas mist netting is time intensive and requires specialized training, it has certain advantages over visual and aural population monitoring techniques. Mist nets can sample species that are poorly detected by other means, counts are not subject to observer bias, netting effort is easily standardized, and each bird counted can also be examined in the hand. Capture allows birds to be aged, sexed, and marked to allow individual identification in future encounters. In addition, extra data can be collected that also contribute to population studies, such as breeding status or sub-species identification. Data can be collected for other research purposes at the same time (e.g., physiological state, molt, parasite loads, DNA sampling). Because mist netting is one of the most efficient means of capturing many bird species, especially those that are insectivorous, the technique is often used in mark–recapture studies.

In this paper, we discuss the strengths and limitations of mist netting for population monitoring applications, and summarize the literature in which population parameters based on mist-net captures were evaluated by comparing them with data from independent data sources. In addition, we review the main sources of potential bias in population indices based on numbers of birds captured, and discuss some ways to address such bias. Ralph et al. (*this volume a*) should be regarded as a companion paper to this one, because it recommends best practices in mist netting, accompanied by the reasons why recommended procedures will improve monitoring capability.

SPECIES COMPOSITION

Mist netting is often used as a tool to determine what species are present in a study area. The technique is a valuable component of species inventory because it detects more cryptic, ground-foraging, and non-singing birds than aural or visual surveys (Blake and Loiselle 2001, Rappole et al. 1993, 1998, Wallace et al. 1996, Whitman et al. 1997). Further, results are relatively unaffected by the bird identification skills of observers (Karr 1981a; although misidentification may still occur, Dale *this volume*). However, netting is often a less efficient means of species inventory than censuses such as point counts, in terms of species detected per unit effort (Ralph et al. 1995, Gram and Faaborg 1997, Whitman et al. 1997). Moreover, netting is known to under-sample or completely miss some species (such as aerial foraging swallows, or raptors), regardless of season (Wang and Finch 2002). As a result, most authors have recommended that mist netting be used as a supplement to visual or aural surveys when a species inventory is being prepared, rather than as a sole source of data (Faaborg et al. *this volume*, Whitman *this volume*). Kendall et al. (*this volume*) provide information on using mark–recapture techniques to estimate the total species present, even though only a proportion has been detected.

RELATIVE ABUNDANCE AND TRENDS

Mist-netting studies are commonly used to document differences in abundance indices among species, locations, years, or age classes (see next section), and to detect trends in population indices over the long term. No matter what count methods are used to obtain abundance indices, the proportion of the true population that is counted will likely vary over time and space, introducing bias, which we discuss below. Nonetheless, evaluation studies have shown that abundance indices derived from mist-net sampling often compare well to independent data on the parameters of interest.

For example, species rankings based on relative abundance in breeding season mist-net samples were usually correlated with abundance rankings based on point counts at the same locations (Table 1), although individual species' rankings sometimes differed markedly between count types (DeSante et al. *this volume*, Kaiser and Berthold *this volume*). Similar studies in wintering areas gave mixed results, in that agreement of species' rankings between methods was quite good for some data sets (e.g., Wallace et al. 1996 *this volume*), but very poor in others (Blake and Loiselle 2001). Faaborg et al. (*this volume*) found good correspondence for year-round residents but very little for wintering species, and Lynch (1989) found that level of correspondence differed among habitats. In the migration season, birds are perhaps less selective of specific habitat types (Moore et al. 1995). For example, Wang and Finch (2002) found good correspondence between mist-net and point-count abundance rankings of species during migration in all habitats studied.

Within species, annual abundance indices have been shown to fluctuate in parallel with indices based on other data sources (Table 1). Repeated mist netting throughout the breeding season gave indices that paralleled abundance data derived from spot mapping, in 3 of 4 species studied by Silkey et al. (1999, from a single netting station) and in 9 of 21 species studied by Peach et al. (*this volume*, pooling data from many locations). No comparable studies have been conducted during the wintering season. For the migration season, Dunn et al. (*this volume a*) showed that annual abundance indices based on daily mist-net samples were strongly correlated with indices based on a standardized daily census in 73% of 64 species.

Several comparisons have been made between long-term trends in abundance indices based on netting data and trends from independent sources (Table 1). Pooled data from constant-effort mist netting at many locations during the breeding season corresponded with regional population trends based on spot mapping in 15 of 21 species (Peach et al. 1998, *this volume*). Trends in numbers of migrants captured were often correlated with Breeding Bird Survey trends from regions to the north where the migrants were assumed to have originated (Hagan et al. 1992, Dunn and Hussell 1995, Dunn et al. 1997, Francis and Hussell 1998, Berthold *this volume*, Rimmer et al. *this volume*). Correlations were strongest when statistical techniques were used that compensated for variation in daily bird numbers caused by weather and date in the season, and precision of long-term trends has been shown to improve when netting at a single station is more frequent (Thomas et al. *this volume*). However, as noted by Rimmer et al. (*this volume*), birds from diverse portions of the breeding range are typically sampled at a single location, making direct comparisons between mist-net capture rates and Breeding Bird Survey trends difficult.

DEMOGRAPHIC MONITORING

Monitoring of productivity is a special case of abundance monitoring, in which abundance of adult and young birds is assessed separately. Because capture probabilities differ between age classes (Ballard et al. *this volume*, Burton and DeSante *this volume*, Nur et al. *this volume*), the relative proportions of young to adults cannot be regarded as absolute measures of the number of young produced per adult, but rather are indices of productivity (Bart et al. 1999). Productivity indices from constant-effort mist netting in the breeding season have been compared to the numbers of nestlings found during intensive nest monitoring (Table 1). In some, but not all species, these estimates fluctuated in parallel between years (Nur and Geupel 1993b, du Feu and McMeeking *this volume*). Discrepancies may have resulted from post-fledging dispersal of young (e.g., Anders et al. 1998, Vega Rivera et al. 1998), so that mist-net samples represented local productivity in some species and regional productivity in others. Differences in mist-net based productivity indices among stations within a region (as found by Ralph et al. *this volume b*) could therefore result from true differences in local productivity, or from post-fledging redistribution of birds. Therefore, unless pilot work has demonstrated that productivity indices from mist netting accurately reflect local productivity in the target species, site-specific indices of productivity based on mist netting should at least be augmented by intensive nest monitoring (e.g., Gates and Gysel 1978, Roth and Johnson 1993).

In contrast, it has been demonstrated that collecting data from multiple netting stations is a good means of tracking regional productivity (Bart et al. 1999; Table 1). Cooperative programs that pool data from constant-effort sampling at many mist-net stations in a region include MAPS (Monitoring Avian Productivity and Survivorship; DeSante et al. *this volume*), the British Trust for Ornithology's

TABLE 1. COMPARISON OF POPULATION DATA COLLECTED BY MIST NETTING WITH DATA FROM INDEPENDENT SOURCES

Parameter	Season	Source of data for comparison	Correspondence of parameter between data sets	Source
Relative abundance of species	Breeding	Point counts	Correlated at 34 of 37 locations	DeSante et al. *this volume*, Kaiser and Berthold *this volume*
	Winter	Point counts	Roughly correlated in some data sets; not in others	Lynch 1989, Wallace et al. 1996, Blake and Loiselle 2001, Faaborg et al. *this volume*
	Migration	Point counts	Correlated in all habitats	Wang and Finch 2002
Annual abundance indices for individual species	Breeding	Spot mapping	Often correlated, but not in all species	Silkey et al. 1999, Peach et al. *this volume*
	Migration	Transect	Correlated in 73% of 64 species	Dunn et al. *this volume a*
Daily abundance indices	Migration	Point counts	Corresponded only roughly	Simons et al. *this volume*
	Migration	Radar	Corresponded only roughly	Simons et al. *this volume*
Population trends	Breeding	Spot mapping	Corresponded in 15 of 21 species	Peach et al. 1998, *this volume*
	Migration	Spot mapping	Often corresponded	Berthold *this volume*
	Migration	Breeding Bird Survey	Often corresponded	Hagan et al. 1992, Dunn and Hussell 1995, Dunn et al. 1997, Francis and Hussell 1998, Rimmer et al. *this volume*
Local productivity	Breeding	Nest monitoring	Corresponded in 4 of 4 species	du Feu and McMeeking *this volume*
	Breeding	Nest monitoring	Corresponded in 1 of 2 species	Nur and Geupel 1993b
Regional productivity	Breeding	Nest monitoring	Corresponded in 1 of 2 species	Nur and Geupel 1993b
	Breeding	Population model[a]	Corresponded (1 species studied)	Bart et al. 1999
Survivorship	Breeding	Resighting	Corresponded (1 species studied)	Nur et al. *this volume*
	Breeding	Band recoveries	Corresponded roughly (5 species studied)	Peach and Baillie *this volume*
	Breeding	Correlation with causal factor	Several examples	Peach et al. 1991, 1999
Sex ratio		Shooting	No correspondence (2 species)	Mawson 2000
Capture rate	Breeding	Other trap types	Does not always correspond	Bauchau and Van Noordwijk 1995, Collister and Fisher 1995

[a] A model containing results from annual range-wide counts and annual survival rates was used to estimate range-wide productivity in Kirtland's Warbler (*Dendroica kirtlandii*).

CES Scheme (Constant Effort Sites; Peach et al. *this volume*), the German MRI Program (Mettnau-Reit-Illmitz-Program; Kaiser and Berthold *this volume*), and the STOC program in France (Suivi Temporel du niveau d'abundance des populations d'Oiseaux terrestres Communs; Vansteenwegen et al. 1990). An evaluation of CES productivity indices (Peach et al. 1996) showed that although there was variation in capture rates and age proportions among locations, annual changes in age proportions at individual stations were similar in direction and magnitude across habitats and regions (Peach et al. 1996). Productivity indices based on pooled data also were similar among a cluster of stations in California (Ralph et al. *this volume b*), and pooled data from CES stations had acceptably low standard errors (Peach et al. *this volume*).

Migration data also may be useful for tracking regional productivity, as represented by the proportion of young birds in fall mist-net samples. However, this hypothesis has been little tested (Hussell *this volume*). It will be difficult to validate productivity indices that are based on capture of fall migrants, because independent productivity data from the breeding grounds will rarely be available (because breeding locations are unknown or unstudied). Nonetheless, some approaches to evaluation have been suggested for future research (Dunn et al. *this volume b*).

MAPS, CES, and the other cooperative demographic monitoring programs mentioned above are designed to collect information not only on productivity, but also on apparent survival rates. Whereas survival rates could be estimated for any season in which birds are site faithful and relatively sedentary, these cooperative studies estimate annual survival between breeding seasons. Average survival can also be estimated for individual netting stations, although sample sizes are usually too low to document annual differences (Faaborg and Arendt 1995, Hilton and Miller 2003).

There are fewer validation studies of survivorship estimates than of productivity indices, because independent estimates of survivorship are harder to obtain. Nur et al. (*this volume*) showed that survivorship of one species estimated from mist-net recaptures was similar to estimates based on resighting of marked individuals. Peach and Baillie (*this volume*) found that across five species, there was an overall (but non-significant) relationship between survivorship estimates based on CES and those based on band recoveries. Survival rates from CES were lower, probably because birds that emigrate from a station cannot be distinguished from birds that die, but the authors presented cogent arguments supporting the usefulness of CES estimates as indices of survival. There have also been several studies showing that change in annual survival rates was correlated with events likely to have had a strong effect on mortality (Peach et al. 1991, 1999).

POTENTIAL BIAS IN MIST-NET SAMPLES

As with bird counts obtained through visual and aural surveys, the numbers of birds captured in mist nets are indices of abundance, rather than total counts. Use of standardized, constant effort protocols will reduce variation in capture rates caused by uneven effort or net avoidance (Ralph et al. *this volume a*). However, even completely standardized operations capture only a proportion of all birds present, and that proportion will vary with species, habitat, weather, and other factors unrelated to true population size. Sauer and Link (*this volume*) showed that capturing different proportions of the true population could lead to false conclusions in comparison of samples, so it is important to investigate the potential for bias and to estimate its magnitude.

Capture rates at all seasons are affected by a multitude of factors, including distribution of nets with respect to territory size (Remsen and Good 1996, Ballard et al. *this volume*, Nur et al. *this volume*), mesh size of nets (Heimerdinger and Leberman 1966, Pardieck and Waide 1992, Jenni et al. 1996), season (Pagen et al. 2002), species (Jenni et al. 1996, Wang and Finch 2002), age class (Ballard et al. *this volume*, Burton and DeSante *this volume*, Nur et al. *this volume*), factors affecting movement rates (e.g., whether birds are incubating or molting), activity height (Remsen and Good 1996), and vegetation and habitat structure (Pagen et al. 2002, Ballard et al. *this volume*, Kaiser and Berthold *this volume*, Mallory et al. *this volume*, Whitman *this volume*).

Capture rates of migrants are also affected by most of these factors. Weather has a particularly strong effect on migrant numbers, because it influences rate of daily influx and departure from a location, and weather effects may be especially marked at stations near the edges of migration routes (Simons et al. *this volume*). In addition, during migration there will be daily variation in the proportion of birds migrating past the study site that actually stop there (Dunn and Hussell 1995). Migrating birds may be less selective of habitat during migration than are breeding birds, however, so habitat biases may be lower during migration than in other seasons.

After a review of sources of bias in mist-net captures, Remsen and Good (1996) concluded that unadjusted capture rates should not be used in quantitative comparisons of relative abundance, either among species, or within species among habitats. On the other hand, there is much evidence that a strong signal can be obtained from standardized index counts (Table 1). Whereas descriptive, non-qualitative results alone can be useful for land managers (e.g., Humple and Geupel 2002), information on relative abundance can add a great deal of value, particularly when conclusions are tempered by explicit discussion of the potential for bias and its possible magnitude. Moreover, long-term trend monitoring will not be compromised by the fact that numbers captured are only a proportion of true population size, as long as there are no temporal trends in the capture proportions themselves. In most studies such stability is assumed rather than directly tested, but Dugger et al. (2000) found that capture proportions in a neotropical study area remained relatively stable over time within species and locations. However, relatively small changes in a species' mean peak of activity can have a large effect on capture rates (Remsen and Good 1996). Long-term habitat change is the most likely source of systematic bias in long-term trends based on mist netting (Ralph et al. *this volume a*), and such change may be difficult to prevent even with regular management of the vegetation (Kaiser and Berthold *this volume*).

Mark–recapture methods can help to reduce the potential for bias caused by variation in capture proportions among mist-net samples (Sauer and Link *this volume*). Mark–recapture modeling estimates the proportion of all birds that is actually captured, which can then be used to estimate total population size (e.g., Kaiser and Bauer 1994, Kaiser and Berthold *this volume*). Peach and Baillie (*this volume*) and Kendall et al. (*this volume*) provided background on the uses of mark–recapture for this purpose, as well as for estimating adult survival, recruitment, and proportion of transients in a sample. The technique may have more limited value for migration studies, because the high rate of turnover in the birds present at a study location precludes using recapture rates to estimate population size. It should be noted that capture–recapture estimates of population size and capture probability are model-based, and the assumptions associated with any model must be considered when interpreting results.

Another means of addressing biases that may exist in mist-net samples is to adjust numbers of birds captured according to independent data on abundance. Although no count methods are completely problem-free, a few techniques have been developed that produce relatively unbiased estimates

of density (Buckland et al. 2001, Bart and Earnst 2002, Thompson 2002). These methods can be used in combination with mist-netting studies to evaluate the presence and potential magnitude of bias in the mist-net samples. Once capture proportions have been quantified, the density estimation data can be used to adjust the mist-net samples during analysis.

FUTURE RESEARCH

The strengths and limitations of mist netting for population monitoring have received considerable attention in recent decades, but much remains to be learned. We suggest the following topics as priorities for research:

• The factors affecting the proportion of the true population captured need to be better quantified in a wider variety of species. In particular, more work is needed on effects of vegetation structure, habitat, and net avoidance.

• For programs that pool data from many stations, more work is needed on the most appropriate number and distribution of stations to ensure representative sampling at chosen geographic scales, the effects on results of frequency of operation, and on effects of station turnover.

• Additional validation studies are needed on abundance and demographic indices based on mist netting (including fall age ratios in migrating birds), and on population trends of temperate migrants sampled in their wintering areas.

• There is little information on age- or sex-specific differences in dispersal and habitat preference, or on degree of annual variation in these factors. Such knowledge is important for interpreting spatial and temporal differences in productivity indices.

• Mark–recapture methods are improving rapidly, but better models are needed to address dispersal of juveniles or previous breeders, and for pooling of data from multiple stations (especially when there is turnover in the sample of stations). Use of mark–recapture for migration studies also needs further investigation.

CONCLUSIONS

Mist netting as an extremely valuable tool for many kinds of population monitoring, not only for detecting the presence of species and counting individuals, but as an efficient means of capture to age individuals and mark them for future identification. It is almost unique among methods in providing demographic estimates in all seasons, for many species of birds. Although mist netting is especially effective as a monitoring technique when used in mark–recapture studies, it can also provide valuable indices of relative abundance. In addition, mist-net samples can be used to track long-term trends in abundance and productivity.

ACKNOWLEDGMENTS

This paper benefited from discussion among all authors and workshop participants (see list in preface.) We especially appreciate the contributions of K. M. Burton, J. Faaborg, C. M. Handel, G. R. Geupel, N. Nur, W. J. Peach, C. C. Rimmer, L. Thomas, C. Vansteenwegen, and A. A. Whitman, and a review by C. M. Francis.

Studies in Avian Biology No. 29:7–11

EFFECTS OF MIST-NETTING FREQUENCY ON CAPTURE RATES AT MONITORING AVIAN PRODUCTIVITY AND SURVIVORSHIP (MAPS) STATIONS

KENNETH M. BURTON AND DAVID F. DESANTE

Abstract. Data from the Monitoring Avian Productivity and Survivorship (MAPS) Program were analyzed to evaluate the effect of frequency of operation (number of days per 10-day period) of mist nets at MAPS stations on capture rates of adult and young birds. A negative relationship existed between netting frequency and the number of captures of adult birds per unit effort. This suggests that net avoidance by adult birds can be an important consideration at higher frequencies. There also was a negative relationship between netting frequency and the rate of capture of individual adults; this demonstrates saturation of effort. With regard to young birds, however, netting frequency had no effect on either type of capture rate. These results indicate that data from stations run at high frequencies will produce inflated productivity indices by lowering capture rates of adults but not of young. Thus, when pooling data from stations operated at differing frequencies for large-scale demographic monitoring, the data must be adjusted to control for netting frequency. We interpret these findings and suggest more rigorous approaches to the study of these phenomena.

Key Words: capture rate, MAPS, mist net, net avoidance, netting frequency, productivity.

Constant-effort mist netting has been shown recently to be a viable method of monitoring demographic parameters of landbird populations (Baillie 1990; Baillie et al. 1986; Butcher et al. 1993; DeSante 1992; DeSante et al. 1993a,b; Nur and Geupel 1993a,b; Peach et al. 1991, Ralph et al. 1993). However, many questions remain regarding the optimal design of monitoring programs using mist netting, not least of which concerns the frequency at which mist nets should be operated (Nur and Geupel 1993b, Ballard et al. *this volume*). The question of how often to operate mist nets is not merely academic. Mist netting, although providing information not readily obtainable by other methods, such as point counting, is relatively labor intensive. Managers and researchers need to know what sampling effort is required to produce accurate and precise estimates of the target parameters (e.g., population size, productivity, survivorship, recruitment) in the most efficient manner possible. Furthermore, to avoid undue disturbance to the birds themselves, netting should not be conducted at a frequency higher than that necessary to obtain the desired information.

From a bird's point of view, there is no reward associated with being captured in a mist net. Common sense and anecdotal evidence suggest that after such an experience (particularly if repeated), birds are likely to stay away from the net for some time. This phenomenon is known as "net avoidance" or "net shyness," although it is debatable whether birds are avoiding the nets themselves, the net sites, both, or neither. The existence, magnitude, and duration of net avoidance undoubtedly vary among species and probably among individuals, and are likely to increase with repeated capture. At the population level, different age classes are likely to show different degrees of net avoidance due to behavioral differences and degree of naiveté. The degree of net-site avoidance undoubtedly depends to some extent on the site's proximity to a bird's nest in the breeding season, and on its proximity to food, shelter, or other resources, and thus net-site avoidance may vary seasonally.

Net avoidance is generally assumed to exist in mist-netting studies, but few studies have been conducted to examine its magnitude and effects on indices and estimates of population parameters. Stamm et al. (1960) documented steady declines, which they attributed to net shyness, in capture rates of all species combined immediately before and after spring migration in Maryland. As further evidence, they found a marked increase in capture rate, followed by another decline, after relocating their nets (an indication that birds learned to avoid the site of capture, rather than recognizing the nets *per se*). Swinebroad (1964), however, was unable to demonstrate net avoidance in a New Jersey Wood Thrush (*Hylocichla mustelina*) population and in fact had a higher-than-expected proportion of recaptures (based on population estimates from spot mapping); he concluded that placement of nets in areas of high activity within actively defended thrush territories resulted in a disproportionately high rate of repeat captures.

The variation in the results of these studies is further evidence that the intensity of net avoidance varies according to species, season, and perhaps even to population. However, Stamm et al. and Swinebroad banded at highly irregular intervals ranging from 1 to 21 days, making meaningful interpretation and comparison of their results difficult.

Because of territoriality, there is a limited pool of adult birds available at a given site. After these birds have been captured in a given year, an increase in effort will not increase the number of resident individuals captured, although non-breeding birds will continue to be captured. Thus, in a closed population, the capture rate of new individuals (i.e., first captures) is likely to decline as effort is increased, a phenomenon known as "saturation of effort." The length of time taken to reach saturation is dependent on population size, capture probability, and net density, in addition to sampling frequency.

Ballard et al. (*this volume*) found that nets operated five days a week (about 7 days out of 10) captured 50% more locally produced hatch-year Wrentits (*Chamaea fasciata*) than did nets run in the same study plot either once every ten days or twice a week (about three days out of ten). However, the number of locally breeding adult Wrentits captured did not differ significantly among the various regimes. These results suggest that saturation is a more significant issue with adult birds than with young; this is what one would expect, since adults tend to be more sedentary than young birds during the breeding season.

Monitoring Avian Productivity and Survivorship (MAPS) Program protocol (DeSante 1992; DeSante et al. 1993b, 2002) is for nets to be operated on one day per 10-day period. This recommendation was made to increase the number of stations by making them easier to operate, decrease the variability among stations, and minimize disturbance to the birds. Nur and Geupel (1993a,b), however, recommend that nets be operated as frequently as possible to increase annual capture probabilities, and to distinguish between residents and transients, based on multiple captures of the former, so as to be able to exclude the latter from survivorship estimations. Nur et al. (*this volume*) found that locally breeding Wrentits were captured repeatedly at their study site, while non-breeders were not. Furthermore, Sauer and Link (*this volume*) suggest that estimation of the degree of bias in population-parameter indices is possible by estimating capture probability, the reliability of which will be improved by increasing the number of samples. On the other hand, Pradel et al. (1997) suggest that sufficiently spaced capture sessions nearly always will preclude multiple captures of transients, making them easier to identify and exclude from survivorship analyses.

Obviously, no single netting regime is optimal for all purposes. Our contention has been that, for demographic-monitoring purposes, operation of nets once per 10-day period over at least six periods will provide sufficient within- and between-year recaptures to discriminate effectively between residents and transients, and that if additional effort is possible, more information would be provided by the establishment of additional stations than by increased effort at existing stations.

Some MAPS stations (mostly stations operated by bird observatories and other avian research centers and established prior to the inception of the MAPS Program) operate their nets more frequently than once per 10-day period. Thus, data from MAPS stations provide an excellent opportunity to examine the effects of netting frequency on capture rates across a wide spectrum of sites.

METHODS

MAPS mist-netting protocol is described in DeSante (1992) and DeSante et al. (1993b, 2002). At the end of each breeding season, banding data (including species, age, sex, and band number) are submitted to the Institute for Bird Populations (IBP) for analysis, along with detailed information on mist-netting effort (date, number of nets, opening and closing times, total net hours). Baseline descriptions of each station, including primary habitat type, are kept on file at IBP.

We used 1992 MAPS banding data to assess the relationship between netting frequency (number of days of operation of mist nets per 10-day period) and total capture rates (numbers of all captures, including repeats, per unit effort) as a measure of net avoidance. We also examined the relationship between netting frequency and rate of first capture (numbers of newly captured individuals, excluding repeats, per unit effort) as a measure of saturation. We used 600 net-h as the unit of effort; this represents one season's effort at a station consisting of ten 12-m nets operated for 6 h/day at a frequency of 1 day/period for 10 periods.

Stations were grouped into four primary habitat types: "forest," "woodland," "scrub," and "meadow." We first conducted ANOVAs using netting frequency and habitat and their interaction as main effects. Habitat had highly significant effects on both total and first capture rates (all age classes pooled; $F_{3,166} = 18.61$, $P < 0.001$). Forest and meadow habitats were underrepresented at netting frequencies higher than 1 day/period, so we excluded from further analysis stations in these two habitats. Capture-rate data from woodland and scrub habitats were log transformed prior to further analysis in order to meet the assumptions of the models used; frequency data did not require transformation.

Mean values ±1 SE are reported. Gallinaceous birds and hummingbirds were excluded from analysis because most MAPS operators do not have permits to band them.

RESULTS

Data from 76 MAPS stations in woodland and scrub habitats were available for analysis. Netting frequency at these stations ranged from 0.8 to 5.2 day/period (day/p) with a mean of 1.4 ± 0.10 day/p over an average of 9 ± 0.26 periods. Total capture rate of adults ranged from 23.2 to 357.6/600 net-h (mean = 139.6 ± 9.21); total capture rate of young ranged from 7.4 to 818.9/600 net-h (mean = 98.8 ± 13.46). Rate of first capture ranged from 16.6 to 343.5/600 net-h for adults (mean = 113.9 ± 7.62) and from 7.4 to 786.7/600 net-h for young (mean = 92.0 ± 12.83).

The effect of netting frequency on capture rates did not differ between the two habitats analyzed (woodland and scrub) for either adults or young (frequency × habitat effect, $F_{1,73} = 0.7$, $P = 0.42$).

Combining habitats, increasing netting frequency significantly reduced total capture rate of adults ($F_{1,73} = 6.9$, $P = 0.01$); however, it did not affect total capture rate of young ($F_{1,73} = 0.4$, $P = 0.51$). Netting frequency also affected first capture rate of adults ($F_{1,73} = 9.3$, $P < 0.01$) but not of young ($F_{1,73} = 1.3$, $P = 0.26$). Figures 1–4 illustrate, using non-transformed data, the trends for each of the two habitats. The slopes were negative in all cases, regardless of statistical significance. However, the r values were all less than 0.3, indicating that netting frequency did not explain much of the variance in capture rates, even for adults.

DISCUSSION

We found that net (or net-site) avoidance (as measured by decline in total capture rate) and effort saturation (as measured by decline in rate of first captures) can be significant in constant-effort mist-netting operations. Net avoidance and effort saturation during the breeding season appear to operate primarily on adults (presumably territorial, breeding individuals). The difference between adults and young is likely due to the higher degree of mobility among young during the breeding season.

Net avoidance and saturation, although distinct phenomena, have a similar effect on bird population studies: they result in inflated indices of productivity by lowering the capture rates of adults, but not of young. Statistics developed by Baillie et al. (1986) for the Constant Effort Sites Scheme, and adopted in

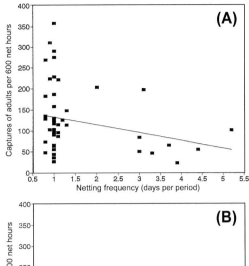

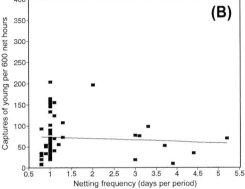

FIGURE 1. Total capture rates of (A) adults and (B) young vs. netting frequency at 54 MAPS stations in woodland habitats in 1992. (A) r = 0.25, slope = −18.7; (B) r = 0.07, slope = −3.6.

the MAPS Program, use the number of individuals captured, rather than capture rates, in population size and productivity analyses. Stations are almost certain to capture more individuals by increasing their netting frequency and thus would contribute more data to these analyses, but, at least in regard to adults, this increase is not proportional to the increase in effort. Due to saturation, one cannot simply divide the number of individuals by the frequency of effort, as this would underestimate adult-population size and overestimate productivity. This is documented by DeSante et al. (*this volume*) in the case of a single station operated nearly daily. One solution might be to select data from a single day of operation from each period, either randomly or by some other criterion, for use in these analyses. DeSante et al. (*this volume*) demonstrate that this technique produces valid results. Another approach might be to calculate the total number of individuals captured using only the first day in each period, then only the second, and

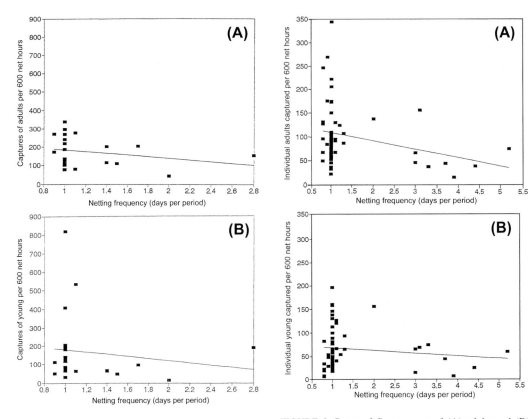

FIGURE 2. Total capture rates of (A) adults and (B) young vs. netting frequency at 22 MAPS stations in scrub habitats in 1992. (A) r = 0.25, slope = –46.1; (B) r = 0.14, slope = –59.32.

FIGURE 3. Rates of first capture of (A) adults and (B) young vs. netting frequency at 54 MAPS stations in woodland habitats in 1992. (A) r = 0.27, slope = –17.1; (B) r = 0.13, slope = –5.9.

so on, and use the average. The first approach would be the simpler, whereas the second could increase the accuracy and precision of the indices.

The problem of net avoidance becomes significant in breeding-bird monitoring programs in two cases. One is when nets are operated prior to the period under investigation, because resident or early-arriving breeders could be captured during this time and might not be captured again that year due to net avoidance. This is especially true if the nets are operated prematurely and frequently, as for a spring-migration monitoring program. This could act to decrease adult population size indices, increase productivity indices, and reduce survivorship estimates.

The second case in which net avoidance may affect population studies is when a station is operated at a very high frequency. Survivorship models using within-year recaptures to identify residents require a certain period of time between captures, typically 10 days (Buckland and Baillie 1987, Peach

1993, Peach et al. 1990). Stations operated at very high frequencies actually may lower their ability to identify residents, since these birds may be captured several times in rapid succession and avoid the nets thereafter, thus not reappearing in the data set after the necessary time interval has elapsed.

An additional issue is the relationship between annual recapture probability and netting frequency. Increasing recapture probability increases the precision of survival estimates, as does increasing the number of samples (Pollock et al. 1990). For the purpose of estimating interannual survivorship, however, an entire season represents a single sample, regardless of netting frequency. Increasing netting frequency undoubtedly does increase recapture probability, but the exact relationship between these two variables has not been examined across a broad spectrum of sites. Increasing netting frequency certainly does not proportionately add adult birds to the catch.

A more formal approach to the study of net avoidance, but beyond the scope of this paper, would be to

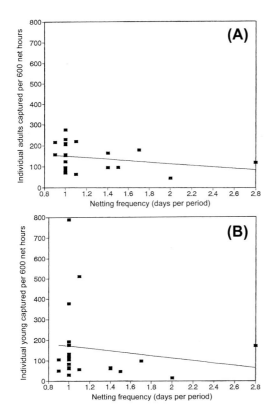

FIGURE 4. Rates of first capture of (a) adults and (b) young vs. netting frequency at 22 MAPS stations in scrub habitats in 1992. (a) r = 0.25, slope = −35.4; (b) r = 0.14, slope = −58.2.

estimate within-year recapture probabilities. Such an approach has been used in closed population estimation models that allow for capture probability to vary by response to capture (Otis et al. 1978), but to our knowledge has not been used to assess the effects of sampling frequency. Such a study could be done on a station-by-station basis, using only a single species or group of related species and a set of stations in similar habitat operated at various frequencies, and it would need to be limited to resident individuals.

Ultimately, the optimum frequency at which to operate a constant-effort mist-netting station will be determined by the specific objectives of the project and the resources available. Data from stations operated at varying frequencies can be combined for large-scale analyses, provided those from stations operated on multiple days per period are adjusted appropriately. In general, however, additional effort, when possible, likely will be more valuable to large-scale monitoring programs if used for establishment of additional stations nearby in similar habitat, rather than repetition. Increasing the number of stations providing data and standardizing the effort expended at these stations will increase the precision and reliability of regional monitoring indices and estimates. Furthermore, clusters of similar stations may provide valuable dispersal and philopatry information, as well as giving more accurate pictures of local conditions and trends.

ACKNOWLEDGMENTS

We wish to thank all 1992 MAPS-station operators and field crews for providing the data used in this paper. Participants in the 1993 mist-net workshop offered valuable comments and suggestions pertaining to this analysis. D. K. Rosenberg provided statistical assistance. B. G. Murray, Jr., W. J. Peach, and C. Vansteenwegen reviewed earlier drafts of the manuscript. We thank the long list of financial supporters, detailed in DeSante (*this volume*). This is Contribution No. 28 of The Institute for Bird Populations.

Studies in Avian Biology No. 29:12–20

MONITORING PRODUCTIVITY WITH MULTIPLE MIST-NET STATIONS

C. John Ralph, Kimberly Hollinger, and Sherri L. Miller

Abstract. We evaluated data from 22 mist-net capture stations operated over 5 to 13 years in northern California and southern Oregon, to help develop sampling designs for monitoring using mist nets. In summer, 2.6% of individuals were recaptured at other stations within 1 km of the original banding station, and in fall, 1.4% were recaptured nearby. We recommend that stations be established 1–5 km apart to promote independent sampling. Percent of young birds in the total captured was similar among stations, both in summer and fall, indicating that large numbers of stations might not be necessary to sample age structure for an entire region, at least for common species. We examined the percent of young captured in fall and summer to determine whether some stations consistently captured lower proportions of young across all species, and found no consistent pattern. Power analysis indicated that about 10 stations were required to detect a 50% change in percent young between years for the Song Sparrow (*Melospiza melodia*), a common species. To detect a 25% change, 10 stations still sufficed in fall, but about 3× more were required in summer. Summer results were similar for the Yellow-breasted Chat (*Icteria virens*). More stations would be needed to reach similar precision targets for uncommon species, and probably also in regions of more heterogeneous habitat. Although the capture rates at stations in our region increased during the study, the capture rates at individual stations declined significantly after the first year of operation.

Key Words: bird, migration, mist net, monitoring, productivity.

Constant-effort mist netting can be used to estimate population composition, species abundance, and demographic parameters such as survivorship and productivity. Coupled with habitat surveys and trend analyses, demographic monitoring has been suggested as a necessary minimum for meeting the monitoring obligations of various resource-management agencies, and for interpreting differences in bird abundance among habitats and over time (e.g., Butcher 1992, Manley 1993). Central to planning and execution of monitoring with mist netting is knowledge of the number of stations necessary to characterize population parameters for a region or a habitat.

Determining the number of netting stations needed to most efficiently monitor birds in a target region requires a balance between effort and the power of the results. If stations produce relatively uniform results, few stations will be needed, as long as sample size requirements can be met. For example, Bart et al. (1999) found that 7 stations could monitor productivity in Kirtland's Warbler (*Dendroica kirtlandii*), using the proportion of young in the total catch as the index of productivity, but the study took place in uniform habitat, for a single species, and in a small area. By contrast, Peach et al. (*this volume*) found that for 17 of 23 species captured, 40–70 netting stations were required to detect annual changes across England with precision of 5% mean standard error. Number of stations required for monitoring productivity at a target level of precision may also differ

between the summer season and fall, when more migrants than summer residents are captured.

In this paper, we examine the number of stations needed to sample productivity in summer and fall, in an area approximately 25–50 km in radius and sampled in reasonably homogenous habitat. We also analyzed data from a dense configuration of stations in a larger region of northwestern California and southern Oregon, most established since 1992 to monitor the birds of the region. Our stations were established in riparian habitats along river and stream corridors, and near mountain meadows. We were interested in monitoring permanent and summer residents, as well as migrants, and in monitoring the very important post-breeding period of late summer and fall.

Specifically, this paper addresses the following questions:

(1) To what degree do nearby stations share the same individuals? If movement rates among stations are relatively high, such that nearby stations capture a high number of the same individuals, then stations must be located farther apart to achieve statistical and biological independence of samples.

(2) How much variation is there in percent of young within and among stations? If stations are similar to each other in their percent young, then fewer stations may be needed to provide a good estimate of annual changes in productivity for the region.

(3) How many stations are needed in a region to detect a specific change in our demographic measure of productivity, percent of young?

12

(4) Is there a consistent effect of year-of-operation on capture rate, which could affect interpretation of trend results?

METHODS

With several cooperators, we established 34 constant-effort stations in northwestern California and southern Oregon, in what is referred to as the Klamath-Siskiyou bioregion. A sub-set of 22 stations with the most similar operating years, schedules, and effort was selected for the analyses presented here (Table 1, Fig. 1). Stations were located along the Klamath River and its tributaries, the major riparian corridors of northwestern California, as well as some nearby rivers. All stations were located in riparian areas bordered by coniferous forests; on the main stem of a river, on a tributary, or in upper elevation meadow–riparian areas. Two coastal stations were in riparian areas within the coast redwood (*Sequoia sempervirens*) zone, and two were along the riparian margin of a coastal pine (*Pinus contorta*) forest.

At each station, 10–12 mist nets were operated during the breeding season, and usually during fall migration as well. Nets were placed in the same locations each year. Except for two stations (HOME and PARK), each station was consistently operated one day during each 10-day period beginning in early May and continuing to the end of August (defined here as the breeding season). During September and October (our definition of the fall migration season), nets were operated once per week. Since 1992, the HOME station has been operated during the breeding season twice every 10 days and in the fall for 3 days a week (usually with at least 1 day between sessions). PARK station was operated during the breeding season once every 10 days, and in the fall for 2 days a week. Regardless of season, nets were opened at all stations from within 15 min of dawn and operated for five hours, weather permitting. Other net operations and processing of birds followed the guidelines in Ralph et al. (1993) and Hussell and Ralph (1998).

Most analyses in this paper included data for the most frequently-captured species; 14 in summer, and 12 in fall (Table 2). The dates defined above for these seasons cover the majority of the breeding and migration seasons of the species involved. However, in many species, at least a proportion of the population does migrate earlier than September. Stations used for each analysis varied (Table 1). Because the effort was similar at all stations, except where otherwise indicated, we did not weight stations in the analyses according to effort.

To determine whether stations close together were sampling the same local population (and therefore not collecting independent samples), we determined the percent of individuals captured between stations as a function of distance. We confined this analysis to eight of the closest stations (analysis A in Table 1).

We used the percent of young of the total of birds captured as an index to productivity. Stations used for this analysis (analysis B in Table 1) represent an area of about 120,000 ha, near the average size of a Forest Service District in the national forests of the Klamath River region. For some of the stations operated for five or more years during the period of 1992–2001, we computed the average annual percent young for each species in summer and fall. To test for differences of the average percent young among stations, we used ANOVA and Duncan's multiple range test (Zar 1984).

To test whether annual percent young was consistently low or high at a given station across species, we calculated an index of productivity for each station. We first calculated the range of percent young for each species over the years of the study period at that station, then calculated an index representing the annual percent young relative to the range of percentages of young of that species captured at that station. For example, if the range for Black-headed Grosbeaks (scientific names of all species are in Table 2) was 25–75% over 10 years at a station, and the percent young in a given year was 65%, 10% lower than maximum value, the relative value for that species at that station was $0.80 (= 1 - (0.10 / (0.75-0.25)))$. We used a General Linear Model (SAS Institute 1996) to compare the means of these relative percent young by species over all the years when the species was captured (in some years at some stations a species may not have been captured).

We estimated the power of detecting a change in the proportion of young in the total number of birds captured ($\hat{d}$), by species and season (analysis C in Table 1), for two common riparian species, Song Sparrow and Yellow-breasted Chat. We tested for differences in percent young $H_0 : d = 1$ vs. $H_1 : d \neq 1$ (Cochran 1977), for all pairs of years from 1992 to 1995. We estimated the power of detecting a 50% ($d = 0.5$ or 1.5) or 25% ($d = 0.25$ or 1.25) decrease or increase, over a range of sample sizes (number of stations) from one to 50.

To determine if capture rate at a station changed according to year of operation, we compared annual capture rates for the first year of operation (1991, 1992, 1993 or 1994) to the three subsequent years for 17 of the stations (analysis D in Table 1). We used a mixed-effects model (Littell et al. 1996) to estimate the structure of capture rates with year of operation (Year 1, Year 2, Year 3 or Year 4) and capture year (1991–1997), testing capture year both as a categorical and as a continuous variable. We used Tukey-Kramer test for multiple pairwise comparisons of capture rates by years and by year of operation. Station was the random effect in the model, and we accounted for potential serial correlation among years assuming an autoregressive correlation structure (SAS Institute 1996).

RESULTS

INDEPENDENCE OF STATIONS

For the stations less than 1 km apart, 2.6% of individual birds were recaptured at another station in the summer, and 1.4% in fall (Table 3). At stations more than 1 km from the original capture stations, in both

TABLE 1. Mist-net capture stations, the analyses in which the station's data were used, number of nets, the years operated, and seasons of operation (S = summer, F = fall).

Station	Operator	Analyses[a]	N nets	1992	1993	1994	1995	1996	1997	1998	1999	2000	2001
Aiken's Creek (AKEN)	Redwood Sciences Laboratory	A	10	S	–	–	–	–	–	–	–	–	–
Antelope Creek (ANT1)	Klamath National Forest	D	10	–	–	S,F	S,F	S,F	S,F	S,F	S,F	S,F	–
Big Bar (BBAR)	Trinity National Forest	B	12	S,F	S	S,F	S	S,F	S	–	–	–	–
Bondo Mine (BOND)	Redwood Sciences Laboratory	A, B, C, D	10	S	S	S	S	S	–	–	–	–	–
Camp Creek (CAMP)	Redwood Sciences Laboratory	A, B, C, D	10	S,F	S,F	S,F	S,F	S,F	S,F	S,F	S,F	S,F	S,F
Red Cap Creek D (CAPD)	Redwood Sciences Laboratory	A, B, C, D	13	S,F	S,F	S,F	S,F	S,F	S,F	S,F	S,F	S,F	S,F
Carberry Creek (CARB)	Rogue River National Forest	D	10	–	–	S,F	S,F	S,F	S	–	–	–	–
Emmy's Place (EMMY)	Redwood Sciences Laboratory	D	10	–	–	S,F	S,F	S,F	S,F	–	–	–	–
Grayback Creek (GBCR)[b]	Siskiyou National Forest	D	8	S	S	S	S	S	S	S	S	S	–
Grove's Prairie (GROV)	Redwood Sciences Laboratory	D	10	–	–	S,F	S,F	S,F	S,F	S,F	S,F	S,F	S,F
HBBO HQ (HOME)	Humboldt Bay Bird Observatory	A	17.5	S,F	S,F	S,F	S,F	S,F	S,F	S,F	S,F	S,F	S,F
Indian Valley (INVA)	Redwood Sciences Laboratory	D	10	–	–	S,F	S,F	S,F	S,F	S,F	S,F	S,F	S,F
Delaney Farm (LADY)	Redwood Sciences Laboratory	A, B, C, D	10	S,F	S,F	S,F	S,F	S,F	S,F	S,F	S,F	S,F	S,F
Long Ridge (LORI)	Siskiyou National Forest	D	10	S	S	S	S	S	S	–	–	–	–
Molier (MOLI)	Redwood Sciences Laboratory	A, B, C, D	12	S	S	S	S	S	–	–	–	–	–
DeMello pasture (PARK)	Humboldt Bay Bird Observatory	A	14	S,F	S,F	S,F	S,F	S,F	S,F	S,F	S,F	S,F	–
Pacific Coast Trail 1 (PCT1)	Klamath National Forest	B, D	13	–	S,F	S,F	S,F	S,F	S,F	S,F	S,F	–	–
Redwood Creek (RECR)	Redwood Sciences Laboratory	D	11	–	–	S,F	S,F	S,F	S,F	S,F	S,F	S,F	S,F
Red Cap Creek 2 (RED2)	Redwood Sciences Laboratory	A, B, C, D	13	S,F	S,F	S,F	S,F	S,F	–	–	–	–	–
Whitmore Creek (WHIT)	Redwood Sciences Laboratory	A	10	S	–	–	–	–	–	–	–	–	–
Wright Refuge (WREF)	Humboldt State University	D	10	–	S,F	S,F	S,F	S	S	–	–	–	–
Yager Creek (YACR)	Pacific Lumber Company	D	12	–	–	S,F	S,F	S,F	S	S	S	S	S

Notes: "–" denotes no data were taken.

[a] Stations used in each analysis: A = Independence between stations from movement among stations (includes all years); B = Variation in percent young among stations and years (1992–1995); C = Number of stations needed to detect declines in productivity (includes years 1992–1995); D = Effect of running nets on capture rate (includes summer data from first four years of operation – years used indicated with underline).

[b] This station was also operated in the summer of 1991.

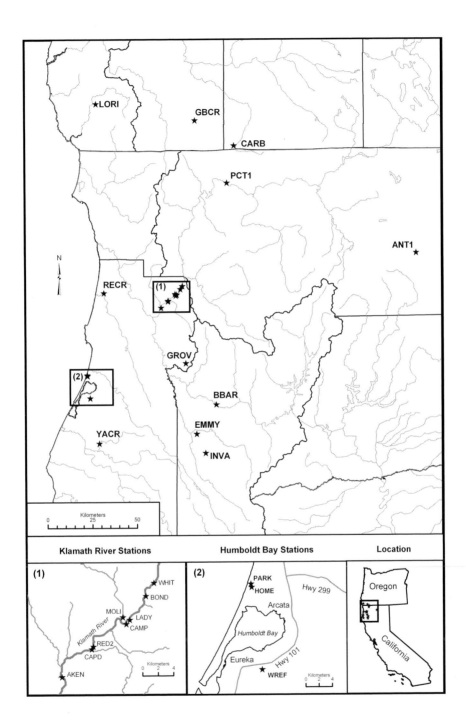

FIGURE 1. Locations and four-letter code names of each of the 22 stations used in this study, with county and state borders (black lines) and river systems (gray lines). Insets show details of the Klamath River and Humboldt Bay intensive study areas.

TABLE 2. SPECIES USED IN THE ANALYSES FOR EACH SEASON

Code	Species	Summer	Fall
WIFL	Willow Flycatcher (*Empidonax trailii*)	X	X
PSFL	Pacific-slope Flycatcher (*E. difficilis*)	X	
BUSH	Common Bushtit (*Psaltriparus minimus*)	X	
RCKI	Ruby-crowned Kinglet (*Regulus calendula*)		X
SWTH	Swainson's Thrush (*Catharus ustulatus*)	X	X
HETH	Hermit Thrush (*C. guttatus*)		X
AMRO	American Robin (*Turdus migratorius*)		X
VATH	Varied Thrush (*Ixoreus naevius*)		X
WREN	Wrentit (*Chamaea fasciata*)	X	X
OCWA	Orange-crowned Warbler (*Vermivora celata*)	X	
YWAR	Yellow Warbler (*Dendroica petechia*)	X	
MYWA	Myrtle Warbler (*D. coronata*)		X
MGWA	MacGillivray's Warbler (*Oporornis tolmiei*)	X	
WIWA	Wilson's Warbler (*Wilsonia pusilla*)	X	
YBCH	Yellow-breasted Chat (*Icteria virens*)	X	
WETA	Western Tanager (*Piranga ludoviciana*)	X	
SPTO	Spotted Towhee (*Pipilo maculatus*)	X	X
FOSP	Fox Sparrow (*Passerella iliaca*)		X
SOSP	Song Sparrow (*Melospiza melodia*)	X	X
GCSP	Golden-crowned Sparrow (*Zonotrichia atricapilla*)		X
BHGR	Black-headed Grosbeak (*Pheucticus melanocephalus*)	X	

seasons, the number of birds recaptured was ≤0.5%, indicating that stations more than 1 km apart were collecting largely independent samples.

CONSISTENCY IN PERCENT OF YOUNG AMONG STATIONS

Percent of young differed little among stations for most species in summer (Table 4). Six of the stations were quite close together, in similar riverine–riparian habitat, and had statistically indistinguishable percents of young. Two more distant stations (BBAR and PCT1) appeared to have lower percents of young for some species (Table 4). However, each of these stations also had the highest percent young for at least one species. Two resident species, Wrentit and Song Sparrow, tended to have more variable percents of young among stations than did the other species, most of which are migratory.

In the fall, percent young was more consistent

TABLE 3. PERCENT OF INDIVIDUALS CAPTURED AT A STATION LOCATION OTHER THAN WHERE PREVIOUSLY CAPTURED, 1992–2001

Distance between capture and recapture locations	Summer		Fall	
	Total captures	Percent recaptured	Total captures	Percent recaptured
< 1.0 km	5646	2.65	5243	1.39
≥ 1.0 ≤ 5.0 km	4326	0.46	1924	0.10
≥ 5.1 ≤ 10.0 km	3719	0.22	1142	0.09
≥ 10.1 ≤ 17.5 km	1483	0.20	0	–

among stations than during the summer (Table 5). However, for five species, the BBAR station had significantly different percent young than the other stations.

We did not find a pattern in standardized percent young that would indicate consistently low or high productivity across years at some stations (all target species combined; Table 6). BBAR was consistently lowest in percent young in summer across all years, although the difference was significant in only one year. In the fall, CAPD usually had the highest percent young, but this was significantly higher in only one of the years.

A station with the highest percent young in one year did not necessarily have the highest in other years. The percent young was indistinguishable across all stations in the summers of 1992 and 1995, and in the falls of 1993 and 1995. However, in the summer of 1993, three stations had fewer young than the other stations. In summer 1994, stations were evenly divided, with some stations having higher percents of young and others having lower percents.

NUMBER OF STATIONS NEEDED TO DETECT ANNUAL CHANGES IN PRODUCTIVITY

Power analysis showed that for the Song Sparrow, 10 stations were required in summer to detect a 50% change in percent young between years with a 0.95 probability and a significance level of 0.05 (Table 7). The number of stations required to detect a 25% change at the same level of probability is three times as large, at 32 stations. In the fall, when percent young was more consistent among stations, only four stations were needed to detect a 50% change, and 10 to detect a 25% change. Summer data for the much-less common Yellow-breasted Chat gave similar results (Table 7; this species is not captured in fall). With 10 stations, the probability of detecting a 50% change in percent young between years was

TABLE 4. PERCENT OF YOUNG (SUMMER) AVERAGED OVER 10 YEARS (1992–2001)

Species code	BBAR	BOND	CAMP	CAPD	LADY	MOLI	RED2	PCT1
				Station				
PSFL	88.8	76.4	49.6	73.0	70.2	66.3	72.8	47.6
	A[a]	AB	B	AB	AB	AB	AB	AB
WIFL	93.3	85.3	84.0	80.7	77.6	94.7	78.7	46.1
	A	A	A	A	A	A	A	B
BUSH	50.9	79.2	0	94.5	100	–	60.0	65.8
	AB	AB	B	A	A	–	AB	AB
WREN	100.0	71.8	58.9	76.1	65.2	64.6	73.1	79.2
	A	BC	C	BC	C	C	BC	AB
SWTH	58.3	44.5	37.3	31.2	18.2	21.8	32.8	23.8
	A	AB	B	B	B	B	B	B
OCWA	21.3	30.6	33.2	48.5	51.0	74.0	59.7	19.5
	B	B	B	AB	AB	A	AB	B
MGWA	3.9	39.7	31.0	42.9	40.2	39.5	35.9	35.6
	B	A	AB	A	A	A	AB	AB
WIWA	1.8	53.6	32.1	61.4	59.3	67.5	60.9	2.9
	B	A	AB	A	A	A	A	B
YWAR	16.6	55.0	17.6	56.5	36.2	38.3	33.3	32.6
	A	A	A	A	A	A	A	A
YBCH	25.8	39.4	49.2	44.1	30.4	34.2	28.2	44.5
	A	A	A	A	A	A	A	A
WETA	52.6	63.7	54.9	75.5	61.8	54.2	68.3	77.8
	A	A	A	A	A	A	A	A
BHGR	13.3	75.2	58.8	69.6	62.2	69.8	68.4	60.3
	B	A	A	A	A	A	A	A
SPTO	67.6	70.1	61.8	74.2	66.9	70.1	81.0	72.6
	A	A	A	A	A	A	A	A
SOSP	61.5	68.9	54.0	70.7	35.9	50.2	56.9	68.0
	ABC	A	ABC	AB	C	BC	ABC	AB

Note: Species codes are explained in Table 2.
[a] Stations with the same letter are not significantly different in average percent young (ANOVA, Duncan's multiple range test, P > 0.05).

0.97, and 29 stations were needed to detect a 25% change with 0.95 probability.

CHANGE IN CAPTURE RATE ACCORDING TO YEAR OF OPERATION

We compared capture rates in the first and subsequent three years of station operation to test the assumption that there is no effect of year of operation on capture rates. When capture rate was calculated by the year of operation (i.e., Year 1, Year 2, Year 3 and Year 4) for all 17 stations combined, there was a noticeable (>20%) decline after Year 1 (Table 8). However, many stations were established in the same years, so the decline could have been related to differences in bird abundance among years. To determine if the decline was significant, and related to initiation of the mist-net station or simply a difference in bird abundance, we examined

two models: year of operation and capture year as categorical variables and then as continuous variables. Both year of operation and capture year had significant effects on capture rates, in both models (year of operation: categorical, $F = 6.81$, $P = 0.002$, continuous, $F = 11.65$, $P = 0.003$; capture year: categorical, $F = 2.52$, $P = 0.043$, continuous, $F = 6.63$, $P = 0.021$). The predictability of the alternate models, as measured by the estimated variance of a single prediction, was similar. The AIC_c value was considerably lower for the categorical model, 760.4 vs. 845.3, indicating the categorical model was a better fit to the data.

Capture rate at the 17 stations generally increased from 1991 to 1997, with stations that began operation later in the period tending to have higher captures rates. At each individual station, however, capture rates declined after the first year. The mean capture rate averaged over all 17 stations for the first

TABLE 5. PERCENT YOUNG (FALL) OF THE MOST COMMON SPECIES CAPTURED OVER 10 YEARS (1992–2001)

Species codes	Station					
	BBAR	CAMP	CAPD	LADY	RED2	PCT1
WIFL	100.0	97.1	96.7	89.1	96.0	100.0
	A[a]	A	A	A	A	A
RCKI	0.0	35.8	60.7	54.2	20.0	54.8
	A	A	A	A	A	A
SWTH	100.0	67.9	76.5	69.4	74.9	79.9
	A	B	B	B	B	B
HETH	22.9	71.4	78.2	70.8	78.2	78.6
	B	A	A	A	A	A
AMRO	50.0	50.0	75.9	44.1	44.4	49.0
	A	A	A	A	A	A
VATH	0.0	60.6	45.8	66.8	40.0	60.0
	A	A	A	A	A	A
WREN	–	97.5	96.0	94.9	80.6	96.0
	–	A	AB	AB	B	AB
MYWA	–	82.3	94.1	94.0	85.2	86.2
	–	A	A	A	A	A
SPTO	13.9	87.6	86.8	81.4	92.7	85.4
	B	A	A	A	A	A
FOSP	22.9	53.2	69.2	60.8	60.2	72.6
	B	A	A	A	A	A
SOSP	57.8	79.6	71.4	76.6	72.8	82.0
	A	A	A	A	A	A
GCSP	21.4	59.0	57.6	45.6	62.0	62.1
	B	A	A	A	A	A

Note: Species codes are explained in Table 2.
[a] Stations with the same letter are not significantly different in average percent young (ANOVA, Duncan's multiple range test, $P > 0.05$).

year of operation was significantly higher than the capture rate in years 2, 3, and 4.

DISCUSSION

INDEPENDENCE OF STATIONS

Recapture rate between stations >1 km apart was very low. We make the conservative recommendation that stations be established a minimum of 1–5 km apart to approach independence of sampling, while still allowing multiple samples to be collected within an area of relatively homogeneous habitat.

CONSISTENCY IN PERCENT OF YOUNG AMONG STATIONS

If stations in an area are similar in percent of young, then relatively few stations should be needed to sample regional productivity at target levels of precision. The few differences we found between stations in percent young captured in summer seemed to reflect distance from other stations, rather than differences in habitat. Six of the stations used in this

analysis (Table 4) were in similar, riverine–riparian habitat, in close proximity on a 12-km section of the main stem Klamath River near Orleans (Fig. 1). The two more distant stations appeared to have, in general, lower productivity. The BBAR station on the Trinity River, a tributary of the Klamath, and PCT1 (109 km upstream along the Klamath River) had the lowest percent young for five of the 14 species analyzed. Together, these two stations accounted for most of the significant differences in percent young among stations. Percents were not consistently low, however, as each of these stations also had the highest percent young for at least one species.

Some resident species had more variable annual percent young than migratory species (Table 4; Wrentit and Song Sparrow), suggesting that there might be real spatial differences in local productivity. It is possible that residents are better able to fine tune their productivity to local conditions, whereas productivity of migrant species might be more affected by wintering ground conditions and factors operating on a broader scale. Variability among stations in percent young for resident species may

TABLE 6. STANDARDIZED PERCENT YOUNG FOR ALL TARGET SPECIES COMBINED, BY STATION AND SEASON, FOR 1992–1995

	Summer				Fall			
Station	1992	1993	1994	1995	1992	1993	1994	1995
BBAR	38.3	17.6	33.2	29.6	63.9	–	20.0	–
	A[a]	D	B	A	AB		C	
BOND	50.1	78.2	47.4	57.7	–	–	–	–
	A	A	B	A				
CAMP	59.4	41.5	38.2	52.8	61.1	37.4	70.0	39.4
	A	DC	B	A	AB	A	AB	A
CAPD	61.2	60.5	86.6	48.6	82.9	61.2	81.2	71.2
	A	AB	A	A	A	A	A	A
LADY	63.3	28.0	50.0	58.4	58.7	58.0	69.4	37.8
	A	DC	B	A	AB	A	AB	A
MOLI	45.7	66.9	64.2	56.2	–	–	–	–
	A	AB	AB	A				
RED2	43.6	68.7	60.1	54.6	32.1	49.4	49.9	43.7
	A	A	AB	A	B	A	B	A
PCT1	–	52.8	39.0	56.7	–	40.0	85.8	70.7
		ABC	B	A		A	A	A

Notes: See Methods for means of standardization. Species codes are explained in Table 2.
[a]Stations with the same letter are not significantly different in average percent young (ANOVA, Duncan's multiple range test, $P > 0.05$).

TABLE 7. PROBABILITY OF DETECTING ANNUAL CHANGE (DECLINE OR INCREASE) IN THE PERCENT OF YOUNG CAPTURED, WITH A SIGNIFICANCE LEVEL OF 0.05, AMONG KLAMATH RIVER STATIONS

		Number of	Probability of detecting	
Species	Season	stations	50% change	25% change
Song Sparrow	Summer	4	0.78	0.37
		6	0.86	0.49
		8	0.91	0.58
		10	0.95	0.65
		32	>0.99	0.95
	Fall	2	0.92	0.58
		4	0.98	0.75
		6	>0.99	0.86
		8	>0.99	0.92
		10	>0.99	0.95
Yellow-breasted Chat	Summer	6	0.72	0.26
		8	0.79	0.33
		10	0.97	0.60
		29	>0.99	0.95

reflect differences in the quality of the immediate and nearby habitats, allowing us to identify source and sink areas. However, Nur and Geupel (1993b) showed that summer mist-net captures reflected local productivity in Song Sparrows, but not Wrentits. In many species, percent young in summer and fall, when dispersers and migrants are being captured, may represent average productivity across the region rather than local productivity at each netting station. In the Klamath network, many species use the riparian habitats during migration, and variability in percent young is low among stations. That fewer stations are needed in fall than in summer to detect annual changes in percent young is an indication that young and adults are distributed among stations in more even proportions during the fall.

TABLE 8. SUMMER CAPTURE RATES OVER THE FIRST FOUR YEARS OF MIST-NET OPERATIONS (17 STATIONS). YEAR 1 RANGED FROM 1991 TO 1994

Year	Mean annual capture rate	SE
1	567.77	29.40
2	440.07	20.72
3	448.99	25.27
4	412.97	23.06

NUMBER OF STATIONS NEEDED TO DETECT ANNUAL CHANGES IN PRODUCTIVITY

For two species in our region, 10 stations were needed to detect a 50% annual change in regional productivity at target precision levels, and about 30 to detect a 25% change (at least in summer). If detecting changes smaller than 25% is of interest, or for detecting similar changes in less common species, a larger number of samples may be required. More stations may also be needed if habitat is more heterogeneous than in our study area.

Here we examined changes in productivity between adjacent years of sampling, both consecutive and non-consecutive years. When additional years of sampling are available, we will examine our power for detecting multi-year trends in productivity.

CHANGE IN CAPTURE RATE IN FIRST AND SUBSEQUENT YEARS

The decline in capture rates following the first year of operation is perplexing. The drop could be due to several causes, including net shyness. The presence of investigators even for as little as one morning in 10 could result in birds avoiding the study area, or, alternatively, learning the location of nets and avoiding them in subsequent years. Net avoidance resulting from long-term memory would result in capture rates suggesting a decline in abundance when none actually occurred. If net shyness was the cause, then decline of captures should be greater in adults than young of the year, so percent young should increase after the first year of operation. This will be tested in future work. It is crucial to that we continue to investigate patterns in capture rate at mist-netting stations that may affect interpretation of monitoring efforts using this technique.

ACKNOWLEDGMENTS

We thank the cooperators at the stations in our network for providing their data for analyses: J. Alexander (Klamath Bird Observatory), L. Angerer (Mendocino National Forest), S. Chinnici (The Pacific Lumber Company), S. Cuenca (Klamath National Forest), W. DeLaney (land owner – Camp Creek, Orleans), C. DeMello (land owner – "PARK" station, Arcata), C. Dillingham (Siskiyou National Forest), L. George (Humboldt State University), M. Mamone (Rogue River National Forest), G. Rible (Rogue River National Forest), B. Rogers (Shasta-Trinity National Forests), H. Sakai (Redwood National and State Parks), and D. Vroman (Siskiyou National Forest). We especially note the numerous biologists, interns, and volunteers who manned the stations of the Klamath Demographic Network over the years. We thank J. Baldwin, E. H. Dunn, T. Matsumoto, and C. P. Ralph for much help and encouragement on the manuscript.

Studies in Avian Biology No. 29:21–27

INFLUENCE OF MIST-NETTING INTENSITY ON DEMOGRAPHIC INVESTIGATIONS OF AVIAN POPULATIONS

Grant Ballard, Geoffrey R. Geupel, and Nadav Nur

Abstract. We evaluated capture rates of juvenile and adult passerines, comparing two different netting regimes on the same study plot at the Palomarin Field Station, Point Reyes National Seashore, California. One set of nets was run approximately 5× as often as the other during the breeding season. For four resident species breeding in the immediate vicinity of the nets, results were compared to direct measures of productivity and breeding density as determined from nest monitoring, color banding of nestlings, and known densities of adults from spot-mapping censuses of color-banded individuals. Nets run 6 days/week captured an average of 42% of the Song Sparrows (*Melospiza melodia*) breeding within 100 m of the nets, whereas nets run 1 day/week averaged 10%. Capture rates of adult Wrentits (*Chamaea fasciata*) did not differ significantly between netting regimes. Nets run with higher frequency detected direction of change in productivity in Song Sparrows accurately, whereas nets run with lower frequency did not. The reverse was true for Wrentits, though Wrentit fledglings were twice as likely to be caught in the higher frequency nets. Distance from nest to net also influenced juvenile capture probability. Results indicate the importance of using standardized netting protocol, and show that demographic indices based on mist netting should not be directly compared among species. Optimal netting frequency to attain study goals should be evaluated separately for each species. We caution investigators from drawing conclusions regarding songbird population size and demography based on mist-netting data alone.

Key Words: capture probability, *Chamaea fasciata*, demographic monitoring, *Melospiza melodia*, mist netting, passerine, population size, sampling effort, spot mapping, Song Sparrow, Wrentit.

Constant effort mist-netting has been widely used as a method for monitoring breeding populations of passerines (DeSante 1991b, Ralph et al. 1993), although few studies have attempted to validate the technique (but see du Feu and McMeeking 1991; Nur et al. 2000, *this volume*; S. Baillie et al. unpubl. report).

In this paper we compare capture rates in two arrays of mist nets operated with different protocols, established on a plot where spot-mapping and nest-monitoring of color-banded individuals of four species provided an independent measure of population parameters (Lebreton et al. 1992). The two netting regimes differed in both the frequency of netting and the number of nets employed. We examine whether more intensive mist-netting effort leads to more accurate estimates of population size, productivity, and survivorship.

The use of mist nets to estimate the size of a breeding population requires knowledge of the likelihood of capture of adults (Jenni et al. 1996, Sauer and Link *this volume*). Capture likelihood could vary with many factors, including bird species, distance of territory to nets, number of intervening territories, year, and netting intensity (Nur et al. *this volume*). Here we compare capture rates of adults of four species for individuals known to be breeding within 100 and 200 m of each set of nets in each year.

Another important variable for estimating population size is the breeding status of individuals that are caught. Nur and Geupel (1993b) found that varying percent of breeding season captures consisted of transient individuals that did not breed on the study area, and Nur et al. (*this volume*) found that most Wrentits (*Chamaea fasciata*) captured during the breeding season were not territory holders. Whether or not an individual is recaptured at least once within a season has been used as a means of separating transients from local breeders (Peach 1993, Chase et al. 1997, Gardali et al. 2000). We compare within season recapture rates of known breeders between the two netting regimes.

If mist nets recapture sufficient numbers of individuals from one year to the next, the data may be used in adult survivorship calculations (Clobert et al. 1987, Nur et al. 1999). Knowledge of adult survivorship is important to understanding population dynamics. We examine recapture rates of breeders known to have bred in 1992 that returned to breed on the study plot in 1993, for each netting regime and study species.

Finally, mist netting can be used to estimate productivity of breeding populations (DeSante and Geupel 1987, DeSante et al. 1993, Nur et al. 2000). Capture rates of hatch year (HY) individuals are often assumed to be an index of annual productivity. However, due to variation in natal dispersal strategies and catchability of juveniles produced from nests close to nets, the area being sampled is difficult or impossible to determine (Baker et al. 1995). We compare numbers of HY individuals caught with each netting regime to numbers known to have been produced on the study plot, and we determine the proportion of individuals produced locally and subsequently caught in each netting regime.

METHODS

Field work was conducted on a 36-ha plot at the Palomarin Field Station in the Point Reyes National Seashore in central coastal California. Densities of Song Sparrows (*Melospiza melodia*), Wrentits, Spotted Towhees (*Pipilo maculatus*), and Nuttall's White-crowned Sparrows (*Zonotrichia leucophrys nuttalli*) were determined by almost daily spot-map censusing throughout the breeding season (mid-March to July 31). These four species are obligate coastal scrub breeders at Palomarin; that is, 90% of their territories are located in scrub habitat as opposed to in adjacent forested habitats (Geupel and Ballard 2002; Point Reyes Bird Observatory [PRBO], unpubl. data). We located and monitored most nests of the study species, as described by Geupel and DeSante (1990) and Martin and Geupel (1993). In summary, we individually color-banded all nestlings surviving until their primaries broke sheath (usually a few days before fledging). Nestlings missing from the nest after banding were presumed fledged unless there was evidence of depredation. We recorded each nest's location, and its distance from the nearest mist net in each of the two net arrays. Further description of the study site and methods have been provided elsewhere (DeSante 1981, Geupel and DeSante 1990, Johnson and Geupel 1996, Nur et al. *this volume*).

Two arrays of 12-m mist nets were run with different frequency during the summers (May 1 to August 18) of 1992 and 1993 (Fig. 1). One array (the "daily nets") consisted of 20 nets placed relatively close together at 14 sites (6 were stacked 2 high), situated near the southeastern edge of the study area close to the border of coastal scrub and mixed evergreen forest (DeSante and Geupel 1987, Johnson and Geupel 1996). These nets were run at least 6 days/week during both breeding seasons. The other array (the "weekly nets") consisted of 10 nets at ten sites spaced at maximum

distances for safe operation (usually 5–20 m), situated in the center of the study area in continuous coastal scrub habitat. These nets were operated once and occasionally twice in 10 days through both breeding seasons. Captured birds were aged by combination of skull pneumatization and plumage characteristics (Pyle et al. 1987). Unbanded birds were given new bands. Netting effort was consistent for the two years of the study. Nets were made by Avinet (Dryden, New York), and were 36- and 30-mm mesh.

We evaluated the differences between netting regimes using log-likelihood tests (G-test) or Fisher's exact tests, depending on sample size (we used the latter where sample size was small). Results were considered significant if $P < 0.05$. We used logistic regression to model the effect of distance from nest to nearest net on capture probability.

RESULTS

CAPTURE RATES OF ADULTS

The weekly nets captured 10% of adult Song Sparrows breeding within 100 m of nets, significantly fewer than the daily nets, which captured 42% (G-test, controlling for year, $G = 7.22$, df = 1, $P = 0.007$) (Table 1, Fig. 2). For Wrentits, the netting regimes did not differ significantly, with 42% of those breeding within 100 m captured in the daily nets and 36% in the weekly nets ($G = 0.15$, df = 1, $P = 0.69$). There was no significant change in the proportion of breeders captured when we extended the distance to include all breeders within 200 m. No Wrentit breeding more than 150 m from either set of nets was captured (Fig. 2).

WITHIN-SEASON RECAPTURE RATES OF ADULTS

Song Sparrows were more likely to be caught twice or more within a season in the daily nets than in the weekly nets (Table 2). In fact, no Song Sparrows at all were recaptured in the weekly nets (Fisher's exact test, pooling years, $P = 0.025$). The

TABLE 1. CAPTURE RATES FOR BREEDERS NESTING AT DIFFERENT DISTANCES FROM NETS, COMPARING DAILY TO WEEKLY NETS

| Species | Netting intensity | Year | Breeders within 100 m | | | Breeders within 200 m | | |
| | | | Number present | Captured | | Number present | Captured | |
				Number	Percent		Number	Percent
Song Sparrow	Daily	1992	13	5	39	22	6	27
		1993	9	4	44	23	4	17
	Weekly	1992	18	2	11	49	3	6
		1993	13	1	8	37	1	3
Wrentit	Daily	1992	18	6	33	32	6	19
		1993	12	6	50	30	7	23
	Weekly	1992	50	20	40	66	20	30
		1993	45	14	31	65	17	26

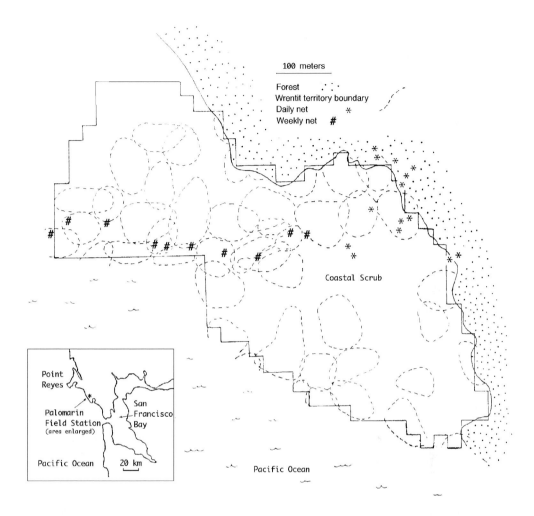

FIGURE 1. The study plot at the Palomarin field station of the Point Reyes Bird Observatory (boundary shown with solid lines). Examples of typical Wrentit territories (as determined from spot mapping in 1985) are marked by dashed lines.

difference between capture rates for Wrentits breeding within 100 m of either set of nets was not significant (G = 2.14, df = 1, P = 0.14; Fisher's exact test, pooling years, P = 0.137). Within a season, both regimes were more effective at recapturing Wrentits than Song Sparrows.

BETWEEN-YEAR RECAPTURE RATES OF ADULTS

The daily nets caught more returning Song Sparrows than did the weekly nets, which recaught none (P = 0.044; Table 3). The daily nets caught fewer returning Wrentits than the weekly nets, but this difference was not significant (P = 0.668). Thus, for Song Sparrows, but not for Wrentits, between-year capture rates declined as netting frequency declined.

Nonetheless, capture–recapture rates for Wrentits, but not for Song Sparrows, were high enough from both the weekly and daily nets for us to calculate adult survivorship after an additional year of netting (Nur et al. 1999).

CAPTURE RATES OF HY BIRDS COMPARED TO NUMBER FLEDGED

For Song Sparrows, the capture rates of hatching year birds in the daily nets reflected a decrease in productivity between 1992 and 1993, showing an 11% decrease in HY birds/100 net-h, and thus matched the change in productivity known to have taken place over the entire study plot (–13%), but underestimated the change for birds nesting within

Song Sparrow

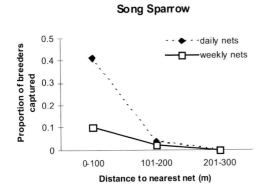

Wrentit

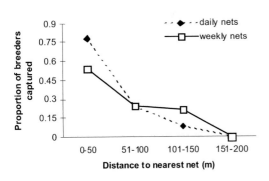

FIGURE 2. Recapture rates of adult breeding Song Sparrows and Wrentits related to distance from nest or territory center to nearest mist net.

200 m of nets (−28%; Table 4). Capture rates in the weekly nets failed to track the number of nestlings known to have fledged at either distance from nets. In fact, capture rates went up whereas the number fledged went down.

For Wrentits, capture rates in the daily nets did not reflect productivity changes at any distance, showing a 32% decrease in HY birds caught/100 net-h between 1992 and 1993 whereas known productivity went up 39% overall, and up 20% within 200 m of nets. The weekly nets performed better; capture rates went up 21% whereas total number fledged on the study plot went up 39%, though within 200 m they went up by 98%. Thus, whereas capture rates

TABLE 2. PROPORTION OF BREEDERS WITHIN 100 M OF THE NETS THAT WERE CAUGHT MORE THAN ONCE PER YEAR, 1992 AND 1993, COMPARING DAILY TO WEEKLY NETS

Species	Netting intensity	Year	Breeders	Captured > once	Percent
Song Sparrow	Daily	1992	13	2	15
		1993	9	2	22
	Weekly	1992	18	0	0
		1993	13	0	0
Wrentit	Daily	1992	18	3	17
		1993	12	4	33
	Weekly	1992	50	9	18
		1993	45	2	4

in the weekly nets reflected the general direction of productivity change on the study plot, they did not reflect the magnitude of this change, particularly for Wrentits breeding closer to the nets.

CAPTURE RATES OF FLEDGLINGS PRODUCED ON THE STUDY PLOT

Compared to weekly nets, the daily nets caught significantly more locally produced White-crowned Sparrows (G = 8.65, P = 0.003) and Song Sparrows (G = 20.12, P < 0.001), and more (but not significantly more) Spotted Towhees and Wrentits (Table 5). For White-crowned Sparrows and Song Sparrows, the ratio of captures was about 5 to 1 (daily vs. weekly), similar to the ratio in netting frequency. For Spotted Towhees, the ratio was 2.5 to 1, and for Wrentits, only 1.17 to 1 (i.e., 17% more HY birds were caught in the daily nets compared to the weekly nets).

The number of fledglings captured was biased somewhat by differing distributions of breeding birds in relation to the different netting regimes. That is, the weekly nets were located closer to higher bird densities, especially for Wrentits. Using logistic regression to control for the effect of proximity, the predicted capture probability of a Wrentit fledged 100 m from the daily nets (combining both years) was 0.35. For the weekly nets it was 0.17 (Table 6). This difference was significant (P < 0.01). Thus, the daily nets were approximately twice as likely as the

TABLE 3. RETURN RATES OF BANDED BREEDERS NESTING WITHIN 100 M OF THE NEAREST NET, COMPARING DAILY TO WEEKLY NETS

Species	Daily nets			Weekly nets		
	Number returning	Number captured	Percent captured	Number returning	Number captured	Percent captured
Song Sparrow	6	3	50	9	0	0
Wrentit	7	2	29	19	8	42

TABLE 4. DETECTING PRODUCTIVITY WITH DAILY AND WEEKLY NETTING

Species	Netting intensity	Year	HY birds captured	Number/ 100 net-h	Number fledged In study plot	Number fledged <200m
Song Sparrow	Daily	1992	77	0.75	76	21
		1993	66	0.67	66	13
Percent change				-11%	-13%	-28%
	Weekly	1992	16	1.40	76	47
		1993	13	1.67	66	43
Percent change				+19%	-13%	-9%
Wrentit	Daily	1992	77	0.75	86	24
		1993	51	0.52	120	29
Percent change				-32%	+39%	+20%
	Weekly	1992	41	3.60	86	45
		1993	34	4.35	120	89
Percent change				+21%	+39%	+98%

weekly nets to catch Wrentits fledged 100 m from the closest net. There were too few captures to carry out similar analyses for other species.

DISCUSSION

We demonstrated important differences in capture rates among species and netting strategies, which argue against drawing conclusions regarding adult survivorship, breeding population size, or productivity from mist-netting data alone. For one species, increased effort increased the proportion of the actual breeding population sampled, whereas for another this was not true. Increased effort increased proportion of the locally produced young captured in all four species evaluated, but not to the same extent. There was also substantial annual variation in these parameters, as N. Nur and G. Geupel (unpubl. report), using the same daily nets in the period 1980–1991, found that 71% (versus our 17 to 33%) of Wrentit breeders were caught more than once within a given year. Given this level of annual variation in capture probability, the importance of standardization of techniques among years and study sites cannot be overstated.

Numerous factors have been shown to affect capture rates, and these should be expected to vary among species. For example, differences in post-fledging movement may have been responsible for our low capture rates in weekly nets for locally fledged sparrows, but not Wrentits. Song Sparrows have higher dispersal distances and tend to be less sedentary than Wrentits (Nur and Geupel 1993b; PRBO, unpubl. data). It is likely that young Song Sparrows range farther from their natal territories and do this relatively abruptly, therefore spending less time in the vicinity of mist nets that intersect their territories (Nice 1937). Wrentit juveniles have been observed to stay with family groups near their natal territory an average of thirty days after fledging, and thus have a greater likelihood of being captured in mist nets, even if these nets are run only once or twice per week (Geupel and DeSante 1990). However, Song Sparrows are probably more similar to most North American passerines in dispersal strategy, flying ability, and escape frequency than Wrentits, which are known for their uniqueness in these areas (Geupel and Ballard 2002).

Other studies have also found different capture rates for different species. Du Feu and McMeeking

TABLE 5. PROPORTION OF LOCALLY PRODUCED FLEDGLINGS CAUGHT DURING 1992 AND 1993 COMBINED, COMPARING DAILY WITH WEEKLY NETS

Species	Number fledged	Daily nets Number captured	Daily nets Percent captured	Weekly nets Number captured	Weekly nets Percent captured	P	Ratio (daily:weekly)
White-crowned Sparrow	76	12	15.8	2	3.9	0.003	6.0
Song Sparrow	142	34	23.9	8	5.6	<0.001	4.3
Spotted Towhee	39	5	12.8	2	5.1	ns	2.5
Wrentit	206	41	19.9	35	16.9	ns	1.2

TABLE 6. EFFECT OF DISTANCE TO NEAREST NET ON CAPTURE PROBABILITY OF LOCALLY PRODUCED WRENTITS, COMPARING DAILY WITH WEEKLY NETS

Distance from nest to nearest net (m)	Daily nets		Weekly nets	
	Capture probability estimate	95% confidence interval	Capture probability estimate	95% confidence interval
0	0.488	0.33–0.65	0.221	0.14–0.33
100	0.350	0.12–0.47	0.169	0.12–0.23

Notes: Results of logistic regression analysis. P < 0. 001 for model including distance and netting frequency.

(1991) found that a netting regime's captures of Eurasian Blackbirds (*Turdus merula*) was correlated with local productivity, but that with Song Thrushes (*Turdus philomelos*) this correlation did not exist. Also, Nur and Geupel (1993b), using 12 years of data from the same daily nets we used, found that HY Song Sparrow capture rates mirrored true local production whereas capture rates of HY Wrentits did not.

Net shyness is another factor that probably differs among species. The fact that breeding Wrentits were caught less frequently in the daily nets than in the weekly nets may indicate learned net avoidance. If nets are run infrequently, it may be harder for birds (Wrentits, at least) to remember net locations (see also Faaborg et al. *this volume*). However, analyses conducted by Nur et al. (*this volume*) using capture–recapture techniques indicated no evidence of learned net avoidance in Wrentits, as recapture probability in the daily nets was high (71%) 1981–1991, and all breeders with territories within 50 m of nets were recaptured each year. Also (in our study), Song Sparrows were not captured unless nets were run fairly often, and therefore net avoidance did not appear to be a factor.

Habitat may also affect capture rates differently between species (Ballard et al. 2003). In our study, the daily nets were situated closer to and in the forest adjacent to the coastal scrub study plot. All study species nested in much higher densities in coastal scrub habitat at Palomarin than in the forested habitat. Neither Wrentits nor Song Sparrows regularly held territories in the forested habitat, so forest nets were not expected to capture as many of either species. Still, it is possible that Song Sparrows were more likely than Wrentits to venture into the forest habitat, which could also be an explanation for why the daily nets captured more of this species. It would be instructive to evaluate the effect of habitat by repeating our study using a design that varies netting frequency within each habitat type.

We did not test for effects of net density on capture rates, but this factor should also be expected to affect species differently, depending on territory size and movement patterns.

Other authors have related differences in capture rates between species to the birds' different morphologies. Jenni et al. (1996) found that all study species showed similar ability to avoid nets, but that certain species were significantly less likely to escape from the net after being caught. They related this finding to skull width and overall size and mass of the bird. Wrentits and Song Sparrows are relatively similar in size and weight, but Wrentits have longer tarsi, which may be more easily tangled in nets (Wrentit: mean = 25.07 mm, N = 238, SE = 0.24; Song Sparrow: mean = 21.07 mm, N = 216, SE = 0.32).

Capture rates are probably influenced also by the placement of individual nets, but this is difficult to assess (Ballard et al. 2003, Berthold *this volume*). Micro-habitat differences, exposure to sun or wind, and density of net placements relative to number of bird territories are some of the variables that could have significant effects on the effectiveness of different nets for different species. We found that individual nets caught a high percentage of Song Sparrows, and other nets caught a high percentage of the Wrentits. In fact, nets side by side often had completely different capture rates (PRBO, unpubl. data). Jenni et al. (1996) found that exposure to wind and sunlight both affected capture rates, varying by habitat and bird-species composition. These considerations warrant further investigations of sampling effectiveness of various net locations.

For most species at our site, capture rates were not high enough for estimating relative abundance, adult survivorship, or relative productivity of our locally breeding birds. Increased effort generally improved our ability to determine these population parameters, even for species in which net shyness may have been an issue (see above), but never reached an adequate sample size for most other species breeding nearby. Possibly we could increase netting intensity without increasing frequency (e.g., use

100 nets, each run 1 day in 10, rather than running the same 10 nets daily). However, as the coverage area is increased, details of local populations might be lost. Our nets captured a surprisingly small segment of the local population (birds breeding within 200 m, at best), and sometimes only if nets were run with high frequency.

CONCLUSIONS

Our results and others discussed here indicate the importance of standardizing all aspects of mist netting, from using the same net locations to maintaining the same netting frequency throughout a study. However, regardless of netting frequency, different species were not equally represented in mist nets. To obtain sufficient sample size to attain study objectives, it may not be possible to use the optimal netting frequency for each species individually.

Validation of results provided by mist nets requires knowledge of true population size and productivity data, which are best provided by daily nest-searching and territory mapping of color-banded individuals. We recommend continued investigations of true breeding population sizes for disparate species and locales, which will greatly enhance the interpretability of data gathered by mist-netting alone.

ACKNOWLEDGMENTS

We thank the many volunteers, interns, and staff of the Palomarin Field Station for their hours in the poison oak cutting net lanes, nest-searching, and attending mist nets. Thanks also to the membership and board of Point Reyes Bird Observatory for their continued enthusiastic support of research in avian ecology. This manuscript benefited greatly from the comments of several reviewers, particularly C. J. Ralph, E. H. Dunn, and L. Thomas. This is PRBO contribution number 1095.

Studies in Avian Biology No. 29:28–45

METHODOLOGICAL CONSIDERATIONS OF THE MONITORING AVIAN PRODUCTIVITY AND SURVIVORSHIP (MAPS) PROGRAM

DAVID F. DESANTE, JAMES F. SARACCO, DANIELLE R. O'GRADY, KENNETH M. BURTON, AND BRETT L. WALKER

Abstract. The Monitoring Avian Productivity and Survivorship (MAPS) Program is a cooperative program to generate annual indices of adult population size, post-fledging productivity, and estimates of adult survivorship for landbirds at multiple spatial scales. The program consists of a network of constant effort mist-netting and banding stations spread across North America. We use MAPS data collected from 1989 through 1993 (1995 for one analysis) to investigate methods of data collection and analysis, focusing on the following critical areas: density of nets, starting and ending dates each year, number of days of operation per 10-day period, verification of data, pooling of data for between-year comparisons, comparison of indices of adult population size from mist netting and point counts, and the use and interpretation of mark–recapture analyses. Results provide justification for current recommended MAPS methodology: operation of about ten 12-m, 30-mm-mesh mist nets over an area of about 8 ha, for six morning hours per day, for one day per 10-day period, and for six to ten 10-day periods (depending on latitude), with operations beginning after and ending before most of the migrant individuals have passed through the local area.

Key Words: constant-effort mist netting, MAPS, methods, population size, productivity, survivorship.

The Monitoring Avian Productivity and Survivorship (MAPS) Program is a North America-wide constant effort mist-netting program that was established to collect large-scale, long-term demographic data on landbirds. Its primary purposes are to (1) help identify causal factors driving population trends documented by other North American avian monitoring programs, such as the Breeding Bird Survey (BBS), Breeding Bird Census, Winter Bird Population Study, and Christmas Bird Count; (2) help formulate management actions to reverse population declines and maintain stable or increasing populations; and (3) help evaluate and enhance the effectiveness of implemented management actions (DeSante 1991a, 1992; DeSante et al. 1993a,b, 1995, 2001). BBS and other monitoring programs have supplied convincing evidence for recent declines in many landbird species, including many that winter in the Neotropics (Robbins et al. 1989, Terborgh 1989), and those findings were the major impetus leading to the establishment of the Neotropical Migratory Bird Conservation Program, "Partners in Flight." By themselves, however, the monitoring programs listed above provide little direction on management needed to reverse population declines. They provide no information on primary demographic parameters (productivity and survivorship), and thus fail to distinguish problems caused by birth-rate effects on the breeding grounds from problems caused by death-rate effects that may operate primarily on the wintering grounds or migration routes (Temple and

Wiens 1989, DeSante 1992). MAPS is designed to fill this information gap.

MAPS is a cooperative effort among public agencies, private organizations, and individual bird banders. It was established in 1989 by The Institute for Bird Populations and was patterned to a large extent after the Constant Effort Sites (CES) Scheme, operated by the British Trust for Ornithology (BTO) since 1981 (Baillie et al. 1986, Peach et al. *this volume*). MAPS has grown continuously since 1989 to over 500 stations operated continent-wide during 2002.

In this paper we discuss some of the reasoning and testing behind the methods chosen for the MAPS protocol, and the ramifications of both field and analytical methods on the accuracy and precision of results. We also identify some unresolved methodological and analytical difficulties regarding the interpretation of MAPS data, and indicate where additional work is needed to resolve these issues.

METHODS

The following terminology is used in this paper. Post-fledging "productivity" is an index of the relative number of hatch-year birds that attain independence from their parents and begin post-juvenile dispersal, and is represented by proportion of young in the catch. Adult "survivorship" is a measure of death rate and is estimated by mark–recapture analyses as the apparent annual survival probability of adults; that is, the probability of an adult bird surviving and returning in year $i+1$ to the location where it was marked in year *i*. Survivorship thus includes components of actual survival and site fidelity. "Recapture probability" is the conditional probability of recapturing a marked bird in year *i*+1, given that it survived from year *i* to *i* +1 and returned in year *i*+1 to the location where it was marked in year *i*. "First capture" refers to the first capture of a bird in year *i*, regardless of whether or not it had been captured in a previous year. Effort "saturation" is said to have occurred in a closed population when rate of first captures declines due to most birds already having been captured once. "Net avoidance" refers to lowered recapture probability of individual birds that have been captured (or, perhaps, hit a net and bounced out), as a result of learning to avoid nets or specific net sites.

The overall design of the MAPS Program and methods used to establish and operate MAPS stations have been described in detail in DeSante et al. (1993a,b, 2002). Analysis methods are detailed in DeSante et al. (1993b, 1995, 1996), DeSante and Burton (1994), and Nott and DeSante (2002), and are only briefly outlined here. Indices of annual population size are calculated as the numbers of first captures of adult birds of each species (and of all species pooled) in each year, pooled over all stations of interest (e.g., grouped by geographic region, habitat characteristics, or population trends of a target species) that lie within the breeding range of each species. Similar calculations are completed for first captures of young birds, and indices of productivity are then calculated for each species (and for all species pooled) as the proportion of young in the total catch. Following Baillie et al. (1986), the significance of annual changes is inferred statistically from confidence intervals calculated from the standard errors of the mean percent changes (Baillie et al. 1986, DeSante et al. 1993a, DeSante and Burton 1994). Peach et al. (1996) give revised formulae that take into account between-station heterogeneity in capture trends. We infer the statistical significance of regional between-year changes in adult population size and productivity by means of binomial tests on the proportion of target species that increased in each region. Annual adult survival rates and adult recapture probabilities are estimated from modified Cormack-Jolly-Seber (CJS) mark–recapture models (Clobert et al. 1987, Pollock et al. 1990, Lebreton et al. 1992)

Miscellaneous analyses were conducted in support of the results and discussion to follow. For purposes of clarity, we include details related to each analysis along with the relevant results. Results are given as means ±SE unless stated otherwise.

RESULTS AND DISCUSSION

FIELD METHODS

Net characteristics

Number and density of nets can have important effects on the precision of mark–recapture estimates of adult population size and adult survivorship. Spreading nets as widely as possible will tend to

increase the number of territories intersected, and thus the population size sampled, but will tend to decrease recapture probability for the birds on any single territory, and vice versa. There should exist some intermediate net density that will simultaneously optimize both the number of different individual adults captured and the recapture probability of these adults, although this optimal net density is likely to differ among species and among habitat types.

Figure 1 presents a plot of total capture rate (including recaptures) of adult birds (all species pooled), as a function of net density. Data were collected in 1990 from 25 MAPS stations located in forest or forest-edge habitats, all using 12-m nets, and all operated for one or two days per 10-day period. (Stations that were operated for more than two days per 10-day period were excluded from this analysis because of potential saturation and net-avoidance problems; see Burton and DeSante *this volume* and below). Highest capture rates appeared to occur at net densities between about 0.6 and 1.7 nets per ha, although variance was high. As a rule of thumb, therefore, we suggest that MAPS stations operate 12-m nets at net densities between about 1.0 and 1.5 nets per ha, and recommend that 10 nets be operated in an 8-ha netting area (1.25 nets per ha). The upper limit on the number of nets that can be used at any station, and the lower limit on net density, should be set by the number of people available to operate a station. Operators must be able to visit all net locations within 10–15 min if no birds are caught (Ralph et al. 1993). We suggest that the 8-ha netting area be centrally located in a 20-ha study area of similar habitat that defines the MAPS station and its boundaries.

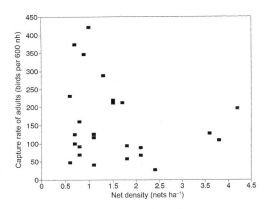

FIGURE 1. Capture rate of adult birds (all species pooled) at varying net densities. Data are from 25 MAPS stations operated in forest or forest-edge habitats for one or two days per 10-day period in 1990.

To provide optimal coverage, nets should be placed relatively uniformly throughout the netting area. Within this general constraint, however, nets should be placed opportunistically at locations where birds can be captured most efficiently, such as brushy portions of wooded areas, forest breaks, and near water. This is because larger sample sizes and higher recapture probabilities contribute to stronger inference in analyses (as well as being more interesting for station operators).

To promote similarity of species' catchability among stations, we recommend that all stations use the same type of net. For maximum captures of small birds (most target species weigh less than about 30–35 g), and for ease of extraction of birds of all sizes, we suggest the use of 30-mm mesh, four-tier, tethered, black nylon mist nets (Heimerdinger and Leberman 1966, Pardieck and Waide 1992). All nets should be 12 m in length, for uniformity and ease of handling. If nets of other lengths must be used, netting effort should be calculated accordingly (e.g., the use of a 6-m net for one hour should be counted as 1/2 net-h).

Schedule of operation

Start and end times.—The breeding season is divided into 12 equal 10-day periods between May 1 and August 28 (although some stations in extreme southern United States may start earlier). It is important that the first netting session take place after the vast majority of spring migrant individuals of the target species have moved through the study area. This is because inclusion of migrating adult individuals in the data will negatively bias both productivity indices and survivorship estimates, since low (or zero) recapture rates of migrants can be mistaken as high mortality in adults.

For example, we estimated adult survival probabilities (all species pooled) from three years of mark-recapture data for each of eight stations operated in 1989–1991. Four of these eight stations were also migration-banding stations, and submitted data to the MAPS Program that were collected during the latter part of the migration season. Annual survival estimates for various species from these eight stations ranged from 0.05 to 0.38 (mean = 0.27 ± 0.04), and were only 50–60% of the generally expected values for temperate-zone passerines (Loery et al. 1987, Karr et al. 1990a, Pollock et al. 1990, Peach 1993). Moreover, data from these early netting sessions cannot simply be dropped from analysis, because this could introduce another negative bias in survival

estimates if locally-resident birds that are captured during these early netting sessions display net avoidance and are not captured during subsequent netting sessions (Burton and DeSante *this volume*).

Even though mark-recapture analysis models have recently been developed to account for the presence of transient individuals (Peach et al. 1990, Peach 1993, Pradel et al. 1997, Nott and DeSante 2002; also see DeSante et al. 1995 and below), it is likely that these models will perform better with data free from large numbers of migrant individuals. To avoid operating MAPS stations while large numbers of spring migrants are still passing through, we have established a tiered schedule for beginning the operation of MAPS stations (Fig. 2) that ranges from Period 1 (May 1–10) in the extreme southern parts of the United States through Period 5 (June 10–19) over most of Canada and Alaska. We strongly discourage netting at MAPS stations prior to the appropriate time for beginning operation of the station.

At the other end of the season, we originally recommended that all MAPS stations be operated through Period 12 (August 19–28), even though fall migration of target species may already be underway. We reasoned that data from later periods (e.g., Periods 11 and 12) could be eliminated prior to analysis if desired, especially as very few adults breeding at MAPS stations are captured for the first time late in the season. Moreover, excluding late netting sessions from British CES analysis did not significantly change regional productivity indices, but tended to increase precision of the estimates (Baillie et al. 1986, Peach et al. *this volume*). This led to recommendations in the CES Scheme to operate each station, if possible, for all twelve 10-day periods.

Similar analyses of MAPS precision have not yet been conducted. However, using data from six stations in each of three regions, we compared productivity indices based on data collected over all or only part of the 1992 season. In all three cases, we found highly significant correlation between the productivity indices from the two time periods (Fig. 3), although this might have been expected because data from the truncated period were included in the data from the entire time period. At Shenandoah (Fig. 3A), where only one netting session was run after August 8, the slope of the regression was not significantly different from 1.0 (P = 0.30). At Wenatchee (Fig. 3B) and Flathead (Fig. 3C), which each had two netting sessions after August 8, the slopes were significantly or near significantly different from 1.0 (P = 0.03 for Wenatchee and P = 0.07 for Flathead). In all three locations, data from the longer time period

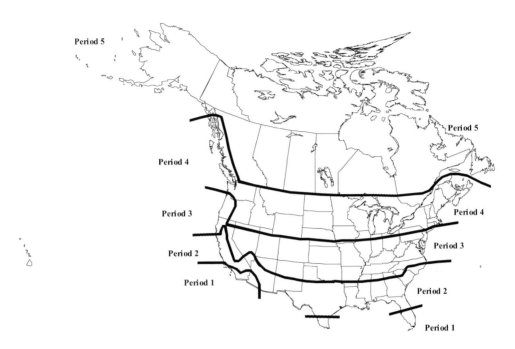

FIGURE 2. Recommended starting periods for MAPS stations in five geographic regions. Period 1 = May 1–10; Period 2 = May 11–20; Period 3 = May 21–30; Period 4 – May 31 –June 9; Period 5 = June 10–19.

gave higher productivity indices. Differences, however, were small between productivity indices calculated from the truncated period and those calculated from the entire period (averaged over species for which at least 10 aged individuals were captured during the entire period): 0.03 ± 0.02 (N = 11 species) at Shenandoah, 0.09 ± 0.02 (N = 24) at Wenatchee, and 0.08 ± 0.02 (N = 20) at Flathead. Results for individual species were similar; most showed higher productivity indices when these were calculated over the longer period, and in most of the relatively common species these increases were small (<0.10, including ten of the 11 species studied at Shenandoah, 15 of 24 at Wenatchee, and 14 of 20 at Flathead). Despite the small magnitude of difference, the lower productivity indices calculated without data from the last two netting periods may provide a more representative index of local productivity, rather than being confounded by an influx of migrating individuals from further north.

To gauge the extent to which migrating individuals might be occurring at MAPS stations and to assess the timing of their occurrences, we analyzed levels of subcutaneous fat found on birds captured at MAPS stations during 1992–1995 as a function of geographical region and 10-day period (Fig. 4). Throughout the breeding season (June through early August), substantial numbers of birds (10–30% depending on region) had very light fat deposits (fat classes 1 or 2). Few birds (generally <5%) had light-moderate fat deposits (fat class 3) and very few (generally <1%) had moderate-heavy or heavy fat deposits (fat class 4 or greater). In sharp contrast, during Periods 1–3 (May 1–30, although the total numbers of captures were low during these periods because most stations delayed initiating station operation according to the schedule presented in Fig. 2) and Periods 11–12 (August 9–28), substantial numbers of birds (generally >10%) had moderate to high fat deposits (fat classes ≥3).

These data suggest that substantial numbers of migrating individual birds are being captured at MAPS stations in all geographic regions during Periods 11 and 12, and that the operation of MAPS stations should be curtailed after Period 10 (July 30–August 8). This will likely have a negligible effect on recapture probabilities of locally resident adults, because few such birds are captured during Periods 11–12 that were not already captured earlier in the season. It will, however, provide productivity indices more representative of the local area in which the station is located, and will reduce the time commitment and expense of operating MAPS stations by 17%–25%, depending on the starting date of the station. This recommendation was included in standardized MAPS protocol beginning in 1997.

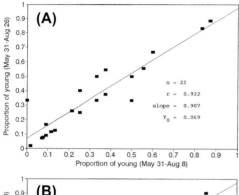

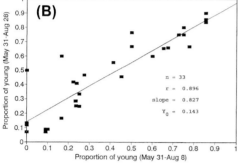

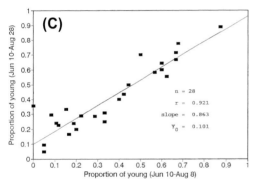

FIGURE 3. Regression of the proportion of young caught during all 10-day periods vs. the proportion of young caught in all but the last two 10-day periods during 1992 for all stations (N) at three stations.

The difference between North America and Britain is apparently that huge numbers of long-distance migrant landbirds from farther north pass through North American MAPS stations during mid-late August, whereas relatively few such migrants from north of Britain pass through British CES stations during that time.

Netting frequency.—Increasing the number of days of operation per 10-day period will, of course, increase the number of birds captured. However, there is also likely to be a rapid fall-off in captures after two or three days of operation because of

saturation and net-avoidance effects (Burton and DeSante *this volume*). Another potential problem of netting too often is that disturbance to captured birds might contribute to nest failures or to birds moving out of the netting area.

Surprisingly little is known about the extent and role of saturation and net avoidance in affecting the results of mist-netting studies. Kaiser (1993b) showed that migrating birds may sometimes avoid specific capture locations after first capture, but do not recognize nets in other locations as something to be avoided. How long avoidance of capture location may last is poorly known. MAPS data collected during the breeding season showed that some adult individuals of certain species (e.g., Swainson's Thrush [scientific names in tables], MacGillivray's Warbler, Lincoln's Sparrow) are often recaptured later in the season in the same net in which they were first captured (Institute for Bird Populations, unpubl. data). The actual extent of net avoidance probably varies among species, possibly differs between the breeding season (when birds are faithful to a nest site) and non-breeding seasons, and may even differ among individuals within a species. Recent advances in mark–recapture software (RELEASE) provide goodness-of-fit tests that can detect net-avoidance effects (Pradel 1993). However, such tests have not yet been applied to MAPS data.

Burton and DeSante (*this volume*) suggested that both saturation and net-avoidance effects seemed to occur in adults but not in young birds, and appeared to increase with increasing frequency of operation. We tested this by establishing two adjacent MAPS stations in a single habitat type at the Patuxent River Naval Air Station and operating one for one day per 10-day period and the other for two days per 10-day period (usually consecutive days), over two years (1992 and 1993). In both years, the rate of first captures for young birds (all species pooled) was roughly the same between stations; i.e., about twice as many individual young birds were captured at the two-day station as at the one-day station (Table 1). This was expected, because there was constant turnover of young birds through dispersal, such that net avoidance should not have been a serious problem. By contrast, the rate of first captures for adult birds (all species pooled) was lower at the two-day station than at the one-day station by 22.2% in 1992 and by 35.7% in 1993. As a result, the productivity index was 9% higher at the two-day station in 1992 and 42% higher in 1993. Clearly, increasing the frequency of operation at a station tends to bias productivity indices positively.

TABLE 1. NUMBERS OF INDIVIDUAL ADULT AND YOUNG BIRDS CAPTURED PER 600 NET-HOURS AND THE PROPORTIONS OF YOUNG IN THE CATCH AT TWO ADJACENT MAPS STATIONS

Species	1992							1993						
	One-day station			Two-day station				One-day station			Two-day station			
	Adult	Young	Proportion young	Adult	Young	Proportion young	Difference[a]	Adult	Young	Proportion young	Adult	Young	Proportion young	Difference
Yellow-billed Cuckoo (*Coccyzus americanus*)	-	-	-	0.0	0.6	1.00	-	0.9	0.0	0.00	0.5	0.0	0.00	0.00
Red-bellied Woodpecker (*Melanerpes carolinus*)	-	-	-	1.2	0.0	0.00	-	1.8	0.0	0.00	-	-	-	-
Downy Woodpecker (*Picoides pubescens*)	1.2	-	0.00	0.6	0.0	0.00	-	-	-	-	0.0	0.5	1.00	1.00
Northern Flicker (*Colaptes auratus*)	1.2	-	0.00	-	-	-	-	-	-	-	-	-	-	-
Eastern Wood-Pewee (*Contopus virens*)	-	-	-	0.6	0.0	0.00	-	1.0	0.0	0.00	-	-	-	-
Acadian Flycatcher (*Empidonax virescens*)	2.5	0.0	0.00	2.3	1.2	0.33	+0.33	7.0	1.0	0.12	4.6	1.8	0.29	+0.17
Great Crested Flycatcher (*Myiarchus crinitus*)	1.2	0.0	0.00	-	-	-	-	0.9	0.0	0.00	-	-	-	-
White-eyed Vireo (*Vireo griseus*)	3.8	0.0	0.00	2.9	0.0	0.00	-	2.8	1.8	0.40	1.0	1.0	0.50	+0.10
Yellow-throated Vireo (*V. flavifrons*)	-	-	-	0.6	0.0	0.00	-	-	-	-	-	-	-	-
Red-eyed Vireo (*V. olivaceus*)	13.8	1.2	0.08	8.8	1.8	0.17	+0.09	11.0	0.0	0.00	5.1	1.0	0.17	+0.17
Blue Jay (*Cyanocitta cristata*)	-	-	-	-	-	-	-	-	-	-	1.5	0.5	0.25	-
Carolina Chickadee (*Poecile carolinensis*)	1.2	0.0	0.00	1.8	0.6	0.25	+0.25	2.0	0.0	0.00	3.7	0.9	0.20	+0.20
Tufted Titmouse (*Baeolophus bicolor*)	3.8	5.0	0.57	2.9	2.9	0.50	-0.07	1.8	3.7	0.67	3.1	4.1	0.57	-0.10
Carolina Wren (*Thryothorus ludovicianus*)	5.0	3.8	0.43	3.5	5.3	0.60	+0.17	1.8	3.7	0.67	3.1	6.1	0.67	0.00
Veery (*Catharus fuscescens*)	1.2	0.0	0.00	-	-	-	-	0.5	0.0	-	0.5	0.0	0.00	-
Wood Thrush (*Hylocichla mustelina*)	2.5	2.5	0.50	3.5	1.8	0.33	-0.17	5.5	0.9	0.14	5.6	1.5	0.21	+0.07
American Robin (*Turdus migratorius*)	-	-	-	-	-	-	-	0.9	0.0	0.00	-	-	-	-
Gray Catbird (*Dumetella carolinensis*)	1.2	0.0	0.00	0.6	0.0	0.00	-	-	-	-	1.0	0.0	0.00	-
Brown Thrasher (*Toxostoma rufum*)	-	-	-	0.6	0.6	0.50	-	-	-	-	0.5	0.0	0.00	-
Pine Warbler (*Dendroica pinus*)	-	-	-	0.6	0.0	0.00	-	-	-	-	0.5	0.5	0.50	-
Black-and-white Warbler (*Mniotilta varia*)	-	-	-	0.0	0.6	1.00	-	0.0	2.8	1.00	0.5	2.5	0.83	-0.17
American Redstart (*Setophaga ruticilla*)	-	-	-	1.2	0.0	0.00	-	-	-	-	-	-	-	-
Prothonotary Warbler (*Protonotaria citrea*)	-	-	-	-	-	-	-	0.9	0.0	0.00	0.5	1.0	0.67	-
Worm-eating Warbler (*Helmitheros vermivorus*)	2.5	0.0	0.00	1.8	1.8	0.50	+0.30	0.9	0.9	0.50	3.1	2.5	0.46	+0.17
Ovenbird (*Seiurus aurocapillus*)	5.0	1.3	0.20	-	-	-	-	5.5	2.8	0.33	0.0	1.0	1.00	+0.13
Louisiana Waterthrush (*S. motacilla*)	-	-	-	-	-	-	-	1.8	0.9	0.33	5.1	3.1	0.38	+0.77
Kentucky Warbler (*Oporornis formosus*)	8.8	5.0	0.36	2.9	0.0	0.00	-0.36	5.5	2.8	0.33	1.0	0.0	0.00	+0.05
Common Yellowthroat (*Geothlypis trichas*)	-	-	-	-	-	-	-	0.9	0.0	0.00	3.6	1.0	0.22	-
Hooded Warbler (*Wilsonia citrina*)	3.8	0.0	0.00	5.3	0.0	0.00	-	12.0	1.8	0.13	0.5	0.0	0.00	+0.09
Yellow-breasted Chat (*Icteria virens*)	-	-	-	-	-	-	-	0.5	0.0	-	1.5	0.0	0.00	-
Summer Tanager (*Piranga rubra*)	-	-	-	-	-	-	-	0.9	0.0	0.00	0.5	0.0	0.00	-
Scarlet Tanager (*P. olivacea*)	1.2	-	-	1.2	0.0	0.00	-	-	-	-	0.5	0.0	-	-

TABLE 1. CONTINUED

Species	1992 One-day station Adult	Young	Proportion young	1992 Two-day station Adult	Young	Proportion young	Difference[a]	1993 One-day station Adult	Young	Proportion young	1993 Two-day station Adult	Young	Proportion young	Difference
Northern Cardinal (*Cardinalis cardinalis*)	2.5	0.0	0.00	4.7	0.6	0.11	+0.11	4.6	0.9	0.17	2.0	0.5	0.20	+0.03
Eastern Towhee (*Pipilo erythrophthalmus*)	–	–	–	–	–	–		0.9	0.0	0.00	0.5	0.0	0.00	
Swamp Sparrow (*Melospiza georgiana*)	–	–	–	0.6	0.0	0.00		–	–	–	–	–	–	
Common Grackle (*Quiscalus quiscula*)	–	–	–	0.6	0.0	0.00		3.7	0.0	0.00	1.0	0.0	0.00	
Brown-headed Cowbird (*Molothrus ater*)	1.2	0.0	0.00	0.0	0.6	1.00	+1.00	–	–	–	–	–	–	
All species pooled	62.5	18.8	0.23	53.3	18.1	0.25	+0.02	73.7	25.8	0.26	47.4	27.5	0.37	+0.11
Number of species	18	6		22	12		7/10 +	22	13		25	16		11/14 +
Total number of species	18			25				23			27			

Notes: Data were from stations operated at the Patuxent Naval Air Station.
[a] Difference in proportion of young between 2-day and 1-day stations; shown only for cases when at least one station had a non-zero value.

We found similar results in 1990 and 1991 data obtained from the Palomarin MAPS station operated by the Point Reyes Bird Observatory (Table 2). This station is typically operated every day from May 1 through August 28. We compared productivity indices obtained from all 10 days of operation per 10-day period (the all-days method) with those obtained from only the first complete day of operation in each 10-day period (the first-day method). Analyses were conducted for all species pooled, and for 16 target species in which at least 10 first captures of adult birds were recorded during all days of operation in either year. In 1990, the all-days method showed 9.8% higher productivity for all species pooled, and 13.8% higher for the 16 target species. In 1991, the all-days method increased productivity for all species pooled by 7.2%, and for the target species by 15.1%. However, the two methods detected similar differences in productivity between 1990 and 1991. For all species pooled, productivity decreased 9.8% according to the all-days method and 7.6% according to the first-day method. For the 16 target species, the decreases were 9% and 10%, respectively, for the all-day and first-day methods. These results suggest that net avoidance may not affect the estimation of annual changes in productivity. However, this will only be true if the number of netting days in each netting session remains constant across all netting sessions at the station, both within and between seasons.

Another important conclusion is that a single day of operation per 10-day period is sufficient to provide accurate information on between-year changes in productivity indices, at least for the more common species. Because adding more stations will improve precision of regional productivity estimates more than will adding days of effort at a single station (Burton and DeSante *this volume*), we recommend that the best use of excess manpower would be to establish several (or larger) MAPS stations that operate for one day per 10-day period, rather than operate for additional days at a single station.

In accordance with the CES protocol (Baillie et al. 1986) and the data presented above, we strongly recommend that MAPS stations be operated for only one day in each 10-day period, with visits in adjacent periods being at least six days apart. Beginning in 1992, virtually all MAPS stations have used this recommendation for implementing the MAPS protocol.

Daily timing.—MAPS protocol recommends operating the entire array of nets for at least 4 h and, preferably, for 6 h per day beginning at local sunrise. This covers the period of the day when birds are

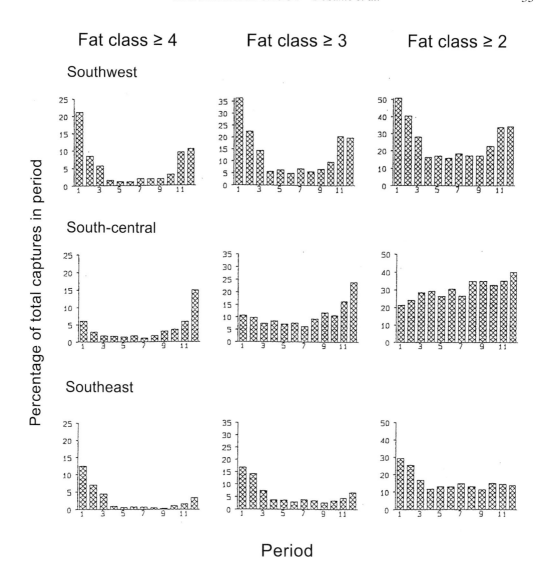

FIGURE 4. Frequency distributions of classes of subcutaneous fat carried by birds captured in the MAP Program as a function of 10-day period for three southern regions. Periods: 1 = May 1–10; 2 = May 11–20; 3 = May 21–30; 4 = May 31– Jun 9; 5 = Jun 10-19; 6 = Jun 20-29; 7 = Jun 30–Jul 9; 8 = Jul 10–19; 9 = Jul 20–29; 10 = Jul 30–Aug 8; 11 = Aug 9–18; 12 = Aug 19–28. (Continued on next page.)

most active. We recommend that nets not be operated if the average wind speed exceeds 10 knots (or gusts exceed 20 knots) or if other weather variables (i.e., precipitation or extreme heat or cold) are likely to endanger captured birds. If nets are closed early or opened late due to inclement weather or other unforeseen circumstances, we recommend that the missing hours be made up with netting in the equivalent time period on another day within the same 10-day period (or early in the next period). However, we only recommend making up lost effort if half or more of a normal day's operation is missed.

Standardization

All aspects of station operation must be kept constant through all years of operation. Otherwise, changes in numbers of birds captured could reflect changes in netting protocol, rather than changes in population characteristics. This is the reason for specifying the MAPS protocol in such detail. There may be large differences between stations in the numbers and ages of birds captured, but this should not affect regional estimates of annual change in productivity as long as the protocol at each station

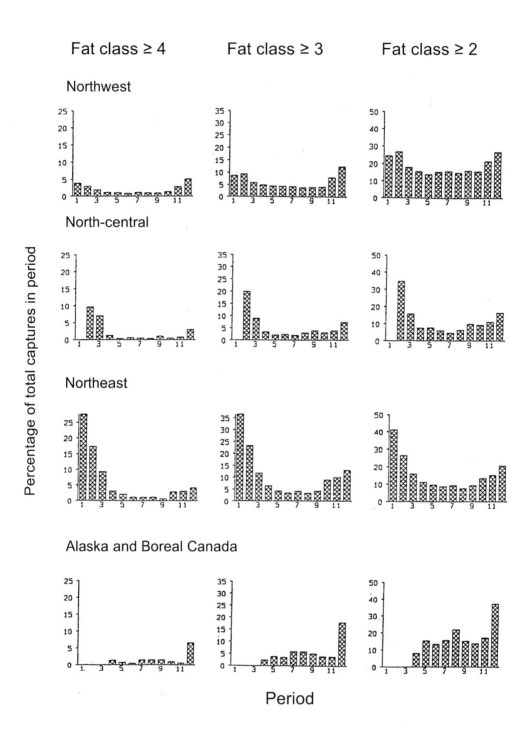

FIGURE 4. Continued. Four northern regions.

TABLE 2. PRODUCTIVITY INDICES (PROPORTION OF YOUNG IN THE CATCH) CALCULATED BY TWO METHODS FROM DATA COLLECTED AT A MAPS STATION OPERATED DAILY

Species	1990				1991				Difference: 1991–1990		
	N[a]	All days[b]	First day[c]	Difference[d]	N	All days	First day	Difference	All days	First day	Difference
Pacific-slope Flycatcher (*Empidonax difficilis*)	16	0.91	0.85	+0.06	35	0.73	0.53	+0.20	-0.18	-0.31	+0.14
Warbling Vireo (*Vireo gilvus*)	23	0.23	0.33	-0.10	9	0.18	0.00	+0.18	-0.05	-0.33	+0.28
Tree Swallow (*Tachycineta bicolor*)	12	0.00	0.00	0.00	12	0.00	0.00	0.00	0.00	0.00	0.00
Barn Swallow (*Hirundo rustica*)	14	0.65	0.57	+0.08	9	0.44	0.00	+0.44	-0.21	-0.57	+0.36
Chestnut-backed Chickadee (*Poecile rufescens*)	12	0.80	0.75	+0.05	12	0.79	0.81	-0.02	-0.01	+0.06	-0.07
Bushtit (*Psaltriparus minimus*)	7	0.67	0.00	+0.67	10	0.66	0.83	-0.18	-0.01	+0.83	-0.85
Bewick's Wren (*Thryomanes bewickii*)	12	0.73	0.67	+0.07	13	0.63	0.56	+0.07	-0.11	-0.11	+0.01
Swainson's Thrush (*Catharus ustulatus*)	45	0.39	0.25	+0.14	54	0.34	0.31	+0.03	-0.05	+0.06	-0.11
Wrentit (*Chamaea fasciata*)	12	0.78	0.56	+0.23	19	0.80	0.83	-0.04	+0.01	+0.28	-0.26
Orange-crowned Warbler (*Vermivora celata*)	51	0.45	0.50	-0.05	40	0.48	0.20	+0.28	+0.04	-0.30	+0.34
Wilson's Warbler (*Wilsonia pusilla*)	40	0.75	0.65	+0.11	45	0.63	0.47	+0.17	-0.12	-0.18	+0.06
Song Sparrow (*Melospiza melodia*)	25	0.67	0.83	-0.17	15	0.78	0.88	-0.10	+0.11	+0.04	+0.07
White-crowned Sparrow (*Zonotrichia leucophrys*)	7	0.76	1.00	-0.24	13	0.80	1.00	-0.20	+0.04	0.00	+0.04
Purple Finch (*Carpodacus purpureus*)	48	0.44	0.45	-0.02	54	0.29	0.21	+0.08	-0.14	-0.24	+0.10
Pine Siskin (*Carduelis pinus*)	14	0.39	0.25	+0.14	29	0.15	0.00	+0.15	-0.24	-0.25	+0.01
American Goldfinch (*C. tristis*)	9	0.10	0.00	+0.10	20	0.23	0.25	-0.02	+0.13	+0.25	-0.12
All species pooled	415	0.66	0.60	+0.06	472	0.60	0.56	+0.04	-0.06	-0.05	-0.02
Mean of 16 species		0.55	0.48	+0.07		0.50	0.43	+0.07	-0.05	-0.05	-0.00
SE of the mean		±0.07	±0.08	±0.05		±0.07	±0.09	±0.04	±0.03	±0.08	±0.07
Prop. species increase[e]				0.63				0.56			0.63

Notes: Data were from the Palomarin Field Station, operated by the Point Reyes Bird Observatory. Results are shown for species with at least ten first captures of adult birds in either year, and for all species pooled.
[a] Number of first captures of adult birds during all days of operation.
[b] Calculated using data from all days of operation each 10-day period.
[c] Calculated using data from only the first complete day of operation each 10-day period.
[d] Difference in proportion of young (or difference between the 1990–1991 difference in proportion of young) calculated by the two methods (presented as all-days method minus first-day method).
[e] Proportion of species for which the increase was positive.

remains constant from year to year. Consistency is needed in the numbers and design of nets used, their placement, and schedule of operation (time of starting and ending each day, number of days/10-day period, start and end date in the season). Finally, nets should be opened, checked, and closed in the same order, and that sequence should remain constant for all days and years of operation.

COLLECTION OF DATA AT A MAPS STATION

The following data are required for all birds captured in the MAPS Program, including recaptures, because they are required by the banding offices or are needed for calculation of productivity indices and survivorship estimates: station code, net number, date, time of capture (net-run time), band number, capture code (newly banded, recaptured, band changed, unbanded), status code (whether or not released back into the population), species, age, how aged, sex, and how sexed. In contrast, the following data are considered supplemental and are used in verification programs designed to identify questionable or contradictory species, age, and sex determinations: degree of skull pneumatization, extent of cloacal protuberance or brood patch, extent of body molt, type of flight-feather molt, extent of juvenal plumage, extent of primary-feather wear, wing chord, body mass, fat class, and bander's name. We strongly encourage all MAPS cooperators to collect these supplemental data, for without them there is no way of verifying the accuracy of the species, age, and sex determinations (see also Ralph et al. 1993). All other data that might be collected on mist-netted birds (e.g., tier of the net in which it was captured, direction bird entered the net, etc.) are not needed for the MAPS Program, although we accept any notes cooperators wish to add regarding any capture record. We require that all MAPS data be submitted using standardized metrics and codes provided by the MAPS Program.

We also require MAPS cooperators to provide detailed data on mist-netting effort, including station code, date, times of opening and closing each net array (or individual nets, if some are opened or closed earlier or later), and, if possible, starting times for all net runs. All times are rounded to the nearest 10-min (0700, 0710, 0720, etc.). These effort data are necessary for standardizing the effort at each station from year-to-year, for selecting data to be used in each year-to-year comparison (see below), and for estimating the effects of missed effort.

ANALYTICAL METHODS

Data verification

Each year, about 1/3 of all MAPS stations were operated by field biologist interns trained and supervised by biologists from The Institute for Bird Populations. Because these interns frequently had relatively little prior experience with mist netting and banding, we began their work periods with an intensive three-week training program. In addition, we developed data checks designed to catch errors during data entry and to provide a pre-analysis verification of the data. Verification procedures included four types: (1) checks that assured that entered codes were valid and that data fell within accepted ranges; (2) comparisons of species, age, and sex determinations against the supplemental data used to make those determinations (i.e., degree of skull pneumatization; presence of cloacal protuberances, brood patches, or juvenal plumage; and extent of body and flight-feather molt and primary-feather wear) that flagged discrepancies or suspicious data; (3) checks that identified unusual band numbers or band sizes for each species; and (4) checks that screened original banding and recapture data from all years of station operation for inconsistencies in species, age, and sex determinations for each band number.

An analysis of intern-collected data for 1993 showed that these four verification procedures flagged 4.7% of 16,790 capture records (Table 3). Although the majority of flagged records involved contradictions within a given capture record, a substantial proportion involved inconsistencies among different capture records. Of these, many were not errors at all, but cases in which recaptures provided additional information that allowed resolution of "unknown" codes in the earlier records.

The most frequent corrections to the data set were for sex determination (3.2% of total records). Most of these involved changing an unknown to a known sex upon recapture or, to a lesser extent, vice versa. The latter cases often involved birds questionably or erroneously sexed by small cloacal protuberances or light brood patches early in the season. Changes in age determination were less frequent (1.7% of total records) and usually involved questionable or erroneous skull determinations, often caused by confusion between a fully pneumatized (adult) and a nearly completely non-pneumatized (young) skull, with errors being detected upon recapture. Questionable sex determinations often led to questionable age determinations and vice-versa; both age

TABLE 3. RESULTS OF MAPS DATA VERIFICATION PROCEDURES FOR ALL 1993 DATA VERIFIED AGAINST 1992 OR OTHER PREVIOUS YEARS, SHOWING NUMBER (N) AND PERCENT OF RECORDS REQUIRING A CHANGE IN THE DATABASE

	Data collected by					
	Institute interns		Independent station operators		Both groups combined	
Datum needing alteration	N	Percent	N	Percent	N	Percent
Sex	533	3.2	1,104	3.6	1,637	3.5
Age	284	1.7	643	2.1	927	2.0
Species or band number	78	0.5	22	0.1	100	0.2
All changes combined	781	4.7	1,658	5.4	2,439	5.1
Total records	16,790		30,696		47,486	

and sex were changed in 0.6% of records. Species (or band number) was by far the least often changed determination (0.5% of total records). Most changes in species determinations were caused by misread bands on recaptured birds (which sometimes resulted in age or sex changes as well). These findings suggest that, after verification and correction, errors remaining in intern-collected data were essentially negligible for species determinations, well below 1% for age determinations, and less than about 1% for sex determinations.

After data verification, only 21 (0.1%) of the 29,299 intern-collected capture records during both 1992 and 1993 were given unknown species determinations, 407 (1.4%) were given unknown age determinations and 14,152 (48.3%) were given unknown sex determinations. Of the 16,486 intern-collected capture records of adult birds during both 1992 and 1993, only 17.9% (mostly of sexually monomorphic species) were given unknown sex after data verification, thereby indicating that most of the unsexed birds in the total sample were young birds.

Verification procedures were also applied to the approximately 2/3 of the total data that were submitted from independent stations (i.e., stations not operated by IBP trained and supervised interns). We detected a slightly higher proportion of "errors" in species, age, or sex determinations (5.4% of 30,696 records) than in intern-collected data, although the relative frequency among the error types was similar (Table 3). We were surprised by this error rate, because most independent stations were operated by experienced banders with Master banding permits (although some data may have been collected by sub-permittees). Our results suggest either that the quality of our intern training was exceptionally good, or that the training of licensed banders in North America could stand improvement. Data collected by Dale (*this volume*) support the second conclusion. As a result of these studies, the Institute for Bird Populations in 1995 spearheaded the creation of

the North American Banding Council that, by 2002, had developed standardized training materials and certification programs for banders. Such programs previously existed in a number of European countries, including Finland and the United Kingdom, and most CES Scheme ringers (banders) were known to be highly experienced or were observed in action by BTO staff on ringing courses. Thus, the quality of ringing data collected there is assumed to be higher than in North America, and ringing data submitted to the CES Scheme are analyzed without any verification.

Pooling data from different stations

Analysis methods require pooling of data from multiple stations. Although MAPS protocol recommends one day of netting per 10-day sample period, a few stations net more frequently; this was especially true in the early years of MAPS. Using data from one MAPS region, we analyzed the effect of pooling data from stations using different netting schedules on between-year changes for 1990–1991 and for 1991–1992 (Table 4). Data were pooled in four ways for analysis. Using data from all days of operation in each 10-day period, we calculated one index uncorrected for effort, and another corrected to birds/600 net-h. We also calculated unadjusted and effort-adjusted totals using data only from the first complete day of operation in each netting period. The all-days, unadjusted index method tends to weight the data from each station roughly according to effort expended at the station. (Because of saturation and net-avoidance effects, however, a station operated on a daily basis will generally not capture 10× as many birds, especially adults, as a station operated only one day per 10-day period.) In contrast, the all-days, effort-adjusted index method tends to weight each station equally. (Again, however, because of saturation and net-avoidance effects, stations operated on multiple days in each 10-day period will generally be relatively under-weighted relative

TABLE 4. CHANGES IN THE NUMBERS OF ADULT AND YOUNG BIRDS AND THE PROPORTION OF YOUNG FROM 1990 TO 1991 AND FROM 1991 TO 1992

Species	N^c	Percent change in numbers of adults				N	Percent change in numbers of young				N	Change in proportion of young			
		All days^a		**One day^b**			**All days**		**One day**			**All days**		**One day**	
		Birds^d	Birds/600 nh^e	Birds	Birds/600 nh		Birds	Birds/600 nh	Birds	Birds/600 nh		Birds	Birds/600 nh	Birds	Birds/600 nh
Changes between 1990 and 1991															
Dusky Flycatcher (*Empidonax oberholseri*)	2	+19	+144	+33	+15	1	-76	-78	-91	-92	1	-0.26	-0.26	-0.34	-0.34
"Western" Flycatcher (*E. difficilis or occidentalis*)	4	+58*	+33**	+38	+26	4	-37**	-38*	-6	-26	4	-0.18	-0.19	-0.09	-0.13
Swainson's Thrush	6	+7	+49	-10	+22	6	+17	+16	+26*	+12	6	+0.02	-0.06	-0.07	-0.03
American Robin	6	+31	+19	+36	+37	2	+100	-95	-100	-100	5	+0.02	-0.14	-0.07	-0.13
Warbling Vireo	5	-8	-10	+4	-6	4	-33*	-13	-35	-29	4	-0.06	-0.02	-0.09	-0.06
Orange-crowned Warbler	5	+3	+30	+88	+37	4	-16*	-18	+21*	+9	4	-0.04	-0.07	-0.08	-0.03
Yellow Warbler (*Dendroica petechia*)	5	-23	+5	+8	+18	5	+8	+53	0	+3	5	+0.08	+0.08	+0.02	-0.02
MacGillivray's Warbler (*Oporornis tolmiei*)	4	+20	-18	+22	-1	5	-12	-1	-22	-21	4	-0.08	+0.02	-0.12	-0.08
Wilson's Warbler	4	+40	+43	+59	+55	4	-23	-55	+25	+74	4	-0.14	+0.02	-0.02	+0.06
Song Sparrow	5	-15	-20	-7	-10	5	+53	+30	+91	+47	5	+0.12	+0.10	-0.15	+0.11
Lincoln's Sparrow (*Melospiza lincolnii*)	2	+14	+54	+56	+53	2	0	+50	+500	+525	2	-0.03	-0.01	-0.20	+0.20
Dark-eyed Junco (*Junco hyemalis*)	5	+70*	+45*	+82	+63	4	+5	-44*	-16	-36+	4	-0.10	-0.22**	-0.22**	-0.22**
All species pooled	6	+23*	+22	+29*	+24	6	+4	+1	+32	+3	6	-0.04	-0.05	-0.00	-0.05
Proportion increasing^f		0.75	0.75	0.83*	0.75		0.42	0.42	0.42	0.50		0.33	0.33	0.33	0.25
Changes between 1991 and 1992															
Dusky Flycatcher (*Empidonax oberholseri*)	6	-10	-12	-31+	-32*	6	+85	+2	+550**	+750+	2	+0.09	+0.08	+0.22	+0.22
"Western" Flycatcher	10	-13	+1	+13	+8	9	+86**	+105+	+125*	+147*	8	+0.16	+0.10	+0.15	+0.09
Swainson's Thrush	9	-5	-2	-3	-6	6	+141**	+180**	+191**	+206**	6	+0.23*	+0.26	+0.28*	+0.29
American Robin	10	-23	-19	-34	-33	7	-20	+15	+67	+63	8	+0.07	+0.06	+0.09	+0.08
Warbling Vireo	10	-28*	-18	-11	-13	8	+133*	+46	+86	+55	8	+0.25**	+0.13	+0.16	+0.12
Orange-crowned Warbler	9	+105	+161	+86	+155	10	+204**	+237**	+261**	+238*	9	+0.06	+0.02	+0.03	-0.01
Yellow Warbler	7	-17	-17+	-25*	-26*	7	+48	+38	+80**	+68*	7	+0.12	+0.08	+0.12	+0.11
MacGillivray's Warbler	10	-3	-8	-13	-14	11	+71**	+62	+82*	+70+	9	+0.14	+0.14	+0.18	+0.17
Wilson's Warbler	11	-1	+46	-1	+27	11	+167**	+135*	+178*	+152*	11	+0.26	+0.12	+0.25	+0.17
Song Sparrow	9	-14	-22	-17	-20	10	+14	+14	+6	+33	8	+0.05	+0.09	+0.05	+0.08
Lincoln's Sparrow	4	-20	-22*	-42**	-42*	5	+41+	+28	+39		4	+0.13	+0.08	+0.18**	+0.16*
Dark-eyed Junco	10	-3	+1	+8	+7	9	+120	+229+	+215*	+214+	9	+0.20*	+0.29**	+0.27*	+0.27*
All species pooled	11	-11+	-1	-7	-2	11	+93**	+136**	+113**	+137**	11	+0.19**	+0.21**	+0.20**	+0.22**
Proportion increasing^f		0.08*	0.33	0.25	0.33		1.00**	1.00**	1.00**	1.00**		1.00**	1.00**	1.00**	0.92**

Notes: Data from the Northwest MAPS region, pooled in four different ways (see text).

[a] Calculated using data from all days of operation during each 10-day period.

[b] Calculated using data from only the first complete day of operation during each 10-day period.

[c] The number of stations from which data were recorded. At least one bird of the relevant age had to have been captured in one or other of the two years being compared. For calculating change in proportion of young, at least one bird (any age) had to have been captured in each of the years being compared.

[d] Total number of first captures.

[e] Total number of first captures/600 net-h.

[f] Proportion of the 12 target species for which increases were recorded. Significance is from a one-sided binomial test showing whether the proportion of increasing species differs from 0.50.

+ denotes 0.05 ≤ P < 0.10, * denotes 0.01 ≤ P < 0.05, ** denotes 0.001 ≤ P < 0.01, *** denotes 0.0001 ≤ P < 0.001.

to stations operated only one day per 10-day period.) The one-day, unadjusted index method weights each station according to the number of nets used and the length of time they are operated each day, whereas the one-day effort-adjusted index method weights each station equally.

The four methods often produced substantially different regional between-year changes in the numbers of first captures of adults and young, and substantial, but perhaps smaller, differences in regional changes in proportion of young (Table 4). Differences among the four methods were generally less for all species pooled than for individual species. Note particularly the differences among the four methods in the 1990–1991 between-year changes in numbers of adult Swainson's Thrushes, numbers of young Orange-crowned and Wilson's warblers, and proportion of young Wilson's Warblers.

Data for Swainson's Thrush show the effect that particular stations can have on these results, depending on which pooling method is used (Table 5). Station 103 (which comprised over 50% of first captures) drove the 1990–1991 comparison in the all-days unadjusted index method, because this station was weighted as if it were 10 stations. If between-year changes in adult numbers are not homogeneous across an entire region, then regional changes produced by this method will be severely biased toward the stations that are operated most often. The opposite bias occurred when data were standardized to first captures/600 net-h. This was true whether all days per 10-day period were used or only the first day per 10-day period. In both of these cases, Station

105, which had the smallest total effort, drove the regional increases in adult capture rates.

Finally, it should be noted that differences in results from the four methods were more pronounced for 1990–1991 than for 1991–1992. This was not only a result of differing effort among stations included in each comparison, but also because the underlying changes between 1990 and 1991 may in fact have differed between coastal lowland and interior montane stations (DeSante et al. 1993a). Pooling data over stations where bird populations may be subject to different demographic stressors, such as critical weather factors, can mask important differences in population and demographic changes and, thus, may be inappropriate. This caution, of course, applies to all large-scale monitoring programs, including the Breeding Bird Survey, that pool data from multiple stations or routes to provide regional indices.

The pooling method we have adopted is to use only one day of data from each 10-day period for all stations (thus converting all stations to one-day stations). Next, we adjust each station's numbers to ensure equal effort (at each station but not among stations) in the two years being compared. For each netting period, the time during which each individual net was open is compared between years. Any bird captured at a time when that net was not open during the comparison year is excluded from the comparison. We then use the total number of first captures (rather than first captures/600 net-h) from those single days in each period, such that stations are weighted according to the number of birds that they contribute to the regional total.

TABLE 5. Station-specific indices and changes between 1990 and 1991 in regional indices of adult population size for Swainson's Thrush

	1990						1991					
	All days per period[a]			One day per period[b]			All days per period			One day per period		
Station number	Total net-h	Birds[c]	Birds/ 600 nh[d]	Total net-h	Birds	Birds/ 600 nh	Total net-h	Birds	Birds/ 600 nh	Total net-h	Birds	Birds/ 600 nh
101	360.00	3	5.0	360.00	3	5.0	360.00	2	3.3	360.00	2	3.3
102	324.00	1	1.9	324.00	1	1.9	324.00	2	3.7	324.00	2	3.7
103	13518.50	45	2.0	1440.00	9	3.8	12399.00	54	2.6	1440.00	9	3.8
105	216.00	0	0.0	216.00	0	0.0	216.00	4	11.1	216.00	4	11.1
106	2007.70	36	10.8	1039.60	25	14.4	1987.60	29	8.8	1041.60	18	10.4
107	1222.75	1	0.5	437.83	1	1.4	1345.67	1	0.4	518.92	0	0.0
Total		86	20.1		39	26.4		92	30.0		35	32.3
Percent changes between 1990 and 1991 in number of adults captured							+7%		+49%		-10%	+22%

Notes: Data from the Northwest MAPS region, analyzed with four different methods (see text).

[a] Using data from all days each period that the station was run.

[b] Using data from only the first complete day each period that the station was run.

[c] Using the total number of first captures of adults.

[d] Using the number of first captures of adults/600 net-h.

Validation of MAPS population size indices

MAPS indices of adult population size were compared to independently derived indices of abundance, to determine whether different sources of data would give similar results. For each of 36 Washington and Oregon MAPS stations operated in 1992, we established nine point-count locations, 150 m apart, generally in a 3 × 3 array. We replicated 10-min counts at these nine points three times, once in each of the first three 10-day periods that each station was operated. Most of these 36 stations were located at the edge between a mixed coniferous forest and a montane meadow or riparian corridor. All point counts at a given station were conducted by the same observer, but different observers conducted point counts at different stations. For each station, we ran correlation analyses between species-specific indices of relative abundance derived from mist nets (total number of first captures of adult birds during the entire season) and analogous indices derived from point counts (total number of individual adult birds detected at all distances from the points, excluding flyovers, from all three replicates combined). Data were included from each species detected by at least one of the count methods.

Indices of adult population size from the two methods for the various species were significantly (P < 0.05) correlated at 33 of the 36 stations; highly significant (P < 0.001) correlations were obtained for 25 stations (Table 6; mean over 36 stations: r = 0.61 ± 0.06, range = 0.09–0.94). Lack of correlation at the other three stations resulted from capture or counting of large flocks of apparently non-breeding adult birds (usually Pine Siskins or Evening Grosbeaks [*Cocothraustes vespertinus*]). These results suggest that constant effort mist netting according to MAPS protocol effectively sampled adult birds in proportion to their relative abundance as determined by point counts. Kaiser and Bauer (1994) also found significant correlation between first captures of adult birds and numbers of adult birds detected on point counts (r = 0.83, N = 29, P < 0.001).

Cormack-Jolly-Seber analyses of mark–recapture data

One of the important goals of MAPS is to detect differences and changes in annual adult survival, using CJS mark–recapture analyses. These analyses do not require constant effort data, as the estimation

TABLE 6. CORRELATION BETWEEN INDICES OF ADULT POPULATION SIZE DERIVED FROM MIST-NETTING DATA AND ANALOGOUS INDICES DERIVED FROM POINT-COUNT DATA

Station	N[a]	r	Station	N[a]	r
Mount Baker NF			*Siuslaw NF*		
Frog Lake	25	0.74 ***	Mary's Peak	26	0.89 ***
Murphy Creek	19	0.80 ***	Nettle Creek	28	0.68 ***
Beaver Lake	27	0.80 ***	Beaver Ridge	26	0.88 ***
Copper Creek	15	0.52 *	Homestead	26	0.94 ***
Perry Creek	23	0.52 *	Cougar Creek	30	0.69 ***
Monte Cristo Lake	33	0.59 ***	Crab Creek	26	0.76 ***
Wenatchee NF			*Willamette NF*		
Timothy Meadow	44	0.48 ***	Ikenik	46	0.69 ***
Quartz Creek	30	0.39 *	Fingerboard Prairie	40	0.39 *
Two Point	45	0.32 *	Strube Flat	28	0.34 +
Pleasant Valley	37	0.63 ***	Clear Cut	38	0.71 ***
Rattlesnake Spring	42	0.16	Major Prairie	31	0.45 **
Deep Creek	30	0.09	Brock Creek	40	0.59 ***
Umatilla NF			*Fremont NF*		
Buzzard Creek	36	0.82 ***	Sycan River	46	0.57 ***
Brock Meadow	37	0.42 **	Deadhorse	49	0.48 ***
Fry Meadow	38	0.61 ***	Cold Creek	38	0.82 ***
Coyote Ridge	44	0.37 *	Augur Creek	46	0.50 ***
Buck Mt. Meadow	38	0.84 ***	Island	45	0.68 ***
Phillips Creek	45	0.62 ***	Swamp Creek	29	0.86 ***

Notes: Data collected in 1992, from 36 MAPS stations in six National Forests in Oregon and Washington. Mist-netting data were the total number of first captures of adult birds during the entire season. Point-count data were the total number of detections (excluding flyovers) during nine unlimited-distance point counts replicated three times, once during each of the first three 10-day periods the station was operated.

[a] Number of species for which adults were detected by either mist netting or point counts.

+ denotes 0.05 ≤ P < 0.10, * denotes 0.01 ≤ P < 0.05, ** denotes 0.001 ≤ P < 0.01, *** denotes 0.0001 ≤ P < 0.001.

of recapture probability takes into account differences in effort between years. However, estimating regional survivorship precisely requires pooling of data among stations, and recapture probabilities are likely to differ among stations because of variation in habitat and operation (number, density, and location of nets). Although Carothers (1973, 1979) showed that bias in survival estimates produced by heterogeneous recapture probabilities was frequently small, Peach (1993) suggested that effects of among-station heterogeneity in recapture probability should be checked before pooling data among stations. Current analyses of MAPS data from Alaska and western boreal Canada indicate that MAPS recapture probabilities are generally best modeled as a function of sex but not as a function of geographic area or habitat type (Institute for Bird Populations, unpubl. data).

Using the computer program SURGE4, and pooling three years (1990-1992) of mark-recapture data from each of 27 stations east of the Rocky Mountains, we calculated maximum-likelihood estimates for annual adult survival and recapture probabilities for 13 individual target species; for all permanent resident,

short-distance migrant, and long-distance migrant species pooled; and for all species pooled (Table 7). In the following discussion, we assume that heterogeneity in recapture probability was small or, if not small, did not seriously bias estimates of survival and recapture probability.

Estimates of survival and recapture probability for the 13 target species (Table 7) generally compared favorably to those from the longer-term British CES Scheme. For example, Peach (1993) found that the estimated average annual adult survival rate (1983–1991), based on pooled mark–recapture data from multiple CES ringing stations for six target species in Britain, was 0.44 (range 0.32–0.57). Our mean estimated adult survival rate was 0.42 (range 0.19–0.85). The precision of survival estimates from MAPS, however, was lower than those from the CES, probably because of the lower sample sizes resulting from just three years of MAPS data compared to eight years of CES data. Recapture probabilities from MAPS for the 13 target species ranged from 0.03–0.66, averaged to 0.35, and were again roughly similar to estimates from the CES Program.

In contrast, estimates of annual adult survival

TABLE 7. MODIFIED CORMACK-JOLLY-SEBER CAPTURE–RECAPTURE ANALYSES FOR SELECTED TARGET SPECIES DERIVED FROM THE CAPTURE HISTORIES OF ADULT BIRDS

Species	Number of			Survival probability[a]		Recapture probability[b]	
	Stations[c]	Individuals[d]	Captures[e]	Estimate ± SE	CV	Estimate ± SE	CV
Black-capped Chickadee	21	253	346	0.55 ± 0.29	51.8	0.16 ± 0.10	58.0
Veery	12	245	449	0.39 ± 0.08	20.4	0.63 ± 0.13	20.4
Wood Thrush	17	302	427	0.19 ± 0.07	38.4	0.65 ± 0.24	36.7
Gray Catbird	21	1,260	1,953	0.29 ± 0.04	14.1	0.66 ± 0.09	13.7
Red-eyed Vireo	21	311	397	0.24 ± 0.10	41.4	0.61 ± 0.25	40.8
Yellow Warbler	16	450	608	0.46 ± 0.20	43.2	0.22 ± 0.11	49.7
American Redstart	15	204	249	0.44 ± 0.30	68.3	0.17 ± 0.13	76.6
Ovenbird	20	329	421	0.24 ± 0.13	56.4	0.47 ± 0.27	57.9
Common Yellowthroat	25	643	878	0.35 ± 0.13	35.6	0.23 ± 0.09	39.2
Northern Cardinal	21	359	459	0.55 ± 0.20	36.3	0.24 ± 0.10	41.2
Indigo Bunting (*Passerina cyanea*)	14	202	269	0.85 ± 0.73	85.6	0.12 ± 0.11	90.4
Song Sparrow	22	653	1,133	0.47 ± 0.18	38.2	0.33 ± 0.14	41.2
American Goldfinch	21	686	784	0.48 ± 0.30	62.5	0.03 ± 0.02	78.9
Group means for							
Target Species	19	454	644	0.42 ± 0.21	45.6	0.35 ± 0.14	49.5
All Resident species	27	1,490	1,858	0.45 ± 0.09	21.0	0.21 ± 0.05	23.4
All short-distant migrant species	25	3,317	4,252	0.33 ± 0.06	19.6	0.21 ± 0.04	21.2
All long-distant migrant species	27	4,918	6,865	0.31 ± 0.03	10.6	0.42 ± 0.05	11.1
All species	79	9,725	12,975	0.33 ± 0.03	8.7	0.31 ± 0.03	9.3

Notes: Calculated using the computer program SURGE4, for species for which more than 200 capture histories were available from a total of more than ten stations where the species was known to be breeding.

[a] Defined as the probability of an adult bird surviving and returning in 1991 to the area where it was captured in 1990.

[b] Defined as the conditional probability of recapturing an adult bird in 1991, given that it did survive and return in 1991 to the same area where it was captured in 1990.

[c] Number of stations operated for three consecutive years (1990–1992) where the species was known to be breeding.

[d] Number of individual adult birds captured during the three years (1990–1992) at stations where the species was breeding; thus, the number of capture histories.

[e] Total number of captures (including recaptures) during the three years (1990–1992) at stations where the species was breeding.

rates of temperate-zone passerines from other studies, which used traps at nest sites or food-baited traps during the winter, were often somewhat higher than estimates from MAPS or CES. For example, the average annual survival rate of ten Maryland-wintering species was 0.54 ± 0.03 (Karr et al. 1990a), that for Black-capped Chickadee (*Poecile atricapilla*) in Connecticut was 0.59 ± 0.02 (Loery et al. 1987, Pollock et al. 1990), and that for European Dipper (*Cinclus cinclus*) in France was 0.57 ± 0.08 (Lebreton et al. 1992). A likely reason for lower survival estimates from MAPS (and CES) is the inclusion in the sample of captured birds of transient individuals that are unlikely to be recaptured in subsequent years. Such transients can include late spring migrants, floaters, individuals breeding just outside the study area, post-breeding dispersing adults, and early fall migrants. Despite protocols that generally exclude late spring and early fall migrants from MAPS data (see section on netting schedules), substantial numbers of transient individuals are still likely to be included in the data.

Results of pooling species having various migration strategies illustrate a possible effect of including transients in mark–recapture analyses (Table 7). The survival probability of all permanent resident species pooled was higher than that for both short- and long-distance migrant species pooled, each of which might be expected to have more transients in the captured sample than would permanent resident species. On the other hand, the differences in survival between resident and migrant species might be real if migration causes enhanced mortality. Until the effects of transient birds can reliably be excluded from analyses, it will be difficult to interpret the biological significance of survival estimates.

Major advances in reducing the effects of transient individuals on survival estimates have been obtained in recent years (Peach et al. 1990, Peach 1993, Pradel et al. 1997, Nott and DeSante 2002, Kendall et al. *this volume*). Pradel et al. (1997) essentially uses an ad hoc approach that consists of ignoring the first observation of each individual bird and then proceeding as usual with the left-truncated capture histories. This method effectively permits estimation of an unbiased survival rate for resident birds and estimation of the proportion of transients among newly marked birds. DeSante et al. (1995) tested this model on four years of mark–recapture data from MAPS (1990–1993). Using this model, estimates of survival probability increased for eight species by 51%, from an average of 0.40 to 0.61, and estimates of recapture probability likewise increased by 60%, from an average of 0.32 to 0.51. The precision of the estimates was also increased for both survival (by 11%) and recapture probability (by 24%). In addition, the estimated proportion of transients was high, about 65%. More recently, Nott and DeSante (2002) included Pradel et al.'s (1997) suggestion for a within-year length-of-stay addition to the transient model. The inclusion of the length-of-stay model further increased the precision of the survival estimates for resident individuals by an average of 16% for 10 species without substantially affecting the survival estimates themselves (survival estimates increased for 5 species and decreased for 5 species; Nott and DeSante 2002).

It must be emphasized, however, that regardless of whether or not a transient model is employed, survival rate estimates derived from CJS mark–recapture analyses are apparent survival rate estimates in which mortality and permanent emigration are confounded; low apparent survival could be caused either by high mortality or by high permanent emigration rates. The low survival for Wood Thrush (Table 7), for example, could result either from high mortality, presumably during the non-breeding season, or from a high emigration rate (caused perhaps by high rate of nest predation, or by breeding habitat alteration). In the latter case, management for Wood Thrush should be focused on the temperate breeding grounds, whereas low survival during the non-breeding season would call for management directed at the migration routes or tropical wintering grounds.

Thus, there exists a pressing need to design studies to distinguish the effects of permanent emigration from mortality. This will be difficult, because rigorous separation of their effects requires extensive networks of nearby stations to identify movements of birds between them. Effects of movements could then be separated from mortality using multi-state models, such as those described by Hestbeck et al. (1991). Nichols (in DeSante 1995) suggested another technique that calls for the establishment of nested study areas of increasing size and the estimation of survival rates over each area. Peach (1993) and, more recently, Cilimburg et al. (2002) investigated the effects of sampling area on survival rates and found that, in some cases, survival rates could be increased by as much as 23% by increasing the sampling area so as to include individuals that emigrated from the smaller-sized study area. Despite the fact that CJS mark–recapture models applied to data from small study areas, such as the 20-ha areas (with nets placed within the central 8 ha) used by MAPS, provide only estimates of apparent survival, it seems likely that geographic or habitat variation in apparent survival within a given species could provide important management information, regardless of whether the low apparent survival rates are caused by high mortality or high emigration rates.

Finally, CJS mark–recapture methods can also be used to provide estimates of actual adult population size, complete with standard errors; that is, they can provide essentially unbiased abundance estimators. Such estimates can be compared with indices of abundance derived from constant effort mist netting (or from point counts or other methods of indexing relative abundance), to identify and estimate the magnitude of biases in those indices. These data can then be used to determine whether bias in the various indices remains constant among species, locations, or years, a constancy that is often assumed in analyses but which may not hold true (Sauer and Link *this volume*). Such analyses have not yet been conducted using MAPS data.

PEER REVIEW

A detailed evaluation of the statistical properties of MAPS data collected during the 1992–1995 MAPS pilot study (Rosenberg 1997), and an evaluation of the appropriateness and efficacy of the field and analytical methods being used by the MAPS Program (DeSante 1997), was completed in 1996. These evaluations were subjected to peer review by a panel of experts in mark–recapture modeling and population dynamics analyses at USGS/BRD Patuxent Wildlife Research Center (Geissler 1997), which concluded that "MAPS is technically sound and is based on the best available biological and statistical methods. The pilot substantially exceeded expectations in rapidly expanding the number of sites supported by independent agencies and organizations. MAPS complements other land bird monitoring programs such as the BBS by providing useful information on land bird demographics that is not available elsewhere. MAPS is the most important project in the nongame bird monitoring arena since the creation of the BBS." Results of this review and evaluation have been published in several papers (DeSante et al. 1999; DeSante 2000; Rosenberg et al. 1999, 2000).

CONCLUSION

Initial analyses of the first five years of MAPS data (1989–1993) suggest that the field and analytical techniques currently in use can provide important information regarding between-year changes, as well as longer-term trends and spatial differences, in annual indices of productivity and estimates of survivorship. The accuracy and precision of these indices and estimates, however, and thus their ultimate usefulness, depend on assumptions regarding age-, species-, and station-specific differences in dispersal characteristics, numbers of transients in the populations being sampled, and heterogeneity of recapture probabilities, as well as upon the basic statistical properties of the data, including the numbers and distributions of individuals that can be sampled at the various stations. The validity of several, but not all, of the assumptions underlying the field and analytical techniques has recently been verified and these results (e.g., DeSante 2000; DeSante et al. 1999, 2001; Nott and DeSante 2002; Nott et al. 2002) have further supported the usefulness of MAPS data. Two important questions that still need further investigation are (1) the degree that young concentrate in various habitats, and the effect of that on productivity indices; and (2) an assessment of the actual effect of permanent emigration on adult survival estimates. Also currently lacking is information on the sensitivity of results to violations of the assumptions, and on the sampling effort necessary to attain targeted levels of precision, although studies on the latter question are currently underway.

ACKNOWLEDGMENTS

We thank all of the MAPS station operators and field crews who provided data used in this paper, and E. Feuss, E. Ruhlen, and H. Smith for verifying data and aiding in analysis. We thank W. L. Kendall, J. D. Nichols, W. J. Peach, D. K. Rosenberg, and J. R. Sauer for help and advice on statistical aspects of data analysis, especially regarding the mark-recapture analyses reported here. We appreciate the many helpful comments on earlier drafts of this manuscript provided by V. A. Kaiser and W. J. Peach, and the editing help of E. H. Dunn. Financial support for the MAPS Program has been provided by the U.S. Fish and Wildlife Service, National Biological Service (now Biological Resources Division of the U.S. Geological Survey), National Fish and Wildlife Foundation, and Denali and Shenandoah National Parks; Regions 1 and 6 of the U.S. Forest Service and Flathead National Forest; the U.S. Department of Defense Legacy Resource Management Program, Department of the Navy, and Texas Army National Guard; and the Yosemite Association, Sequoia Natural History Association, and Confederated Salish and Kootenai Tribes. We thank them all for their support. This is Contribution Number 27 of The Institute for Bird Populations.

Studies in Avian Biology No. 29:46–56

CURRENT PRACTICES IN THE BRITISH TRUST FOR ORNITHOLOGY CONSTANT EFFORT SITES SCHEME AND COMPARISONS OF TEMPORAL CHANGES IN MIST-NET CAPTURES WITH CHANGES IN SPOT-MAPPING COUNTS AT THE EXTENSIVE SCALE

WILL J. PEACH, STEPHEN R. BAILLIE, AND STEPHEN T. BUCKLAND

Abstract. The Constant Effort Sites (CES) scheme of the British Trust for Ornithology (BTO) aims to monitor changes in abundance, breeding productivity, and survival rates for a range of common passerines breeding in scrub and wetland habitats in Britain and Ireland. Changes in the size of the annual catch from a set of standard mist nets operated during 12 summer (May–August) visits, are combined across stations to produce estimates of the percent change in adult and juvenile numbers. We use the proportion of juveniles in the catch as a relative measure of breeding productivity. Methods are presented for calculating standard errors of between-year changes in both adult and juvenile catches, and changes in the proportion of juveniles. We compared the changes in the numbers of adults caught between 1982 and 1992 with changes in the numbers of territories counted on farmland and woodland Common Birds Census (CBC) plots. For 9 of 21 species considered, between-year changes in catches and counts were significantly and positively correlated, and long-term trends in abundance were consistent across the two monitoring schemes. For six species, long-term trends, but not between-year changes, were consistent across the two monitoring schemes. For a further six species, between-year changes and long-term trends were inconsistent between monitoring schemes, although for several of these species the disparity may be due to heterogeneous population trends across habitats. We discuss priorities for further validation studies of CES, including possible effects of habitat succession and station turnover on long-term trends in catch sizes.

Key Words: abundance monitoring, Common Birds Census, Constant Effort Sites, productivity, validation.

The Constant Effort Sites (CES) scheme is organized by the British Trust for Ornithology (BTO), and aims to monitor changes in the abundance, breeding success, and survival rates of a range of common passerine species breeding in wetland and scrub habitats in Britain and Ireland. Standardized mist netting and banding are used to assess changes in the abundance of adult and juvenile birds. The percent of young birds in the overall catch is taken as an index of annual productivity, while between-year recaptures are used to estimate apparent survival (i.e., return rates) of adults. Changes in the catches of adults and young of 23 species (including eight warblers and five finches), and updated trends in abundance and productivity, are published annually (e.g., Balmer and Milne 2002, Baillie et al. 2002). The CES scheme complements other BTO monitoring schemes that provide information on changes in population levels (Common Birds Census; Waterways Bird Survey; and, since 1994, the Breeding Bird Survey), nesting success (Nest Records Scheme), and survival rates (Ringing Scheme). The BTO has developed an Integrated Population Monitoring (IPM) programme, which aims to monitor changes in bird populations and to identify the mechanisms and causes of these changes (Baillie 1990, Greenwood et

al. 1993, Thomson et al. 1997). The most important contribution of the CES scheme to the IPM programme is the provision of demographic information (productivity and survival), although for species that are difficult to census by traditional counting methods (e.g., Reed Warbler) the information on changes in the abundance of breeding adults will also be important.

The CES scheme was initiated in 1981 as a pilot project with a volunteer organizer. From an initial set of 17 participating study locations in 1981, the scheme expanded to 47 stations by 1984. Following an evaluation of the scientific potential of the CES scheme (Baillie et al. 1986), the BTO took over full responsibility for the project and devoted approximately half of one full-time staff member to its organization and promotion. The popularity of the CES scheme has continued to grow, and in 2000 data were received from 144 stations.

In this paper we describe the methodology of the CES scheme and the data currently being collected. Methods are presented for estimating between-year changes and associated standard error of adult and juvenile catches, and changes in the proportion of young birds (Peach et al. 1996). Finally, we compare between-year changes and trends in the numbers of adult birds caught on CE stations between 1982 and 1992 with changes in the numbers of territories counted on CBC plots during the same period. Since undertaking the work reported here, we have developed methods for modelling long-term changes in numbers and productivity from CES data (Peach et al. 1998). Results of these analyses are now reported annually along with those from other BTO monitoring schemes (Baillie et al. 2002).

STUDY SITES AND METHODS

STATION COMPOSITION AND NETTING REGIMES

All CE stations are operated by one or more fully trained volunteer banders who have proposed their study sites for registration in the national project. British and Irish banders are encouraged to propose locations at which experience has shown that reasonable numbers of passerines are netted during spring and summer. Under-represented regions (such as Scotland and Ireland) and species (such as Redpoll and Linnet; scientific names in Table 1) are highlighted in articles and publicity sent to banders and in presentations given at conferences and meetings. Proposed locations have generally been accepted into the scheme provided they do not contain a significant growth of coniferous trees (which will increase in height at a relatively rapid rate) and provided banders undertake to operate the station in a standardized manner for at least four years. Although banders are encouraged to control scrub growth, particularly around net positions, in most cases where this is attempted, it probably only entails the cutback of growth on the tops and sides of bushes.

At the time of proposing a new station, the bander must also specify the number and positions of a set of standard mist nets. These are usually determined by the bander based on previous experience of netting at the station. Once agreed, these net positions are not normally changed. Banders proposing locations at which they have not previously netted are usually asked to experiment with net positions during an initial trial year, after which the fixed set of standard CES nets is determined. In 1992 the mean standard net length on the 111 stations at which at least eight main visits were completed was 110.2 m (range 46–274 m). There are currently no guidelines concerning the density or number of nets to be used, because when the scheme was initiated it was felt that individual station characteristics and the number of banders available would have a large influence on the number and spacing of nets. We are now encouraging groups of banders to operate relatively large stations and to erect as many standard nets as possible. In

TABLE 1. MEAN STANDARD ERRORS (PERCENT) OF BETWEEN-YEAR CHANGES IN CATCHES, AND MEAN NUMBERS (IN PARENTHESES) OF CE SITES CONTRIBUTING DATA, DURING THE PERIOD 1987–1988 TO 1991–1992

Species	Adults (visits 1–6)		Adults (visits 1–12)		Juveniles (visits 1–12)		Percent juveniles (visits 1–12)	
Wren (*Troglodytes troglodytes*)	7.7	(79.0)	7.0	(67.2)	7.7	(68.2)	2.5	(66.8)
Dunnock (*Prunella modularis*)	6.6	(78.4)	6.7	(67.0)	9.8	(67.2)	3.4	(66.6)
Robin (*Erithacus rubecula*)	9.1	(75.2)	9.0	(64.6)	7.1	(67.8)	2.3	(65.6)
Blackbird (*Turdus merula*)	6.5	(80.6)	6.5	(68.2)	10.3	(65.4)	3.9	(66.2)
Song Thrush (*T. philomelos*)	10.8	(71.2)	10.8	(62.8)	16.2	(59.0)	5.1	(54.4)
Sedge Warbler (*Acrocephalus schoenobaenus*)	8.2	(51.4)	8.0	(47.0)	12.6	(46.0)	4.8	(43.0)
Reed Warbler (*A. scirpaceus*)	7.2	(41.6)	5.8	(41.0)	10.3	(42.8)	3.9	(38.0)
Lesser Whitethroat (*Sylvia curruca*)	11.9	(46.0)	10.8	(42.8)	16.4	(49.0)	5.9	(36.2)
Whitethroat (*S. communis*)	10.7	(53.2)	11.4	(48.0)	13.6	(52.4)	4.6	(45.4)
Garden Warbler (*S. borin*)	9.7	(62.2)	9.5	(56.0)	17.0	(56.8)	5.2	(51.6)
Blackcap (*S. atricapilla*)	8.6	(69.4)	7.5	(61.8)	11.2	(63.2)	3.8	(60.4)
Chiffchaff (*Phylloscopus collybita*)	14.2	(47.2)	14.8	(50.8)	12.1	(57.6)	3.7	(50.6)
Willow Warbler (*P. trochilus*)	4.9	(78.4)	5.1	(66.6)	7.0	(68.2)	3.1	(67.0)
Long-tailed Tit (*Aegithalos caudatus*)	14.3	(64.0)	14.2	(56.0)	22.6	(52.4)	4.4	(49.2)
Blue Tit (*Parus caeruleus*)	9.1	(79.0)	8.3	(67.6)	9.3	(68.4)	2.7	(68.2)
Great Tit (*P. major*)	9.6	(74.6)	8.9	(64.2)	11.3	(67.2)	3.2	(64.6)
Treecreeper (*Certhia familiaris*)	35.6	(36.6)	24.2	(32.8)	16.8	(49.4)	6.9	(36.0)
Chaffinch (*Fringilla coelebs*)	9.2	(66.6)	9.9	(58.0)	23.4	(46.4)	6.3	(50.2)
Greenfinch (*Carduelis chloris*)	25.7	(34.8)	23.0	(35.2)	27.3	(23.4)	11.2	(23.8)
Linnet (*C. cannabina*)	21.6	(20.6)	20.5	(20.0)	34.4	(15.8)	8.3	(13.8)
Redpoll (*C. flammea*)	29.4	(26.2)	27.3	(24.0)	33.6	(13.2)	11.6	(13.6)
Bullfinch (*Pyrrhula pyrrhula*)	9.1	(70.2)	7.5	(63.4)	14.9	(55.4)	4.4	(59.0)
Reed Bunting (*Emberiza schoeniclus*)	9.9	(50.0)	9.3	(45.0)	20.5	(36.4)	6.5	(37.4)

Notes: Species are separated into taxonomic groups. For a station to be included in the analysis, at least eight out of 12 paired visits must have been completed (or four out of six paired visits for adults caught during visits 1–6). The precision of changes in adult captures is presented for all 12 CES visits (1–12) and for the first six visits only (see text for rationale).

1992 the median number of individual birds of all species trapped in standard nets at stations at which at least eight visits were completed was 112 adults (range 28–262) and 174 juveniles (range 43–425).

All CES banders are asked to make 12 visits to their stations between early May and late August, one in each of 12 10-day or 11-day periods. The dates of these periods vary slightly from year to year to ensure that at least three non-working days (weekends or public holidays) are included in each visit period. The interval between main visits should normally not be less than 6 days and must be at least 3 days. At least 10 of the 12 main visits were completed at 87% of all CES stations in 1991 (N = 108) and at 84% of all stations in 1992 (N = 122). Banders are asked to operate their set of standard nets for a set duration of at least 6 h on each visit, and to standardize their chosen netting duration across years, but not necessarily across visits within a year. A typical regime would be to begin netting at dawn and continue until midday on each of the 12 visits. Different netting durations between visits is allowed for in the analysis by only comparing between-year changes in catches for paired visits (i.e., visits completed in both years under consideration; see below).

To increase volunteer participation in the CES scheme, banders have the option of carrying out extra visits to their CE stations between May and August, and of erecting additional nets during main CES visits. However, extra visits are not permitted during the three days preceding a main visit and the length of additional netting should not exceed the combined length of all the standard nets. During 1989 a mean of 3.0 extra visits were made per CE station with no extra visits being made at 53% of stations. The mean length of additional netting per visit in 1989 was 8.6% of the standard net length. Captures made during extra visits or from additional nets are collected and computerized but are not used in calculations of between-year changes in catch sizes. These captures are used in analyses of mark–recapture data and might also contribute to analyses of adult:juvenile ratios.

DATA COLLECTION AND ROUTINE ANALYSIS OF BETWEEN-YEAR CHANGES

For each bird trapped on a CE station between May and August the following information is recorded in a station- and year-specific file on the BTO computer: band number, species, age ("adult" = after hatching year or "juvenile" = hatching year), sex (in the case of adults), date(s) of capture, and an additional net code to indicate whether the bird was trapped in a standard CES net or in an additional net. To minimize the costs of collecting and computerizing the CES data, information on biometrics, molt, and brood patches have not been collected routinely as part of the CES scheme. However, most banders now submit these data electronically as part of their main banding returns and they can be linked to the CES files as required. In particular, CES banders have been encouraged since 2001 to record brood patches to provide information on the length of the breeding season. Until 1993, simple, descriptive habitat

information was collected, accompanied by detailed station sketch maps. Starting in 1994, habitat codes, vegetation height, and scrub density were recorded on each side of each standard mist net.

CES capture data are submitted either on paper forms or on computer disc. Paper submissions are computerized and checked by BTO staff, after which printouts of the data are returned to the bander for final checking. The BTO has developed various computer software packages for banders that enable the user to computerize their banding and recapture data and to carry out most of the paperwork required for administrative purposes (Coker 1993, Cubitt 2002). The latest software is freely available and includes a program to extract CES capture data from larger data sets. In 1992, data from 35 out of 122 stations were submitted on disc and this figure rose to 130 out of 144 stations operated in 2000.

CALCULATION OF THE MAGNITUDE AND PRECISION OF BETWEEN-YEAR CHANGES IN ADULT AND JUVENILE ABUNDANCE

Between-year changes in the catches of adults and young birds (r) are computed by aggregating the numbers of birds caught across those stations at which at least eight paired visits (at least four out of the first six visits, and four of the second six visits) were completed in each of the two years under consideration. Only captures from paired visits contribute to the annual total. For example, if all 12 visits are completed in year one but only visits 1 to 10 in year two, then the comparison of between-year change is based upon catches from the 10 paired visits only. Stations are excluded from the analyses of between-year change if netting effort was not standardized or if major habitat changes occurred.

An index of between-year changes in the adult or juvenile catch at CE stations is calculated as

$$r = \frac{\sum\limits_{j=1}^{n} y_j}{\sum\limits_{j=1}^{n} x_j}$$

where x_j = last year's catch at station j, y_j = this year's catch - last year's catch at station j, n = the number of stations worked in the same way during both years. We define $q = 100(r)$ = percent change between years.

The measure of change r is a ratio estimator with approximate standard error (Cochran 1963)

$$SE(r) = \sqrt{\frac{n\sum\limits_{j=1}^{n}(y_j - r \cdot x_j)^2}{(n-1)\left(\sum\limits_{j=1}^{n}\right)^2}}$$

and the standard error of q is found as

$$SE(q) = 100\ SE(r)$$

An approximate 95% confidence interval for the true ratio R (after Cochran 1963) is

$$r\left\{\frac{\left(1-1.96^2\,c_{\overline{yx}}^{\overline{}}\right)\pm1.96\sqrt{\begin{array}{c}\left(c_{\overline{yy}}^{\overline{}}+c_{\overline{xx}}^{\overline{}}-2c_{\overline{yx}}^{\overline{}}\right)-\\1.96^2\left(c_{\overline{yy}}^{\overline{}}c_{\overline{xx}}^{\overline{}}-c_{\overline{yx}}^2\right)\end{array}}}{1-1.96^2\,c_{\overline{xx}}^{\overline{}}}\right\},$$

where

$$c_{\overline{xx}}^{\overline{}}=\left\{c.v.(\overline{x})\right\}^2=\left\{\frac{\sum_{j=1}^{n}\left(x_j-\overline{x}\right)^2}{n\,(n-1)\left(\overline{x}\right)^2}\right\},$$

$$c_{\overline{yy}}^{\overline{}}=\left\{c.v.(\overline{y})\right\}^2=\left\{\frac{\sum_{j=1}^{n}\left(y_j-\overline{y}\right)^2}{n\,(n-1)\left(\overline{y}\right)^2}\right\},$$

and $c_{\overline{yx}}^{\overline{}}=\left\{\dfrac{\sum_{j=1}^{n}y_j\left(x_j-\overline{x}\right)}{n(n-1)\,\overline{x}\,\overline{y}}\right\}$

These limits should be multiplied by 100 to give limits for Q, the true percentage change between years.

The formulae presented here do not require that be-tween-year changes in captures be homogeneous across CE stations. The calculation of a binomial standard error for a between-years change would not be valid because some individuals are caught in both years under consideration and because of the observed heterogeneity in capture trends across stations (see below). The methods presented here are appropriate for any monitoring programs that aim to draw inferences from between-year changes in abundance at a sample of stations or plots.

Standard errors of between-year changes in the numbers of territories on Common Birds Census or Waterways Bird Survey plots have until recently been calculated using a modification of Cochran's (1963) cluster sample method. Cluster sampling would be appropriate if a random sample of stations (clusters) was drawn, and the fate of all birds in sampled stations was recorded. That is clearly not the case in monitoring programs. The ratio sampling method requires only the first of these two assumptions.

CALCULATION OF THE MAGNITUDE AND PRECISION OF THE BETWEEN-YEAR CHANGE IN THE PERCENT OF JUVENILES

A simple estimate of change in productivity between years i-1 and i is

$$v_i-v_{i-1}$$

where v_i and v_{i-1} are the proportions of young birds in the entire catches, summed over all stations operated in the

same manner in year i and year i-1.

In any year,

$$v_i=\frac{\sum_{j=1}^{n}b_j}{\sum_{j=1}^{n}(a_j+b_j)}$$

where b_j is the number of juveniles caught at the jth station in any year i, and a_j is the number of adults caught at the jth station. The standard error of the overall proportion v_i is then calculated as

$$\mathrm{SE}\,(v_i)=\sqrt{\frac{n\sum_{j=1}^{n}\left(b_j-v\left(a_j+b_j\right)\right)^2}{\left(n-1\right)\left(\sum_{j=1}^{n}\left(a_j+b_j\right)\right)^2}}$$

The standard error of the difference v_i-v_{i-1} is

$$\mathrm{SE}\,(v_i-v_{i-1})=\sqrt{(\mathrm{SE})^2+(\mathrm{SE})^2}.$$

ADULT CAPTURES COMPARED TO TERRITORY COUNTS

The Common Birds Census

Between 1962 and 1994, the Common Birds Census (CBC) was the main monitoring scheme for common breeding birds in the United Kingdom. The scheme involves the counting of breeding territories on typically 200–300 plots in farmland and woodland each year using the spot-mapping method. Farmland plots can be any type of arable, horticultural, or grazing land (except unenclosed sheepwalk), and must be at least 40 ha, and preferably 60 ha, in area, which can include up to 10% of small woods and copses. Woodland plots include all kinds of semi-natural and broadleaved woodlands, but not parkland, scrubby heathlands, or coniferous plantations, and must be at least 10 ha in area. For a full account of the methods, history, and long-term trends of bird species monitored by the CBC, see Marchant et al. (1990).

The CBC provides an independent source of information on between-year and long-term changes in abundance for 21 of the 23 species currently monitored by the CES scheme. The CBC has been the subject of a large number and wide range of validation studies (O'Connor and Marchant 1981, O'Connor and Fuller 1984, Baillie and Marchant 1992) and is generally accepted to provide reliable extensive information on population changes of a wide range of common bird species in lowland Britain. If strong positive correlations exist between population changes as measured by CBC and CES data, then this would constitute good evidence that the latter is providing meaningful measures of changes in the size of the breeding population. However, a lack of correlation between measures of population change would be more difficult to interpret, because the two schemes are using different methods to assess changes in population size in different habitats. The CBC measures changes in the numbers of territories, whereas the CES scheme measures changes in the numbers of adult birds caught, which might include transient or non-breeding individuals. The CBC covers woodland and farmland whereas most CES plots are located in scrub and reedbed habitats. Although the CBC methodology is generally considered to be reliable for most territorial passerines, it may not perform well for some species, such as those having short song periods or very large or highly aggregated territories (Bell et al. 1968, Fuller and Marchant 1985). A lack of correlation between the CBC and CES might also occur if the population level of a species had remained unchanged during the period of study. Between-year changes would then largely reflect sampling error, rather than real changes in the bird population.

A further question considered here is whether between-year changes in adult captures made during the first six CES visits correlate more strongly with those measured from the CBC, or are more precise than those derived from captures made during all 12 visits. CBC census workers carry out their field work between late March and early July, which corresponds more closely with the first six CES visits (May–June) than the full 12 visits (May–August). For most species a high proportion of adults are caught during the first six visits (Baillie et al. 1986) and late season captures might include a relatively high proportion of transients, as well as individuals embarking on second or late breeding attempts. If changes in adult captures from the first six CES visits were more closely correlated with changes from the CBC (or were much more precise) than changes based on captures from all 12 visits, then it might be concluded that adult abundance on CE stations would be better monitored using captures from the first six visits only.

Analysis

Weighted correlation was used to compare between-year changes in the number of territories recorded on farmland and woodland CBC plots during the period 1983–1984 to 1991–1992 with changes in the captures of adults on CES stations during visits 1–6 and during visits 1–12. Each pair of between-year changes was weighted by the reciprocal of the mean of the standard errors of the between-year changes from the CBC and CES schemes. This weighting procedure has the effect of down-weighting changes from the early years of the CES scheme when fewer stations were operated and precision was relatively poor.

At the time of conducting these analyses, methods for the indexing of long-term monitoring data were under development (Peach and Baillie 1994, Peach et al. 1998, Siriwardena et al. 1998) and in this paper we use the simple chain index in which successive between-year changes in abundance are linked together around an arbitrary base year (Marchant et al. 1990). Although the chain indexing method has various shortcomings (Peach and Baillie 1994), we use it here to compare long-term trends in abundance across monitoring schemes and not to draw biological conclusions concerning changes in abundance. Our approach therefore assumes there is no differential sensitivity of the two

monitoring schemes to the use of the chain index. We recommend that the chain index should not be used for future analyses of CES trends, as more robust methods are now readily available (Peach et al. 1998, Baillie et al. 2002).

Long-term trends in chain indices derived from the CBC and CES data for the period 1982 to 1992 were compared using a test for homogeneity of linear slopes. This involved fitting an analysis of covariance model using the GLM procedure of SAS (SAS Institute 1988) in which year was the covariate and monitoring scheme the main factor, with an interaction term between year and scheme. A significant interaction term was taken as evidence of different average rates of change in the abundance of adult birds as measured by the two monitoring schemes. Comparisons of slopes from the CBC and CES schemes were carried out for both farmland and woodland CBC indices and for CES indices derived from visits 1–6 and visits 1–12. In all such analyses, indices were weighted by the square root of the sum of the number of birds caught, or the number of territories counted, during the year of the index and the preceding year. We note that the use of linear regression to assess the significance of trends in chain indices may be statistically unreliable (because the observations are not independent), and more robust techniques have been developed since these analyses were conducted.

Finally, we compare the precision of between-year changes in captures of adults on CE stations based on captures during the first six visits and all 12 visits.

RESULTS

PRECISION OF BETWEEN-YEAR CHANGES IN CATCHES

The precision with which between-year changes in abundance are measured by the CES scheme has increased as the number of contributing stations has risen. The average precision attained for between-year changes in the catches of adults, young and the percent of young during the period 1988–1989 to 1991–1992 for 23 species is summarized in Table 1. For 16 of the 23 species, between-year changes in the catches of adults (between May and August) are currently estimated with standard errors of 10% or less. Between-year changes in the catches of juveniles are more variable across stations, with mean standard errors of 10% or less being attained for only seven species. Between-year changes in the percent of young birds caught are measured with mean standard errors of 5% or less for 17 of the 23 species (Table 1).

ADULT CAPTURES COMPARED TO TERRITORY COUNTS

Average standard errors of between-year changes in CES adult captures are presented in Table 1. Weighted correlation coefficients comparing between-year changes in abundance of common passerines on CBC plots and CE stations are presented in Table 2, whereas tests for differing overall trends in abundance between the two monitoring schemes are summarized in Table 3. The information summarized in Tables 1–3 is considered below according to the taxonomic groupings used in the tables.

Resident insectivores and thrushes

For this group of five common species, between-year changes in adult CES catches were highly correlated with changes in counts in both woodland and farmland CBC plots (Table 2), suggesting that the CES is providing reliable measures of changes in adult abundance for all five species. Temporal trends in abundance were generally consistent across the two monitoring schemes (Table 3), although catches of Blackbirds have declined at a greater rate on CE stations than have territory counts on CBC plots. Exclusion of late season adult captures did not improve precision of between-year changes, and, in the case of Wren, resulted in lower precision (Table 1).

Migratory warblers

For this group of eight species, comparative CBC data were available for all species except Reed Warbler. For Sedge Warbler, Whitethroat, and Chiffchaff, between-year changes in CES catches were generally consistent with changes in counts on CBC plots (Table 2). In the case of Whitethroat, trends in CES catches were more consistent with trends in CBC counts on farmland when captures made during July and August were excluded (Table 3). The precision of between-year changes in the captures of adult Whitethroats (and Chiffchaffs) was also higher when data from July and August were excluded (Table 1). For Blackcap, Willow Warbler, and Lesser Whitethroat, long-term trends were reasonably consistent across the two schemes (Table 3). In the case of Willow Warbler, there was some evidence of a greater rate of decline in CE catches compared to territory counts on farmland CBC plots (Table 3).

TABLE 2. WEIGHTED PEARSON'S CORRELATION COEFFICIENTS COMPARING BETWEEN-YEAR CHANGES (1983/1984 TO 1991/1992) IN THE NUMBER OF ADULTS CAUGHT ON CE SITES AND THE NUMBERS OF TERRITORIES RECORDED ON CBC PLOTS IN FARMLAND AND WOODLAND

Species	Farmland CBC		Woodland CBC	
	CES 1–6	CES 1–12	CES 1–6	CES 1–12
Wren	0.97 ***	0.92 ***	0.93 ***	0.87 ***
Dunnock	0.95 ***	0.90 ***	0.79 *	0.82 **
Robin	0.97 ***	0.96 ***	0.84 **	0.79 *
Blackbird	0.83 **	0.78 *	0.65 (*)	0.63 (*)
Song Thrush	0.89 **	0.84 **	0.68 *	0.68 *
Sedge Warbler	0.78 *	0.76 *	–	–
Reed Warbler	–	–	–	–
Lesser Whitethroat	-0.29	-0.22	–	–
Whitethroat	0.86 **	0.86 **	0.93 ***	0.96 ***
Garden Warbler	-0.47	-0.51	0.35	0.13
Blackcap	0.57	0.47	0.59	0.64 (*)
Chiffchaff	0.72 *	0.80 **	0.65 (*)	0.74 *
Willow Warbler	0.38	0.50	0.34	0.43
Long-tailed Tit	0.71 *	0.75 *	0.58	0.62
Blue Tit	0.24	0.15	-0.07	-0.07
Great Tit	-0.24	-0.71 *	-0.11	-0.41
Treecreeper	-0.29	0.09	0.01	0.14
Chaffinch	-0.11	0.03	-0.67 *	-0.31
Greenfinch	0.27	0.33	-0.06	-0.14
Linnet	0.13	0.17	-0.09	-0.01
Redpoll	–	–	–	–
Bullfinch	0.46	0.18	–0.15	–0.30
Reed Bunting	-0.10	-0.10	–	–
Number significant	9+	9+, 1-	5+, 1-	6+

Notes: Changes in the numbers of adults caught on CE stations were considered using data from all 12 visits (May–August) and from the first six visits only (May–June). Species are separated into groups as in Table 1.
*** denotes $P < 0.001$; ** denotes $P < 0.01$; * denotes $P < 0.05$; (*) denotes $P < 0.10$; – denotes no comparative CBC data available.

Trends in the catches of adult Garden Warblers on CE stations differed significantly from trends in abundance on both woodland and farmland CBC plots (Table 3), although the difference was only marginally significant on woodland ($0.05 < P < 0.06$). Trends in the abundance of Garden Warblers also differed between woodland and farmland CBC habitats ($P < 0.02$). Catches of Garden Warblers on CE stations have declined since 1982, whereas numbers on CBC plots have increased on farmland and shown no trend in woodland.

Tits and Treecreeper

For Long-tailed Tit, both between-year changes and long-term trends in abundance were consistent between the CBC and CES schemes (Tables 2 and 3), particularly for annual indices derived from CES visits 1–6 (Table 3). Between-year changes

in the catches of adult Treecreepers were generally not consistent between the two monitoring schemes (Table 2). However, long-term trends in the catches of Treecreepers made during all 12 CES visits did not differ significantly from those derived from CBC counts in both woodland and farmland habitats (Table 3). Relatively small numbers of adult Treecreepers are caught on CE stations (for example the 1991–1992 change was based upon 59 adults trapped in 1991 and 41 in 1992) and hence between-year changes are measured imprecisely (Table 1).

The most pronounced inconsistencies between long-term trends in CES catches and CBC counts were for Blue Tit and Great Tit (Table 3). In the case of Great Tit, between-year changes in abundance were negatively correlated (Table 2). For both species, CES captures have declined strongly since 1982, whereas there have been no significant trends in counts of tits on either farmland or woodland CBC habitats.

TABLE 3. COMPARISON OF LONG-TERM TEMPORAL TRENDS IN CHAIN INDICES DERIVED FROM CBC AND CES DATA (1982–1992)

Species	Farmland CBC		Woodland CBC	
	CES 1–6	CES 1–12	CES 1–6	CES 1–12
Wren	0.00	0.72	0.32	0.08
Dunnock	2.90	1.64	0.00	0.28
Robin	0.41	0.06	3.90	1.14
Blackbird	3.62	5.98 *	4.55 *	7.17 *
Song Thrush	0.03	0.11	5.43 *	3.08
Sedge Warbler	2.12	0.23	–	–
Reed Warbler	–	–	–	–
Lesser Whitethroat	1.32	1.19	–	–
Whitethroat	1.36	8.47 **	0.01	2.94
Garden Warbler	17.26 ***	12.49 **	11.73 **	4.35 (*)
Blackcap	2.59	3.42	0.47	0.78
Chiffchaff	1.99	2.90	0.00	0.17
Willow Warbler	5.46 *	4.04 (*)	0.04	0.74
Long-tailed Tit	1.62	5.90 *	0.21	2.56
Blue Tit	19.13 ***	39.13 ***	20.91 ***	45.58 ***
Great Tit	9.87 **	13.42 **	21.10 ***	26.06 ***
Treecreeper	7.36 *	0.27	12.21 **	0.05
Chaffinch	21.02 ***	8.98 **	7.73 *	0.90
Greenfinch	7.54 *	6.12 *	14.86 **	17.65 ***
Linnet	3.42	16.96 ***	0.49	5.31 *
Redpoll	–	–	–	–
Bullfinch	2.86	0.89	2.77	0.63
Reed Bunting	41.72 ***	10.12 **	–	–
Number of species with different trends	8/21	11/21	8/18	6/18

Notes: F-statistics and associated significance levels are presented for the interaction between monitoring scheme (factor) and year (continuous covariate). Significant interactions indicate different average annual rates of change in abundance. Changes in the numbers of adults caught on CES stations were considered using data from all 12 annual visits (May–August) and from the first six visits only (May–June).

*** denotes $P < 0.001$; ** denotes $P < 0.01$; * denotes $P < 0.05$; (*) denotes $P < 0.10$; – denotes no comparative CBC data available.

Finches and Reed Bunting

For one of the six species in this group (Redpoll) there are no comparable CBC data. For Chaffinch, between-year changes in CES captures were not positively correlated with those derived from CBC data (Table 2), and long-term trends in CES catches were inconsistent with trends in counts on farmland, but not woodland (Table 3). Woodland is probably the preferred breeding habitat of Chaffinches in Britain (Gibbons et al. 1993).

For Greenfinch and Linnet, trends in abundance were generally inconsistent between the two monitoring schemes, although not when CES catches of Linnets were limited to the first six visits (Table 3). For both of these species, changes in adult abundance are measured with relatively low precision by the CES scheme (Table 1), due to small sample sizes.

Bullfinch is a relatively late-breeding species and a relatively high proportion of adults are caught for the first time in any year during visits 7–12 (Baillie et al. 1986). Between-year changes are therefore measured with greater precision when they are based upon captures from all 12 visits, rather than only from the first six visits (Table 1). Although between-year changes were not consistent with those derived from CBC data (Table 2), longer-term trends in abundance were consistent across the two monitoring schemes (Table 3).

In the case of Reed Bunting, between-year changes in CES catches and counts on CBC farmland plots were not correlated (Table 2), and long-term trends in abundance differed significantly (Table 3). However, changes in numbers on farmland may not be representative of wider population changes because wetland habitats are the main and probably preferred breeding habitat for this species (Gordon 1972, Gibbons et al. 1993). Drier farmland probably serves as a suboptimal, overspill habitat for Reed Buntings when population levels in wetland habitats are high (Bell 1969, Marchant et al. 1990).

DISCUSSION

COMPARISON OF CES AND CBC

Despite the problems of interpretation outlined above, several general conclusions emerge from this analysis.

(1) For at least nine species, between-year changes in adult captures combined across CE stations were consistent with extensive changes in abundance as measured by spot-mapping of breeding bird populations. These species are Wren, Dunnock, Robin, Blackbird, Song Thrush, Sedge Warbler, Whitethroat, Chiffchaff, and Long-tailed Tit (Table 2).

(2) For a further six species, long-term trends in CES captures (but not between-year changes) were generally consistent with trends in abundance derived from extensive CBC counts (Table 3). These species are Blackcap, Willow Warbler, Treecreeper, Linnet, Bullfinch, and Lesser Whitethroat.

(3) For the remaining six species, between-year and long-term changes in CES adult catches were inconsistent with concurrent changes in territory counts on CBC plots for at least one of the two CBC habitats. In the case of Reed Bunting, this may reflect the unrepresentative habitats covered by the CBC. In the cases of Garden Warbler, Chaffinch, and Greenfinch, trends in abundance differ significantly between woodland and farmland CBC plots suggesting that population processes may differ between habitats. The preferred habitats of Garden Warblers are probably woodland and scrub close to canopy closure (Gibbons et al. 1993). Because the CES monitors Garden Warblers mainly in scrub and woodland habitats it is perhaps not surprising that the trend in abundance on CE stations is more similar to the CBC trend for woodland than for farmland (Table 3).

In the case of the two titmouse species (Blue Tit and Great Tit), trends in abundance were consistent across CBC woodland and farmland habitats, but inconsistent between the CBC and CES data. Because between-year changes in the numbers of adult titmice caught at CE stations were measured with reasonable precision (Table 1), the observed disparity between the CES and the CBC data is difficult to explain, and casts some doubt over the reliability of the CES data for these species. One possible cause of declining catches of adult tits on CE stations could be net-avoidance, which might be promoted by winter and spring mist-netting activities on or adjacent to constant effort stations, often in association with artificial feeders. Such netting activities would be unlikely to involve other species caught on CE stations. This possibility could be investigated by comparing trends in captures on stations with and without winter and spring mist-netting activities. Habitat succession on CE stations might also serve to reduce catching efficiency as tits in mixed-aged flocks tend to fly along the tops of bushes and trees. As the vegetation grows higher, fewer of these flocks might be caught in mist nets.

(4) For most species monitored by the CES

scheme, there was little difference in between-year changes, long-term trends, and precision based on captures made during all 12 visits and captures made during visits 1–6 only. However, in the case of Whitethroat, long-term trends in catches were more strongly correlated with trends in counts on CBC plots, and the precision of between-year changes was higher, when CES changes were based upon captures during visits 1–6 only. Similarly, long-term trends in the captures of Linnets and Long-tailed Tits were more closely correlated with those derived from CBC data when the CES changes were based on captures made during visits 1–6 only. For these three species, changes in adult abundance might be better measured by using captures from the first six CES visits only.

For Treecreeper and Bullfinch, long-term trends in CES captures were more closely correlated with those from the CBC, and precision of between-year changes improved, when captures from all 12 visits were used.

To summarize, for 15 of the 21 species considered, long-term trends in the abundance of adult songbirds as recorded by spot-mapping (CBC) and standardized mist netting (CES) were similar (see also Peach et al. 1998). This suggests that, for most common songbirds, the CES methodology is providing reliable information on extensive changes in the size of breeding populations. Our conclusions are broadly similar to those of Silkey et al. (1999) who found that capture rates from standardized mist netting in coastal scrub did reflect changes in breeding densities for three out of four species considered. These authors noted that the form of the relationship between capture rates and breeding densities differed between species, thus highlighting the need for caution when relating changes in catch rates to breeding densities.

PRIORITIES FOR FURTHER VALIDATION OF CES

Effects of habitat succession

Successional changes at CE stations could cause two potentially serious problems for long-term monitoring. First, the catching efficiency of particular net locations may decline as the vegetation height increases and birds increasingly fly over the tops of nets. Second, the composition of breeding passerine communities can be sensitive to successional changes to the vegetation (Fuller 1987, 1995), and therefore long-term population trends derived from CES data may be negatively biased for species which

prefer early successional habitats, and positively biased for species which prefer later successional habitats. Little is known about the habitat preferences of juvenile passerines during the post-fledging period, though successional changes on CE stations have the potential to bias CES results for both adult birds and young birds.

A new system of habitat recording was introduced in 1995 to collect quantitative information on the extent and rate of habitat change on CE stations. This system involves the collection of three types of information describing an area extending 10 m from both sides of each standard mist net: (1) five habitat codes giving details of the major habitat type (following Crick 1992) and the presence of water; (2) the average maximum height of the scrub vegetation within 5 m of the net; and (3) the percent scrub cover within 10 m of the net. Fuller (1987) has shown that percent scrub cover is a useful predictor of the overall density of passerine birds and the total number of species breeding in scrub in southern England. Habitat codes are also requested for land surrounding the CE station.

At a smaller sample of CE stations we plan to collect net-specific capture and habitat data, which should allow us to consider relationships between habitat changes and capture rates at a finer scale. It might also be useful to have CE banders manage and maintain vegetation at fixed heights at some of their standard net locations (i.e., through regular cut back) while allowing the vegetation to grow up at others, and comparing changes in catch rates in managed and unmanaged net locations on the same stations.

Some insight into the likely importance of habitat succession as a factor affecting capture rates might be gained through analyses of the existing CES data. Trends in catch rates of species thought to be sensitive to successional change or changes in species composition could be compared in habitats considered to be sensitive and insensitive to successional change (e.g., scrub and woodland respectively). Analyses might allow for widescale population changes through the calculation of station-specific deviations in catches from those expected according to known regional population changes (derived, for example, from the British Breeding Bird Survey).

Effects of station turnover

Each year a number of CE stations drop out of the scheme and a number of new stations are enrolled. During the period 1987–1993, the average loss rate of CE stations was 8% per annum. If between-year changes in catches differ between stations which have just entered the scheme and stations just about to leave the scheme, then bias could be introduced into long-term indices of abundance or productivity. This might be the case if stations tended to be registered when they were catching relatively large numbers of birds and tended to be discontinued when they were catching relatively small numbers of birds.

Analyses of existing data could compare between-year changes in captures for stations at the beginning of their (CES) lives with those at stations that have been operated for some minimum number of years, or which are in their last few years as CE stations. This sort of analysis has been applied to CBC territory count data (S. Baillie and S. Gates, unpubl. data) and for most species considered, between-year changes in territory counts did not differ between plots at the beginning and end of their lives.

Representativeness of CE stations

For practical reasons relating to the efficiency of mist netting in different habitats, most CE stations are operated in either scrub or wetland habitats, and fewer than 10% of stations are operated in deciduous woodland. The CES scheme therefore monitors bird populations only in these habitats. Because banders choose the locations of their CE station, the national sample of CE stations may not be representative of scrub, wetland, and woodland habitats within Britain and Ireland.

Various land-use databases are now available for the U.K. region that could be used to examine the degree to which CE stations are representative of the wider landscape. The Centre for Ecology and Hydrology (CEH) has provided the BTO with re-motely sensed land cover data for each 1-km square of Great Britain (Fuller et al. 1993). In 1990, the percent of each of 25 land cover types was measured in each 1-km square. The 25 land cover types are general categories such as "lowland bog," "scrub/orchard," and "deciduous wood." Recently a further land-cover survey has been completed and more up-to-date data are now available (Fuller et al. 2002). Such information will be used to assess whether the habitat within 1-km squares containing CE stations is broadly representative of the squares containing predominantly scrub and wetland (and perhaps woodland) habitat. This could be done both for the entire United Kingdom and within broad regions. An obvious problem here will be the definition of a subset of squares which represents the "scrub and wetland" component of Great Britain.

Validation of annual CES productivity indices

The proportion of young birds in catches made on CE stations represents an integrated measure of annual productivity, which incorporates the number of nesting attempts per pair, nesting success, and im-mediate post-fledging mortality. Any comparative assessment of annual productivity should ideally incorporate all these factors.

Each year the BTO Nest Records Scheme collects information on approximately 30,000 nest histories (Greenwood et al. 1993). This information can be used to estimate average laying dates, clutch sizes, egg survival rates, and chick survival rates for a wide range of species, including most of those currently being monitored by the CES scheme. For some CES species, annual estimates of post-fledging mortal-ity could be attained from the U.K. national band-ing recovery data using the methods developed by Thomson et al. (1999).

For species that are essentially single-brooded (like Willow Warbler and the *Parus* tits), it should be possible to combine estimates of nesting success with those for post-fledging mortality, producing independent annual estimates of productivity that could be compared with the percent of young birds caught at CE stations. For multi-brooded species, it may be difficult to obtain any extensive measure of the number of breeding attempts. The distribution of laying dates from nest record cards, or the temporal distribution of heavy (gravid) females (Naylor and Green 1976) or brood patches at differing stages of development (Boddy 1992) as recorded by banders, may provide some information on annual variation in the number of breeding attempts, although all such approaches would require critical evaluation. Intensive studies may be required to measure annual variation in the number of breeding attempts.

Comparison of results from CES and intensive studies

Intensive local studies have an important role to play with respect to both the validation and the interpretation of data generated through extensive monitoring programs like the CES scheme. Where possible, intensive studies should be replicated across many locations in order to allow general con-clusions to be drawn.

For example, independent assessments of the abundance of adults birds on CE stations would be useful to compare against catches. Between 1985 and the early 1990s, timed point counts were carried out during May and June at a sample of CE stations (34 stations in 1985 and 10 stations in 1993). These count data will provide useful independent estimates of local breeding population sizes and between-year changes in those populations. Some additional comparative count data are available from a small number of stations in the form of intensive territory mapping counts (e.g., Peach et al. 1995).

Another source of high quality count data is observation of individually marked adult birds, which can also provide a range of information concerning territorial and breeding behavior and site fidelity. Color-banding of chicks or of juveniles could provide useful information on site fidelity and dispersal, and could be a useful tool for the study of net avoidance.

Intensive banding programs for nestlings can provide useful information on local nesting success, for comparison with productivity indices from mist netting (as shown by Nur and Geupel 1993b, du Feu and McMeeking *this volume*). Species using nest boxes are obviously convenient for such studies, whereas finding nests of open-nesting passerines can be time consuming. If a high proportion of locally fledged young are banded as chicks, then it is also possible to apportion the total juvenile catch into local and non-local components. For some species, a high proportion of the total juvenile catch may be of non-local origins (Naylor and Green 1976, Nur and Geupel 1993b).

Finally, the BTO is seeking to develop a small network of Integrated Population Monitoring (IPM) Stations at which intensive standardized mist netting is combined with intensive territory mapping, nest-finding, and color-banding of nestlings and adults. The main aim of these IPM stations is to generate high quality demographic data over long runs of years, but a secondary aim is to provide locations for replicated validation studies.

ACKNOWLEDGMENTS

We are grateful to the many volunteer banders who have devoted so much time and energy to the operation of Constant Effort Sites. The CES scheme was organized in a voluntary capacity by M. Boddy during the early 1980s, and by J. Marchant and B. Holden between 1986 and 1988. The Constant Effort Sites scheme is funded by a partnership of the British Trust for Ornithology and the Joint Nature Conservation Committee (on behalf of English Nature, Scottish Natural Heritage, and the Countryside Council for Wales, and also on behalf of the Environment and Heritage Service in Northern Ireland). The contribution of STB was partially supported with funds from the Scottish Office Agriculture and Fisheries Department, while he was employed by the Scottish Agricultural Statistics Service. WJP is grateful to D. F. DeSante and The Institute for Bird Populations for kind assistance with travel expenses, and to the Point Reyes Bird Observatory for hosting the workshop. We thank J. R. Sauer, N. Nur, J. H. Marchant, M. Boddy, C. Vansteenwegen, and R. J. O'Connor for improving earlier drafts of the manuscript.

Studies in Avian Biology No. 29:57–62

RELATIONSHIP OF JUVENILES CAPTURED IN CONSTANT-EFFORT NETTING AND LOCAL ABUNDANCE

Chris R. du Feu and John M. McMeeking

Abstract. Numbers of juvenile Blackbirds (*Turdus merula*), Song Thrushes (*T. philomelos*), Blue Tits (*Parus caeruleus*), and Great Tits (*P. major*) caught during constant effort mist-netting were compared with numbers of nestlings of these species banded during the years 1979–2002 in Treswell Wood, Nottinghamshire, England. There was a significant relationship between the annual numbers of juveniles captured and the annual numbers of nestlings banded in all four species. Mortality and immigration between fledging and mist-netting periods probably vary among years, reducing the strength of correlation. Results suggest that number of young birds captured in the British Trust for Ornithology Constant Effort Sites scheme across many sites is a good index of the number of young in the population following juvenile dispersal.

Key Words: constant-effort mist netting, Constant Effort Sites, productivity, banding.

The index of productivity used by the Constant Effort Sites (CES) scheme of the British Trust for Ornithology is the ratio of juveniles to adults totalled over a large number of study sites (Peach and Baillie 1990). The assumption underlying this index is that the numbers of adults and young birds captured are proportional to the true numbers of each age group in the population. This has been tested for adults by comparing CES data from many sites with results from the Common Birds Census (Peach et al. *this volume*), with positive results. Here we present evidence to support the assumption that young birds are also captured in proportion to their abundance, using data from a single site. Some of the data were previously published (du Feu and McMeeking 1991), but this paper includes additional data and discussion.

We compared numbers of nestlings banded that were deemed to have fledged with numbers of young birds captured in mist nets during the summer. There are many reasons to expect that these numbers might not be correlated. Not all birds produced at the study site will be banded as nestlings. All nestlings do not fledge at the same time as each other, or at the same time each year, which affects numbers captured in mist nets. Dispersal and mortality of young occurs throughout the netting period, and captures are affected by weather. Captures of juveniles of flocking species in mist nets may not be independent of each other. Such factors could potentially invalidate the use of juvenile captures in mist netting as an index of local fledging success.

METHODS

Treswell Wood is composed of 47 ha of mature broad-leaved trees, mainly ash (*Fraxinus excelsior*) with some oak (*Quercus robur*), with an understory predominantly of hazel (*Corylus avellana*). It is an ancient woodland designated as a Site of Special Scientific Interest, owned and managed by the Nottinghamshire Wildlife Trust. Since 1972 the Trust has restored the traditional system of "coppice with standards" (Cramp and Simmons 1977) to parts of the wood.

We have carried out year-round constant-effort mist netting at seven sub-sites in Treswell Wood since 1978. Our netting regime differs from that of the CES regime, which specifies 12 evenly spaced visits to each site throughout the months May to August inclusive. Instead, we visit each of our seven sites in the Wood five times a year, approximately once every 10 weeks. The exact order of visiting the sites varies according to weather, for some sites are more affected by wind than others, but it is kept as constant as possible from year to year. On each visit we use ten 18-m nets, in fixed positions, set for five hours from shortly after dawn. If conditions allow, extra nets are erected. Such extra nets are not sited immediately adjacent to the standard nets, to prevent interference with the standard nets. Birds caught in additional netting are not included in our constant effort analyses.

About 100 nest boxes, primarily for tits (*Parus* spp.), have been placed in the northern two-thirds of the wood. The number and distribution of boxes have remained relatively constant since 1979. We record all nests in boxes, and band all chicks. Although we make no attempt to find non-box nests, we record all natural nests of any species we detect while on the nest box rounds (e.g., when an adult is flushed from the nest), and chicks in those nests are also banded. Nest checks have been done by the same person (CdF) each year. Because the distribution of boxes is much the same from year to year, the opportunity for finding other nests is also approximately the same. No nestling tits have been banded other than those in boxes, but we have banded enough Blackbirds (*Turdus merula*) and Song Thrushes (*T. philomelos*) to analyze them here.

We assume that any bird banded has also fledged, unless

there is evidence to the contrary. Such evidence includes finding carcasses of young in the nest when the boxes are emptied at the end of the season. Sometimes predators attack nests and leave a few partially dismembered bodies, in which case we assume that all chicks failed to fledge. Evidence for success includes finding undamaged but flattened empty nests with many flakes of feather sheath, nestlings capable of fledging when last seen in the nest, and newly fledged juveniles in the vicinity of nest boxes. There have been almost no direct observations of birds fledging from nests.

A Common Bird Census (CBC) is carried out in the wood by other workers. For all years, we have a record of the total numbers of territories recorded, but a breakdown of where these territories lay within the Wood is available only for some years (1981–1994 and 1997–1998).

In this paper, we compared the numbers of banded Blackbirds and Song Thrushes deemed to have fledged each year with the numbers of free-flying juveniles caught in mist nets between 28 May and 15 August (1979–2002). These dates correspond approximately to the CES breeding season sampling period. We also compared the numbers of nestling Blue Tits (*Parus caeruleus*) and Great Tits (*P. major*) fledging from boxes with the numbers of juveniles

mist netted in the same period. We use the terms "sampling period" for the late May through August netting period and "study period" for the years 1979–2002.

Because data for both numbers of nestlings banded and juveniles caught are count data, we used log(N+1) transformations in correlation analyses, as described in Fowler and Cohen (1986). Scatter diagrams were plotted on logarithmic axes and all regression lines were fitted using the model 2 reduced major axis regression described by Fowler and Cohen (1986).

RESULTS

Annual numbers of each species banded as nestlings within the wood, and the numbers of juveniles captured in constant effort nets in the sampling period are given in Table 1. We found a significant, positive correlation between these annual numbers for all four species: Blackbird (r = 0.49, N = 24, P = 0.02), Song Thrush (r = 0.40, N = 24, P = 0.05), Blue Tit (r = 0.64, N = 24, P = 0.001), Great Tit (r = 0.46, N = 24, P = 0.03). Only four points lay more than two standardized residuals away from any regression line

TABLE 1. NUMBERS OF NESTLINGS BANDED AND FLEDGED AND OF JUVENILES CAPTURED IN CONSTANT-EFFORT MIST NETTING BETWEEN 28 MAY AND 15 AUGUST EACH YEAR

	Blackbird		Song Thrush		Blue Tit		Great Tit	
Year	Nestlings banded	Juveniles captured	Nestlings banded	Juveniles captured	Nestlings banded	Juveniles captured	Nestlings banded	Juveniles captured
1979	14	16	33	2	91	0	65	4
1980	9	8	10	4	222	7	51	5
1981	0	5	6	4	215	45	55	9
1982	0	3	4	2	171	10	49	0
1983	7	4	14	4	117	5	48	5
1984	12	5	27	2	147	8	60	5
1985	9	10	14	0	175	11	104	3
1986	13	9	26	2	226	0	125	0
1987	3	3	15	1	261	30	133	30
1988	5	2	6	0	104	8	74	5
1989	0	5	3	2	242	46	132	14
1990	0	0	0	1	173	17	38	2
1991	3	0	0	0	120	1	44	4
1992	0	0	4	4	130	0	66	9
1993	0	1	0	0	85	1	22	0
1994	0	6	6	6	120	4	21	1
1995	5	6	8	0	171	18	66	2
1996	4	6	2	2	113	3	18	3
1997	3	6	0	0	93	2	65	2
1998	0	1	0	1	41	1	20	2
1999	0	4	0	2	108	2	90	6
2000	3	1	5	2	88	0	43	1
2001	4	1	0	0	87	0	46	1
2002	4	2	8	2	63	2	70	3
Totals	96	104	191	43	3363	221	1505	116

(Fig. 1). These were the points for Blue Tit in 1986 and 1998 and for Great Tit in 1986 and 1996.

There was significant correlation between numbers of Song Thrush nests (1981–1994 and 1997–1998) and the numbers of Song Thrush territories recorded by CBC in the section of the Wood in which boxes were present (r = 0.77 for transformed annual indices, N = 16, P < 0.001; Fig. 2). The correlation for Blackbirds was not significant (r = 0.39, N = 16, P = 0.14).

DISCUSSION

Here we examine some of the probable causes of variance in the correlations between number of nestling-banded birds deemed to have fledged and number of juveniles captured during summer mist netting.

PROPORTIONS BANDED

The relationship between nestlings banded and juveniles captured was weaker for Song Thrush and

Blackbird than for the tit species. A contributing factor was the relatively low proportions of the nestling populations of Song Thrush and Blackbird that were banded. The correlation between Song Thrush nests found and CBC territories (Fig. 2) suggests there was fairly constant nest finding effort, although data for Blackbirds do not support this as strongly. Nest-finding effort was not exhaustive, however, and although 605 Blackbird and 327 Song Thrush CBC territories were recorded in the study period, only 55 and 104 nests were found, respectively. Because both species are multiple brooded, the overall percentage of nests found is unlikely to be higher than 10%. The percentages of juveniles banded at nests and later caught in constant effort nets, 0% for Blackbirds and 9.7% for Song Thrushes, are compatible with this low figure. The number of juvenile Song Thrushes netted has always been so low that chance factors are relatively important in determining variation in numbers. Thus, it is not surprising that the correlation between the numbers of nestlings banded and the numbers of juveniles netted was weakest in this species.

For tits, the number of nests in natural sites is

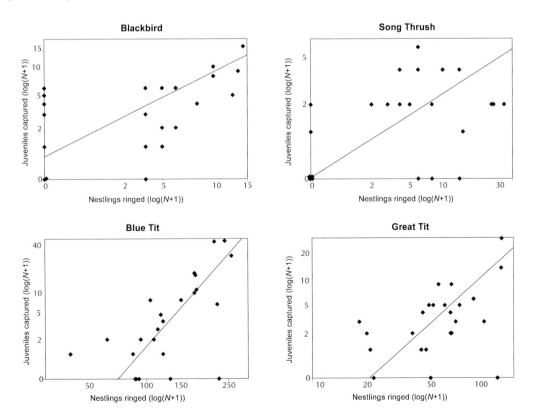

FIGURE 1. Nestlings banded and juveniles captured in constant-effort mist nets in Treswell Wood, 1979–2002 (model 2 reduced major axis regression method).

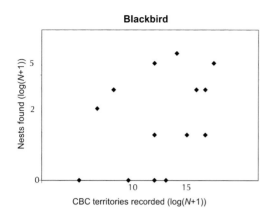

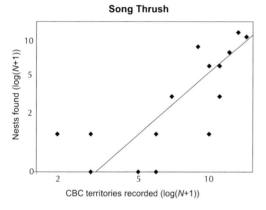

FIGURE 2. Blackbird and Song Thrush Common Bird Census (CBC) territories recorded vs. nests found, 1981–1994 and 1997–1998.

unknown, as is the number of young fledged from such sites. We have never banded nestling tits in natural sites. During the study period, 41% and 37% respectively of the juvenile Great Tits and Blue Tits captured in constant effort nets in the sampling period had been banded as nestlings. This suggests either that there are many natural nests (producing up to 60% of all nestlings), or that many juveniles captured in mist nets had moved in from elsewhere (see below). Several lines of evidence indicate that the first explanation is correct and the second has little influence.

Over 24 years, the percent of adult female tits captured in the spring in constant-effort mist nets that were later found nesting in boxes was 27% for Great Tits and 17% for Blue Tits. These percentages are lower than those given by Perrins (1979) for the percentage of these tits using boxes in Wytham Wood. However, in Treswell Wood we did not capture all females nesting in boxes every year. (For Blue Tits, 86% of females nesting in boxes were captured, but

the figure for Great Tits was only 56%.) Moreover, one-third of the Wood contained no nest boxes. Another estimate of the proportion of tits nesting in boxes is the ratio of occupied nest boxes to the number of CBC territories found in the same part of the Wood. This ratio was 0.29 for Great Tit nests and 0.31 for Blue Tits, although the ratio may be biased by miscounts due to unsuccessful and replacement clutches, and by the use of nest box data in CBC.

Whereas all lines of evidence indicate that less than half of nestling tits were banded each year, the proportion is much higher than for Song Thrush and Blackbird, and is less likely to have varied among years simply as a result of chance.

FLEDGING PERIOD

Song Thrush and Blackbird are multi-brooded, and it is probable that many of the year's juveniles were already dead by the time the sampling period began, whereas others had not yet fledged. Because mist-net data were collected over several visits, however, the total sample of juveniles should be relatively unaffected by variation in timing of the breeding season. Tits, on the other hand, are almost exclusively single brooded, all fledge within a relatively short period, and fledging dates vary from year to year. This means that in late years there were fewer mist-netting sessions after nestlings had fledged and become available for capture.

To gain insight on the effect of fledging date variation on the correlation between nestlings banded and juveniles captured, we reanalysed data omitting the last two netting visits in each year. Although correlations remained more or less the same for the two thrushes and Blue Tits, the correlation was considerably weakened for Great Tits. In Treswell Wood, Great Tits nest nearly a week later than do Blue Tits. This result demonstrates the importance of ensuring that sampling periods extend far enough into the summer to ensure a representative number of individuals will be trapped.

It is likely that the complete absence of juvenile tits captured in 1986 (Table 1) was primarily a consequence of the very late season (which was also followed by high post-fledging mortality caused by lack of food late in the season). The percentage of nest box-banded birds recaptured by the end of the study period was also lower for the 1986 cohort than for any other year.

MOVEMENT AND DISPERSAL

Lack of correspondence between mist-net samples of juveniles and number of locally banded nestlings could reflect changes in the local population of young birds between the two samples. Such changes could reflect dispersal and immigration, or mortality.

Perrins (1979) states that after the first month after fledging, there is local redistribution of tit populations, with some new birds moving into the area and some natives moving out. Our sampling period ends during this redistribution period, and we have only a little evidence for it. Two young Blue Tits and one Great Tit were captured between 4 and 8 km away from the Wood within the sampling period, and several more were captured elsewhere shortly after the end of the sampling period. Evidence of movement into the Wood came from one Blue Tit that fledged from a nest box on a farm to the south of the Wood and was captured 1.5 km away within 10 days, in the northern part of the Wood. However, because the proportions of nest box-banded tits captured later in constant effort netting were so close to the estimates of percentages of all nests that were in boxes, it appears that juvenile dispersal did not have a great effect by the time our sampling period ended.

Reanalysis of the data with the last two sessions removed made little overall difference to the strength of the relationships for the three earliest fledging species. This provides further evidence that any local dispersal has not had a major impact by the time the sampling period ends.

MORTALITY

Two of the four points in Figure 1 with standardized residuals >2 were 1996 for Great Tits and 1998 for Blue Tits (the left-most points on the graphs in Fig. 1). In both of these years there was massive mortality of nestlings in nest boxes, largely through predation. Both species suffered in each of these years, although Great Tits rather more in 1996 and Blue Tits more in 1998. It is not known whether the predation was equally great amongst tits that nested in natural sites. Neither is it known whether predation of nests was equally great in the area surrounding the Wood. Although very few juveniles were mist netted in the standard nets in these years (three Great Tits 1996, one Blue Tit in 1998), these numbers were higher than expected (Fig. 1). Possibly this was a chance result, but may also have represented immigration from areas with lower predation.

Lack (1966) discussed the causes, timing, extent, and variation of post fledging mortality for Great Tits and Blue Tits. He found that there is heavy mortality before the beginning of November, most of it in the first month after fledging. W. Peach (pers. comm.)

suggests that this mortality is greatest in the first few days after fledging. In these few days juveniles will be relatively immobile, waiting high in the tree canopy for parents to bring food, and so are particularly vulnerable to predators. Instances of early death caused by predators have been provided by bands, from one Blue Tit and two Great Tits, recovered from owl pellets within our sampling period. In some years, we also noted very heavy predation on Song Thrush nests, often at a late stage. In some cases a Tawny Owl (*Strix aluco*) systematically raided Song Thrush nests, as shown by bands of nestlings being found in the owl's nest. Blackbirds seem not to have suffered systematic nest predation by the owls, as we have only ever recovered one single Blackbird nestling band from any owl nest.

The level of immediate post-fledging mortality depends, among other things, on population size, weather, food availability, predator activity, and brood sizes. It varies greatly from year to year, and therefore weakens the relationship between number of juveniles mist netted and number of nestlings banded. However, the fact that there is correlation between number of juveniles captured and numbers banded in the nest suggests the immediate post-fledging mortality is generally similar from year to year (with the possible exception of 1986).

CAPTURE PATTERNS

A major problem in any estimate of productivity based on captures of tits in mist nets lies in the erratic nature and non-independence of captures. In the early post-fledging period, tits may remain in family parties. Thus whole families are often captured together rather than as individuals. Later young tits join mixed species flocks and, again, captures tend to be of groups rather than of individuals. The flocks often spend much of their time high in the tree canopy, out of range of mist nets. Therefore tits can be abundant, but not be captured. Nonetheless, there are very few years in which we missed capturing at least some of the flocking birds. The distorting effect of flocking on mist-net captures is well illustrated by the 1980 data. Tits were abundant in 1980 (Table 1) and there was high survival, but the constant effort captures were relatively low. In fact many juvenile tits were caught but, by chance, these captures were in netting that was not part of the constant effort program, and so did not contribute data to this analysis.

CONCLUSION

For all four species considered, there was significant correlation between the numbers of young birds caught in mist nets and the numbers of banded nestlings deemed to have fledged. Despite variance introduced by the factors discussed above, number of juveniles captured in summer appeared to provide a good index of local productivity in most years.

The CES productivity index is compiled using data from many sites (typically well over 100), such that atypical captures at one site are unlikely to bias the national index. Moreover, the CES productivity index is meant to reflect numbers of juveniles surviving the immediate post fledging period, and the index was neither intended nor expected to represent site-specific productivity. Early post-fledging mortality and dispersal therefore pose little problem for the CES scheme. Nonetheless, the fact that relationships can be demonstrated between constant effort captures and known numbers of nestlings on a single site encourages confidence that constant effort data from many sites combined will provide a measure of juvenile abundance that can reliably be used in calculating indices of adult productivity.

ACKNOWLEDGMENTS

We are indebted to the Nottinghamshire Wildlife Trust for permission to band in Treswell Wood since 1972, to the many banders who have been involved in fieldwork, to Margaret Price and her Treswell Wood CBC workers, to R. du Feu and S. Wain for data extraction, and to J. J. D. Greenwood and W. J. Peach for their encouragement and guidance. We are also grateful to the editors and referees for their help in revising our 1991 paper and in translating it from the original English version.

Studies in Avian Biology No. 29:63–70

ESTIMATES OF ADULT SURVIVAL, CAPTURE PROBABILITY, AND RECAPTURE PROBABILITY: EVALUATING AND VALIDATING CONSTANT-EFFORT MIST NETTING

NADAV NUR, GEOFFREY R. GEUPEL, AND GRANT BALLARD

Abstract. We evaluate the use of capture–recapture data gathered with constant-effort mist-netting to infer adult survival, comparing estimates obtained using the program SURGE with direct observations on color-banded individuals. In addition, we determined capture probability of breeding adults in relation to several factors, such as distance from nest to nearest net. Data were collected as part of a long-term, on-going study of species breeding at the Palomarin Field Station, Point Reyes National Seashore, concentrating on Wrentits (*Chamaea fasciata*). Capture probability of breeding Wrentit adults was strongly related to distance from nest to nearest net and, independently, to the number of intervening territories between nest and net. In addition, females (and their mates) laying early in the season were less likely to be caught than those laying later. Breeding adults whose nests were more than 200 m from the closest mist net were rarely caught. Most adults caught were transient individuals, not holding local breeding territories. Territory-holders were caught repeatedly; non-territory holders were not. Recapture probability of territory-holders in the following year (if alive) was estimated at 71%, but only at 5% for those not holding local territories. Survival of Wrentit breeding adults was estimated to be 57%, which was slightly below estimates based on re-sightings (59% to 64%). However, survival estimated on the basis of capture–recapture of all adults (ignoring territorial status) was only 38%. We suggest that, in the absence of information regarding territorial status, survival analyses be restricted to individuals caught at least twice in a season. This is an effective method for screening out transient individuals.

Key Words: capture–recapture, constant effort netting, productivity, survival, transients, validation, Wrentit.

Populations of certain North American landbird species appear to be declining strongly (reviewed in Hagan and Johnston 1992, Finch and Stangel 1993). For effective management responses to be formulated, underlying causal factors responsible for the declines must be identified. To understand the causes of population decline requires detailed demographic information. However, the primary, long-established North American monitoring programs, specifically the Breeding Bird Survey, do not provide this information.

The three most critical demographic processes underlying population growth and decline are (1) adult survivorship, (2) reproductive success (i.e., production of young, or "productivity"), and (3) recruitment of young into the breeding population. These three demographic components are the most critical because the change in breeding population size from one year to the next, representing decline or recovery of a species, can be directly attributed to a combination of these three components (provided that immigration balances emigration). The need for researchers, managers, and agencies to assess such primary demographic parameters has been repeatedly stressed by many authors (Temple and Wiens 1989, DeSante et al. 1993b, Nur and Geupel 1993b).

Mist-netting appears to be a potentially powerful and efficient means of collecting critical data on demographic parameters such as annual survival and reproductive success, and is the cornerstone of several monitoring programs, including the Constant Effort Sites (CES) Scheme of the British Trust for Ornithology (Baillie et al. 1986, Bibby et al. 1992, Peach 1993, Peach et al. *this volume*), and, more recently, the Monitoring Avian Productivity and Survivorship (MAPS) program of the Institute of Bird Populations (DeSante et al. 1993b, *this volume*). However, the accuracy and validity of inferences based on mist-netting data have only recently been studied (though see du Feu and McMeeking 1991), and we know little about the limitations of data derived from constant effort mist-netting (CEM). Finally, in the absence of information on the specific portion of the sampled population to which mist-netted birds belong, it is impossible to develop methods of data collection and data analysis that best measure demographic parameters of the target portions of the population (such as local breeders).

Both CEM and intensive observations of color-banded individuals have been underway at the Point Reyes Bird Observatory (PRBO) since 1980. Because the same population has been studied with different methodologies, we are able to evaluate demographic inferences made using the CEM methodology, by comparing results with inferences made using a second methodology. In addition, we are able to estimate capture probability, which is rarely known for natural populations, and evaluate whether captured individuals are a random sample of those present at the breeding site.

Here we report selected results of a project that we refer to as "The Mist-Net Validation Study," with regard to adult survival, capture probability, and recapture probability. We consider factors influencing capture and recapture probability, which could therefore bias demographic estimates. In this paper, we report results from a single site over the period 1981–1991. Additional aspects of the project have been reported in Silkey et al. (1999) and Nur et al. (2000).

METHODS

The study species is the Wrentit (*Chamaea fasciata*), which has been the subject of relatively little prior study (Erickson 1938, Geupel and DeSante 1990, Geupel and Ballard 2002). Wrentits are monogamous, year-round, territorial residents, and both parents share in parental care such as nest-building and incubation. The Wrentit is considered to be quite sedentary (Erickson 1938, Johnson 1972), and we found that <1% of breeders move their territories between years on our study site (Geupel and DeSante 1990, Geupel and Ballard 2002). This make the species well suited for estimating survivorship on the basis of capture–recapture data. Wrentits maintain year-round territories and that, together with the sedentary nature of this species, makes them good candidates for a validation study, because birds observed on the study grid are likely to be the same ones caught in the nets.

The field work was conducted at PRBO's Palomarin Field Station, located just within the southern boundary of the Point Reyes National Seashore and adjacent to the Pacific Ocean. On the main 36 ha study site, we simultaneously carried out constant effort mist-netting, nest searches, intensive spot-mapping, and behavioral observations of color-banded individuals.

Constant effort mist-netting was conducted using 20, 12-m mist nets comprising 14 netting sites (Fig. 1). Eight sites (14 nets) were located on the edge of mixed, evergreen forest habitat comprised primarily of coast live oak (*Quercus agrifola*), California bay (*Umbellularia californica*), Douglas-fir (*Pseudotesuga menziesii*), and California buckeye (*Aesculus californicus*). The other six single nets were located in disturbed coastal scrub, which is the preferred habitat of Wrentits (Erickson 1938, AOU Check-list 1983). This was composed primarily of coyote bush (*Baccharis pilularis*), California sage (*Artemisa californica*), bush monkey flower (*Mimulus aurantiacus*), poison oak (*Rhus diversiloba*), California blackberry (*Rubus vitifolius*), and California coffeeberry (*Rhamnus*

californica) interspersed with introduced grasses. For further description of the study area see DeSante and Geupel (1987) and Silkey et al. (1999).

Net locations were adjacent to, and extended across, approximately 25% of the 36 ha study plot (Fig. 1). Net locations were selected so as to maximize the number of birds caught (L. R. Mewaldt, pers. comm.). The standardized mist-netting procedure was described by DeSante and Geupel (1987) and continued with only minor change during the study period, 1981–1991. Briefly, nets were run 7 days/week for 6 h, beginning 15 min after local sunrise (weather permitting) from 1 May (from 1 April prior to 1989) to approximately 25 November, and 3 days/week (Wednesday, Saturday, and Sunday) from December through end of March (through end of April, since 1989).

Detailed monitoring of individuals was conducted on the 36-ha study plot and has been described elsewhere (Geupel and DeSante 1990). In brief, identities and territory boundaries of color-marked individuals were determined from detailed spot-mapping censuses conducted a minimum of 3 days/week during the breeding season (15 March–31 July) throughout the 11 years of the study. Each territorial individual was observed a minimum of once every two weeks, and normally at least once per week.

Concentrated efforts were made to locate and monitor all nest attempts of all territorial pairs on the study area from 1981 through 1985, and from 1987 through 1991. No attempt was made to locate nests in 1986 and effort was reduced in 1980, hence we excluded those years from analyses of fledged young. The method of locating and monitoring Wrentit nests was described in Geupel and DeSante (1990). Nearly all successful nests (those fledging one or more young) were found before fledging, and nestlings were individually color-banded. Additional individuals were color-banded when first caught in mist-nets as hatching year (HY) or as after-hatching year (AHY) birds.

Here we analyze survival and capture probability with respect to territorial status; all individuals were classified as "territory holders" or "non-territory holders" according to whether or not they were known to maintain breeding territories on or adjacent to the study grid. Whereas all territory holders were presumed breeders (which could be confirmed through nest-finding and monitoring), non-territory holders were mostly transient individuals. Non-territory holders may have been "floaters" (*sensu* Stutchbury and Zack 1992), but it is also possible that some individuals bred outside the study area. Note that some non-territory holders were floaters displaying local site fidelity (Nur et al. 2000).

We examined differences in capture rates (per season and over the observed lifetime of individuals) for adults, comparing territory holders and non-territory holders, using Poisson regression (StataCorp 1997). We used linear models to test for differences in capture dates between known territory holders and non-territory holders (Neter et al. 1990), after determining that assumptions of this method were met (Nur et al. 1999). We evaluated differences in capture probability of territorial (breeding) adults with respect to distance of the nest from nearest net, number of

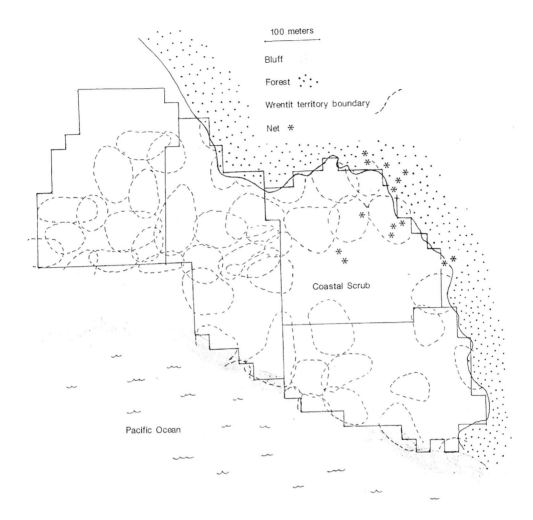

FIGURE 1. Palomarin Field Station, Point Reyes National Seashore. Nest-searches and territory-mapping of color-banded birds took place in the four contiguous area marked by solid, rectilinear lines, totaling 36 ha. Constant effort mist-netting was conducted at nets marked with asterisks. Dotted lines enclose Wrentit territorial boundaries for a typical year (1985).

territories between a bird's territory and the nearest net, sex, age, and various measures of reproductive success (date of completion of first clutch, number of young hatched or fledged, the number of clutches or broods), using multiple logistic regression (Hosmer and Lemeshow 2000). Date of clutch completion was transformed to the square of the number of days since 21 March (two days prior to the earliest first-egg date in the sample).

To analyze survival probability and recapture probability (i.e., the probability a bird that has survived to year x is caught in year x), we used the statistical program SURGE (Lebreton et al. 1992, Cooch et al. 1996). All analyses were conducted on the mist-net capture–recapture data from 333 different individuals caught over 11 years, and the results compared with detailed observations on individually color-banded Wrentits (244 different individuals for a total of 523 breeder-years). We first analyzed all captures, stratifying

on territorial status, and then carried out analyses on capture data that pooled all adults.

Statistical analyses were carried out using STATA 5.0 (StataCorp 1997). Results give estimates ± SE, unless otherwise stated, and were considered significant if $P < 0.05$.

RESULTS

INFLUENCES ON CAPTURE PROBABILITY OF ADULTS

Territorial status

Most of the adult Wrentits caught in the study did not hold territories within the study area (Table 1). In general, there were about three times as many non-territory holders as territory holders (means = 26.4 and 8.4, respectively; Table 1), although the

TABLE 1. CAPTURE OF AHY WRENTITS OVER 10 YEARS IN RELATION TO TERRITORIAL STATUS

Year	Number of local breeders	Number of non-territory holders	Percent local breeders
1981	8	35	19
1982	8	33	20
1983	12	30	29
1984	10	9	53
1985	9	28	24
1986	7	47	13
1987	8	32	20
1988	10	35	22
1989	5	14	26
1990	6	12	33
1991	10	16	39

Notes: Local breeders were birds known to hold territories in the study area. Non-territory holders were birds that either did not breed, or bred off the study area.

proportion of territory holders was unusually high in 1984 (53%). The number of non-territory holders varied more markedly among years than did the number of territory holders (Table 1), but the ratio of territory holders to non-territory holders did not vary significantly between years (Likelihood Ratio Statistic [LRS] = 26.94, df = 10, P = 0.076). Results were quite similar when only breeding season captures were considered.

Territory holders and non-territory holders were caught throughout the netting season. The two groups did not differ in mean first capture date (24 May ± 35.3 days [SD] for territory holders vs. 29 May ± 29.6 days [SD] for non-territory holders; ANOVA, P > 0.15). In general, fewer adults were captured in July and August (whether territory holders or non-territory holders).

Territorial status influenced the number of times an individual was recaught in the same season (Table 2). Non-territory holders were usually caught only once during a given year (78%), whereas local breeders were usually caught multiple times (71% more than once; 53% three or more times in the same year).

Over the entire study period, 66% of territory holders were recaptured at least once, whereas 56% were recaught more than once and 31% were recaught six times or more. Only four territory holders (out of 59) had any breaks in their capture–recapture records (i.e., a year in which they were not caught, flanked by one or more years in which they were caught). By contrast, only 20% of non-territory holders were recaptured at least once, and only 5% more than once. The difference in number of total captures

for the two groups was highly significant (P < 0.001, Poisson regression).

Most (74%) non-territory holder birds were first caught in the winter or spring as after-hatching year individuals (i.e., they were neither locally fledged young nor caught in the nets in their first calendar year of life). In contrast, 52% of territory holders caught in nets were locally fledged young or were caught in nets in their first calendar year of life.

Capture probability of territory holders in relation to distance from nets

Over the 11-year study period, 523 breeders were identified on the study grid through intensive observations of color-banded individuals (the same individual was counted multiply if it bred in more than one year). Of these, 93 (17.8%) were captured in mist nets some time during the year, nearly all during the breeding season. By far the most important influence on capture probability was distance between the nest and the nearest mist net. All individuals breeding within 50 m of a net were caught (N = 40), while those breeding more than 200 m from the nearest net were rarely caught (0.8%, N = 389; Fig. 2). In between 50 and 200 m, the proportion of breeders caught in nets declined in a smooth fashion (Fig. 2), ranging from 82% caught among those breeding 50–75 m from a net, to 17% caught among those breeding 175–200 m from a net. The statistical significance of distance to the net in predicting capture of a known local breeder was very high (P < 0.001, logistic regression).

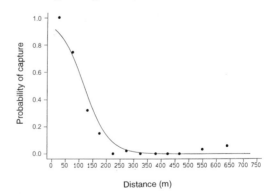

FIGURE 2. Capture probability of Wrentit breeders in relation to distance (m) from the nest to the nearest mist net, 1981–1991. Filled circles show proportion of breeders caught for breeders grouped in 50 m intervals: 0–50 m, 50–100 m, etc. Beyond 500 m, data are shown in 100 m intervals. Solid line gives the best fit to the data using logistic regression.

TABLE 2. FREQUENCY OF CAPTURE AND RECAPTURE OF WRENTITS WITHIN A YEAR, IN RELATION TO TERRITORIAL STATUS. (INCLUDES ONLY INDIVIDUALS CAUGHT AT LEAST ONCE DURING THE BREEDING SEASON)

	Local breeders			Non-territory holders	
N times captured	Frequency[a]	Percent	N times captured	Frequency[a]	Percent
1	22	29	1	196	78
2	14	18	2	37	15
3	10	13	3	9	4
4	12	16	4	3	1.2
5	5	7	5	3	1.2
6	3	4	6	1	0.4
7	6	8	7	2	0.8
8–14	4	5	–	–	–
Total	78	100	Total	251	100

[a] Individuals were included more than once if caught in multiple years.

To examine whether territorial boundaries influenced capture probability, we compared proportion captured with respect to the number of territories a Wrentit had to traverse to reach the nearest net (Table 3). This analysis was restricted to birds breeding within 200 m of a net, because we showed above that Wrentits breeding at a greater distance from any net were rarely caught. Where a net was included within a Wrentit's territory, the Wrentit was almost always caught; conversely, Wrentits breeding more than two territories away were never caught (Table 3). Distance to nearest net and number of intervening territories to nearest net had independent and statistically significant effects on capture probability ($P = 0.001$ and $P = 0.011$, respectively).

Other factors influencing capture probability of breeders

Date of first clutch completion varied widely in the sample of breeders (minimum, median, and maximum first clutch completion dates were 23 March, 26 April, and 30 June, respectively). Earlier-breeding birds were less likely to be caught than those breeding in the middle or later in the breeding season (Table 4). However, for all breeders whose first clutch was completed from about 21 April on, capture probability was similar, at about 26%. First clutch completion date had a significant effect on capture probability when distance to nearest net was statistically controlled ($P = 0.044$).

Among breeders, there was a correlation between age and capture probability (one-year old individuals were more likely to be caught than older birds), but this relationship was not significant after controlling

TABLE 3. CAPTURE PROBABILITY IN RELATION TO TERRITORY LOCATION INCLUDING ONLY WRENTITS BREEDING WITHIN 200 M OF THE NEAREST MIST NET

Territory location[a]	Number of birds	Percent caught
0	56	96.4
0.5	24	62.5
1	15	6.7
1.5	7	14.3
2	12	25.0
2.5–3	4	0.0

[a] Coding for N territories: 0 = net was within Wrentit's territory; 0.5 = net was in territorial no-man's land (outside territorial boundary but not within neighbor's territory); 1, 2, 3 = net was one, two or three territories away; 1.5, 2.5 = as with 0.5, but an additional territory or two away.

for distance to nearest net ($P > 0.1$). Capture probability showed no significant association with the number of young hatched or fledged, the number of clutches or broods, or the sex of the breeder ($P > 0.4$ in each analysis).

SURVIVAL AND RECAPTURE PROBABILITY

Analyses stratified according to territorial status (territory holder vs. non-territory holder) resulted in estimated survival probabilities of 57% and 38%, respectively (Table 5). Recapture probability was estimated to be 71% for territory holders and 5% for those who were not. The difference in recapture probability between the two groups was significant (LRS = 14.69, $P = 0.001$), but the difference in survival probability was not ($P > 0.3$), due to lack of precision regarding the estimate of non-territory holder survival. Low precision was related to the fact that this category of individual was very unlikely to be recaptured the next year.

Annual survival of territory-holding birds caught in mist nets varied from 17–82%, and usually (7 out of 10 years) in a narrower range of 41–78%. Survival of territory holders did not vary significantly with age (LRS = 7.96, $P > 0.5$) or year (LRS = 8.26, $P > 0.5$). However, survival estimates showed a tendency

TABLE 4. EFFECT OF BREEDING DATE (DATE FIRST CLUTCH COMPLETED) ON CAPTURE PROBABILITY OF WRENTITS

Date 1st clutch completed	Number of breeders	% caught
Before 11 Apr	65	7.7
11–20 Apr	63	14.3
21–30 Apr	67	26.9
1–10 May	49	26.5
11–21 May	33	21.2
after 22 May	36	27.7

Note: Date categorized into 10-day intervals.

TABLE 5. RESULTS OF SURGE ANALYSIS ON MIST-NET CAPTURES OF WRENTITS, BY TERRITORIAL STATUS

	Survival		Recapture	
	probability	95% CI	probability	95% CI
Local breeders	0.574	0.47 – 0.67	70.8	0.53 – 0.84
Non-territory holders	0.376	0.13 – 0.72	4.8	0.01 – 0.18

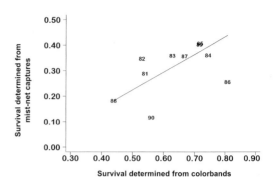

FIGURE 3. Comparison of Wrentit survival indices. Values for each year are shown by two digit codes. 1985 and 1989 are superimposed. On the *x*-axis is survival as estimated by resighting of color-banded individuals. On the *y*-axis is the SURGE estimate of survival using the pooled data (not differentiated by breeding status). Because 1986 was an aberrant year (see text), the best least-squares fit to the data excludes 1986.

to increase with age, consistent with our observations on the color-banded population (Geupel and Ballard 2002).

Analysis of resightings of color-banded birds gave an estimated survival probability of 58.3 ± 2.9% and resighting probability of 91.5 ± 3.1% for females. For males, the estimates were 69.1 ± 2.4%) and 93.4 ± 1.9%. Survival based on resightings differed for the two sexes (likelihood ratio test, P = 0.004), but resighting probability did not. Mean adult survival (averaging values for males and females) based on resighting data was 63.7%, which was somewhat greater than the adult survival estimate obtained from capture data for territory-holding individuals (57.4%), but the confidence intervals of the two estimates overlapped. Thus, survival estimates based on capture–recapture analyses of territory holders caught in mist nets were consistent with those derived from sighting–resighting analyses of color-banded territory holders.

Most investigators running a constant-effort mist-netting program can not distinguish local breeders from non-territory holders. We therefore analyzed data for all mist-net-caught adults, pooling data from territory holders (59 different individuals) and non-territory holders (274 different individuals). The pooled analysis showed no significant variation with year or age, and gave a survival estimate of 30.6% (95% Confidence Interval of 22–41%), vs. 57% for local breeders alone. Recapture probability was estimated at 38.2% (95% CI of 23–56%), as opposed to 71% for known local breeders.

Even though analysis of capture–recapture data gives skewed estimates of survival when non-territory holders are included, it may still provide a reasonable index of annual survival. We investigated whether such an annual index could reliably predict annual survival, by comparing it with survival analyses based on resightings of color-banded birds. There was a trend for the two survival estimates to vary in the same direction (Fig. 3), but the correspondence between the two indices was not significant ($R^2 = 0.252$, P = 0.14, linear regression). The year 1986 was an outlier, yielding the highest survival estimate of the ten years according to resighting,

but a relatively low estimate of survival according to capture–recapture data (third lowest). That year was aberrant in other respects (DeSante and Geupel 1987), and if 1986 was excluded, there was a significant correlation between the two survival indices ($R^2 = 0.518$, P = 0.029, linear regression).

DISCUSSION

The most important determinant of capture probability for adults in our study was distance from the net. A similar result was obtained for juveniles (see Nur et al. 1995), but the quantitative relationship between distance and capture probability differed for the two classes. For adults, few were captured that bred more than 200 m from the nearest net. Juveniles, however, were caught with a near-constant probability of ~14% beyond 300 m, up to a least 700 m. The catchment area for juveniles was likely more than a kilometer, maybe several. Thus, the populations being sampled by nets were very different for the two age classes. This has implications for the use of estimates of productivity derived by dividing the number of HY birds caught by the sum of AHY + HY captures (as is the practice of the Constant Effort Sites Scheme and MAPS program). This will not pose a serious problem if the numbers of HY birds within 200 m of nets (the area which samples adults) always fluctuate in parallel with numbers of HY birds further from the nets, but this may not be the case, and the subject deserves greater study.

Other than distance from the net, there appeared to be no important factors influencing capture probability of breeders, except that the earliest breeding birds were less likely to be caught. We have no explanation for this result. We speculate that seasonal differences in vegetation (and thus conspicuousness of the nets) may be responsible, but this needs to be examined directly.

The difference in year-to-year variability in number of breeders as opposed to number of transients caught reflected the greater constancy of capture among breeders, presumably because all those breeding close to the nets were caught in every year, whereas all those breeding some distance away were almost never caught. Annual fluctuations in the number of transients is discussed elsewhere (Nur et al. 2000), and is influenced by demographic processes such as last year's production of fledglings and breeding population size.

The most important result of the study was that survival derived from mist net capture–recapture data was underestimated unless local breeders and non-territory holders could be differentiated, due to an almost 18-fold difference between the two groups in recapture probability. If true non-breeders could be distinguished from those transient birds that bred off the study area, then at least non-breeding transients could be excluded from survival analyses. Unfortunately, Wrentit breeders and non-breeders cannot be distinguished in the hand, because both groups commonly display partial brood patches (PRBO, unpubl. data). The same problem is likely to apply to other species as well, such as those in which males do not develop brood patches. Even when the female brood patch is more highly developed among breeders than non-breeders in part of the breeding cycle (e.g., during incubation and the brooding phase), such differences are unlikely to persist throughout the three months or more that constant effort mist netting is conducted. Date of capture might provide some clues as to breeding status, but at least in the Palomarin Wrentit population, breeders and non-breeders cannot be distinguished by this means, and we expect this would also hold true for many other species.

One solution to the problem of differentiating local breeders and transients (whether the latter are breeders or non-breeders) would be to establish the identity of territory-holders within range of mist-nets through the use of unique color-bands or other markings, as in this study. For Wrentits, this identification need be done only within 200 m of the nets, but for other species a greater range would be prudent (perhaps 500 m or more, depending, in part, on territory size). Such an effort would be more time-consuming than the standard mist-netting protocol, but might be justified for a species of high concern.

A second, more expedient solution relies on our observation that non-territory holders were rarely recaptured within the same season, whereas territory holders were usually recaptured (Table 2). Survival could be estimated from only those individuals that had been recaptured in the same season. This would not eliminate the problem of transients, but should definitely reduce its magnitude. Data from some true breeders would be discarded, but at least in Wrentits, only 29% of breeders were not recaught at least once in the same year. An implication of this approach is that, in establishing a constant-effort mist-netting program, one goal would be to maximize the number of adults recaptured, as opposed to number of first captures. Running nets as many days per 10-day period as is feasible would further that goal, but would only be helpful if there was no net-avoidance. The fact that breeding Wrentits were caught so often in the same year, and usually in the breeding season, implies little net-avoidance in this species, even though these birds had ample opportunity to learn where nets were placed. Nets were in permanent locations, and operated at least 3 times/week (daily for more than 6 months of the year).

We applied the within-season recapture criterion to survival analyses of Wilson's Warbler (*Wilsonia pusilla*) capture–recapture data from the Palomarin Field Station (Chase et al. 1997). Individuals were classified as non-transient or transient on the basis of whether they were or were not caught two or more times in the breeding season, at least 7 days apart. Recapture probability for putative transients was only one-fifth that of non-transients (likelihood ratio test, P < 0.001). The survival estimate for all individuals pooled was 31%, whereas the estimate exclusive of putative transients was about 46%. True survival in this population was unknown, but is likely to be about 50%.

We have also analyzed data for the Song Sparrow (Nur et al. 2000), with similar results. Territory-holders and non-territory holders had very different recapture probabilities and pooling the two classes of adults resulted in low (biased) survival estimates, whereas distinguishing the two classes of individuals improved survival estimates. One difference between Palomarin Song Sparrows and Wrentits was that for the former, survival estimates for mist-net-caught, known territory holders were still substantially lower than survival as determined from analysis of resightings of color-banded breeders (47% vs. 60%, respectively; Nur et al. 2000). However, for the Song

Sparrow, the double-capture criterion (by which individuals caught twice in the same breeding season are considered non-transients) was very effective in yielding a survival estimate which matched the estimate obtained from capture–recapture analyses of color-banded individuals (both methods yielded estimates of 60% survival for males and females pooled). Thus, the use of the double-capture criterion was substantiated for the Song Sparrow, and that finding supports its use in analyses of Wilson's Warbler survival (Chase et al. 1997). Similar results were obtained by Peach (1993) for several European passerine species.

Even though Wrentit survival estimates were severely skewed when breeders and transients were not distinguished, there may still be value in a survival index based on year-by-year estimates for pooled data. We could not show a significant correlation between the mist-net survival indices and estimates based on individually marked birds, but there was reasonable correspondence between the two survival measures in most years. Any marked temporal trend in survival would probably be detected by the pooled mist-net survival index. We wish to point out, however, that mist-net studies may or may not be able to accurately assess differences in survival between

sites. To our knowledge, no validation studies have been carried out to date on this topic.

Since this study, mark–recapture models have been developed to deal specifically with the effect of transients (Pradel et al. 1997). It would be valuable to analyze this data set (where territorial status of individuals is known, not inferred) using Pradel's model, to compare results with those based on color-band resighting data, and to analyze capture–recapture data for known local breeders only.

ACKNOWLEDGMENTS

The research presented here was partially funded by a contract with the U.S. Fish and Wildlife Service, Office of Migratory Bird Management. Additional support was provided by Chevron Corporation and by the membership of the Point Reyes Bird Observatory. We thank the numerous intern field biologists who helped collect data reported here and thank O. Williams and B. Hardesty for help in preparing and analyzing field data. We thank the Point Reyes National Seashore for their continued cooperation. Thanks to W. J. Peach, J. Clobert, T. Martin, and especially E. H. Dunn, for valuable comments and improvements to the MS. We are also grateful to L. R. Mewaldt, C. J. Ralph, and D. F. DeSante for their foresight in establishing a long-term monitoring and research program at Palomarin. This is PRBO Contribution Number 1101.

Studies in Avian Biology No. 29:71–74

ESTIMATING ADULT SURVIVAL RATES FROM BETWEEN-YEAR RECAPTURES IN THE BRITISH TRUST FOR ORNITHOLOGY CONSTANT EFFORT SITES SCHEME

WILL J. PEACH AND STEPHEN R BAILLIE

Abstract. Recent developments in the methodology for estimating survival rates from mark–recapture data are summarized. Transient individuals are common in mist-net samples and, unless catered for in the analysis, can cause survival rates to be seriously underestimated. Mark–recapture data from multiple study sites can now be combined analytically to provide regional estimates of survival. Although permanent emigration away from constant effort sites may result in true survival being underestimated, temporal changes in apparent survival may still be useful in highlighting the demographic mechanisms driving population changes.

Key Words: Constant Effort Sites scheme, mark–recapture, survival.

Many passerine species show strong fidelity to breeding sites in successive breeding seasons. This is generally true for long-distance migrants, as well as residents. Consequently, regular captures of marked breeding birds can be an effective means of generating between-year recaptures, and these can be used to estimate apparent survival rates of adult birds. When the sampling effort is standardized across breeding seasons (or at least measured), annual return rates can be estimated with greater precision and less bias.

Birds banded as chicks or as juveniles on constant effort sites have much lower recapture rates in subsequent years than do birds banded as adults (i.e., at least one year old). This is partly because young birds experience higher mortality rates than adult birds, but mainly because many young passerines make their first breeding attempt at sites away from their natal area (Greenwood 1980). For this reason we have not attempted to estimate first-year survival rates using Constant Effort Sites (CES) mark–recapture data (although see Peach et al. 1999). Survival rates of young passerines are probably best estimated using reports of banded birds found dead (Baillie and McCulloch 1993).

In recent years there has been a rapid growth of interest in the application of mark–recapture techniques to the estimation of demographic parameters, in respect to both extensive wildlife monitoring programs and intensive population studies. Comprehensive reviews of the methods and software available for analyzing mark–recapture data have been published (e.g., Pollock et al. 1990, Lebreton et al. 1992, Baillie and North 1999). We have applied these methods to data collected at constant effort sites (Peach et al. 1990, 1995; Peach

1993) and present here a summary of our main findings. For most analyses we recommend the use of program MARK (White and Burnham 1999) combined with program RELEASE (Burnham et al. 1987) for goodness-of-fit tests.

MODELING SURVIVAL RATES

The estimation of survival rates (strictly, return rates) involves the fitting of open population Jolly-Seber models parameterized in terms of survival and recapture rates (Pollock et al. 1990, Lebreton et al. 1992). An important starting point for many analyses is the Cormack-Jolly-Seber (CJS) model in which both survival and recapture rates are time-dependent (Cormack 1964, Jolly 1965, Seber 1965). Following the notation of Lebreton et al. (1992), models are referred to in terms of survival rate (ϕ) and recapture probability (p) with the subscript t denoting time-dependence. The CJS model is therefore referred to as (ϕ_t, p_t).

The CJS model assumes that survival does not vary according to the age of animal, and this is probably reasonable for adults of most short-lived small passerines (e.g., Buckland and Baillie 1987, although see Loery et al. 1987). The choice of a starting model will depend partly on biological knowledge or intuition, and it may be important to consider age-dependent survival models in relatively long-lived species. The goodness-of-fit tests provided by the software RELEASE, now available in the package MARK (White and Burnham 1999), provide explicit tests of the general suitability of the CJS model.

Having decided upon a biologically reasonable starting model that fits the data, the analyst can then test a series of simpler models, each having fewer parameters than the starting model. For example, an obvious simplification of the CJS model is to constrain recapture probability to be constant over time (ϕ_t, p). If the sampling effort has remained relatively constant during each of the sampling periods, as is the case at constant effort sites, then the simpler (ϕ_t, p) model should provide a more parsimonious description of the data than the (ϕ_t, p_t) model. Estimating fewer parameters from the same data increases the precision of the estimates, although at the risk of introducing bias. Likelihood ratio tests can be used to test specific hypotheses about model structure, and Akaike's Information Criterion (Akaike 1973) can be used to compare large numbers of candidate models without conducting large numbers of statistical tests (Lebreton et al. 1992, Burnham and Anderson 1998). The aim of the modelling procedure is to identify the simplest model that provides an adequate description of the data.

Program MARK has the useful facility of allowing the user to test for linear relationships between time-dependent model parameters and environmental variables (Lebreton et al. 1992, White and Burnham 1999). This can serve both as an aid to model simplification and as a means of testing biological hypotheses about factors affecting survival rates. This facility has, for example, allowed analysts to establish strong relationships between annual survival rates of two long-distance migratory bird species and annual rainfall in the African winter quarters (Kanyamibwa et al. 1990, Peach et al. 1991). It is better to test for relationships between time-dependent survival rates and external variables using the link functions available in MARK, rather than using ordinary least squares approaches, because the latter make no allowance for autocorrelation of successive survival estimates (Lebreton et al. 1992).

If capture effort has varied between sampling periods (e.g., years), then time-dependence in recapture probability can in principal be explained by some measure of capture effort, which can then be incorporated into the model (Clobert et al. 1987). However, in our experience simple measures of capture effort do not always correlate with or explain temporal variation in recapture rates, and we strongly advocate standardization of capture effort whenever this is possible.

THE PROBLEM OF TRANSIENTS IN COHORT SAMPLES

Estimates of survival between the year of capture and the first year of recapture may be biased downwards if cohort samples contain transient individuals

that are unlikely to be retrapped in subsequent years (Buckland 1982). One possible approach to this problem is to restrict analyses to individuals recaptured in years after their first year of capture (equivalent to excluding all first encounters). However, in short-lived species this often involves the loss of a high proportion of the available survival information with a consequent loss of precision (Peach et al. 1990).

Pradel et al. (1997) developed a new approach to the problem of transients that involves estimating the proportion of resident birds in banded samples, in addition to apparent survival and recapture rates. This method has the advantage of removing bias on survival estimates and of providing an estimate of the proportion of transient individuals in cohort samples. A disadvantage of Pradel's method is that for all cohorts the estimate of survival during the year after initial capture remains biased, and this may be a particular problem for short-lived species where a high proportion of all recaptures occur during the first recapture period.

An alternative approach is to use within-year recaptures to identify residents in newly banded cohorts (Buckland and Baillie 1987, Peach et al. 1990). Most constant-effort banding schemes involve repeated sampling of study areas throughout each breeding season, and transient birds should have a lower probability of being retrapped within the same season than resident individuals (note the probability of retrapping transients in subsequent years is, by definition, zero; Pradel et al. 1997). Thus, birds retrapped more than some specified minimum number of days after first being trapped are considered "residents" whereas individuals not retrapped over the same period are considered to be a mixture of "residents" and "transients." We have tended to use 6–10 days as the minimum period that must separate same-year captures of an individual during the first year in which it was encountered for it to be considered resident (Peach 1993). This information is included in the analysis by expanding the encounter histories for each bird to have a single additional encounter period immediately after the first encounter. Modelling then proceeds with a dummy "age" structure that partitions survival and recapture rates between first encounter and subsequent same-year recapture (within-year survival and recapture rates), from same-year recapture and the following breeding season (between-year survival and recapture rates). In this way, individuals not retrapped more than 6–10 days apart in the first year of capture but retrapped in subsequent years, are correctly classified as residents and do contribute to subsequent estimates of annual survival. Within-year survival and recapture rates can be modelled as constant across years or year-specific. These "within-year" transients models are straightforward to fit using program MARK.

The effect of the "within-year recapture" transients models is to substantially reduce, but not remove, the negative bias on apparent survival estimates caused by the presence of transient individuals in cohort samples (Peach et al. 1990, Peach 1993). However, our approach maximizes the precision of survival estimates by fully using recapture information from the breeding season following initial capture, which often constitute a high proportion of all between-year recaptures for short-lived species. Using within-years recaptures to minimize problems caused by transients will be most appropriate where precision may be limiting statistical inference and small amounts of bias can be tolerated, as is often the case in studies attempting to detect temporal changes in survival rates. The approach is less suited to studies whose primary focus is absolute levels of survival, such as comparative life histories.

COMBINING SURVIVAL INFORMATION ACROSS STUDY SITES

An analytical development of particular importance to the CES Scheme was the capability of programs like SURGE and MARK to handle multiple groups of marked animals within a single analysis (Pradel et al. 1990, White and Burnham 1999). This facility allows the analyst to test for differences in survival or recapture probabilities between groups, which in the CES-context might include study site or sex. The general approach is to fit starting models in which parameters differ between groups, and then to constrain parameters to be identical or even additive across groups (Pradel et al. 1990, Lebreton et al. 1992). In the CES context, this allows the analyst to check whether apparent survival rates differ between sites and, if they do not, to pool survival information across sites to provide more precise regional survival estimates.

The modelling framework for multiple-site analyses is analogous to that used in analysis of variance. An approach that we have adopted in the analysis of CES data is to have a starting model in which survival and recapture probabilities are both year- and site-specific, with an interaction between year and site (Peach 1993). We then attempt to simplify recapture probability, initially by dropping the year-site interaction term, and then by removing the time-dependence. These simplifications are usually parsimonious because of the constant sampling effort maintained at CE sites. Recapture probabilities often differ significantly between sites, which probably reflects the differing numbers and densities of nets at different sites. We then attempt to simplify the survival side of the model, first by seeking to remove the interaction term, and then by removing the site term. We have used this modelling approach to combine mark–recapture data from up to 10 CE sites to provide regional estimates of annual adult survival rates for the Willow Warbler (Peach et al. 1995; scientific names in Table 1).

We compared estimates of adult survival for five passerine species derived from multiple-site CES mark–recapture data (Table 1) with independent estimates from national BTO band recovery data relating to birds found dead (taken from Peach 1993 and Baillie and McCulloch 1993). Survival estimates from recaptures were generally lower than those based on recovery data (Table 1). Although these differences could be a consequence of the differing time periods covered by the two sets of analyses, they are probably partly caused by the permanent emigration of some birds away from constant effort sites (Peach et al. 1990, Cilimburg et al. 2002). Even if apparent survival rates estimated from mark–recapture data do underestimate true survival, they may still constitute a useful index of temporal changes in true survival rates. Moreover, the precision of the survival rates of small passerines estimated from the CES data is generally comparable to or better than that attainable from the national United Kingdom band recovery data, because these species have low band reporting rates (Table 1).

DISCUSSION

Despite the potential problems of negative bias affecting apparent survival estimates, recent developments in both theory and software for analysing mark–recapture data make this aspect of the CES data an exciting prospect for the future. The main application of the CES mark–recapture data will be in the detection of long-term temporal trends in the apparent survival rates of adult passerines, and the testing of relationships between survival and environmental variables such as rainfall in the winter quarters of migrants (e.g., Peach et al. 1991). Knowledge of apparent survival rates is likely to be an important factor affecting the population dynamics of small passerines (Baillie and Peach 1992), and may be critical to our understanding of the mechanisms leading to wide-scale population changes

TABLE 1. ESTIMATES OF AVERAGE ANNUAL ADULT SURVIVAL RATES (AND ASSOCIATED STANDARD ERRORS) DERIVED FROM POOLED MARK–RECAPTURE DATA FROM MULTIPLE CONSTANT-EFFORT BANDING SITES AND FROM RECOVERIES OF DEAD BIRDS BANDED IN BRITAIN AND IRELAND

Species	Mark–recapture analyses (1983–1991)				Recovery analyses (1985–1990)		
	Number of combined	Number of individuals retrapped	Survival rate		Number of recoveries	Survival rate	
			ϕ	SE		S	SE
Willow Warbler (*Phylloscopus trochilus*)	7	183	0.371	0.025	385[a]	0.554	0.056
Blackbird (*Turdus merula*)	4	113	0.566	0.036	1307	0.668	0.020
	4	165	0.581	0.029			
Blackcap (*Sylvia atricapilla*)	3	51	0.443	0.057	197	0.534	0.128
Reed Warbler (*Acrocephalus scirpaceus*)	3	168	0.496	0.026	957[b]	0.558	0.023
Wren (*Troglodytes troglodytes*)	2	29	0.318	0.068	–	–	–
Dunnock (*Prunella modularis*)	1	62	0.422	0.040	265	0.447	0.050

Notes: All survival estimates were derived from time-independent models that fit the data. CE survival estimates are from Peach (1993) and estimates from recoveries are from Baillie and McCulloch (1993).

[a] Estimated from recaptures >5 km from the place of banding.

[b] Estimates based on recoveries of dead birds were supplemented by recaptures >5 km from the place of banding.

(Peach et al. 1999). Other potential applications are the comparisons of apparent annual survival rates between sites (perhaps treatment and control sites), between males and females (e.g., Pratt and Peach 1991), and between different habitats, regions (e.g., Peach et al. 1995), or latitudes.

ACKNOWLEDGMENTS

We thank the many individuals and organizations that have contributed to this work, as detailed in Peach et al. *this volume*.

A EUROPEAN EXAMPLE OF STANDARDIZED MIST NETTING IN POPULATION STUDIES OF BIRDS

ANDREAS KAISER AND PETER BERTHOLD

Abstract. The "MRI-program" is a standardized long-term bird trapping program that has been in existence since 1974. Three central European stations are run daily during the entire autumn migratory period from June through November. Three other stations follow the same highly standardized protocol. In this paper, the field methods are described and standardization is discussed. Advantages of standardization include improved accuracy of capture–recapture estimates of population size and other parameters.

Key Words: capture–recapture, migrant, mist net, monitoring, MRI-program, passerine, standardization.

The standardized study of many different species and populations of birds at the same time, over broad geographic scales, offers valuable opportunities to monitor bird populations and at the same time study factors affecting population dynamics. Two examples of such projects that involve mist netting to capture birds are migration and stopover studies (Bairlein 1998, Bairlein and Giessing 1997, Bairlein et al. 1994), and productivity and survival studies (DeSante 1992, DeSante et al. *this volume*, Peach and Baillie *this volume*). Each of these programs uses highly standardized methods, both to reduce bias in sampling and to facilitate strong statistical analysis. Another example, described here, is the "MRI-program," which currently consists of up to six trapping sites in operation during fall (Fig. 1).

Long-term research programs were begun at three inland stations: the Mettnau peninsula in south Germany, the nature reserve "Die Reit" in north Germany near Hamburg, and in east Austria in the nature reserve at the eastern shore of Lake Neusiedl near Illmitz. Preliminary work was done in 1972 and 1973, and these sites have been run under standard conditions since 1974. Later additions included a banding site at lake Galenbeck in northeastern Germany, and two coastal sites, the Ebro-Delta banding site in Spain and Rybachy at the Kurish Split in Russia (Fig. 1). The latter two sites collaborate closely with the Vogelwarte Radolfzell.

Sites were chosen according to four criteria: (1) at least one site should sample each of the autumn migratory populations of central, northern, western, or eastern Europe, as shown by the atlas of songbird migration (Zink 1973–1985); (2) the stations should be situated in protected areas that would not be disturbed during long-term studies; (3) the areas should have a high degree of climax vegetation and thus show relatively few changes over the long term; and

(4) the areas should be excellent bird conservation areas with rich bird life during the breeding season as well as the migration period. In addition to these considerations, the suitability of the areas was tested by sample trapping during the pilot years.

The program was designed so that a number of questions could be answered, including five main topics:

(1) *Population dynamics and demography*: Short-term and medium-term fluctuations in numbers of migrants, as well as long-term population

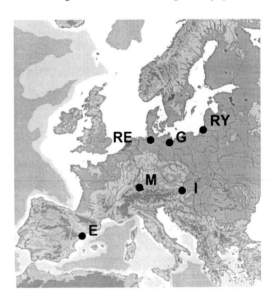

FIGURE 1. Banding sites of the Mettnau-Reit-Illmitz-program in Europe and sites in cooperation with the "Vogelwarte Radolfzell" (German bird-banding office). M=Mettnau (Lake Constance), RE=Reit (Hamburg), I=Illmitz (Lake Neusiedl, Austria), G=Galenbeck (Lake Galenbeck), RY=Rybachy (Rossitten, Russia), E=Ebro-Delta (Tarragona, Spain).

changes and their magnitudes, with a special focus on decline of small birds (Marchant 1992, Berthold et al. 1993, Böhning-Gaese 1995, Kaiser and Berthold 1995). Demographic studies were to look at age and sex differences and their role in migratory and stopover behavior, habitat preference, nutrition, and many other topics.

(2) *Migration*: Phenology of migration, migration routes, and strategies of migration and stopover (Berthold 1996, 2001). Also studied are the dependence of these features on sex, age, the breeding area and range of the populations, and seasonal and climatic factors. Finally, questions are investigated on migratory physiology, such as fat deposition, the control of migration, stopover behavior, and the interplay of molt, migration, and energy balance (Berthold et al. 1991; Kaiser 1992, 1993b, 1996).

(3) *Biorhythmicity*: Special attention is given to daily activity patterns of staging individuals, molt (Kasparek 1981), and to the variation in migration patterns from year to year (Bairlein 1981, Brensing 1989).

(4) *Ecosystem research*: Resource partitioning and utilization of stopover sites are of interest, including the role of habitat (Streif 1991), nutritional preferences (Brensing 1977, Grosch 1995), mobility (Bastian 1992), stopover period (Kaiser 1993b), population size and turnover (Kaiser 1995), and competition. Other studies investigate the carrying capacity of a stopover area for small birds and how such an area can be made optimal.

(5) *Methodological research:* Repeatability and observer bias in wing length measurements, fat scoring, and ageing techniques were studied (Berthold and Friedrich 1979; Kaiser 1993a, 1993b). Capture–recapture and other counting methods look at frequency and intensity of operations of the nets required to gain an adequate sample size.

In this paper, we discuss features of the MRI-program that are particularly relevant to population monitoring.

METHODS

The trapping site at Mettnau is typical of the operation of a single large-scale netting station in the MRI-program, and is described as an example. This site is an area of approximately 1 km², situated on the Mettnau Peninsula nature reserve east of Radolfzell at Lake Constance (Berthold et al. 1991). There are 52 mist nets in use, placed in a single transect through a *Phragmites* reed swamp, but sampling all habitat types characteristic of the peninsula (Streif 1991). Distance between nets and release (banding) site range from 55 to 360 m. Operations are run daily through the fall season (30 June–6 November). Nets are open 24 h. Nets are checked at fixed intervals over the entire day (hourly, except half-hourly in poor weather). No activity is permitted near nets between net checks, and all captures are passive (no chasing or tape lures).

As noted by Bibby et al. (1992), standardization in capture and census methods is needed to reduce bias, and all MRI procedures are highly standardized (Berthold and Schlenker 1975). The number of nets, net locations, hours of operation, timing of net rounds, sequence of checking nets, and height of shelf strings on each net pole are all constant from year to year. Also standardized are all instructions and materials (bands, color rings, balance, tools, rulers). Vegetation is cut back in the off-season to keep habitat and vegetation structure as stable as possible.

Data recorded in the MRI-program include the following:

(1) *Trapping status*: first capture, within-site retrap from the same season, retrap from previous years, or banded elsewhere in the same or an earlier season (foreign retrap). Retraps are handled like first traps except that retraps from the same season do not have wing and foot remeasured, and for same-day retraps, sex, age, and molt are skipped.

(2) *Band number*

(3) *Date*

(4) *Capture time*: time when the net was checked and the bird removed from net.

(5) *Program status*: indicates whether species are study targets (full data collected) or non-target (full data collected only if there is time). Up to 41 species are targets at each site, whereas there are up to 100 non-target species.

(6) *Species-code*: German or Latin abbreviation, or species number

(7) *Net, shelf, and side of net in which the bird was trapped*: net shelves counted from ground upwards, 1 to 4. Left or right of nets are marked by signs at each nets. Data are recorded on a slip of paper placed into the carrying bag for each bird.

(8) *Sex*: recorded only when accurately determinable; otherwise coded as undetermined

(9) *Age*: two age classes are defined: this-year birds (juveniles, yearlings) and adults (older birds, born in the previous calendar year or earlier). Age is recorded only if accurately determinable, for example, by skull pneumatization or by molt limits in the wing (Jenni and Winkler 1994); otherwise coded as unknown age.

(10) *Molt*: body molt is recorded using methods described by Berthold et al. (1970), whereas wing feather molt follows Berthold et al. (1991). Tail feather molt is not recorded.

(11) *Length of the third primary*: length of third wing feather (counting from the outside) gives a relative wing measure that is more convenient to measure than wing chord (Berthold and Friedrich 1979, Svensson 1992).

(12) *Special data for species identification*: notch of the second primary and foot span are measured, to allow discrimination of *Acrocephalus* species.

(13) *Fat class*: using methods of Kaiser (1993a).

(14) *Body mass*: weighed to the nearest 0.1 g within 1 h of capture, using an electronic balance.

RESULTS AND DISCUSSION

Here we discuss some results from the MRI-program that are relevant to the use of mist nets for monitoring, and that illustrate the value of standardization.

STANDARDIZATION

Our results have shown that different species, and different numbers of each species, are caught in different habitats (Bairlein 1981, Streif 1991, Mädlow 1994). Therefore, moving or changing the total number of nets within or between seasons will alter numbers captured and affect annual indices of abundance. In capture–recapture studies, more birds may be recaptured if nets are relocated frequently (see below), but this would alter the probability of capture and recapture in complex ways that would be very difficult to model in analyses. Only in standardized capture–recapture studies are basic model assumptions met and resulting estimates precise (Otis

et al. 1978). We therefore recommend that a station should run with the same number of nets in exactly the same positions each year. For the same reason, it is important to prevent habitat change at the net sites, because habitat change affects capture–recapture probabilities in a manner analogous to moving nets among habitats.

With standard net locations, some species will have low capture probability because relatively little of their specialized habitat is sampled (e.g., Lesser Whitethroat, *Sylvia curruca*; Kaiser 1993b). It is therefore important to determine which species are the targets of study before determining where nets should be placed.

At the main MRI study site, the frequency of all first captures differed among habitats, but the proportions were fairly constant from year to year over a 22-year period (Fig. 2). However, capture indices decreased slightly in the four bushy habitats and increased in reed habitat C. To examine the effect of habitat change, we calculated species-specific long-term population trends separately for the birds

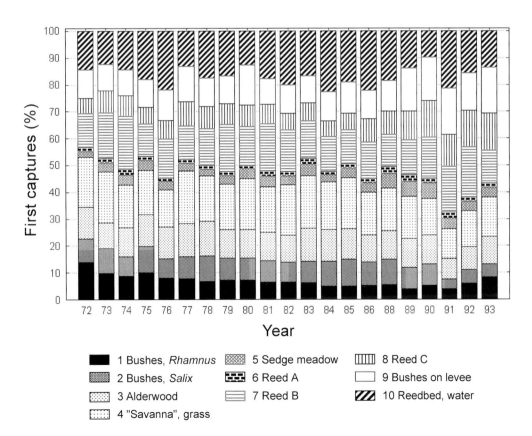

FIGURE 2. Percent of birds captured during June to November at Mettnau in different habitats and years. 1987 missing due to flood.

TABLE 1. LONG-TERM POPULATION TRENDS (1972–1993) FOR FIRST-CAPTURES IN DIFFERENT HABITATS AT METTNAU, GERMANY (KAISER AND BERTHOLD 1995)

Species	1	2	3	4	5	6	7	8	9	10	All habitats	N
Wryneck (*Jynx torquilla*)	ns	ns	—	ns	—	—	—	ns	ns	ns	-0.65**	153
Wren (*Troglodytes troglodytes*)	-0.51*	-0.46*	ns	ns	ns	—	ns	ns	ns	-0.49*	ns	1,280
Dunnock (*Prunella modularis*)	ns	ns	-0.50*	ns	ns	—	ns	0.70*	0.62*	ns	ns	1,331
Robin (*Erithacus rubecula*)	-0.62*	ns	ns	0.56*	0.54*	0.60*	0.58*	ns	ns	ns	ns	9,619
Nightingale (*Luscinia megarhynchos*)	ns	—	—	ns	ns	—	—	—	—	—	0.52*	219
Bluethroat (*L. svecica*)	—	—	—	—	ns	—	ns	ns	—	ns	-0.44*	177
Black Redstart (*Phoenicurus ochruros*)	ns	ns	0.45*	ns	ns	—	ns	ns	0.48*	ns	ns	516
Redstart (*P. phoenicurus*)	-0.67*	-0.60*	-0.70**	-0.78**	ns	—	ns	ns	-0.56*	-0.54*	-0.77**	939
Whinchat (*Saxicola rubetra*)	—	—	—	—	-0.64*	ns	ns	-0.64*	—	ns	-0.47*	277
Blackbird (*Turdus merula*)	ns	ns	ns	ns	ns	—	ns	ns	ns	ns	ns	2,379
Song Thrush (*T. philomelos*)	0.46*	-0.47*	ns	ns	ns	ns	-0.59*	ns	ns	ns	ns	1,654
Grasshopper Warbler (*Locustella naevia*)	-0.52*	-0.47*	—	ns	ns	ns	ns	ns	ns	ns	-0.69**	1,087
Savi's Warbler (*L. luscinioides*)	—	—	—	—	—	—	—	—	—	ns	ns	144
Aquatic Warbler (*Acrocephalus paludicola*)	—	—	—	—	ns	ns	-0.66*	—	—	—	-0.72**	49
Sedge Warbler (*A. schoenobaenus*)	0.89*	ns	-0.80**	ns	ns	ns	-0.84**	ns	ns	ns	-0.49*	1,333
Marsh Warbler (*A. palustris*)	-0.73**	-0.58*	-0.51*	-0.54*	ns	ns	-0.45*	ns	-0.49*	-0.56*	-0.77**	1,435
Reed Warbler (*A. scirpaceus*)	ns	ns	—	-0.72*	ns	0.49*	-0.65*	0.74**	ns	ns	ns	39,309
Great Reed Warbler (*A. arundinaceus*)	—	ns	ns	—	—	—	ns	ns	ns	-0.64*	-0.75**	329
Icterine Warbler (*Hippolais icterina*)	-0.60*	-0.55*	-0.60*	ns	—	—	ns	ns	ns	—	ns	580
Lesser Whitethroat (*Sylvia curruca*)	-0.65*	-0.56**	ns	-0.75**	ns	ns	ns	ns	-0.47*	ns	-0.79**	2,235
Whitethroat (*S. communis*)	ns	ns	—	ns	ns	ns	ns	ns	ns	ns	ns	456
Garden Warbler (*S. borin*)	-0.68**	-0.56*	-0.46*	ns	0.49*	—	0.67**	ns	ns	0.49*	ns	9,579
Blackcap (*S. atricapilla*)	-0.45*	ns	ns	ns	0.86**	ns	0.70**	0.60*	0.71**	0.50*	0.43*	13,615
Wood Warbler (*Phylloscopus sibilatrix*)	—	ns	—	ns	ns	—	ns	—	ns	ns	-0.62**	72
Chiffchaff (*P. collybita*)	-0.72**	-0.82**	-0.43*	-0.60*	ns	ns	0.46*	ns	ns	ns	ns	17,608
Willow Warbler (*P. trochilus*)	-0.86**	0.55*	-0.64**	-0.83**	ns	ns	ns	ns	ns	ns	-0.81**	7,419
Goldcrest (*Regulus regulus*)	ns	ns	ns	0.53*	—	—	—	—	—	—	ns	451
Firecrest (*R. ignicapillus*)	ns	ns	ns	ns	—	—	—	—	—	—	ns	184
Spotted Flycatcher (*Muscicapa striata*)	ns	ns	ns	-0.60*	ns	ns	—	—	—	ns	-0.60**	807
Pied Flycatcher (*Ficedula hypoleuca*)	ns	ns	ns	ns	ns	ns	—	—	—	—	ns	656
Blue Tit (*Parus caeruleus*)	-0.60**	—	ns	-0.52**	ns	ns	—	—	—	ns	-0.44*	5,563
Red-backed Shrike (*Lanius collurio*)	—	ns	—	ns	—	—	—	—	—	—	-0.49*	153
Goldfinch (*Carduelis carduelis*)	-0.66*	ns	ns	ns	—	—	—	—	—	—	ns	481
Bullfinch (*Pyrrhula pyrrhula*)	-0.56*	ns	ns	0.52*	-0.45*	ns	-0.48*	—	—	—	ns	999
Reed Bunting (*Emberiza schoeniclus*)	ns	-0.60*	ns	-0.52*	ns	ns	ns	ns	ns	ns	ns	7,960
All species combined	-0.76**	-0.60*	-0.57*	-0.55*	ns	ns	ns	0.50*	ns	ns	ns	130,478

Notes: Trends are coefficients of annual capture totals linear regressed on year. See Fig. 2 for definition of habitats.
* denotes P < 0.05; ** denotes P < 0.001; ns denotes P > 0.05.

captured in each habitat. Differences in trend among habitats would suggest that habitat change has been taking place over time. For the most part, the trends were very consistent within species among habitats (Table 1). However, in the habitat with dense bushes of buckthorn (habitat 1), the Garden Warbler (*Sylvia borin*), Blackcap (*S. atricapilla*), Robin (*Erithacus rubecula*), and Bullfinch (*Pyrrhula pyrrhula*) were decreasing and the Marsh Warbler (*Acrocephalus palustris*) was increasing, whereas in other habitats population trends of these species were in opposite directions. The Chiffchaff (*Phylloscopus collybita*) showed negative trends in some habitats, but a positive trend in reed B (Table 1). Other species were also captured in remarkably high numbers in later years in reed habitats, and this may be related to an increase in the number of buckthorn bushes within the reed. These results illustrate the importance of maintaining habitat at the same stage over time.

Another possible reason for change in the numbers of birds captured in each habitat could be changes in food abundance, such as fruit patterns related to the height of mist nets or outbreaks of insects in particular habitat types. This kind of variation cannot be controlled with habitat management, but food abundance is not expected to change in a systematic way over time, so long-term trends should be unbiased by this variation.

Timing of operations should be standardized, as well as number and location of nets. Data collected both during migration (Brensing 1989) and during the breeding period (A. Kaiser, unpubl. data) show a strong peak in the number of captures early in the morning, and a second (much lower) peak before dusk. Equal net-hours each day are not equivalent, therefore, unless those net-hours are from the same portion of each day (Karr 1981a). Expressing total number of birds captured as birds/net-h is therefore an ineffective way of controlling for variation in effort, and the schedule of netting operations should instead be standardized.

RELATIVE ABUNDANCE

To test the efficiency and accuracy of mist nets for species inventory and estimates of relative abundance, we compared mist-net counts with different counting methods during the main breeding period from May to July. During this period, population size of adults can be assumed to be relatively constant. At an isolated study plot in south Germany near Espasingen we used a net density of 35-m net/ha in a 9-ha site (and 45-m net/ha in a nearby site of 3 ha), and achieved high capture (and recapture)

probabilities. The correlation between number of all species of breeding birds detected by mist-net captures (first captures only) and point counts was strongly positive (r = 0.83, P < 0.001), but netting totals were nearly always higher than point count totals (Fig. 3; Kaiser and Bauer 1994). The study suggested that netting can be used to sample a consistent percent of a population (although that percent may differ widely among species). Mist-net captures may therefore be a particularly good means of sampling migrants, because it takes place over many hours (unlike transect or point counts) and does not require birds to be singing for them to be detected.

POPULATION TRENDS

The length of a long-term population monitoring project should be at least 15–20 years to cover natural population fluctuations (Berthold and Querner 1978, Tucker and Heath 1994). Analyses of first capture data from the MRI-program for long term trends have been published regularly (Berthold et al. 1993, Kaiser and Berthold 1995, Berthold *this volume*). Böhning-Gaese (1995) determined that species with similar year-to-year population fluctuations do not necessarily have similar long-term trends. Moreover, results of small-scale study on migration season population trends cannot be taken to represent population change on larger spatial scales in the absence of information on which breeding population is being sampled at the migration station (see Dunn and Hussell 1995).

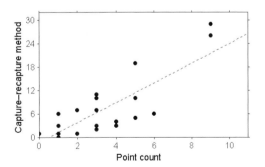

FIGURE 3. Number of local breeders captured (calculated from the number of adult first captures divided by 2 for an estimate of "pairs") compared to point count estimates at a woodland near Espasingen, Germany during the breeding period 1992 (Kaiser and Bauer 1994). Each point represents one species. Linear regression, r = 0.83, R² = 0.70, P < 0.001, N = 29.

CAPTURE–RECAPTURE STUDIES: BREEDING SEASON

Capture–recapture data are affected by net avoidance by birds that have already been captured once (Kaiser 1995). Recapture rate is generally much lower than expected when trapping is frequent (Buckland and Hereward 1982), although some species do not change their behavior drastically after the first catch. The extent of bias can sometimes be tested using mathematical models. We suggest two types of behavioral response to mist netting: (1) if many nets are used in comparison to the size of the study site, most birds learn to avoid the nets; and (2) intensive netting can cause too much direct human disturbance, causing birds to leave the area. These predictions have to be tested further, for example, in combined capture–recapture and telemetry studies.

In the breeding season, leaving up to 6 days between netting sessions increased capture and recapture rates (Dorsch 1998). One strategy for reducing net avoidance (other than reducing netting frequency) is to change net locations, but this compromises standardization (see above). Despite the problem of net avoidance, the MRI-program continues with daily netting in fixed locations, in part because net avoidance is a smaller problem with migrating birds (see below), and because our main objective is to analyze patterns of first captures under standard conditions.

Mist-net samples do not capture all the birds present, and capture–recapture models can be used to determine total population size. For example, in a study of a Reed Warbler (*Acrocephalus scirpaceus*) population at Lake Galenbeck, 254 adult Reed Warblers were caught at least once, with a total of 106 retraps (Fig. 4). Program CAPTURE (Otis et al. 1978) was used to estimate population size. The appropriate time effects and behavioral response model (White et al. 1982) estimated a population size of 500 birds, and the average estimate of all models was 430 (Fig. 5).

CAPTURE–RECAPTURE STUDIES: MIGRATION SEASON

Population size estimates during the migration period are more difficult to calculate than for breeding populations, because a set of well-defined assumptions of models for open population are violated and recapture numbers are not high (Kaiser 1995). To optimize sampling, density and distribution of nets is important. To obtain more recaptures, their density and distribution has to be adapted to the behavior of passerines stopping over. The interaction between capture behavior, recapture probability, disturbance,

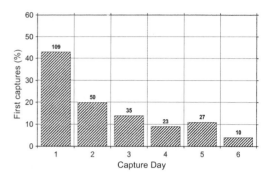

FIGURE 4. Decline in number of first captured Reed Warblers during the first 6 d of the MRI-program, i.e., at the end of the breeding period, at Lake Galenbeck, Germany.

and other biases (Pollock et al. 1990) was discussed by Kaiser (1993b, 1995).

During migration seasons, there is high turnover in individuals present (as shown by the low proportion of retraps), so number of first-time captures is increased by daily netting, and there are few birds stopping over that will develop net shyness (Kaiser 1993b). Nonetheless, Dorsch (1998) has shown that net avoidance may also be an issue with birds that are spending many days at a stopover site. Recapture probabilities during migration must be especially high (>0.2) to estimate other parameters, such as body mass change in relation to capture behavior. At some sites this is feasible, as shown by the 36% retrap rate obtained during 1988–1989 at the Mettnau Peninsula (Kaiser 1995).

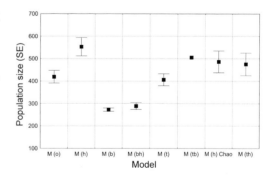

FIGURE 5. Number of breeding Reed Warblers estimated with different models of program CAPTURE (Otis et al. 1978). Capture probabilities are constant in model M_o, or vary by time (M_t), due to behavioral response (M_b), by individual birds (M_h), or by two sources of variation in its capture probabilities (M_{tb}, M_{th}, M_{bh}). Data from Lake Galenbeck, Germany, 1991 and 1992. Point estimates (means) with standard error. Number of first captures was 254, and mean populations size of all models 430.

Mobility of stopover populations was studied by examining the exchange rate of individual birds captured at five banding sites at the Mettnau peninsula during the migration period (Kaiser 1995). With knowledge of the exchange rate, an estimate of the size of the stopover population in the isolated nature reserve was derived from Jolly-Seber estimates. True average stopover time was estimated at 16 days, and it was shown that there were temporal behavioral responses to mist netting and ringing. Nonetheless, variation in capture probability was detected in birds according to differences in body condition, molt, mobility, and behavioral response to mist netting (Kaiser 1993b, 1995). The release of birds at the processing site, up to 500 m away from the trapping site, might affect retrap probabilities by causing the bird to shift its center of activity. Lastly, social interactions, like territorial defense, have an influence on recapture probabilities. All these potential problems should be investigated in further studies. Nonetheless, the capture design chosen in the MRI-program has given clear results for questions of migration patterns, habitat use, and condition of first captures (Berthold et al. 1991, Kaiser 1996).

ACKNOWLEDGMENTS

We thank C. D. Otahal, C. J. Ralph, and L. Thomas for their helpful comments on the manuscript. This final version greatly improved due to the critical input of E. H. Dunn.

Studies in Avian Biology No. 29:82–91

DETERMINING PRODUCTIVITY INDICES FROM AGE COMPOSITION OF MIGRANTS CAPTURED FOR BANDING: PROBLEMS AND POSSIBLE SOLUTIONS

DAVID J. T. HUSSELL

Abstract. Year, location, day, moon phase, and weather all influenced the daily proportion of young birds captured in nine species of passerines in fall migration at three stations on Long Point, Ontario, in 1961–1988. The proportion of young tended to be higher on days following nights when conditions for nocturnal migration were good. Annual proportions of young may be inconsistent indices of productivity, unless they are adjusted for the daily effects of confounding variables. For single species, correlations between annual proportions of young (adjusted and raw) and fall/spring population ratios were usually low and non-significant. In most species, the annual proportion of young did not explain significant amounts of variation in trend analyses of annual population indices. Nevertheless, adjusted proportions of young performed better than raw proportions in these analyses, suggesting that the proportion of young in populations of migrants does contain useful information about productivity. However, the assumption that proportions of young reflect productivity should not be accepted uncritically. More research is needed to determine how best to use information on ages of fall migrants to elucidate their demography.

Key Words: age proportions, fall migration, Long Point, Ontario, passerine migrants, productivity indices.

The age composition of migrants captured for banding is widely assumed to provide information on the productivity of the preceding breeding season (e.g., Ralph et al. 1993). However, it is not clear whether a direct relationship exists between productivity and the proportion of young birds captured in fall migration. The proportion of young captured over a single migration season at a single station could be influenced by many confounding factors, including differing vulnerability to capture, differing timing and speed of migration of age classes, habitat and coastal effects (e.g., Murray 1966; Ralph 1971, 1981; Hussell 1982, 1991; Dunn et al. *this volume* b), and perhaps by weather. Very little research has been done to determine what effects, if any, these factors have on the daily and annual proportions of young captured during migration and consequently upon annual measures of productivity.

Weather has profound effects on numbers of birds migrating and on the numbers occurring (and therefore available for capture) at a station (e.g., Richardson 1978). If the effects of weather differ among age classes, then even consistently collected data on the number of young and adult birds captured at a single station could be biased by year-to-year variations in weather. Given these potential biases, can we derive a consistent annual index of productivity from migrant age data and can we test that such an index does in fact reflect productivity?

I used regression analysis to examine the effects of weather, moon phase, date, and station on the daily proportion of young birds of nine species captured by personnel of the Long Point Bird Observatory at three stations on Long Point during the autumn migrations of 1961–1988. I calculated two annual indices of productivity: (1) the proportion of young birds (hatched in the preceding breeding season) captured over the entire migration at all stations; and (2) an adjusted proportion of young birds, derived from the regression analysis.

Indices of population size for spring and fall migrations at Long Point were also available (calculated by methods similar to those described by Hussell et al. 1992). If age proportions indicate productivity, and if the population size indices reflect population change, then the annual ratio of the fall to spring population index should be positively correlated with the annual proportion of young birds. This is the case because a high proportion of young birds in the fall population should usually be associated with a high fall population relative to that of the previous spring. The strength of this correlation should provide an independent means of evaluating the effectiveness of methods of calculating population and productivity indices.

If productivity fluctuates from year to year, and if age proportions reflect productivity, we might expect deviations of annual fall population size indices from their general trend to be positively correlated with the proportion of young birds captured in the fall.

Therefore, I tested whether the proportion of young explained additional variability in regression analyses of trends in fall population indices.

METHODS

STUDY LOCATION, SPECIES, AGING

I examined age proportions of nine species captured commonly in fall migration at Long Point, Ontario (approximately 42°33'N, 80°10'N): Swainson's Thrush (*Catharus ustulatus*), Red-eyed Vireo (*Vireo olivaceus*), Tennessee Warbler (*Vermivora peregrina*), Magnolia Warbler (*Dendroica magnolia*), Yellow-rumped Warbler (*D. coronata*), Blackpoll Warbler (*D. striata*), American Redstart (*Setophaga ruticilla*), White-throated Sparrow (*Zonotrichia albicollis*), and White-crowned Sparrow (*Z. leucophrys*).

Data were recorded at three stations: Station 1 at the eastern tip of Long Point; Station 2, 19 km west of Station 1; and Station 3, 9 km west of Station 2. Nearly all the data from Station 2 were collected after 1974 and nearly all from Station 3 after 1983. Nearly all birds were captured in mist nets or Heligoland traps (Woodford and Hussell 1961), but a few were taken in other types of baited ground traps. Trapping and netting effort (including numbers, types, and locations of traps and nets) varied both from year-to-year and day-to-day. I excluded birds captured or killed during nocturnal migration when they were attracted to the lighthouse at Station 1.

Red-eyed Vireos and White-crowned Sparrows were aged as either young (hatched in the current year) or adult (hatched earlier) primarily by eye color and plumage differences, respectively, and I analyzed all data from 1961–1988. Other species were aged mainly by the degree of skull pneumatization (birds with incompletely pneumatized skulls were aged as young) or by obvious plumage characteristics (e.g., adult male American Redstarts and some young Swainson's Thrushes), and I used data only from 1966–1988, because skull examination was not used at Long Point prior to 1966.

For each species, a fall migration period ("migration window") was selected that was identical to that used previously for analysis of migration counts (Hussell et al. 1992). Individuals occurring outside the migration window were excluded from all analyses.

EFFECTS OF WEATHER, MOON, DAY, AND STATION ON AGE PROPORTION

Daily proportion of young was defined for each species, based on numbers of newly captured (unbanded) birds for each day that at least one bird was captured and aged, as: proportion of young = (number of young birds)/(number of young birds + number of adult birds).

I used multiple regression to examine effects of various potential predictor variables on daily proportion of young. The dependent variable was the arcsine (square root

(daily proportion of young)). Proportions of 0 and 1 were counted as $1/4n$ and $(n - \frac{1}{4})/n$, respectively, where n was the sample size (i.e., the number of young + adults), before transforming to the angular scale (Snedecor and Cochran 1967:327–328). Cases were weighted by $C \times n/N$, where C was the total number of cases (i.e., station-days), n was the sample size for that case (i.e., number of young + number of adults), and N was the sum of n over all cases. This weights in proportion to sample size, and makes the sum of the weights equal to the number of cases. The analysis was otherwise similar to that used for determining indices of abundance (Hussell et al. 1992).

Station-days with captures of aged birds varied from 373 in the White-crowned Sparrow to 942 in the Swainson's Thrush. However, captures and days with captures were not uniformly distributed among stations. If the sum of the case weights for a station was less than 90, it was judged that the coefficients of variables specific to that station could not be adequately estimated and data from that station were excluded from the multiple regression analyses. This criterion excluded Tennessee Warbler, Blackpoll Warbler, and White-crowned Sparrow at Station 3, and White-throated and White-crowned sparrows at Station 2.

I assumed that productivity effects, if they existed, would be associated with year, and would occur across all stations, days of the year (hereafter, "day"), and other conditions. Therefore I included dummy variables for year, as predictor variables in the regression model without interactions with station or any other variables. On the other hand, I assumed that day, weather, and moon effects might be station-specific. Therefore, I designed the regression model to accommodate this assumption by including predictor variables for day, weather, and moon only as interactions with each station.

Age proportion differences between two of the stations were already known to occur in warblers (Dunn and Nol 1980) and preliminary analyses indicated that age proportions change with day of the year, as expected from other research (e.g., Murray 1966, Hall 1981; Hussell 1982, 1991). Therefore, I included dummy variables for station and station-day interaction variables (1st, 2nd, and 3rd order terms in day, D, D^2, and D^3, respectively, where day D was the day of the year, set to zero on a day near the middle of each species' migration window) in the regression model. Inclusion of these predictor variables enables the regression analysis to detect both consistent station effects and different seasonal patterns of change in proportion of young at each station, if they exist in the data.

Moon phase variables were days from new moon (M, or "moonday") and the square of moonday (M^2). These variables enable the analysis to detect an unequal pattern of increase in proportion of young prior to new moon and decrease following full moon, or vice versa, with the possibility of a discontinuity in the proportion of young occurring at full moon. (The sky is moonless late in the night prior to full moon and early in the night following full moon, so the effects of moonlight are likely to by asymmetrical relative to full moon.)

Weather data were from Erie, Pennsylvania (about

50 km south of Long Point on the south shore of Lake Erie) and the variables were identical to those used by Hussell et al. (1992). I used eight variables representing east wind speed, south-east wind speed, south wind speed, south-west wind speed, temperature differences from normal, square root of horizontal visibility, cloud cover, and precipitation. All positive wind speeds indicated direction the wind was coming from, and negative values represented the opposite direction (e.g. a negative south wind speed was the speed of the wind from the north). I reduced the eight weather variables to six weather factors by principal components analysis, followed by varimax rotation. The six weather factors retained 86.2% of the variance of the original eight weather variables. Because the original four wind direction/speed variables were essentially uncorrelated, they loaded heavily on four factors (referred to as the E, SE, S, and SW wind factors for the wind directions involved). Visibility and temperature loaded heavily on the fifth factor (called "Visibility/Temperature"). Precipitation loaded heavily and cloud loaded moderately on the sixth factor (called "Rain/Cloud").

Predictor variables for weather were formed as interactions between station and the factor scores for the six rotated principal components, enabling the regression model to detect station-specific weather effects. By using factors instead of the original weather variables, the number of station-weather interaction variables was reduced from 24 to 18 at a cost of losing 13.8% of the variance in the original eight weather variables.

In summary, the multiple regression contained up to 63 predictor variables, consisting of up to 28 dummy variables for year, two dummy variables for station, nine station–day interaction variables, six station–moon phase interaction variables, and 18 station–weather factor interaction variables.

PROPORTION OF YOUNG INDICES

I calculated an annual raw proportion of young index as (number of young birds)/(number of young birds + number of adult birds), where numbers were the sums of newly captured birds accumulated from all of the stations over each species' autumn migration window. In addition, I calculated an adjusted annual proportion of young index for each of the nine species from the results of the multiple regressions described above. The adjusted annual proportion of young index was the back-transformed adjusted mean for each year. It is an estimate of what the young proportion would have been in a given year, if the values of the regression variables representing weather, dates, and locations of capture had been the same in all years, and were equal to the average values of those variables recorded in the data.

SPRING AND FALL POPULATION INDICES

Spring and fall population indices for each species counted in migration at Long Point in 1961–1988 were calculated as back-transformed adjusted means for year, from a regression analysis in which the dependent variable was

log (daily count + 1). The "daily count" was an estimated total of number of birds of each species occurring in or passing through a defined count area at each station. The estimate was based on a consistent procedure involving a count along a transect route, unstandardized trapping and netting (as described above), and incidental observations by all observers and banders present at the station (Hussell 1981, Hussell et al. 1992). Indices were calculated in the same way as described elsewhere (Hussell et al. 1992), except as indicated below. Three different sets of indices were calculated using the full data set. I had two reasons for using the full data set, instead of data reduced after an initial regression to remove cases with low predicted values (Hussell et al. 1992): (1) it enabled me to use exactly the same data sets for all three sets of indices, and (2) other analyses indicated that trends in annual indices calculated from the full data sets corresponded more closely to trends in Breeding Bird Survey counts in Ontario than trends based on indices calculated with reduced data sets (D. Hussell and L. Brown, unpublished). The three sets of annual population indices differed in the predictor variables used in the regression analyses. Dummy variables for year were included as predictor variables in all regressions, so that adjusted mean for year could be calculated. Index 1 was based on the full model with station, station–day, station–moon phase, and station–weather variables included as predictor variables (as in Hussell et al. 1992). Index 2 used a reduced model with station and station–day predictor variables. Index 3 was based on a model with dummy variables for station as the only predictor variables (in addition to the year dummy variables). I expected that index 1 would best reflect population size, because effects of variation in weather and moon phase are assigned to those variables. Index 3 would likely be the least satisfactory index of population size.

TESTS OF CONSISTENCY OF PROPORTION OF YOUNG AND POPULATION INDICES

The spring population consists of only adult birds, while the fall population has both young and adult birds. If we assume that the mortality rate of adult birds between spring and fall migrations does not vary importantly among years, then the population ratio = (fall population size index)/(spring population size index) should vary in parallel with fall proportion of young. Therefore, I calculated annual population ratios (population ratio 1, population ratio 2 and population ratio 3) based on each of the three population indices (index 1, index 2, and index 3 for spring and fall) for each of the nine species, and correlated them with annual raw and adjusted proportion of young. If adjustments of proportion of young and population indices were effective, we would expect the highest positive correlation to be between adjusted proportion of young and the population ratio for population index 1.

Rates of change in spring and fall migration indices of 42 species in the period 1967–1987 were positively correlated, as expected if spring and fall indices represent the same source population (Hussell et al. 1992). Fall indices, however, generally showed greater variability around the trend than did spring indices (D. Hussell, unpubl. analyses). This may reflect variability in proportion of young in fall populations. If so, proportion of young may explain additional variability in the trend analysis and allow more precise estimation of trends.

I tested for the effects of age proportion on trend in fall population index 1 of each species with the following model:

$$\mathrm{Ln}I_j = a + bY_j + c\mathrm{Ln}H_j + e_j \qquad \text{(Eq. 1)}$$

where I_j was index 1 in year j, Y_j was year j, H_j was either raw or adjusted proportion of young, and e_j was an error term, and a, b, and c were coefficients estimated by the regression analysis.

In addition, I tested the effect of age proportion on combined spring and fall trend in each species with the following model:

$$\mathrm{Ln}I_{jk} = a + bY_j + cS_k\mathrm{Ln}H_j + dS_k + e_{jk} \qquad \text{(Eq. 2)}$$

where I_{jk} was index 1 in year j and season k (spring or fall), Y_j was year j, S_k was a dummy variable for season ($S_k = 0$ for spring, $S_k = 1$ for fall), H_j was proportion of young in year j, $S_k\mathrm{Ln}H_j$ was an interaction term (formed by multiplying S_k by $\mathrm{Ln}H_j$), e_{jk} was an error term, and a, b, c, and d were coefficients estimated by the regression analysis. This model assumed a common trend b for spring and fall indices and tested whether fall proportion of young index H_j had a significant additional influence on the fall indices.

In both models, c was expected to be positive (i.e., the greater the proportion of young birds, the higher the annual fall population). In both analyses, cases were weighted by $C \times n_j / N$ where C was the total number of cases, n_j was the number of station-days of observations in year j used in calculating index I_j, and N was the sum of n_j for all cases. I tested for second and third order effects in year (with predictor variables Y_j^2 and Y_j^3) and, in the second model, for season-trend interactions ($S_k Y_j$, $S_k Y_j^2$ and $S_k Y_j^3$) using a stepwise procedure. Because this involved many tests and the number of variables was large relative to the number of cases, these effects were considered important enough to be included in the model only if they were significant at the 0.01 level.

I used a sign test on the probabilities (P) associated with c in equations 1 and 2 to determine whether the adjusted proportion of young indices were more effective than raw proportion of young indices as predictors of fall population indices. Because low P values with positive estimates of c indicate good prediction and low P values with negative estimates of c indicate poor prediction, I scored P values associated with negative estimates of c as 2 - P for use in the sign test.

In all tests in this section, I used population ratios based on at least 25 station-days of observations in both spring and fall. Population ratios were excluded if either the spring or the fall index (or both) did not meet the criterion. Adjusted and raw proportion of young indices were used only if captures of aged individuals occurred on at least seven days and at least 50 individuals were aged in that year.

RESULTS

EFFECTS OF WEATHER, MOON, DAY, AND STATION ON AGE PROPORTIONS

Samples of aged birds ranged from 1,328 in the Red-eyed Vireo to 5,414 in the Yellow-rumped Warbler (Table 1). Overall proportion of young varied from 0.549 in the White-crowned Sparrow to 0.916 in the Yellow-rumped Warbler. Except for the Blackpoll Warbler, warblers had proportions of young near 0.90, as reported previously (Dunn and Nol 1980).

Predictor variables in multiple regression analyses accounted for a significant proportion of the variation in transformed proportion of young in all species, with R^2 varying from 0.290 in the White-

TABLE 1. SUMMARY OF AGE DATA AND REGRESSION RESULTS FOR NINE SPECIES CAPTURED AT LONG POINT, ONTARIO

Species	Number of first captures		Proportion of young [a]	Number of station-days[b]	R^2 [c]
	Adult	Young			
Swainson's Thrush	937	3,245	0.776	942	0.300
Red-eyed Vireo	172	1,156	0.870	571	0.391
Tennessee Warbler	191	2,006	0.913	530	0.501
Magnolia Warbler	405	3,225	0.888	831	0.515
Yellow-rumped Warbler	453	4,961	0.916	683	0.393
Blackpoll Warbler	1,061	2,173	0.672	561	0.491
American Redstart	160	1,340	0.893	604	0.289
White-throated Sparrow	669	2,133	0.761	583	0.290
White-crowned Sparrow	1,037	1,260	0.549	372	0.484

[a] Proportion of young for the entire sample = (number of young)/(number of young + number of adults).

[b] Number of station-days for which aged birds were available during the species-specific migration window, over all years used in the analyses (1961–1988 for Red-eyed Vireo and White-crowned Sparrow, 1966–1988 for all other species).

[c] R^2 for the multiple regression of arcsine (square root (proportion of young)), on year, station, station-day, station-moonday, and station-weather predictor variables.

throated Sparrow to 0.515 in the Magnolia Warbler (Table 1). A high R^2 may reflect high year-to-year variability in the proportion of young (variance assigned to the year dummy variables), important effects of other variables, or both.

Interpretation of the effects of independent variables in multiple regressions presents some difficulties, both because some variables are correlated with each other and because effects of individual variables do not occur in isolation from those of other variables (especially where there are higher order terms in the same variable). Nevertheless major effects can be discerned. To summarise the effects of variables (other than dummy variables for station and year), I tabulated the number of times (called "cases" below) that a variable had a significant or near significant ($P \leq 0.1$) positive or negative effect on the proportion of young of a species at a station. In addition, I assessed the importance of positive and negative effects of each variable by summing scores (ordered in accordance with significance level) for each positive and negative effect (Table 2).

Station

The station dummy variables for Stations 2 and 3 always had significant or near significant ($P \leq 0.10$) positive effects on the proportion of young. For nine of the 13 dummy variables (in the regressions for nine species) the effect was significant at $P \leq 0.01$. This indicates a strong tendency for there to be a higher proportion of young birds at Stations 2 and 3 than at Station 1, as previously reported for warblers at Station 2 vs. 1 (Dunn and Nol 1980). In addition to warblers, the effect was also strong in Swainson's Thrush ($P < 0.01$ for both stations) and White-throated Sparrow ($P < 0.01$ for Station 3), but relatively weak in Red-eyed Vireo ($0.05 < P \leq 0.10$ at both sites).

Day

Day of the year (D) had significant effects ($P \leq 0.01$) on proportion of young in 17 of 22 station-species cases (Table 2), including one or more stations in all species. The direction of significant effects was always consistent among stations within species, but was not consistent among species. In most species the effect was negative, indicating that proportion of young tended to decline as the season progressed, but Red-eyed Vireo and Yellow-rumped Warbler showed strong and Swainson's Thrush and White-crowned Sparrow showed weak tendencies in the opposite direction. These effects indicate that the timing of peak migration differs among age classes.

The second order term in day (D^2) had significant effects in 13 of 22 cases (Table 2), but the direction of the effect varied. Negative effects predominated. Because day zero was set near the middle of the species' migration window, a negative second-order effect indicates a tendency for the proportion of young to be higher at the middle of the season than at the

TABLE 2. Effects of day, moonday, and six weather factors from principal components analysis on proportion of young captured

Predictor variable	No. of species-stations with significant effects [a]		Score total of strength of effects [b]	
	Positive	Negative	Positive	Negative
Day	7	10	15	26
Day^2	4	9	10	23
Day^3	10	0	25	0
Moonday	3	4	5	8
Moonday^2	5	1	12	2
Visibility/Temperature	5	2	12	4
Rain/Cloud	1	6	3	14
E Wind	2	1	3	2
SE Wind	1	4	3	7
S Wind	3	3	5	7
SW Wind	0	3	0	7

[a] Number of species-station combinations (out of 22) that show positive or negative significant effects of the indicated variable.

[b] Score total indicates the strength of positive and negative effects of variables. Score total = sum of scores assigned to each species-station combination according to the significance level of the effect of the variable. Scores were as follows: score = 1 if $0.05 < P \leq 0.10$, score = 2 if $0.01 < P \leq 0.05$, score = 3 if $P \leq 0.01$. Maximum possible score total is 66.

beginning and end, although this may be modified or reversed (at one end of the season) by the direction and magnitude of the first- and third-order effects. Swainso's Thrush showed a strong tendency for the mid-season proportion of young to be high (P < 0.01 at all three stations). Tennessee Warbler at Station 2, and White-throated and White-crowned sparrows at Station 1, showed strong (P < 0.01) tendencies in the opposite direction: proportion of young tended to be lowest in the middle of the season. These results may indicate that adult Swainson's Thrushes have a long migration period relative to young birds, whereas the opposite is true for Tennessee Warblers, White-throated and White-crowned sparrows.

When present, the effects of the third order term in day (D^3) were consistently positive (Table 2). This indicates that the proportion of young tended to be relatively low near the start of the season and high near the end of the season. However, these effects usually occurred in combination with negative first-order effects, indicating that proportion of young started at a high plateau, declined during the course of the season, then levelled off again near the end of the migration. Such a pattern would be expected if there was a substantial average difference, but much overlap, in the timing of migration of the two age classes. Species showing this pattern strongly at all stations were Tennessee Warbler and Magnolia Warbler.

Moon

First order effects of the number of days from new moon (M) occurred in seven of 22 cases and the results were somewhat equivocal (Table 2). Negative effects in four species all occurred at Station 2, indicating a tendency for the proportion of young to be lower in the days before full moon, when the sky is moonless late in the night, than in the days following full moon, when the moon is above the horizon late in the night. In one of those species (Blackpoll Warbler) a strong opposite effect (P < 0.01) occurred at Station 1.

The important result with respect to moon phase was the strong tendency for second-order effects to be positive (Table 2). In four of five cases, these effects occurred at Station 1, where the presence of a lighthouse may magnify the effect (Dunn and Nol 1980). This result indicates that the proportion of young tends to be lower near new moon than near full moon, when both the size of the illuminated lunar disk and the number of nocturnal hours that it is above the horizon are near their maximum values. Species showing this pattern strongly at Station 1

were Swainson's Thrush, Blackpoll Warbler, White-crowned Sparrow (all P < 0.01), and American Redstart (P < 0.05). Red-eyed Vireo showed a tendency to have a higher proportion of young near full moon at Station 2 (P < 0.10) and a lower proportion of young near full moon at Station 3 (P < 0.05).

Weather

Only 23% (31/132) of weather-station interactions had significant (P ≤ 0.10) effects on the proportion of young. Nevertheless some patterns could be detected. High horizontal visibility and warm temperatures usually had positive effects on the proportion of young (Table 2). In the Red-eyed Vireo, however, the effect was strongly positive at Station 1 but strongly negative at Station 3 (P < 0.01 in both cases). Rain and cloud tended to have negative effects on the proportion of young (Table 2). The single exception was Swainson's Thrush at Station 3, where the effect was positive (P < 0.01).

Effects of wind variables were more erratic. Easterly and westerly winds had little effect. Winds with a southerly component tended to have a negative effect on the proportion of young, scoring 21 negative points versus eight positive points (Table 2).

ANNUAL PROPORTIONS OF YOUNG AND FALL/SPRING POPULATION RATIOS

Annual raw and adjusted proportions of young for each species are shown in Figure 1 (left side). In some species (e.g., Swainson's Thrush, Yellow-rumped Warbler) differences between raw and adjusted proportions were small; in others (e.g., Tennessee Warbler, Magnolia Warbler), there were large discrepancies in some years between adjusted and raw proportions of young. Proportions of young showed substantial year to year fluctuations. There were no very obvious trends, although the proportion of young in White-throated Sparrows was generally higher from 1975 to 1988 than between 1966 and 1972, and there was a tendency for Tennessee Warbler proportions of young to decline between 1975 and 1987.

Fall/spring population ratios also fluctuated (Fig. 1, right side). Again there were few obvious trends. Red-eyed Vireo population ratios tended to decline from 1966 to 1988. Population ratios of Tennessee, Magnolia, and Yellow-rumped warblers were high in the 1975–1980 period, corresponding with a spruce budworm (*Choristoneura fumiferana*) outbreak that peaked in Ontario in 1980 (Hussell et al. 1992).

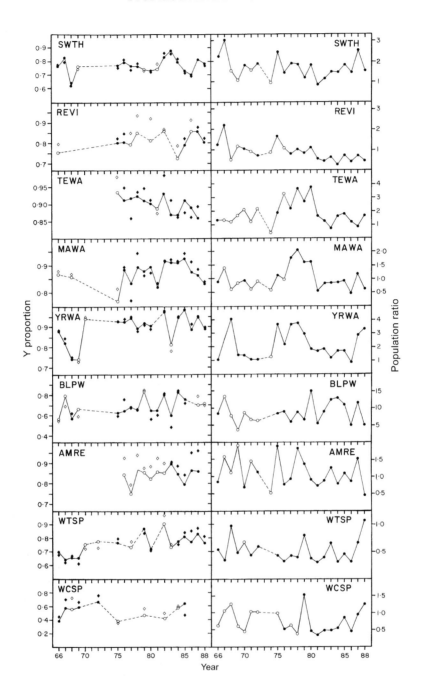

FIGURE 1. Proportion of young (Y proportion, left panels) and fall:spring ratios for population index 1 (right panels) for nine species. Left panels: circles = adjusted proportion of young, diamonds = raw proportion of young; open and closed symbols indicate proportions based on 50–99 and 100+ aged birds, respectively; lines join annual adjusted proportion of young; broken lines span years with missing data. Right panels: closed circles indicate population ratios derived from indices both of which were based on 50+ station-days of observations; open circles indicate ratios calculated from indices at least one of which was based on <50 (25–49) station-days; lines join annual ratios; broken lines span years with missing data. Species Codes: SWTH = Swainson's Thrush, REVI = Red-eyed Vireo, TEWA = Tennessee Warbler, MAWA = Magnolia Warbler, YRWA = Yellow-rumped Warbler, BLPW = Blackpoll Warbler, AMRE = American Redstart, WTSP = White-throated Sparrow, WCSP = White-crowned Sparrow.

For individual species, the only significant correlations between proportions of young and population ratios were those between raw proportion of young and all three population ratios in the White-crowned Sparrow ($r_S = 0.536$ for population ratio 1, $r_S = 0.573$ for population ratio 2, $r_S = 0.664$ for population ratio 3; $N = 11$, $P \leq 0.05$). If proportions of young and population ratios are positively related, however, then the mean correlation coefficient for the nine species should be positive. Mean correlation coefficient between adjusted proportion of young and population ratio 1 was 0.161, which was significantly greater than zero (Table 3). Means of correlations between all other combinations of methods of determining proportion of young and population ratio were non-significant and close to zero. Ranges and standard deviations of the correlation coefficients were lowest when population ratio 1 was used.

The effect of adjusted proportion of young in the trend analyses was positive (in accordance with expectation) in six of nine species for both the fall trend alone and for the combined spring and fall trend (Table 4). Significant or near-significant effects occurred in three and four species for the fall and spring/fall analyses, respectively (Table 4). Raw proportions of young had positive effects in four of nine species in the fall and three of nine species in the spring/fall analyses, with none of the effects significant or near significant. A sign test on the probabilities associated with the effect of proportion of young showed that adjusted proportion of young index was a marginally non-significantly better predictor of fall population indices than raw proportion of young index in the fall trend analyses (seven positive, two negative differences, one-tailed $P = 0.090$). In the spring/fall trend analyses, adjusted proportion of young was a significantly better predictor of the fall population index than the raw proportion of young (eight positive, one negative differences, one-tailed $P = 0.020$).

DISCUSSION

Daily proportion of young was influenced by year, station, date, moon phase, and weather (Table 2). As far as I am aware, this is the first demonstration of effects of weather on the proportion of young captured during fall migration. Although there was considerable variation among species and stations, it appears that there was a general tendency for the proportion of young to be higher when conditions were good for migration than when they were poor. The proportion of young tended to be higher near full moon than near new moon, higher when horizontal visibility was good than when it was poor, higher when there was no rain than when it was raining, and higher when there were tail-winds (northerly component) than when there were head-winds. This indicates that a greater proportion of adult birds land on Long Point when conditions for migration are poor than when they are good. This, perhaps, reflects the relative inexperience of young birds, which are less likely to overfly Long Point when conditions are good.

These effects were detectable despite the fact that capture methods at Long Point were not standardized and varied from day to day and year to year. We do not know to what extent consistent use of the same methods would have improved the precision of the productivity estimates. If the proportion of young captured is influenced by types and siting of traps and nets, then it is likely that the effects of environmental variables, such as station, moon phase and weather, would have been detected even more readily had the data collection been more standardized.

The proportion of young birds varied among the three Long Point stations, with more young recorded at Stations 2 and 3 than at Station 1. Therefore my annual raw proportion of young index (based on numbers of adults and young accumulated over all three stations) is certain to be biased by annual

TABLE 3. SPEARMAN CORRELATION COEFFICIENTS (R_s) BETWEEN PROPORTION OF YOUNG AND POPULATION RATIO FOR NINE SPECIES

Proportion of young		Population ratio model		
		Full	Station + station-day	Site only
Raw	mean	0.072	0.012	-0.020
	min, max	-0.056, 0.434	-0.302, 0.462	-0.496, 0.531
	SD	(0.164)	(0.222)	(0.296)
Adjusted	mean	0.161*	0.070	0.065
	min, max	-0.212, 0.467	-0.212, 0.420	-0.441, 0.420
	SD	(0.202)	(0.242)	(0.314)

* denotes $P \leq 0.05$ for one-tailed t-test for H_o: mean $r_s = 0$.

variations in the proportion of the total captures at each station. This problem exists only if there are significant differences in the proportions of young birds captured among different stations used to calculate a combined raw proportion of young index. If this is so, then the combined proportion of young index should be standardized such that each station is represented in the same proportion in the total index each year.

Overall, the results presented here imply that we should not assume that raw annual age proportions are reliable and consistent indices of productivity (see also Dunn et al. *this volume* b). It may be necessary to make adjustments for the confounding effects of station, day, moon phase, and weather. This conclusion was supported to a limited extent by my tests of consistency of proportion of young indices and population indices.

The annual proportion of young indices that were adjusted for the confounding effects of station, day, moon phase, and weather sometimes differed substantially from raw proportion of young (Fig. 1). The only significant correlation between proportion of young and population ratio was the one that matched adjusted proportion of young with population ratio 1, which was also fully adjusted for effects of day, moon, and weather (Table 3). Adjusted proportion of young was also more effective than raw proportion of young in accounting for variability in trend analyses (Table 4). All of these results suggest that adjusted proportions of young perform better as indices of productivity than do raw proportions of young.

My attempts to validate proportions of young as productivity indices were disappointing, however, in that most of the single-species correlations between proportion of young and population ratios were low and non-significant (Table 3) and, in most species, the effects of proportion of young in the trend analyses were also not significant (Table 4). My analysis is consistent with the view that both age proportions and population ratios contain information about productivity, but one or both of these measures lack precision. Given small sample sizes of aged birds in some years (particularly adults), and variability in migratory populations, it is likely that both age proportions and population ratios lack precision. Nevertheless, my results indicated that adjusted proportions of young performed better than raw proportions of young. Moreover, fully adjusted population indices outperformed other population indices, as is expected because the adjustments are designed to reduce variability that is not attributable to population size.

Inclusion of proportion of young as a predictor variable in trend analyses may enhance precision of estimates of trends in fall populations of some migrants. In several species proportion of young was not significant and it had little effect on the estimate of trend. In other species proportion of young was significant and its inclusion resulted in a relatively large reduction in residual variance, which would allow earlier detection of a trend, if it exists. For example, explained variation (R^2) in fall abundance indices increased by 18.6% in the Tennessee Warbler and 25.4% in the Magnolia Warbler when proportion of young was included as a predictor variable.

These results indicate that either proportions of young or population ratios or both may be useful for

TABLE 4. EFFECT OF PROPORTION OF YOUNG IN TREND ANALYSES OF ANNUAL POPULATION INDICES [a]

| | Sample sizes | | Direction and significance of effect of proportion of young [b] | | | |
| | | | Adjusted proportion of young | | Raw proportion of young | |
Species	Spring	Fall	Fall	Spring/fall	Fall	Spring/fall
Swainson's Thrush	22	18	+	+	−	−
Red-eyed Vireo [c]	22	12	+*	+**	+	+
Tennessee Warbler	22	13	+(*)	+**	−	−
Magnolia Warbler	22	16	+*	+**	+	+
Yellow-rumped Warbler	22	18	−	−	−	−
Blackpoll Warbler	22	17	−	−	−	−
American Redstart	22	12	−	−	−	−
White-throated Sparrow	22	18	+	+	+	−
White-crowned Sparrow	25	13	+	+*	+	+

[a] Except as indicated in footnote c, trends were linear as in equations 1 and 2; that is, there were no higher order or season interaction terms.

[b] (*) = P ≤ 0.10, * = P ≤ 0.05, ** = P ≤ 0.1 in one-tailed test of significance of coefficient c in equation (1) for fall and equation (2) for spring and fall (see METHODS).

[c] Spring and fall linear trends of Red-eyed Vireo differed significantly (P < 0.01). Therefore a season interaction term was included in the spring/fall regression model.

detecting productivity changes in songbird populations, but appropriate adjustments may be necessary to account for effects of confounding variables. Small sample sizes and sampling errors are likely to result in imprecise annual estimates, but long-term trends in productivity should be detectable.

It was notable that in the nine common species selected for analysis here, annual samples of aged birds were often fewer than the 50 that I judged was the minimum acceptable for inclusion in the analyses. Most banding stations probably do not capture large enough samples of more than a few species to be useful for estimating age proportions, unless the data are combined with those from other stations (with appropriate adjustments for station effects). Possibly, much larger samples than this will be needed to obtain precise indices of productivity. Alternatively or additionally, inland stations where higher proportions of adult birds are captured than at Long Point may give more precise estimates and may be less affected by confounding variables.

Validation of productivity indices for small land-bird migrants is a difficult problem because reliable benchmark measures of productivity are generally not available. More research is needed to determine the reliability of indices and required sample sizes and to examine the effects of confounding variables at different stations (inland versus coastal). We need more information on whether different capture methods have an important influence on the proportion of young birds captured. Alternative methods of analysis should also be explored.

ACKNOWLEDGMENTS

Thanks to the staff and numerous volunteers of Long Point Bird Observatory for collecting the age data and counts of migrant birds. C. M. Francis provided me with the age data in 1989 from files obtained from the U.S. Bird Banding Laboratory. Counts were those used by Hussell et al. (1992); assistance and funding for compilation and entry of those data are acknowledged therein. L. Brown, Ontario Ministry of Natural Resources, wrote computer programs to calculate population indices, provided me with computer files of weather data, and assisted in other ways. B. G. Murray, Jr., C. J. Ralph, and W. J. Richardson made helpful comments on a draft of the manuscript. This paper is a publication of Long Point Bird Observatory, Bird Studies Canada, and is Ontario Ministry of Natural Resources, Wildlife Research and Development Section Contribution No. 95-02.

Studies in Avian Biology No. 29:92–96

AN INVESTIGATION OF PRODUCTIVITY INDICES DERIVED FROM BANDING OF FALL MIGRANTS

Erica H. Dunn, David J. T. Hussell, and Raymond J. Adams

Abstract. Indices of productivity were estimated for seven species of birds captured during fall migration at two mist-netting stations less than 1 km apart, in Kalamazoo, Michigan, where those species occur only as migrants. The indices were proportion of hatch-year birds in the fall migration catch, and abundance of hatch-year birds. These values were positively correlated. Within species, mean annual hatch-year abundance often differed in magnitude between the two stations, and in some species annual abundance indices showed long-term trends in opposite directions. Nonetheless, there was evidence of parallel annual fluctuation of both productivity indices, both within and between stations. Fall migration productivity indices will rarely be useful for tracking reproductive success of specific breeding populations, because the areas from which fall migrants originate are large and poorly delineated, but such indices should be useful for other purposes (e.g., comparing regional productivity in wet and dry years). More work is needed to test the effect on fall productivity indices of habitat, net location, and frequency of sampling. Also needed are more comparisons of productivity indices among a larger number of stations, and better validation through comparison with independently derived productivity estimates.

Key Words: age ratio, banding, migration, productivity indices, validation.

Annual productivity is a key component of integrated monitoring (Baillie 1990). At local scales, intensive nest searching can provide data on reproductive success, but most such studies focus on a single species and station, often for just a few years. At slightly broader scales, constant-effort mist netting spanning the post-fledging, pre-migration period has been shown to give estimates of breeding success that correspond well with nest studies, at least in some species (du Feu and McMeeking 1991, Nur and Geupel 1992). Cooperative programs such as the Monitoring Avian Productivity and Survival program (MAPS) in North America (DeSante et al. 1995) and Constant Effort Sites (CES) in Great Britain (Peach et al. 1996) depend on many contributors to track productivity on regional scales. These programs have provided further evidence that summer mist netting reflects true levels of productivity: productivity indices may fluctuate in parallel among stations (Baillie et al. 1986), long runs of data sometimes show patterns and periodic anomalies that correspond well to suspected causal events (e.g., DeSante and Geupel 1987), and large drops in productivity indices may precede declines in breeding populations the next year (DeSante et al. 1998).

Data on birds captured during migration may provide another valuable source of productivity data. In particular, productivity measures from migrants could provide information on species whose breeding ranges are largely inaccessible for other kinds of survey, such as boreal-nesting songbirds. Migrants captured at a single station can come from broad areas of breeding range (Brewer et al. 2000, Wassenaar and Hobson 2001), so it may take only a few stations to provide results representative of a broad geographic area. Finally, fall banding produces relatively large sample sizes compared to MAPS and CES, which may contribute to making productivity indices more robust. However, although there is widespread belief that age data from the migration season reflect annual reproductive success (e.g., Ralph et al. 1993), there are no studies comparable to those for MAPS and CES that have attempted to demonstrate the validity of fall migration productivity indices.

Here we examine two productivity indices for fall migrants captured at two neighboring stations in southern Michigan: the proportion of young birds in the total sample, and an index representing abundance of young birds. Although abundance of young will vary with population size, a portion of the annual fluctuation in numbers of young should reflect variation in productivity. We compare the two indices with each other both within and between stations and to data from the Breeding Bird Survey, and outline needs for further validation.

METHODS

We analyzed age data for 1979–1991 from two banding stations that are about 0.75 km apart, located at Kalamazoo, in southern Michigan. The "River" station had 30–35 12 m, 30 mm-mesh nets in second growth, open riparian woodland, and marsh shrub. The "Marsh" station had 15–20 similar nets in shrub vegetation bordering a marsh and woodland. Mist nets were operated daily (weather permitting) from early August to mid-November, from shortly after dawn until early afternoon. More than 80% of days in the fall migration period were covered annually.

Species chosen for analysis were Gray-cheeked Thrush (*Catharus minimus*), Hermit Thrush (*C. guttatus*), Swainson's Thrush (*C. ustulatus*), Magnolia Warbler (*Dendroica magnolia*), Yellow-rumped Warbler (*D. coronata*), Dark-eyed Junco (*Junco hyemalis*), and White-throated Sparrow (*Zonotrichia albicollis*). None of these species breeds as far south as the study station, so capture of local residents and dispersing juveniles was not a complicating factor in the analyses.

Data were restricted to first captures only, in species-specific migration "windows" (as defined at Long Point, Ontario, 650 km east of Kalamazoo; Hussell et al. 1992). A species was analyzed only if at least 0.2 adult birds/day were captured (on average) within the appropriate migration window, so that results would not be affected by chance variation in low numbers of adults. All birds were aged by the degree of skull pneumatization, and all species chosen for analysis can be aged by this method through the entire migration period. Unaged birds were excluded from the study, and did not exceed 0.3% of the totals for any species analyzed.

We constructed three indices of annual productivity from the number of birds captured, which we term "Raw HY Proportion" (where HY = hatching year birds), "HY Abundance," and "Adjusted HY Proportion." The first index was calculated for each species for each area as (N of HY birds)/(total of HY + AHY birds). To construct the other two indices, annual estimates of abundance for all birds, and for HY birds alone, were calculated from multiple regressions designed to assign variability in daily numbers to date, weather, moon phase, and year. Analysis was identical to that detailed in Dunn et al. (1997). These abundance indices represent the number of all birds, or of HY birds alone, that would be expected in a given year on an average date, under average conditions of moon phase and weather. HY Abundance was simply the abundance index

for HY birds estimated from the regressions. Adjusted HY Proportion was HY Abundance divided by the abundance of all birds, as estimated from the regressions. This figure differed from the Raw HY Proportion in that it was corrected for any variation that may have been caused by weather, moon phase, or date in the season.

Trends in breeding populations for Ontario and Michigan, according to the Breeding Bird Survey (BBS), were obtained from Sauer et al. (2000). Other evidence suggests that migrants at the study stations come from both these areas (Dunn et al. 1997). Trends in HY Abundance were calculated as the slope of the log-transformed annual indices regressed on year, producing an estimated annual percent rate of change that is directly comparable to BBS trends. Trends in HY Proportion were calculated as the slope of the regression on year of the arcsine of the square root of the original indices. Detrended indices (residuals from regression of indices on year) were derived from regression of indices transformed as described above. All other statistics involving HY Proportion were also performed on transformed indices, which normalized their distribution. Results were considered significant if $P < 0.05$.

RESULTS

In all species, annual Raw HY Proportion indices were significantly correlated with annual indices of Adjusted HY Proportion from the same station (r ranged from 0.71 to 0.96, $P < 0.01$ in all cases). However, Adjusted HY Proportion was higher than Raw HY Proportion, and usually had lower variance (Table 1). All remaining analyses were run with both indices, and each produced similar results. In the remainder of this paper, unless noted otherwise, results and discussion are limited to Adjusted HY Proportion (hereafter referred to simply as HY Proportion).

The HY Proportion at both stations averaged about 0.73 (Table 1), which is typical of other inland banding stations in North America (Dunn and Nol 1980). Values were always slightly higher at the River station (Table 1), significantly (or nearly) so

TABLE 1. MEAN RAW AND ADJUSTED HY PROPORTION FOR TWO STATIONS, 1979–1991

	River			Marsh		
Species	Raw	Adjusted	N	Raw	Adjusted	N
Gray-cheeked Thrush	0.64 ± 0.09	0.68 ± 0.08	469	0.54 ± 0.10	0.57+0.11	321
Hermit Thrush	0.82 ± 0.08	0.85 ± 0.07	803	0.75 ± 0.06	0.80+0.07	1,260
Swainson's Thrush	0.82 ± 0.06	0.86 ± 0.08	2,638	0.72 ± 0.13	0.74+0.11	654
Magnolia Warbler	0.71 ± 0.13	0.73 ± 0.07	1,506	0.69 ± 0.13	0.69+0.10	1,101
Yellow-rumped Warbler	0.76 ± 0.09	0.83 ± 0.05	6,862	0.74 ± 0.11	0.79+0.07	754
Dark-eyed Junco	–	–	116	0.65 ± 0.11	0.68+0.09	1,057
White-throated Sparrow	0.64 ± 0.12	0.66 ± 0.08	1,243	0.60 ± 0.10	0.65+0.08	1,348

Notes: Values shown are mean ± SD of indices averaged across years.

for all species except White-throated Sparrow. HY Abundance also differed between stations in six of seven species (Table 2), but there was no consistency in which station had higher mean numbers.

There were no significant long-term trends in HY Proportion, but a few in HY Abundance (Table 3). Direction of trend in HY Abundance at the Marsh station matched direction of BBS trends from Michigan (four species only, all increasing), but not those from Ontario. Trends in HY Abundance at the River station did not agree with BBS trend directions from either region. White-throated Sparrow was notable in showing significant trends in HY Abundance at both banding stations, but in opposite directions.

To determine whether productivity indices fluctuated in parallel, we examined correlation of detrended indices. (Detrending prevents correlation resulting solely from trends in the two sets of indices.) HY Abundance indices were positively correlated between stations, sometimes significantly so, as were HY Proportion indices (Table 4). HY Abundance and HY Proportion tended to fluctuate in parallel with each other within stations.

DISCUSSION

Date, weather, and moon phase had significant effects on HY Proportion in most species (as also found by Hussell *this volume*). Raw HY Proportion is therefore a more biased index than Adjusted HY Proportion, although all analyses gave similar results regardless of which HY Proportion index was used. This suggests that Raw HY Proportion may be a minimally acceptable index of productivity, despite the added variance caused by date and weather effects. More importantly, the similarity of results using both HY proportion indices strengthens our confidence that migration season productivity indices actually reflect proportion of young birds

present in the population, and are not artifacts of weather effects.

Results indicated that young birds of all species were relatively more prevalent than adults at the River station, regardless of which station hosted the higher abundance (Tables 1 and 2). Not only were there differences between stations in absolute values of productivity indices, but occasionally in long-term trends as well (Table 3). HY proportions in migrants are also known to differ markedly between coastal and inland banding stations, and between samples of birds banded and those killed at lighted structures during nocturnal migration (Dunn and Nol 1980, Ralph 1981). These results show that productivity indices derived from migration banding are not reliable indicators of the absolute number of young produced per adult. Similar conclusions have been drawn for productivity indices derived from summer banding, in which there can be higher proportions of HY birds in particular habitats, and in samples of birds captured with particular trapping devices (Peach et al. 1996, Bart et al. 1999, Green 1999, Senar et al. 1999).

Nonetheless, even when summer productivity indices differ in absolute magnitude, they may fluctuate in parallel (Peach et al. 1996, Green 1999), showing that annual changes in the relative proportion of age groups can still be a good indicator of annual shifts in productivity. The same appears to be true of migration season productivity indices (Table 4). In this study, HY Abundance and HY Proportion fluctuated in parallel within and between stations in most species, although many of the correlations fell short of statistical significance. Parallel fluctuation occurred even when trends in these indices did not agree. For example, long-term trends in HY Abundance for White-throated Sparrow were significant at both stations but opposite in sign (Table 3), yet detrended annual indices fluctuated in parallel (Table 4). These results indicate that

TABLE 2. MEAN HY ABUNDANCE FOR TWO STATIONS, 1979–1991

Species	River		Marsh
Gray-cheeked Thrush	0.30 ± 0.11		0.29 ± 0.10
Hermit Thrush	0.72 ± 0.27	***	1.35 ± 0.49
Swainson's Thrush	1.02 ± 0.24	**	0.75 ± 0.29
Magnolia Warbler	0.65 ± 0.18	**	1.16 ± 0.42
Yellow-rumped Warbler	2.14 ± 0.57	***	0.55 ± 0.23
Dark-eyed Junco	0.11 ± 0.05	***	0.89 ± 0.48
White-throated Sparrow	0.64 ± 0.36	+	0.94 ± 0.33

Notes: Values shown are mean ± SD of values averaged across years. Symbols indicate significant difference (see text) between stations (paired t-tests between annual indices): *** = P < 0.001, ** = P < 0.01, * = P < 0.05, + = 0.5 < P < 0.1.

TABLE 3. TRENDS IN POPULATION SIZE AND PRODUCTIVITY INDICES, 1979–1991

	BBS		HY Abundance		HY Proportion	
Species	Ontario	Michigan	River	Marsh	River	Marsh
Hermit Thrush	2.6+	8.1**	2.3	8.5***	0.25	0.84
Swainson's Thrush	-1.2+	–	2.0	5.9	-0.24	-0.85
Magnolia Warbler	3.0+	9.2	-1.8	4.3+	-0.40	-0.63
Yellow-rumped Warbler	-2.8+	4.6*	1.2	3.8	-0.30	0.49
Dark-eyed Junco	-2.8	–	0.1	-4.9	-0.64	-0.18
White-throated Sparrow	-1.3*	1.2	-9.3**	7.4**	0.22	-0.52

Notes: BBS and HY Abundance trends are rates of change (%/yr). Trend in HY Proportion is average annual change (see Methods). Symbols indicate significance of trend (see text): *** = P < 0.001, ** = P < 0.01, * = P < 0.05, + = 0.5 < P < 0.1.

annual fluctuation in HY Abundance is quite strongly affected by reproductive success. Because it is also affected by annual change in population size, however, it is not as useful an indicator of reproductive success as is HY Proportion.

Several factors may have introduced bias into the productivity indices in this study, which could have reduced the strength of evidence for parallel fluctuation. Vegetation increased in height throughout the study period, and while nets at the Marsh station were moved to keep them in shrub habitat, at the River station they were not. Also, in some years there was a large berry crop at one station but not the other, and thrushes were noted to concentrate where berry crops were high, perhaps reducing correlation of HY Abundance between the stations.

In addition, there were methodological differences between the stations that may have affected results. Net numbers were not wholly standardized, with some nets added and others discontinued during the study period, and not all nets were opened on every day that netting took place. Such factors could alter the abundance, proportion, or both of HY birds

at one station relative to the other, particularly if certain nets were more likely to capture birds of a particular age class, or if nets were opened at only one station when there was an influx of birds with unusual age distribution.

The MAPS and CES programs pool productivity data from many stations to calculate regional values, such that anomalies at individual stations are evened out. The same approach with fall migration indices may strengthen results. One difficulty with this approach, however, is defining the region within which all monitoring stations are capturing individuals from the same breeding population. There is evidence, for example, that migrants moving through southern Michigan come from both Michigan and Ontario (Dunn et al. 1997). When BBS trends differ in different parts of the breeding range from which migrants are drawn (as in Yellow-rumped Warbler; Table 3), we do not know which trend is most important for comparison to fall migration productivity indices from southern Michigan. Similarly, we do not know to what extent a more distant station—for example, in central or northern Michigan—would be sampling

TABLE 4. CORRELATIONS OF ANNUAL PRODUCTIVITY INDICES BETWEEN STATIONS, AND WITH EACH OTHER WITHIN STATIONS

	Correlation between River and Marsh		Correlation between HY Abundance and HY Proportion	
Species	HY Abundance	HY Proportion	River	Marsh
Gray-cheeked Thrush	0.33	0.32	0.45	0.61*
Hermit Thrush	0.60*	0.49+	0.08	0.75**
Swainson's Thrush	0.14	0.27	0.44	0.73**
Magnolia Warbler	0.50+	0.93***	-0.19	0.33
Yellow-rumped Warbler	0.46	0.42	0.68*	0.54+
Dark-eyed Junco	0.38	–	0.72*	0.43
White-throated Sparrow	0.51+	0.70**	0.72**	0.04

Notes: Values shown are correlation coefficients between detrended indices (residuals from regression of appropriately-transformed indices on year) and significance levels (see text): *** = P < 0.001, ** = P < 0.01, * = P < 0.05, + = 0.5 < P < 0.1.

the same population as the stations in Kalamazoo. Fall migration productivity data from very nearby stations can certainly be pooled for analysis (assuming stations all follow the same protocol), but it may not be justifiable to pool data from very distant stations.

It will be hard to associate fall migration productivity indices with specific breeding populations because of uncertainty as to breeding origin, so migration season productivity indices will have limited value in assessing impact on productivity of locally varying factors such as predation levels. Nonetheless, accurate information on annual shifts in productivity of migrants should be useful for other purposes. For example, there are known cases of reproductive success varying with weather, either routinely or in response to unusual conditions (e.g., DeSante and Geupel 1987, Bradley et al. 1997). Because weather often affects large geographic areas, data from migrating birds might be especially well suited to the study of such weather effects.

This paper is one of the first to critically examine fall migration productivity indices (see also Hussell *this volume*). Although we found evidence that different stations detected similar annual changes in productivity, our primary conclusion is that a good deal more basic research is in order. A recent study of Pink-footed Geese (*Anser brachyrynchos*) showed the importance of cross-validation and study of biases in data sources, including productivity indices, even for well-studied populations with excellent data (Gantner and Madsen 2001). Similar kinds of work are needed on fall migration productivity indices, including effects of habitat and net location on ages of birds captured, and degree of parallel fluctuation in productivity indices among nearby stations. For example, Harrison et al. (2000) found that habitat change at his late summer banding station altered the relative proportions of age groups in some species but not in others. Similar kinds of research are needed to determine the circumstances and species for which fall productivity indices are meaningful. Even more important is the need to validate migration season productivity indices through comparison with independently collected data on reproductive success. The most suitable comparison would be with MAPS results from probable breeding areas.

In the meantime, we offer several recommendations for the study of productivity through capture of fall migrants. Banders should routinely record the technique they use for ageing each bird handled, and keep careful records of daily effort, net number, and location, so that users of age data can analyze and interpret them correctly. Recording the net number where each bird is captured should permit analysis of net-site effects on age proportion. Capture effort should be as standardized as much as possible (Ralph et al. *this volume a*), to avoid bias in the numbers of each age group captured. Finally, many species have differential timing of fall migration, so it is especially important for avoiding bias to collect evenly spaced (preferably daily) samples throughout the entire migration period of the species.

ACKNOWLEDGMENTS

Thanks are extended to P. B. Blancher, C. M. Francis, and W. J. Peach for helpful reviews. We are especially grateful to the dozens of banders who gathered the data used in our analyses. This paper is Ontario Ministry of Natural Resources, Wildlife Research and Development Section Contribution No. 94-03.

Studies in Avian Biology No. 29:97–111

OPTIMIZING THE ALLOCATION OF COUNT DAYS IN A MIGRATION MONITORING PROGRAM

LEN THOMAS, GEOFFREY R. GEUPEL, NADAV NUR, AND GRANT BALLARD

Abstract. Many migration monitoring stations cannot operate on every day of the migration period. In this paper, we used migration count data from two stations (Point Reyes Bird Observatory fall migration and Long Point Bird Observatory spring migration) to examine the relationship between the proportion of count days (frequency of sampling) and the statistical power to detect long-term population trends. We found that power to detect trends at a single station declined at an accelerating rate as the frequency of sampling decreased. Stations that operate on one or two days per week are unlikely to detect changes in abundance for most species that would be well monitored at higher sampling frequencies. The effect of missing counts can be mitigated to some extent by the choice of sampling design (method of allocating count days over the migration period). We compared a number of candidate designs and found that systematic sampling was the most accurate, although stratified random sampling may be preferred in situations where little is known about the pattern of migration. Designs that clump count days together, such as sampling only at weekends, should be avoided because adjacent count days tend to duplicate the same information.

Key Words: avian migration monitoring, population trends, power analysis, sampling frequency, survey design.

One of the principal objectives of songbird migration monitoring is to determine whether the abundance of birds arriving at a monitoring station has changed over time. To achieve this, birds are surveyed at the station on as many days as possible during the migration season. A number of survey techniques may be employed (including mist netting), depending on the characteristics of the location. Regardless of the survey method used, the daily counts are converted into annual indices of abundance, and population trends are estimated from the annual indices by regression. The use of count data to monitor migration in this way has been reviewed elsewhere (Dunn and Hussell 1995, Dunn in press).

At most of the larger migration monitoring stations in North America (e.g., Long Point, Point Reyes, and Manomet bird observatories), counts take place on essentially every day of the migration season. However, many smaller stations are constrained by funding or by the availability of volunteers and cannot operate every day. Gaps in the daily counts result, which introduce additional variability into the annual index estimates, and in turn reduce the ability of the station to detect population trends. This additional variability is called "sampling variance" and is a function of the "frequency of sampling" (the proportion of days on which counts take place) and the "sampling design" (method of allocating count days over the season). In this paper, we address two questions: (1) To what degree can gaps in the count data reduce our ability to detect long-term trends?

and (2) Can the effect of gaps be minimized by the choice of an appropriate sampling design?

To answer these questions, we used data from two stations where monitoring occurs continually throughout the migration season: Point Reyes and Long Point bird observatories. By analyzing the pattern of counts in these "complete" data sets, we could estimate the sampling variance that would arise from different frequencies of sampling and sampling designs. The two observatories differ in the environment of the stations, the methods of data collection, and the species seen. In addition, we used fall data from Point Reyes and spring data from Long Point. We reasoned that, by using very different datasets, any similarities in the results between stations would be of more general applicability to other migration monitoring stations in North America. This does mean, however, that we cannot interpret any differences in results between the data sets as being due to differences between stations, since they could also be due to differences between season.

The ability of a monitoring program to detect a given trend can be measured using the concept of "statistical power." Statistical power is the probability of getting a significant result in a statistical hypothesis test, given that there is an effect (i.e., trend) of specified magnitude (Cohen 1988, Gerrodette 1987, Nemac 1991, Steidl and Thomas 2001). In the context of avian population monitoring, the Monitoring Working Group of Partners in Flight have proposed that a successful monitoring program is one that has a 90% chance of detecting a 50% decline in a species' population over a 25 year period (Butcher et al. 1993:199). Thus, the importance of gaps in the count data can be assessed by quantifying the impact of sampling frequency on the statistical power to detect a population change of this magnitude. To do this, we estimated statistical power to detect a 50% population change over 25 year for sampling frequencies ranging from one to seven days per week. We assumed that count days are selected at random, that the statistical test used to detect trends is a linear regression of annual indices against time, where annual indices are the mean of the log-transformed daily counts, and that the test was statistically significant when $P \leq 0.05$.

At monitoring stations that do not operate every day, there is often some flexibility in the way that the count days can be allocated through the season. A number of familiar sampling designs are discussed in standard textbooks on sampling (e.g., Cochran 1977), such as simple random, stratified random, and systematic. These designs vary in the ease with which they can be implemented, and in the sampling variance of the resulting annual indices. To quantify the differences in sampling variance that could be expected for migration monitoring, we computed the "design effect" of a number of candidate sampling designs, over a range of sampling frequencies. The design effect is the ratio of (1) the sampling variance obtained from the candidate sampling design divided by (2) the sampling variance obtained from simple random sampling at the same sampling frequency (reference in Cochran 1977:85). Design effects of <1 indicate an improvement in precision over random sampling, and the design with the lowest design effect should be preferred by those designing monitoring programs, all other factors being equal.

This paper is aimed at those designing a migration monitoring program at a single station. We do not consider the trade-off between the frequency of sampling at multiple stations versus the number of stations that can be sampled. The solution to this problem will depend in part upon the variability between stations, which is not well known for migration monitoring. A treatment of the topic in the context of extensive surveys such as the Breeding Bird Survey is given by Link et al. (1994).

METHODS

Data Used

Data from Point Reyes were collected at the Palomarin Field Station in coastal California using constant-effort

mist netting (see DeSante and Geupel 1987 for details of the field methods). We used fall migration data collected between August 18 and November 26 (101 days) in the years 1980 to 1992 (13 years). The field protocol calls for 20 fixed nets to be placed for 6 h each day during the migration period, making 120 net-h in total. However, inclement weather and other eventualities sometimes prevented the protocol from being followed: the mean percent of days when no nets were set was 4.7/year, and the mean net-hours for the remaining days was 110.7. Our analyses required a complete data set, so we substituted for the missing value on days when no nets were run the mean of the counts from the previous two days and the next two days. We standardized all daily counts to the total new birds banded per 120 net-h.

Long Point is a peninsula on Lake Erie, Ontario. There, a combination of standardized transect counts, unstandardized netting, and casual observations were used to produce a daily estimated total of each bird species present at the monitoring station (see Dunn et al. *this volume a*, for a full description of the method of data collection). In this paper, we used spring migration data from the station at the tip of the Point, collected between 1961 and 1993. Of these data, we excluded years with any missing counts, leaving 16 years: 1963, 1967, 1971–1972, 1975, 1978, 1980, 1982–1985, 1987, 1989–1990, 1992–1993. The seasonal timing of data collection varied between years, with a mean starting date of April 10 and ending date of June 13, giving a mean of 65 daily counts per year.

Having derived daily counts from each station, we treated both datasets identically. At each station, we chose migration periods separately for each species using a procedure similar to that of Hussell et al. (1992), as follows. First, we excluded counts in the first or last two weeks of the data collection periods that were separated by more than four days from any other count in any other year. Then we selected start and end dates so as to encompass the middle 98% of days on which the species was recorded. To simplify the comparison of sample designs (see below), we further truncated the data such that all migration periods at the same station began on the same day of the week, and were an integer number of weeks in length.

After the selection of migration periods, species with a mean daily count over all years of less than 1.0 were excluded from the analysis. This criterion was necessary because the methods we used to estimate trends are known to be unreliable for species with low abundances (see DISCUSSION). The counts were then log-transformed (after the adding 0.5 to all counts, to prevent taking the log of a zero count). Annual indices were calculated as the mean of the logged counts.

To better understand our results, we performed a number of descriptive analyses of the log-transformed count data for each species at each station. We studied the frequency distribution of the counts, and the distribution of counts through the migration period. We also plotted "correlograms," which show the correlation between counts taken in the same season against the number of days the counts are spaced apart. Correlation between counts taken in the same season is known as "autocorrelation." The degree of autocorrelation has important implications for the optimal choice of sampling design, as is discussed below.

All of the analyses described here were performed using SAS for OS/2 version 6.10 (SAS Institute 1993).

IMPORTANCE OF SAMPLING FREQUENCY

For each species, we calculated the power to detect a 50% change in annual indices over 25 year under the null hypothesis of no change as

$$power = 1 - \Phi\left(t_{1-\alpha/2,df,\delta}\right) + \Phi\left(-t_{1-\alpha/2,df,\delta}\right)$$

where $t_{x,df,\delta}$ denotes the xth quantile of the noncentral t-distribution, given df degrees of freedom and the noncentrality parameter δ, and $\Phi(t_{x,df,\delta})$ is the cumulative distribution function of the appropriate noncentral t-distribution, evaluated at x (Nemac 1991). The degrees of freedom were 23 throughout (number of years over which we hope to detect the 50% change - 2), and α was set at 0.05. The noncentrality parameter was calculated as:

$$\delta = \frac{(\beta_1 - 0)}{\sqrt{\left(S_{reg}^2 + S_{samp}^2\right)/SS_{yr}}}$$

where β_1 is the slope of the log-linear regression line under the alternate hypothesis (50% change in population size over 25 years is a slope of 0.277 on the log scale), SS_{yr} is the sum of squares of the year variable (which, with 25 years of continuous data, is 1,300), S_{reg}^2 is the variance of the annual indices that is unexplained by the regression line when there are no gaps in the daily count data, and S_{samp}^2 is the additional variance due to missing counts (i.e., the sampling variance). We estimated S_{reg}^2 for each species at each station as the mean square error from the linear regression of annual indices against year. We calculated statistical power at seven levels of S_{reg}^2, assuming sampling frequencies of one to seven days per week and a simple

random sampling design. At a sampling frequency of seven days per week (i.e., no gaps in the count data), $S_{samp}^2 = 0$. At the other six levels of sample frequency, was calculated for each species as the mean sampling variance over all years of count data. The calculation of the sampling variance for each year, assuming a simple random design, is outlined in the next section.

COMPARISON OF SAMPLING DESIGNS

At each station, we calculated the sampling variance for the sampling designs for each species and year and over a range of sampling frequencies. We then calculated the design effect of each sampling design for each species at each sampling frequency as (1) the mean sampling variance over years for the sampling design divided by (2) the mean sampling variance for random sampling at the same sampling frequency. The sampling designs are explained below, and are shown diagrammatically in Figure 1. The sampling frequencies used and the method of comparing sampling designs are described at the end of this section.

In "simple random sampling," our baseline design, the number of count days is fixed, but their location in the season is chosen at random. The variance of the annual index in a single year was calculated as

$$V_{rand} = \frac{S^2}{n} \frac{(N-n)}{N}$$

(Cochran 1977, formula 2.8), where S^2 is the variance of the log-transformed daily counts, N is the number of days in the migration period and n is the number of days on which counts took place. Here, n = frequency of sampling per week × N/7.

In "stratified random sampling," the season is divided into strata and the sample consists of count days randomly selected from within each stratum. For simplicity, we chose to use equal-size strata of one week. We used two different methods to allocate sample days within strata: "proportional

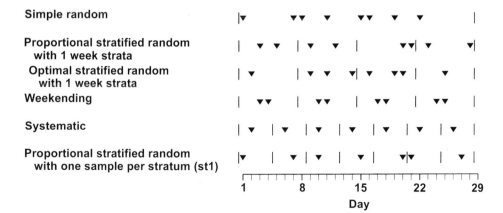

FIGURE 1. A schematic representation of possible sample allocations under six different sampling designs. Vertical lines represent the sampling strata for each design.

allocation" and "optimal allocation." In proportional allocation, the proportion of count days is the same in all strata. Because strata were all the same size, the number of sample days was the same in each stratum. In optimal allocation, strata in which the daily counts are more variable are given a greater frequency of sampling than strata with relatively homogeneous counts. With equal-size strata, the overall sample variance is minimized when the count days are allocated as follows:

$$n_h = n \frac{S_h}{\sum_{h=1}^{H} S_h}$$

(from Cochran 1977, formula 5.26), where n is the total number of count days, n_h is the number of count days in stratum h, and S_h is the standard deviation of the log-transformed daily counts in stratum h ($h = 1 .. H$). Because the timing of migration varied between species and years, no one allocation of count days could be optimal for all species in all years. We thus constructed a compromise allocation scheme at each monitoring station such that the number of count days in each stratum was proportional to the mean of the optimal allocation for that stratum over all years and species. When the compromise allocation of count days was non-integer, we used the nearest integer value, unless that value was zero, in which case we used one, or was greater than seven, in which case we used seven. For both stratified random designs, the sampling variance was calculated as

$$V_{strat} = \frac{1}{H^2} \sum_{h=1}^{H} \frac{S_h^2}{n_h} \left(\frac{N_h - n_h}{N_h} \right)$$

(Cochran 1977, formula 5.6), where H is the number of strata (number of weeks), N_h is the stratum size, n_h is the number of count days, and S_h^2 is the variance of the log-transformed daily counts in stratum h.

In the "weekending" design, counting is concentrated on two consecutive days each week. No formulae are available to determine the sampling variance of the annual indices under such a design, so we calculated the variance empirically. At a sample frequency of two days per week, there were seven possible sample allocations for each year, each subsample consisting of day i, $i+1$, $i+7$, $i+8$, $i+14$, $i+15$,... where $i = 1 .. 7$. We calculated the annual index from each subsample, and used the variance of these seven indices as an estimate of the sampling variance. At higher sample frequencies, additional counts were randomly located during each week, and we used 50 subsamples at each level of i to calculate the sampling variance.

In "systematic sampling," the sample consists of a fixed number of count days spaced at regular intervals throughout the season. The sampling variance is

$$V_{sys} = \frac{N-1}{N} S^2 - \frac{k(n-1)}{N} S_{wsy}^2$$

(Cochran 1977, formula 8.1), where S^2 and N are defined as with random sampling, k is the interval of the count days (e.g., when sampling on alternate days, $k = 2$), n is the number of count days and S_{wsy}^2 is the mean within-sample variance. Here,

$$n = N / k$$

and

$$S_{wsy}^2 = \frac{1}{k(n-1)} \sum_{i=1}^{k} \sum_{j=1}^{n} \left(y_{ij} - \bar{y}_{i\bullet} \right)^2$$

where y_{ij} is the jth log-transformed count in sample i, and $\bar{y}_{i\bullet}$ is the mean of the log-transformed counts in sample i. To simplify the calculations, we removed the last few counts when the migration period was not an integer multiple of the count interval (k). In these cases, we used the same data to calculate the sampling variance for random sampling when determining the design effect.

Systematic sampling is often compared with "proportional stratified random sampling with one sample per stratum" ($st1$) because the two designs differ only in the allocation of samples within strata (Fig. 1). In $st1$, the stratum size is equal to k and one sample is drawn from each of the n strata. We calculated the variance for the $st1$ design using the same data as for systematic sampling and the formula given above for stratified random sampling.

We compared the sampling designs in two groups: (1) proportional stratified, optimal stratified, and weekending, and (2) systematic and $st1$. In the first group, we calculated design effects at all integer sampling frequencies from two to six days per week (two days per week being the minimum for the weekending design). In the second group, we calculated design effects at all integer count intervals from $k = 2$ (sampling every other day) to 7 (once per week), which gave sampling frequencies of 3.5, 2.33, 1.75, 1.4, 1.17, and 1 day per week. For both groups, we performed the comparison using a repeated-measures analysis of variance, with species as the subject and sampling design and sampling frequency as the within-subject factors. Because design effect is a ratio measurement, all comparisons took place on the log scale, and were then back-transformed to the arithmetic scale for the presentation of results.

RESULTS

A total of 38 species was observed at the Point Reyes station in fall, and 81 at Long Point in spring. Of these, six species occurred with a mean count of 1.0 bird/120 net-h or greater during the fall migration period at Point Reyes and 46 species had daily counts of 1.0 or greater during spring migration at Long Point. For these more common species, there was considerable variation in the distribution of the log-transformed daily counts (Fig. 2). Most of the species with low mean counts had very skewed distributions, with a majority of zero counts and a few days when many birds were seen. Species with greater mean counts tended to have less skewed distributions. Some differences were also evident between stations (Fig. 3). Species at Long Point tended

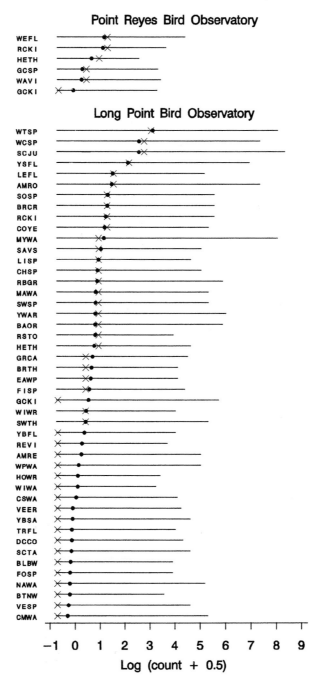

FIGURE 2. The mean (black dot), median (X), and range (horizontal line) of log-transformed daily counts for 52 species at two migration stations (see key to species codes in Appendix A).

to show greater variability in log-transformed counts (larger standard deviation), and have more skewed distributions than at Point Reyes.

The timing of migration varied between species, but the pattern of counts was similar for most species at both stations, showing a rise from low counts to a period of high counts and then a drop-off (Fig. 4). There were, however, distinct differences in the pattern of autocorrelation between the stations (Fig. 5). Species at Point Reyes tended to show an

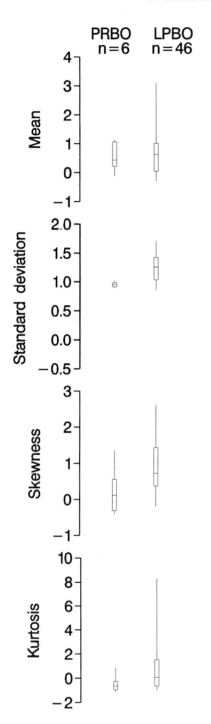

FIGURE 3. Boxplots showing the distribution of four statistics that describe the log-transformed daily counts for six species at Point Reyes Birds Observatory (PRBO) and 46 species at Long Point Bird Observatory (LPBO). The vertical lines show the median, the ends of the box show the inter-quartile range, and the horizontal lines show the range.

approximately linear decline in correlation between counts with increasing separation between count days. A few species at Long Point showed the same pattern, but the majority showed a sharp drop in autocorrelation so that the median correlation between counts spaced three days apart was close to zero. As noted previously, these differences could be due either to differences between stations or between seasons.

IMPORTANCE OF SAMPLING FREQUENCY

Statistical power declined at an accelerating rate with decreasing frequency of sampling for all species (Fig. 6). At Point Reyes, median power declined from 0.78 at a sample frequency of seven days per week to 0.59 at a sample frequency of one day per week. At Long Point, median power declined from 0.60 to 0.28 over the same range of sample frequencies.

The overall rate of decline differed between species, with some showing little effect of decreasing sampling frequency (e.g., Golden-crowned Kinglet [scientific names and key to four-letter codes in the Appendix] at Point Reyes; Slate-colored Junco at Long Point) and others being strongly affected (e.g., Hermit Thrush at Point Reyes; Chestnut-sided Warbler at Long Point). Species little affected were generally those with low power even at high sampling frequencies, while those strongly affected tended to have good power at high sampling frequencies (Spearman's rank correlation between rate of decline in power and power at a sampling frequency of seven days per week: $r_s = 0.89$, N = 6, P = 0.02 at Point Reyes Bird Observatory; $r_s = 0.26$, N = 46, P < 0.001 at Long Point Bird Observatory).

COMPARISON OF SAMPLING DESIGNS

There were consistent differences in design effect (and therefore in sampling variance) among sampling designs. These differences were statistically significant for both groups of sampling designs at Long Point, but not at Point Reyes (Table 1), although the sample size was low at the latter station (six species). Averaged over all sampling frequencies, optimal stratified sampling had the lowest design effect in group 1, and systematic was the lowest in group 2 at Long Point (Table 2). Although direct comparisons between all sampling designs are not strictly appropriate, since the two groups were measured at different sampling frequencies, it is clear that weekending performed very poorly (i.e., had the highest design effect), and the systematic design best (i.e., had the lowest design effect; Table 2). Average design effects were

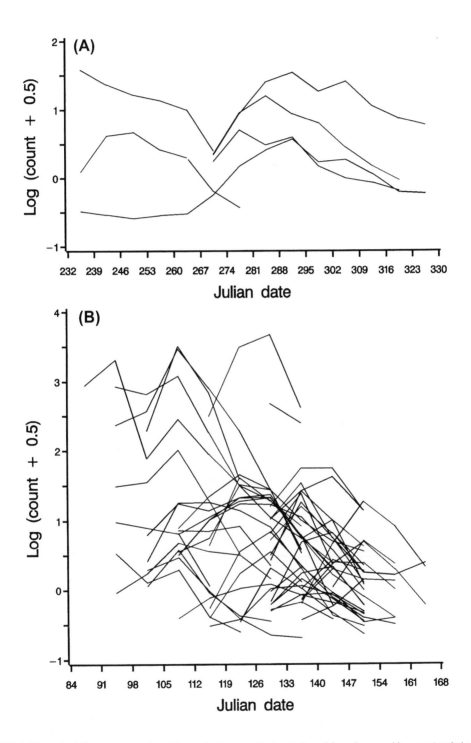

FIGURE 4. Change in daily counts over time at two migration monitoring stations. Lines show weekly mean (pooled across years) of the log-transformed counts during the migration period for each of six species at Point Reyes Bird Observatory (fall migration) and 46 species at Long Point Bird Observatory (spring migration).

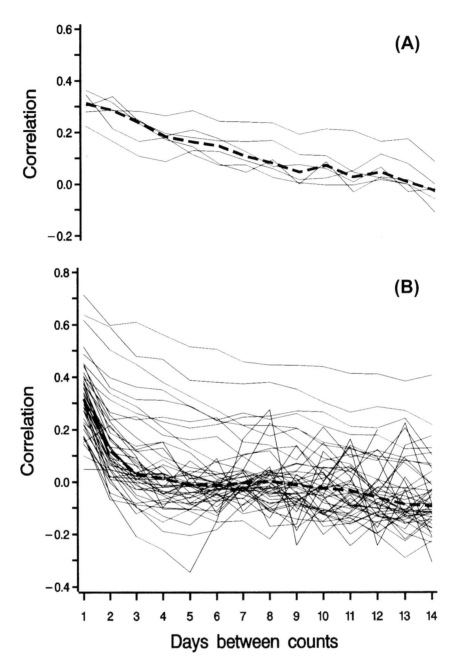

FIGURE 5. Autocorrelation between daily counts at two migration monitoring stations. Thin solid lines show the mean correlation over years between log-transformed counts for each of six species at Point Reyes Bird Observatory and 46 species at Long Point Bird Observatory. The thick dashed line shows the median of the species correlations.

similar among sampling designs at Point Reyes, and were not significantly different (Table 2).

There were also statistically significant effects of sampling frequency on design effect, and interactions between sampling frequency and sampling design

for both groups of sampling designs at Long Point (Table 1). The interactions are shown in Figure 7 (lower panel). For the group 1 designs, weekending performed very poorly at a sampling frequency of two days per week, and was the only sampling design to

TABLE 1. RESULTS OF REPEATED-MEASURES ANOVA TEST OF THE NULL HYPOTHESIS THAT DESIGN EFFECT WAS INDEPENDENT OF SAMPLING DESIGN AND SAMPLING FREQUENCY AT TWO MIGRATION MONITORING STATIONS.

	Point Reyes			Long Point		
Factor	df	F	P	df	F	P
Group 1:						
Sampling design	2, 10	1.37	0.30	2, 90	112.61	<0.001
Sampling frequency	4, 20	1.15	0.36	4, 180	112.04	<0.001
Sampling design × sampling frequency	8, 40	1.52	0.18	8, 360	72.95	<0.001
Group 2:						
Sampling design	1, 5	2.24	0.19	1, 45	44.92	<0.001
Sampling frequency	5, 25	0.70	0.63	5, 225	58.25	<0.001
Sampling design × sampling frequency	5, 25	0.43	0.83	5, 225	4.76	<0.001

Notes: Design effect measures the sampling variance of a sampling design relative to that of random sampling. Response variable was the log-transformed design effect for 6 species at Point Reyes Bird Observatory and 46 species at Long Point Bird Observatory. Group 1 designs (proportional stratified random with 1 week strata, optimal stratified random with 1 week strata, weekending) were tested at sampling frequencies of 2, 3, 4, 5 and 6 days per week. Group 2 designs (systematic, proportional stratified random with 1 sample per stratum) were tested at sampling frequencies of 1, 1.17, 1.4, 1.75, 2.33, 3.5 days per week. The sampling designs are defined in the text.

have a higher sampling variance than simple random sampling (i.e., design effect >1.0). At higher sampling frequencies weekending improved, becoming similar to the proportional stratified random design. Optimal stratified random sampling was similar to the proportional design at low sample frequencies, but improved as the frequency of sampling increased. For the group 2 designs, both systematic sampling and *st1* improved with increasing frequency of sampling, but in an erratic manner such that they were quite similar at a sampling frequency of 1.75 days per week ($k = 4$), but not similar at other frequencies.

At Point Reyes (Fig. 7, upper panel), the weekending design showed the same pattern of convergence upon the proportional stratified design with increasing sampling frequency, but, unlike Long Point, the optimal design and proportional designs were very similar at all frequencies of sampling. The *st1* and systematic designs showed no consistent patterns. For clarity, error bars were not shown on Figure 7, but they were very wide for all designs at

Point Reyes, due to the low number of species in the analysis.

DISCUSSION

Some readers will be disappointed to see that, even when there are no gaps in the count data, the median power to detect a population change of 50% over 25 years was 0.78 for the fall migration data from Point Reyes and 0.60 for the spring migration data from Long Point. This falls short of the goal suggested by the Monitoring Working Group of Partners in Flight (90% chance of detecting a decline of this magnitude; Butcher et al. 1993). However, a number of caveats should be made regarding our power analysis, and we begin the discussion by pointing these out. These limitations affect the level of power assigned to each species when there are no gaps in the count data; they do not greatly alter our main results regarding the relationship between statistical power and sampling frequency, which we

TABLE 2. GEOMETRIC MEAN DESIGN EFFECTS FOR FIVE SAMPLING DESIGNS AT TWO STATIONS. SMALLER DESIGN EFFECTS INDICATE SMALLER SAMPLING VARIANCE (RELATIVE TO RANDOM SAMPLING).

Design	PRBO		LPBO	
Group 1:				
Proportional stratified random with 1 week strata	0.69	A	0.77	B
Optimal stratified random with 1 week strata	0.69	A	0.75	C
Weekending	0.72	A	0.87	A
Group 2:				
Systematic	0.67	B	0.62	E
Proportional stratified random with 1 sample per stratum (st1)	0.66	B	0.70	D

Notes: Means were calculated over six species at Point Reyes Bird Observatory (PRBO) and 46 species at Long Point Bird Observatory (LPBO), and over five sampling frequencies for Group 1 and six sampling frequencies for Group 2. Values in a column with the same letters were not significantly different in paired comparison of means from a repeated-measures ANOVA for each group with log-transformed design effect as the response variable and design and sampling frequency as factors (Bonferroni *t*-tests with experimentwise $\alpha = 0.05$).

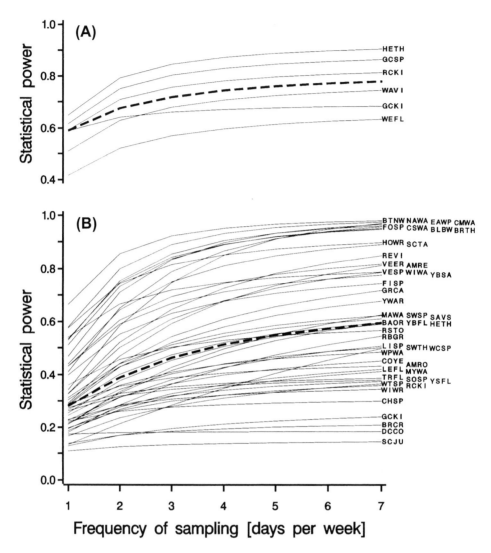

FIGURE 6. Statistical power to detect a 50% change in counts over 25 year and over a range of sampling frequencies at two migration monitoring stations, assuming random allocation of count days. Thin solid lines show the power for each species (species abbreviations at right of plot; see Appendix A for key). The thick solid line shows the median power at each sampling frequency.

discuss next. We finish by discussing the comparison of sampling designs.

LIMITATIONS OF THE POWER ANALYSIS

Our study was not designed as a rigorous evaluation of the ability of the two monitoring stations to detect population trends. To treat all species at both stations in the same manner, and to make the analysis tractable, we made a number of simplifying assumptions. Thus, a number of caveats should be made regarding our results.

First, we assumed that population trends could be estimated using a linear regression of annual indices against time on the log scale. However, for many species the indices do not conform very closely to the assumptions of a linear regression model. A number of other statistical models of trend could be used (such as non-parametric models or empirical smoothing, with different error models; Gerrodette 1987, Thomas and Martin 1996, Thomas 1997), which would almost certainly produce different estimates of power. In addition, we calculated annual indices as the mean of the logged daily counts. However, much of the

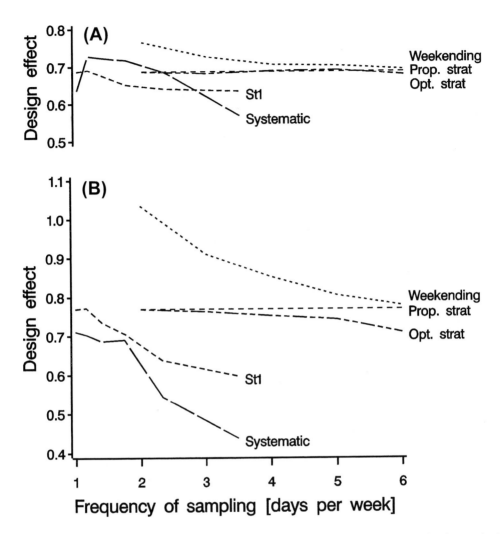

FIGURE 7. Design effect of five sampling designs over a range of sampling frequencies at two migration monitoring stations. Each line is the geometric mean design effect for the sampling design over six species at Point Reyes Bird Observatory and 46 species at Long Point Bird Observatory. Smaller design effects indicate smaller sampling variance (relative to random sampling). See Appendix A for key to species codes.

day-to-day variation in counts may be attributed to environmental factors such as wind direction and phase of the moon. Multiple regression approaches can be used to correct for these factors (e.g., Hussell et al. 1992, Pyle et al. 1994), which can lead to less variability in the trend estimates (Pyle et al. 1994) and increased power to detect trends.

The second caveat regards the selection of data. Our method of selecting a migration period for each species was designed to exclude data collected during the period when the species was not migrating, and also to produce migration periods that were an integer number of weeks in length. Our criterion of

excluding species with mean daily counts of less than 1.0 was designed to minimize the bias associated with adding a constant to the daily counts before log transformation (see below). All such criteria are arbitrary in nature, and differences among analysts will undoubtedly lead to different data being selected and thus to different estimates of power.

Third, we estimated power at only one magnitude of trend (50% over 25 years). Statistical power is dependent upon the size of trend, number of years of monitoring and significance criterion ("α-level"). Thus, even species with low power using our criterion will show a statistically significant trend if the

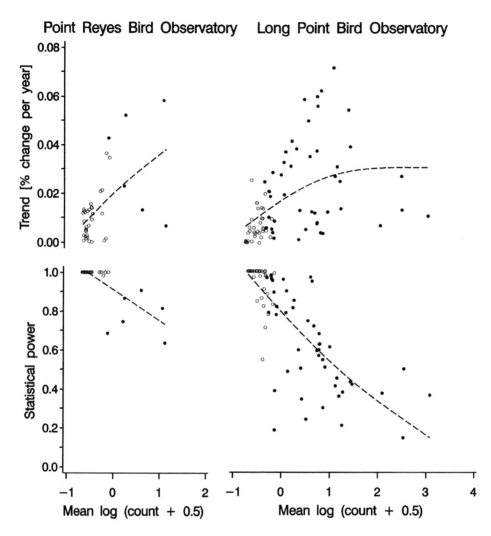

FIGURE 8. Relationship between absolute estimate of trend and statistical power (*y*-axis) and mean log-transformed count (*x*-axis) at two migration monitoring stations. Species that were excluded from our analysis (i.e., with a mean count of less than 1.0) are plotted with an open circle; those that were included are plotted with closed circles. A cubic spline (tension parameter 0.75) has been added to illustrate the pattern.

rate of change is steep enough, if there are enough years of data, or if the significance criterion is raised to greater than the customary level of 0.05. In addition, our analysis used two-tailed tests for population change, while the Partners in Flight criteria only refer to population declines. If we were not interested in detecting population increases then one-tailed tests could be used, which would result in higher statistical power (Gerrodette 1987, Cohen 1988, Steidl and Thomas 2001).

Lastly, we should emphasize that statistical power is a measure of the precision of an estimate,

assuming that the estimator is unbiased. In other words, we assumed that the annual indices, on average, reflect the true patterns of population change in the species they measure. There are two reasons why this may not be the case. Firstly, the estimate of trend will be biased if the proportion of the population that is counted varies with population size (see Sauer and Link *this volume*). The proportion of birds counted is often called the detectability, and cannot be measured directly from count data. Dunn and Hussell (1995) review the factors that may lead to differences in detectability in migration monitoring, and Sauer and

Link (*this volume*) show the statistical consequences. The second possible source of bias in the trend is the statistical procedure used to derive the estimate. In this case we added a constant before log transforming the counts. This is known to bias trend estimates (Link and Sauer 1994, Thomas 1997), causing underestimates of the size of the trend and also decreasing the variance of the estimate. The bias is greater at low abundances, where the constant is large relative to the counts, and so tends to swamp out any natural variability. Thus low abundance species will tend to have artificially high estimates of statistical power (because these estimates are based on the variance of the trend estimate), when in fact the bias towards no trend means that there is little chance of detecting a change in population size if one occurs. In our data, including all species observed at the two stations, there was a clear correlation between the size of species' trend estimates and their mean count, and between statistical power and mean count (Fig. 8). To control this bias, species with low counts are usually excluded from trend analyses that involve log-transformed data (e.g., linear route regression analysis of the Breeding Bird Survey; Geissler and Sauer 1990), as we did in our analyses by excluding species with a mean daily count of less than 1.0. This reduced the correlation between trend estimate and mean count, but the relationship between statistical power and mean count was still quite strong at Long Point (closed circles in Fig. 8). It is thus possible that our estimates of power for low-abundance species were overly optimistic.

In conclusion, due to the limitations outlined above, we caution readers not to place too much emphasis on the actual levels of power assigned to individual species, especially those with low mean counts. Further research is required before we can evaluate the importance of these limitations for assessing the ability of the two stations to detect trends. We do feel, however, that our results regarding the variation in statistical power with sampling frequency are qualitatively robust to these limitations. Because sampling variance increases at an increasing rate with decreasing frequency of sampling, missing count days will always be more important when the overall frequency of sampling is low. We discuss this further in the next section.

IMPORTANCE OF SAMPLING FREQUENCY

Gaps in the daily counts introduce sampling variance into the annual indices, which increases the unexplained variability about the trend line, and thus decreases the statistical power. Our results show that power declines at an accelerating rate with decreasing sampling frequency (Fig. 6), due to the accelerating rate of increase in sampling variance. Hence, a few missing count days have little effect on the power to detect trends for these species, but the effect of additional missing days becomes greater the more there are. Species most affected tended to be those with highest power, that is, those that are the best monitored.

We are reluctant to make general recommendations about a minimum frequency of sampling that should be used, because much depends upon the individual circumstances of each station. However it is plain from our results that frequencies of one or two days per week will likely lead to annual indices for most species that are too imprecise to be able to detect large population trends if they occur. This is supported by the recommendation in Hussell and Ralph (1998) that sampling take place on at least 75% of days within a species' migration window. In addition, if analysis methods that incorporate weather variables are to be used then a large sample of days is required to detect consistent effects (Francis and Hussell 1998).

COMPARISON OF SAMPLING DESIGNS

Many of the differences between sampling designs are explained by two features of the data: the strong seasonality in counts for each species (Fig. 4), and the autocorrelation between counts taken on days that are close to one another (Fig. 5). Seasonality favors sampling designs that lead to counts being taken throughout the migration period; these will tend to consistently capture seasonal variation in counts and, because of this consistency, will have low sampling variance. All of the designs we compared limited the number of count days per week (or per k in the case of systematic sampling and *st1*), and thus had lower sampling variances on average than simple random sampling (i.e., average design effects <1.0). The autocorrelation between counts taken on adjacent days was relatively high (median $\cong 0.3$), and in most species decreased with increasing distance apart of count days (Fig. 5). Thus in the weekending design, with two count days per week, the count data collected on the second day of each "weekend" contained similar information to that already collected on the first day, making it less efficient than the other designs. At higher sample frequencies, additional random days were sampled during the week, and allocation of count days became similar to that of proportional stratified random sampling.

Comparing the systematic and *st1* designs,

Cochran (1977:219–221) has shown that systematic sampling will necessarily have a lower design effect than *st1* if the shape of the correlogram is concave upwards. Many species in the Long Point spring migration data set exhibited correlograms that approximated this pattern, especially at four days between counts and less (Fig. 5). Species in the Point Reyes fall data set did not tend to show the same pattern, and systematic sampling did not appear to be better than *st1*, although the small sample size prevents us from making any strong inferences about differences between the designs at this station.

Overall, our results indicate that systematic sampling should be preferred over the other designs if sampling variance is the sole criterion. Systematic sampling also has the advantage of being easy to implement. However, three drawbacks of the design should be mentioned (see Cochran 1977 and references therein for details). The first is that there is no reliable way of calculating the sampling variance from the sample. Treating the data as if it came from a random sample will almost always result in an overestimate of the true variance. This is not a problem in the current application because the variance of the annual indices does not need to be calculated to estimate the variance of the trend estimate. Secondly, systematic sampling is very imprecise if the counts show a linear trend within the season. This could be a problem for migratory species with breeding populations at the station, because the abundance of birds will tend to show a monotonic increase in the spring and decrease in the fall. However, many migration stations use only the number of new birds captured in mist nets as the daily count (e.g., Point Reyes), or attempt to exclude the resident population from analysis using other techniques (see Dunn and Hussell 1995). We saw little evidence of linear trends in counts at either station in this study (Fig. 4). Where linear trends are suspected, the problem of imprecision may be avoided by making simple adjustments to the formula for calculating annual indices ("end corrections," Cochran 1977). Thirdly, systematic sampling can be very imprecise if the counts show regular periodic variation within the season. This is a potential problem at some stations, such as Long Point, where bird abundance at the station is thought to be related to the regular passage of weather fronts. However, even without adjusting the counts for environmental variables, we found systematic sampling to have a lower design effect than stratified random at Long Point. We thus suspect that imprecision due to periodic variation is unlikely to be a major concern.

Despite the higher expected design effects, stratified random designs have the advantage that it is always possible to derive an unbiased estimate of the sampling variance from the sample. Because of this, stratified random designs are often preferred when little or nothing is known about the distribution of the data being sampled (such as the possibility of periodic variation or linear trends in abundance within the migration period). In this study, optimal allocation performed similarly to proportional allocation at low frequencies of sampling, where the constraint of at least one sample per stratum made the two designs very similar. Even at higher frequencies, the optimal design was only slightly better. It appears that the optimal allocation for individual species were different enough to prevent the compromise optimum allocation from providing much overall benefit. In addition, it should also be noted that a real-life implementation of the optimal allocation formula would not have the true within-stratum variances to work with, but only estimates based on previous years' sampling. We conclude that optimal allocation schemes are probably not worth the extra effort involved in their implementation. If a stratified random design is chosen, perhaps because little is known about the region being sampled, then we recommend a proportional scheme over an attempt at optimization.

Sampling only on two adjacent days (weekending) produced the highest sampling variance of all the designs we compared. We recommend that if constraints are such that sampling can only occur on two days per week, then sampling one day in the weekend and once in the middle of the week should be encouraged.

CONCLUSIONS

1. The frequency of daily sampling will likely have an important effect on the ability of a migration monitoring station to detect trends for some species, regardless of the statistical method used to calculate annual indices and trends.

2. The effect of missing count days is not great when the overall frequency of sampling is high, but increases with decreasing sampling frequency. Species that are well monitored (i.e., high statistical power) are more strongly affected than species that are not well monitored. Single stations that operate on 1–2 days per week are unlikely to be able to detect large changes in the abundance of species that would be well monitored at higher frequencies of sampling.

3. Of the designs we compared, systematic sampling (i.e., counting at regular intervals) performed the best for the Long Point spring migration data,

yielding the lowest sampling variance over a range of sampling frequencies. We had too few species to tell whether the systematic design was any better than the others for the Point Reyes fall data, but it did not appear to be very much different. There are a number of problems associated with systematic sampling, but these are unlikely to be important in the context of migration monitoring. Also, a major advantage of this design is that it is easy to implement, because the sampling days are regular and predictable (e.g., every second day).

4. Stratified random sampling (i.e., dividing the season into one week strata and counting on random days within each week) yielded the next lowest sampling variance for the Long Point spring migration data. Proportional stratified random sampling (i.e., the same number of counts in each week) may be preferred over systematic sampling under conditions where an unbiased estimate of the variance of the annual indices is required. We also evaluated an optimal allocation scheme, which allocated more sampling effort to weeks in which the abundance of birds was more variable. This performed slightly better than proportional allocation, but would be difficult to implement in practice and so is not recommended.

5. Sampling only at weekends produced the largest estimates of variance of the designs we compared. If the station can only be open two days a week, we recommend counting once at the weekend and once during the middle of the week.

ACKNOWLEDGMENTS

We are indebted to the field staff and volunteers at the Palomarin Field Station of Point Reyes Bird Observatory and at Long Point Bird Observatory for their work in collecting the data that we used in this analysis. We thank M. S. W. Bradstreet for permission to use the data from Long Point. Reviews by E. H. Dunn, J. M. Hagan, III, K. Martin, and C. J. Ralph helped to improve earlier versions of the manuscript. This research was supported through grants from the Canadian Wildlife Service (National Wildlife Research Centre) and the Canadian Commonwealth Scholarship and Fellowship Program to L. Thomas and the National Sciences and Education Research Council of Canada to K. Martin.

APPENDIX. KEY TO SPECIES CODES IN FIGURES

Code	Species)
DCCO	Double-crested Cormorant (*Phalacrocorax auritus*)
YBSA	Yellow-bellied Sapsucker (*Sphyrapicus varius*)
YSFL	Northern Flicker (*Colaptes auratus*)
EAWP	Eastern Wood-Pewee (*Contopus virens*)
YBFL	Yellow-bellied Flycatcher (*Empidonax flaviventris*)
TRFL	Alder/Willow Flycatcher (*E. alnorum/E. traillii*)
LEFL	Least Flycatcher (*E. minimus*)
WEFL	Pacific-slope Flycatcher (*E. difficilis*)
WAVI	Warbling Vireo (*Vireo gilvus*)
REVI	Red-eyed Vireo (*V. olivaceus*)
BRCR	Brown Creeper (*Certhia americana*)
HOWR	House Wren (*Troglodytes aedon*)
WIWR	Winter Wren (*T. troglodytes*)
GCKI	Golden-crowned Kinglet (*Regulus satrapa*)
RCKI	Ruby-crowned Kinglet (*R. calendula*)
VEER	Veery (*Catharus fuscescens*)
SWTH	Swainson's Thrush (*C. ustulatus*)
HETH	Hermit Thrush (*C. guttatus*)
AMRO	American Robin (*Turdus migratorius*)
GRCA	Gray Catbird (*Dumetella carolinensis*)
BRTH	Brown Thrasher (*Toxostoma rufum*)
NAWA	Nashville Warbler (*Vermivora ruficapilla*)
YWAR	Yellow Warbler (*Dendroica petechia*)
CSWA	Chestnut-sided Warbler (*D. pensylvanica*)
MAWA	Magnolia Warbler (*D. magnolia*)
CMWA	Cape May Warbler (*D. tigrina*)
MYWA	Yellow-rumped Warbler (*D. coronata*)
BTNW	Black-throated Green Warbler (*D. virens*)
BLBW	Blackburnian Warbler (*D. fusca*)

APPENDIX. CONTINUED

Code	Species
WPWA	Palm Warbler (*D. palmarum*)
AMRE	American Redstart (*Setophaga ruticilla*)
COYE	Common Yellowthroat (*Geothlypis trichas*)
WIWA	Wilson's Warbler (*Wilsonia pusilla*)
SCTA	Scarlet Tanager (*Piranga olivacea*)
RSTO	Eastern Towhee (*Pipilo erythropthalmus*)
CHSP	Chipping Sparrow (*Spizella passerina*)
FISP	Field Sparrow (*S. pusilla*)
VESP	Vesper Sparrow (*Pooecetes gramineus*)
SAVS	Savannah Sparrow (*Passerculus sandwichensis*)
FOSP	Fox Sparrow (*Passerella iliaca*)
SOSP	Song Sparrow (*Melospiza melodia*)
LISP	Lincoln's Sparrow (*M. lincolnii*)
SWSP	Swamp Sparrow (*M. georgiana*)
WTSP	White-throated Sparrow (*Zonotrichia albicollis*)
WCSP	White-crowned Sparrow (*Z. leucophrys*)
GCSP	Golden-crowned Sparrow (*Z. atricapilla*)
SCJU	Dark-eyed Junco (*Junco hyemalis*)
RBGR	Rose-breasted Grosbeak (*Pheucticus ludovicianus*)
BAOR	Baltimore Oriole (*Icterus galbula*)

Studies in Avian Biology No. 29:112–115

USE OF MIST NETS FOR MONITORING LANDBIRD FALL POPULATION TRENDS, AND COMPARISON WITH OTHER METHODS

PETER BERTHOLD

Abstract. In Central Europe, a long-term trapping program based on mist netting has been carried out since 1972. In this "MRI-program," about 40 migratory landbird species are studied annually throughout the fall migratory period. Netting figures from this strictly standardized program are used to monitor trends of populations. Comparisons with other data show that the method can detect trends similar to those from breeding-season studies. Some illustrative examples are presented.

Key Words: migration, mist net, MRI-program, population monitoring.

In 1972, the Max Planck Research Centre for Ornithology, Vogelwarte Radolfzell, initiated a long-term bird trapping program that focuses on a variety of research fields, including migration studies. One of its main purposes is to monitor trends in population size. The program is based on mist netting of about 40 migratory landbird species during the complete fall migratory period. The program was named "Mettnau-Reit-Illmitz-Program" ("MRI-program"), after the large trapping stations in Germany and Austria where it was initially launched. It was extended to five stations in 1992 in eastern Germany and Russia. Up to 1993, about 400,000 individuals (first traps and retraps) were captured. One of the essential characteristics of the MRI-program is to keep the basic conditions for trapping birds as constant as possible, and it is the most standardized long-term trapping program in the world.

Several studies have used annual MRI trapping totals to detect long-term population trends. Trends from the MRI-program for the 10-year period 1974–1983 (Berthold et al. 1986), and from the Mettnau station for the 20-year period 1972–1991 (Berthold et al. 1993) and the 25-year period 1972–1996 (Berthold et al. 1998) were validated through comparison with trends from other studies. Here we show examples for four species.

METHODS

Nets are set up every year on June 30 and used continuously until November 7. Only in 1987 was there no trapping activity, due to flood conditions. All operations of the nets, handling of birds, and data collection have been described in detail elsewhere (Berthold et al. 1991, Kaiser and Berthold *this volume*). All aspects of operations were strictly standardized, even to the extent of nets being set at the same height above the ground each year, and with the same distances between shelf strings.

The study areas are large, mostly with climax vegetation. In addition, vegetation is trimmed to a constant height around the area of the nets.

Because netting is so standardized, there is no need to present results as effort-corrected capture totals, and we use total birds captured within the species-specific fall migration period as the annual index of abundance. Long-term trends in annual indices were calculated as the slope of the regression of annual total number of birds captured on year (Berthold et al. 1993).

RESULTS

Here we compare population data for four species from the MRI-program with independent data from other sources.

The Robin (*Erithacus rubecula*) is one of the few passerine species with no reported recent decline in a central, western, or northern European population. In fact, its populations are considered exceptionally stable (Bezzel et al. 1992, Bauer and Berthold 1997). This is reflected in extremely constant indices according to the Common Breeding Birds Census (CBC) in Britain since the middle 1960s (Marchant et al. 1990; Fig. 1). A strikingly similar pattern was found in the annual netting totals of the MRI-program, with one of the lowest variations from year to year (coefficient of variation 18.96%; Fig. 1).

The Redstart (*Phoenicurus phoenicurus*) is known to be a species with decades-long and essentially continuous decline in large parts of Europe (Hildén and Sharrock 1982, Bauer and Berthold 1997). Only recently have some European populations appeared to stabilize or even increase slightly (e.g., Marchant et al. 1990). Such a long-term decline with a tendency to a possible recent stabilization is also shown in the netting figures from the MRI-program (Fig. 2).

In the Whitethroat (*Sylvia communis*) various investigations have found a population crash of

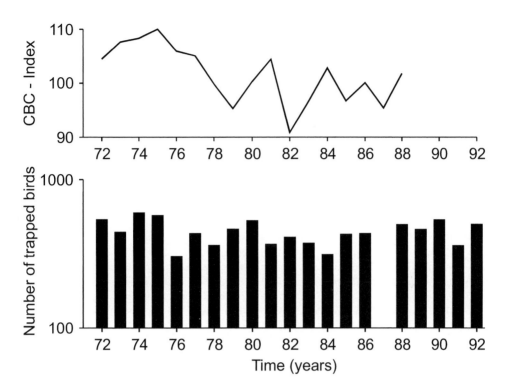

FIGURE 1. Population changes in the Robin. Above: CBC (Common Birds Census) indices from the British Isles (after Marchant et al. 1990). Below: fall netting totals from the MRI-program, Mettnau station, southern Germany (after Berthold et al. 1993).

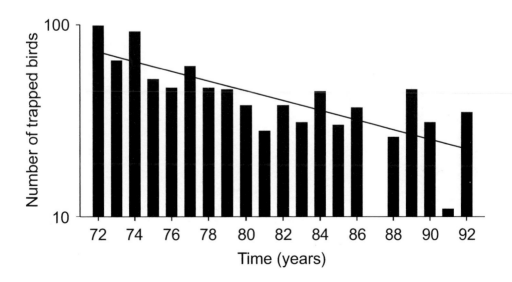

FIGURE 2. Decline in the Redstart, indicated by netting figures (fall totals) and the regression line from the MRI-program, Mettnau station, southern Germany. Slope of the regression analysis = -0.80, N = 909, P < 0.001 (after Berthold et al. 1993).

about 50 to 75% in large parts of Europe since 1968–1969, and a number of local populations have completely disappeared since 1969 (e.g., Berthold 1974, Bauer and Berthold 1997). An exceptionally severe drought in the Sahel zone, south of the Sahara, was recognized as the main cause of this sudden decline (Winstanley et al. 1974). We had just started standardized mist netting in a special "warbler program" on the Mettnau Peninsula in southern Germany in 1968, that is, one year before the population crash of the Whitethroat. These netting activities then merged directly into the MRI-program. They provided the unique opportunity to compare the observed population crash as assessed by our netting figures with the one deduced from the CBC by the BTO in Britain. The patterns of the crash and of the subsequent low population level obtained by the two methods are largely identical (Fig. 3).

The Willow Warbler (*Phylloscopus trochilus*) showed somewhat stable CBC indices in Britain from about 1965 to 1980 (Marchant et al. 1990). Then, it underwent a severe and almost continuous decline of about 60% over the following decade, with only very slight short-term recovery thereafter (Peach and Baillie 1993; Fig. 4). At the Mettnau station, netting rate was fairly constant until 1980, but since 1981 has been gradually dropping. The total decline amounted to 70% between 1981 and 1993. Again, trend in capture rates closely matched the trend in CBC figures for Great Britain (Fig. 4).

DISCUSSION

Factors affecting numbers of migrant birds at a particular stopover site were thoroughly reviewed by Dunn and Hussell (1995). Standardization of effort is important in ensuring that as constant a proportion as possible of the birds that are actually present will be captured on each day and in each year (Ralph et al. *this volume a*). The MRI methodology ensures that this will be the case, such that variation in numbers of birds captured will not simply reflect variation in effort or capture technique.

A crucial aspect of standardization that is often ignored by migration monitoring stations is the need to maintain habitat in the same condition, and vegetation at the same height, from year to year. Even if the same species and number of individuals were present from day to day, growth in vegetation alone could cause changes in the numbers of birds captured. For example, after vegetation grows higher than nets, a higher proportion of birds may fly over nets and avoid capture. Moreover, birds have habitat preferences that will cause them to move elsewhere if there are changes in preferred habitat type and structure (Bairlein 1981; see also Mallory et al. *this volume* regarding capture bias related to habitat structure). MRI stations control vegetation to prevent trends in capture rates over time that could be caused by change in vegetation rather than by change in bird numbers.

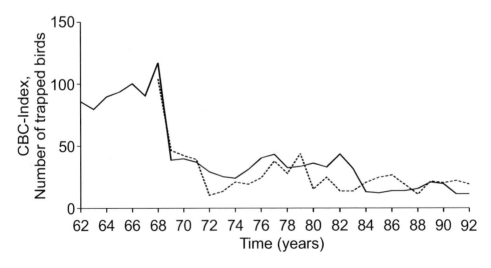

FIGURE 3. Population changes in the Whitethroat. Solid line: CBC indices from the British Isles (after Marchant et al. 1990). Broken line: fall netting totals from the MRI-program, Mettnau station, southern Germany (after Berthold et al. 1993).

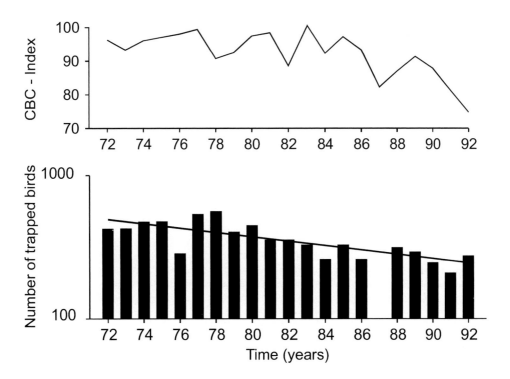

FIGURE 4. Population changes in the Willow Warbler, indicated by netting figures (fall totals) and the regression line from the MRI-program, Mettnau station, southern Germany. Slope of the regression analysis = -0.78, N = 7,240, P < 0.001.

Numbers of migrants captured are also affected by factors other than effort and habitat change, particularly weather (Dunn and Hussell 1995). Although daily sampling reduces the chances that a few days of large migratory flights will not dominate results, log-transformation of daily captures should be routinely used as a minimum treatment for migration counts (Dunn and Hussell 1995). More sophisticated analyses can be used to take into account data on season, weather, and other factors (Dunn et al. 1997, Francis and Hussell 1998), which further reduces variance in the data set and increases precision of population trend estimates (Dunn and Hussell 1995). However, even without any of these treatments, it is clear from the examples in this paper that migration capture data can mirror trends in breeding-population size as determined from independent data sources.

The examples shown compare migration capture data from Germany to breeding-population trends in Great Britain and Germany. Such agreement in the trends as demonstrated would only be expected for species that are changing in the same way over large areas. This will not be true of all species, and one of the unanswered questions for most migration monitoring stations is knowledge of the origin of migrants coming through their sites. In some cases birds from different breeding populations can be distinguished by plumage and measurement differences, and it is important that these data be collected to help identify the breeding populations that are being sampled (Berthold et al. 1991).

ACKNOWLEDGMENTS

I thank J. Dittami, E. Dunn, E. Gwinner, and C. J. Ralph, who have improved drafts of this paper.

Studies in Avian Biology No. 29:116–122

A COMPARISON OF THREE COUNT METHODS FOR MONITORING SONGBIRD ABUNDANCE DURING SPRING MIGRATION: CAPTURE, CENSUS, AND ESTIMATED TOTALS

Erica H. Dunn, David J. T. Hussell, Charles M. Francis, and Jon D. McCracken

Abstract. We compared long-term trends (1984–2001) based on three types of spring migration count data, from the three migration monitoring stations at Long Point Bird Observatory (southern Ontario), for 64 species. The three count methods consisted of daily capture totals from banding, sightings from a daily 1-h count on a fixed route ("census"), and "estimated totals" (ETs). The latter were estimates of birds detected in each study area each day, based on results from banding, census, and unstandardized "other observations." In the majority of species, ET annual indices were significantly positively correlated with both banding and census indices. Banding was not standardized, and variance of annual banding indices was higher than for other count methods, but trends based on banding alone were similar in magnitude to trends from census alone. Relative to trends based on banding or census alone, ET trends were positively biased, possibly as a result of change in estimation methods over time. Nonetheless, because ETs combine data from a variety of count methods, more species can be monitored, with greater precision, than by using one count method alone. Comparison of trends among stations suggested an influence of habitat change at one location. Biases should be minimized with strict standardization of all component count methods, adherence to a clear protocol for ETs, and management of vegetation to prevent systematic habitat change.

Key Words: banding, Breeding Bird Survey, census, estimated totals, habitat bias, migration monitoring, population trend, trend analysis.

Standardized counts of migrating birds can be used to calculate population trends, which have been shown to correlate with trends from the Breeding Bird Survey (BBS; Hussell et al. 1992, Dunn and Hussell 1995, Dunn et al. 1997, Francis and Hussell 1998). Recommended guidelines for migration counting (Hussell and Ralph 1998) state that each monitoring station should select the count method that is most suitable for the location, which may include daily banding, route surveys, counts of birds moving past a fixed point, or some combination of count methods. Different counting techniques may be more suitable for certain types of migratory species, and magnitude of counts will differ among methods, but as long as count protocol at any station is followed consistently, trends should be the same regardless of the type of migration count. However, this assertion has not previously been tested.

Here we present results of separate trend analyses for different count methods from the Long Point Bird Observatory (LPBO), in southern Ontario. At each of three stations (all within 30 km of one another), there was daily banding and a daily "census" (approximately 1-h survey of birds along a fixed route). In addition, records were kept of all birds detected during these and other activities in the day ("other observations"). At the end of the day, all personnel gathered to agree on "estimated totals"

(ETs). These were estimates of the total number of individuals detected in the defined study area that day, based on all available data. We estimated trends based on banding totals, census counts, and ETs separately, then compared them with each other and with trends from BBS.

Whatever methods are selected for migration counts, it is important to use them in a standardized and consistent manner from day to day and year to year, so that variation in counts will not reflect changes in methods (Ralph et al. *this volume a*). At Areas 1 and 2 (the two stations on the Long Point peninsula), early successional dune habitat consists of constantly shifting shorelines and vegetation patches, which has required periodic change in net locations. Moreover, the number of nets that can be operated safely, and the effectiveness of the nets, varies with wind strength at these exposed locations. Areas 1 and 2 each had a Heligoland trap (Woodford and Hussell 1961) that was often used in addition to nets, or in place of nets when weather precluded netting. Banding at Area 3 (the third station, at the mainland end of Long Point) was more standardized in net placement, but not necessarily in number of nets operated or daily operating hours. The census, on the other hand, has always been conducted in a consistent manner at all stations. A comparison of trends based on census or banding alone should therefore allow us to examine the effect of standardization in banding on population trends. Comparison with ET trends should indicate the relative importance of each survey method for particular species, and show whether combining data from different count methods adds to the effectiveness of monitoring.

METHODS

Data were collected from mid-April to early June, 1984–2001, at LPBO's three stations on Long Point, on the north shore of Lake Erie. For each of 64 species of common migrants (Table 1), we calculated annual indices for three data sets (daily banding totals, census, and ETs) for each station separately, and in a composite analysis that produced indices for all stations together.

Banding data were the raw daily banding totals (new captures only), unadjusted for effort. Ideally, capture totals should be corrected for effort either through calculating birds per unit effort (e.g., net-h, trap-h; or, for Heligoland traps, trap-drives), or through including effort as a covariate. However the effort data have not been computerized, and extraction was ruled out for this analysis because time and cost were prohibitive. Even if the data were available, there is no simple way of combining effort-corrected results from each type of capture method.

The Long Point "census" was not a true total count, but rather a daily survey that recorded all birds identified by sight or sound along a fixed route that wound throughout the study area. The census was usually (but not always) done by one observer. Personnel often changed from day to day, and nearly always from year to year, so long-term trends should not be affected by systematic observer bias. Each walk lasted about 1 h and was conducted in early or mid-morning. The route at Area 1 was altered in 1986 and the route at Area 2 in 1988 to accommodate loss of area due to erosion, but otherwise the routes remained fixed.

"Other observations" consisted of sightings within the defined study area additional to census, but there was no standardization of the amount of time expended or number of observers contributing. As noted above, the "defined study area" was altered somewhat at Area 1 in 1986 and at Area 2 in 1988.

ETs were derived jointly at each day's end by all participants. The ETs were intended to be carefully considered estimates of numbers detected in the study area that day, based on banding, census, and other observations. Double-counting was avoided where possible by taking into account numbers retrapped and likelihood that independent sightings were actually of the same birds. The ET procedure was devised in part to overcome the problems posed by a banding program that could not be fully standardized, and the census was intended to provide consistent daily input. ETs were the best estimate by personnel at the station of birds detected each day, regardless of variation in effort put into the various component counts.

Data were included in analyses only for dates within a species-specific time period judged to constitute the spring migration season of each species at Long Point (Hussell et al. 1992). Annual indices were calculated from a regression procedure designed to assign variability in daily counts to date, weather, moon phase, and year (Francis and Hussell 1998). Composite analyses (designed to produce indices combining data from all three stations) also included dummy variables for station, and for interactions between station and all other variables except those for year. Analysis methods are described in detail elsewhere (Hussell et al. 1992, Francis and Hussell 1998), and the following gives only a brief overview.

The dependent variable in the regression analyses was log (daily count + 1), in which the "daily count" was either the daily number of newly-banded birds, the number recorded on the daily census, or the daily estimated total (i.e., the analyses were run three times for each species). The constant was added to allow transformation of zeros, and 1 was chosen because it is the minimum change that can occur in daily counts. The log-transformed daily count was the dependent variable in a regression that included independent variables for year (dummy variables for each year except for one reference year; e.g., Y79 = 1 if the year was 1979, otherwise Y79 = 0), date (first through fifth order day terms), first and second order moon phase variables (days from nearest new moon and its square), and 12 weather variables. Weather variables were constructed using data from Erie, Pennsylvania (40 km south of the study locations), as detailed in Francis and Hussell (1998), and included daily values for horizontal visibility, cloud cover, first and second order terms for temperature difference from normal, and first and second order terms of four wind variables. Annual abundance indices were calculated from the coefficients of the dummy variables for year that were estimated in the regression. The annual abundance index was the adjusted mean for year plus one-half of the error variance of the regression (so the corrected index in the original scale represented an estimate of the mean rather than of the median; see references in Hussell et al. 1992), back-transformed to the original scale. The adjusted mean for year represented the mean of the transformed daily counts under standardized conditions of day, weather, and moon. The annual abundance indices therefore represented the estimated numbers of birds that would be counted each year on the same average date in the season, under average weather and moon conditions.

Trends were calculated as the slope from the weighted linear regression of log-transformed annual indices on year. Weights were proportional to the number of daily counts in the year represented by the index.

We performed bivariate correlations between annual banding and census indices to determine level of correspondence. To determine whether banding and census had independent effects on ET, we performed multiple regressions for each species, with log-transformed ET annual index as the dependent variable, and log-transformed banding and census indices as independent variables.

To detect difference in trends according to count method, we conducted species-specific analyses of

TABLE 1. RELATIONSHIPS AMONG ANNUAL INDICES (1984–2001) FROM BANDING AND CENSUS (DATA FROM THREE STATIONS COMBINED) AT LONG POINT, ONTARIO

Species	Banding-census r^a	Contribution to ET^b		$R^{2\,c}$
		Census	Banding	
Black-billed Cuckoo (*Coccyzus erythropthalmus*)	0.66**	***		0.63
Red-headed Woodpecker (*Melanerpes erythrocephalus*)	0.92***	***		0.93
Yellow-bellied Sapsucker (*Sphyrapicus varius*)	0.74***	***		0.75
Northern Flicker (*Colaptes auratus*)	0.75***	***		0.83
Eastern Wood-Pewee (*Contopus virens*)	0.35	**	+	0.53
Yellow-bellied Flycatcher (*Empidonax flaviventris*)	0.41+	*	***	0.76
Least Flycatcher (*E. minimus*)	0.35		***	0.71
Eastern Phoebe (*Sayornis phoebe*)	0.77***	***	*	0.89
Great Crested Flycatcher (*Myiarchus crinitus*)	-0.04	**		0.28
Blue-headed Vireo (*Vireo solitarius*)	0.90***	*	**	0.90
Warbling Vireo (*V. gilvus*)	0.29	***		0.85
Philadelphia Vireo (*V. philadelphicus*)	0.67**		**	0.72
Red-eyed Vireo (*V. olivaceus*)	0.62**	+	***	0.73
Brown Creeper (*Certhia americana*)	0.85***		**	0.85
House Wren (*Troglodytes aedon*)	0.44+	***	***	0.86
Winter Wren (*T. troglodytes*)	0.76***	***	***	0.94
Golden-crowned Kinglet (*Regulus satrapa*)	-0.28	***	*	0.85
Ruby-crowned Kinglet (*R. calendula*)	0.74***	**	*	0.80
Blue-gray Gnatcatcher (*Polioptila caerulea*)	0.35	***	+	0.73
Veery (*Catharus fuscescens*)	0.59**	**	***	0.89
Gray-cheeked Thrush (*C. minimus*)	0.16	*	***	0.67
Swainson's Thrush (*C. ustulatus*)	0.56*	**	***	0.85
Hermit Thrush (*C. guttatus*)	0.67**		**	0.62
Wood Thrush (*Hylocichla mustelina*)	0.48*	*	***	0.71
American Robin (*Turdus migratorius*)	0.08	***		0.69
Gray Catbird (*Dumetella carolinensis*)	0.88***	**	*	0.91
Brown Thrasher (*Toxostoma rufum*)	0.79***	**		0.75
Tennessee Warbler (*Vermivora peregrina*)	0.81***	*	***	0.88
Nashville Warbler (*V. ruficapilla*)	0.78***	***		0.81
Yellow Warbler (*Dendroica petechia*)	0.73***	***	***	0.97
Chestnut-sided Warbler (*D. pensylvanica*)	0.70**		***	0.69
Magnolia Warbler (*D. magnolia*)	0.47*		***	0.85
Cape May Warbler (*D. tigrina*)	0.82***	**	*	0.86
Black-throated Blue Warbler (*D. caerulescens*)	0.67**		***	0.78
Yellow-rumped Warbler (*D. coronata*)	0.82***	***		0.78
Black-throated Green Warbler (*D. virens*)	0.67**	**		0.60
Blackburnian Warbler (*D. fusca*)	0.43+	*	*	0.55
Palm Warbler (*D. palmarum*)	0.36	***		0.75
Bay-breasted Warbler (*D. castanea*)	0.80***	*	*	0.80
Blackpoll Warbler (*D. striata*)	0.79***	***	**	0.91
Black-and-white Warbler (*Mniotilta varia*)	0.81***	*	+	0.73
American Redstart (*Setophaga ruticilla*)	0.59*		***	0.80
Ovenbird (*Seiurus aurocapilla*)	0.85***	**	***	0.93
Northern Waterthrush (*S. noveboracensis*)	0.79***	**	***	0.93
Mourning Warbler (*Oporornis philadelphia*)	0.33	**	***	0.72
Common Yellowthroat (*Geothlypis trichas*)	0.71**	**	**	0.80
Wilson's Warbler (*Wilsonia pusilla*)	0.20	**	***	0.78
Canada Warbler (*W. canadensis*)	0.34	+	**	0.61
Scarlet Tanager (*Piranga olivacea*)	0.60**	***		0.86
Eastern Towhee (*Pipilo erythropthalmus*)	0.75***	***	+	0.90
Chipping Sparrow (*Spizella passerina*)	0.79***	***	*	0.92
Field Sparrow (*S. pusilla*)	0.55*	**	**	0.76
Vesper Sparrow (*Pooecetes gramineus*)	0.54*	**	+	0.60

TABLE 1.   CONTINUED

Species	Banding-census r[a]	Contribution to ET[b]		R[2 c]
		Census	Banding	
Savannah Sparrow (*Passerculus sandwichensis*)	0.83***	**		0.76
Fox Sparrow (*Passerella iliaca*)	0.63**	***	+	0.85
Song Sparrow (*Melospiza melodia*)	0.77***	*		0.59
Lincoln's Sparrow (*M. lincolnii*)	0.46+	***	***	0.86
Swamp Sparrow (*M. georgiana*)	0.81***	***		0.90
White-throated Sparrow (*Zonotrichia albicollis*)	0.85***		*	0.75
White-crowned Sparrow (*Z. leucophrys*)	0.73***	***	*	0.87
Dark-eyed Junco (*Junco hyemalis*)	0.79***	*		0.55
Rose-breasted Grosbeak (*Pheucticus ludovicianus*)	0.68**	***		0.85
Indigo Bunting (*Passerina cyanea*)	0.88***	*		0.76
Baltimore Oriole (*Icterus galbula*)	0.38	***		0.72

[a] Correlation coefficient between annual indices from banding and census.
[b] Significance of partial correlation coefficient in regression of ET indices on indices for banding and census, indicating whether the count method significantly influenced ET independently of the other count method (* = $P < 0.05$, ** = $P < 0.01$, *** = $P < 0.001$).
[c] Proportion of annual variation in ET indices explained by census and banding indices (R^2 of regression described in footnote b). All R^2 were significant (symbols not shown).

covariance with count method as the factor and year as co-variate. We examined interactions between count method and year. Significant interactions indicated trends that differed in slope.

We compared variability in indices among count methods by calculating variance in the residuals from linear regressions of log-transformed indices on year (thereby removing variability related to long-term trends in the data).

To determine whether trends from different stations or those based on different count methods produced the same magnitude of trend (e.g., comparing the 64 species, trends based on census from Area 1 to those from Area 2), we conducted reduced major axis regression on pairs of trends (Bohonak 2002). If trends from the two sources correspond in magnitude, then the regression results would show an intercept of 0 and a slope of 1.

RESULTS

Analysis of annual indices based on data pooled from all three stations showed that banding and census indices were usually correlated with each other (73% of 64 species). In 35 species, banding and census each had independent influences on annual

ET indices, even though banding and census indices were usually correlated with each other (Table 1). In 20 additional species, banding did not add anything to ETs after census had been taken into account, and in 9 species the reverse was true. For these 29 species, the non-contributing count method usually had much lower mean counts than the other, and thus had little influence on the ET indices whether or not the banding and census indices were correlated with each other. A few species had very low R^2 values (most notably Great Crested Flycatcher [scientific names in Table 1]), indicating that ETs were heavily influenced by observations other than those from banding and census. Results were similar when analysed for each station separately.

Variance of detrended annual indices based on banding was highest at Area 1, lower at Area 2, and lowest at Area 3 (Table 2), but there were no significant differences. Variability of indices based on census was more similar among stations, and ET indices were the least variable, but for all three count methods, variability was lowest at

TABLE 2. COMPARISON OF VARIANCE IN DETRENDED ANNUAL INDICES OVER 17 YEARS FOR DIFFERENT COUNT METHODS AND STATIONS AT LONG POINT, ONTARIO

Station	Mean variance ± SD[a] of indices based on		
	Banding	Census	ET
Area 1	0.47 ± 0.26	0.31 ± 0.21	0.21 ± 0.16
Area 2	0.33 ± 0.25	0.29 ± 0.23	0.22 ± 0.19
Area 3	0.17 ± 0.16	0.21 ± 0.16	0.13 ± 0.07
All stations combined	0.12 ± 0.13	0.11 ± 0.08	0.09 ± 0.05

[a] Mean and SD across species of individual species' variance of detrended annual indices.

TABLE 3. COMPARISON OF TRENDS FROM 1984–2001 BASED ON INDICES FROM DIFFERENT COUNT METHODS AT LONG POINT, ONTARIO

Area	Count methods compared	Slope	Intercept	R²
1	Census vs. band	0.85*	-0.57	0.56
	ET vs. band	0.70**	1.10**	0.73
	ET vs. census	0.83**	1.58**	0.83
2	Census vs. band	1.10	-0.81	0.29
	ET vs. band	0.90	1.40**	0.53
	ET vs. census	0.82**	2.07**	0.70
3	Census vs. band	0.78*	-0.78	0.09
	ET vs. band	0.76**	0.54	0.35
	ET vs. census	0.95	1.36**	0.63
All	Census vs. band	1.02	-0.34	0.51
	ET vs. band	0.93	1.16**	0.64
	ET vs. census	0.91*	1.46**	0.86

Notes: Slope, intercept, and R² from reduced major axis regression of the trends from the two count methods being compared (Bohonak 2002). Significance levels are for test of null hypothesis that slope is 1.0, and intercept is 0 (* = P < 0.05, ** = P < 0.01).

Area 3. Regardless of count method, variability was considerably reduced when indices were based on data from all three stations combined.

Trends from pairs of count methods were compared within stations, using reduced major axis regression. In Table 3, an intercept >0 indicates a tendency to a positive bias in the first count method relative to the second method in each pair. In seven of eight comparisons, ET trends were positively biased relative to banding and census. These eight comparisons also showed slopes <1 (significant in five cases), indicating that the positive bias was less in species with increasing trends than in those with decreasing trends (Table 3, Fig. 1). By contrast, census showed little bias relative to banding, although at two stations the slopes of the relationships were significantly <1, indicating a tendency to a negative bias in census relative to banding in increasing species and the opposite effect in decreasing species (Table 3).

A similar analysis compared trends within count methods between pairs of stations (Table 4). Trends at Area 3 were strongly more negative, for all count methods, relative to trends at Areas 1 and 2 (as shown by the negative intercepts). However, slopes tended not to differ between stations (seven of nine comparisons).

DISCUSSION

Lack of standardization in banding added variability to annual indices. Variability was highest at the station with least standardization (Area 1), and lowest where netting effort was most uniform

(Area 3; Table 2). Increased variability reduces trend precision, such that it will take longer to detect a significant population change. However, increased variance of banding indices did not have a detectable effect on magnitude of estimated trends, which showed the same relationship to census trends at all three stations (Table 3).

The ET procedure incorporates data from census as well as from banding (Table 1), and ET indices were less variable than banding or census indices alone (Table 2). ETs therefore performed their intended function of removing some of the variability from unstandardized banding effort and adding information from other count methods.

Compared to banding and census, ETs tended to be positively biased (Fig. 1). Although we cannot be sure which method best represents actual population trends, there are several reasons to suspect that ETs might be positively biased. First, there appears to have been a change in the way ETs were estimated, starting in about 1993, with observers becoming less conservative in their estimates (E. Dunn et al., unpubl. data). In addition, there may have been an increase over time in the number of personnel, and longer hours spent in the field. We were unable to correct for variable effort in our analyses, and effort-correction is in any case an imperfect and time-consuming solution, particularly when many types of effort are combined. However, additional work could be done to determine the relative importance of these sources of bias. Regardless of the source of bias in historical data at Long Point, bias in trends from other stations or from Long Point in future can be minimized by ensuring that every aspect of data

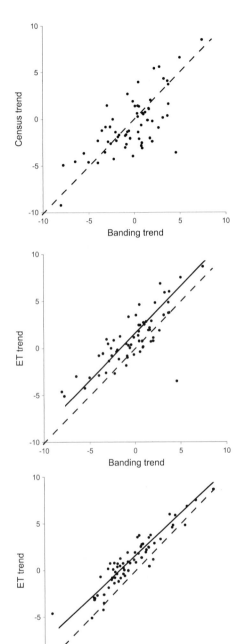

TABLE 4. COMPARISON OF TRENDS FROM 1984–2001 BASED ON INDICES FROM THREE DIFFERENT COUNT AREAS AT LONG POINT, ONTARIO

Count method	Areas compared	Slope	Intercept	R^2
Banding	2 vs. 1	0.75**	-0.41	0.22
	3 vs. 2	1.08	-3.19**	0.12
	3 vs. 1	0.80	-3.79**	0.03
Census	2 vs. 1	0.97	-0.73	0.24
	3 vs. 2	0.84	-2.72**	0.24
	3 vs. 1	0.74**	-3.42**	0.24
ET	2 vs. 1	0.95	0.01	0.30
	3 vs. 2	0.96	-3.35**	0.25
	3 vs. 1	0.91	-3.58**	0.43

Notes: Slope, intercept, and R^2 are from reduced major axis regression of the trends from the two areas being compared (Bohonak 2002). Significance levels are for test of null hypothesis that slope is 1.0, and intercept is 0 (* = $P < 0.05$, ** = $P < 0.01$).

collection is strictly standardized, as recommended by Ralph et al. (*this volume* a).

We found clear evidence of station differences in population trends. We have no reason to suspect that the strongly more negative trends at Area 3, relative to trends at the other two stations, were related to station differences in data collection. One possible explanation is differential habitat change among the three stations. Area 3 is a small woodlot surrounded by marsh and cottage. The vegetation at this station, especially the trees, grew steadily taller throughout the study period and understory was reduced. Many of the species for which the trend at Area 3 was the lowest (most negative) of the three stations, both for banding and census, are large and conspicuous. These species would probably have been detected if present, so we suspect they do not use the location now as often as in the past (e.g., Northern Flicker, Great Crested Flycatcher, nearly all thrushes, Brown Thrasher, Gray Catbird, Rose-breasted Grosbeak, Scarlet Tanager, Baltimore Oriole). However, another 23 species with their lowest trends at Area 3, made up mostly of warblers and vireos, could have been present but detected and captured in mist nets with lower probability as the canopy grew higher and more dense. In contrast to Area 3, Areas 1 and 2 are maintained at relatively early successional stages by storms and shifting of dunes. Although habitat at these two areas is certainly not constant, change appears to be less directional over time.

It is often stated in the migration monitoring literature that habitat change could bias population trends, but this is often ignored when study locations are selected and results are being interpreted. The difference between trends at Area 3 and the other

FIGURE 1. Comparison of population trends at Long Point, Ontario, based on different data sources (data pooled from all stations). ET trends were positively biased relative to trends based on banding or census alone. Dashed line indicates one-to-one correspondence between trends; solid line shows fit according to reduced major axis regression (shown only if different from the dashed line).

two sites at Long Point suggest that habitat effects could be substantial, and emphasizes the importance of having an effective habitat management protocol for long-term studies.

ACKNOWLEDGMENTS

We thank J. Wojnowski and B. Harris for extracting the Long Point banding and census data for this analysis, and the scores of volunteer participants who collected the data. Valuable comments were made on the manuscript by C. J. Ralph, J. Faaborg, G. R. Geupel, and J. R. Sauer. This paper is a contribution of Long Point Bird Observatory, Bird Studies Canada, and is Ontario Ministry of Natural Resources (Wildlife Research and Development Section) Contribution No. 94-02.

Studies in Avian Biology No. 29:123–134

A COMPARISON OF CONSTANT-EFFORT MIST NETTING RESULTS AT A COASTAL AND INLAND NEW ENGLAND SITE DURING MIGRATION

Christopher C. Rimmer, Steven D. Faccio, Trevor L. Lloyd-Evans, and John M. Hagan, III

Abstract. We compared population trends from spring and fall migration capture data from two constant-effort banding stations in New England: one coastal (Manomet Center for Conservation Sciences, hereafter "Manomet") and one inland (Vermont Institute of Natural Science, "VINS"). Data were examined for two time periods, 1981–1992 and 1986–1992. Twelve-year population trends were compared to regional Breeding Bird Survey (BBS) data for the same period. The two migration data sets showed little congruence. Of 22 species examined, Manomet data showed significant declines in 11 during one or both seasons, whereas seven species increased significantly at VINS. The number of significant trends at both sites increased between a 7-year and a 12-year sample. Among six species that were strictly transient at the two sites, five showed the same 12-year trend in fall. In general, Manomet tracked BBS data from the Northern Spruce-Hardwood region reasonably well, while VINS more closely tracked BBS trends from Northern New England. Neither site correlated well with BBS trends from Quebec. VINS captured significantly higher proportions of adult birds than did Manomet in 81% of species examined. However, the two sites tracked trends in age ratios largely independently. Several factors appeared to account for the weak congruence between sites, and we discuss the limitations in comparing these two data sets.

Key Words: age ratios, banding station, capture data, migration, New England, population trends.

Despite an extensive network of migration banding operations in North America and Europe, there have been relatively few studies to establish the validity of migration capture data to monitor bird population changes. Hagan et al. (1992) showed that a 19-year migration data set from the Manomet Center for Conservation Sciences (Manomet) in coastal Massachusetts correlated well with documented population changes in several passerine species that breed in northeastern North America. These included resident species (Tufted Titmouse and Northern Cardinal [scientific names listed in Table 1]), short-distance migrants (Golden-crowned Kinglet and Ruby-crowned Kinglet), and neotropical migrants (Tennessee Warbler, Cape May Warbler, and Bay-breasted Warbler). The Manomet data also corresponded with regional Breeding Bird Survey (BBS) data, as 24 of 38 species examined (63%) showed significant positive correlation of annual indices with those from BBS from at least one northeastern physiographic BBS stratum. Positive correlations between the Manomet and BBS data were more common for physiographic strata close to Manomet, suggesting geographic limitations to the usefulness of migration capture data.

However, Manomet trend data correlated poorly with those from another long-term migration banding station in eastern North America, the Powdermill Nature Reserve, located 800 km west–southwest of Manomet (Hagan et al. 1992). Of 40 species ana-

lyzed in both data sets, only one showed a significant positive correlation between the two sites. This suggested that different source populations undergoing independent changes were likely sampled at each site, and that local habitat changes might have biased samples of migrants through time, particularly at the Powdermill site.

In a study comparing 1979–1991 banding totals among 13 transient species at two Michigan sites 0.75 km apart, Dunn et al. (1997) found significant positive correlations between trends from capture data and those from Michigan and Ontario BBS data. Moreover, the trends between banding and BBS data were of similar magnitude. Although the two sites showed little overall correlation in trends, this was due to discrepancies in one species, and trend differences were small in most cases. These results suggested that standardized mist netting can serve as a useful and accurate population monitoring tool.

Other comparisons of banding capture data with regionally appropriate BBS data have also shown good concordance between the two (Hussell et al. 1992, Dunn and Hussell 1995, Francis and Hussell 1998), but relatively few comparisons between or among migration banding stations have been made. Under the assumption that migration capture data can accurately track population changes, such comparisons might provide valuable information on population trends within a given region. In this study we compare data from two northeastern U.S. migration

TABLE 1. BREEDING STATUS, SAMPLE SIZE, AND POPULATION TRENDS FOR SELECTED SPECIES FROM MIGRATION CAPTURE DATA AT MANOMET AND VINS, AND BBS DATA FROM NORTHERN NEW ENGLAND (NNE) AND NORTHERN SPRUCE-HARDWOOD (NS-H) STRATA, 1981–1992

Species	Code	Status[a] Manomet	Status[a] VINS	N captured Manomet Spring	N captured Manomet Fall	N captured VINS Spring	N captured VINS Fall	Trend (percent/yr) Manomet Spring	Trend (percent/yr) Manomet Fall	Trend (percent/yr) VINS Spring	Trend (percent/yr) VINS Fall	BBS trend (percent/yr) NNE	BBS trend (percent/yr) NS-H
Eastern Phoebe (*Sayornis phoebe*)	EAPH	B	B	63	123	61	373	nd	1.9*	nd	4.9	7.4*	3.9*
Red-eyed Vireo (*Vireo olivaceus*)	REVI	B	B	106	973	33	378	-1.1	-6.8*	nd	7.8	-1.2*	1.7*
Black-capped Chickadee (*Poecile atricapilla*)	BCCH	B	B	760	9,680	158	603	-11.1*	-8.6	8.1*	-3.9	2.8*	1.2
Ruby-crowned Kinglet (*Regulus calendula*)	RCKI	T	T	399	524	134	334	0.8	1.2	6.7	0.7	nd	2.0*
Veery (*Catharus fuscescens*)	VEER	T	B	213	209	25	151	-3.7*	-3.7	nd	7.9*	-0.8	-3.1*
Swainson's Thrush (*C. ustulatus*)	SWTH	T	T	510	358	3	265	-3.4	-2.8	nd	-1.6	nd	-2.9*
Hermit Thrush (*C. guttatus*)	HETH	B	B	537	403	17	573	4.7	2.0	nd	10.6*	10.3*	3.2*
American Robin (*Turdus migratorius*)	AMRO	B	B	370	1,977	70	1,378	-1.8	-6.0	nd	23.4*	0.9	0.7
Gray Catbird (*Dumetella carolinensis*)	GRCA	B	B	471	5,922	177	722	-2.5	-5.9*	3.4	1.4	-1.0	-3.9*
Nashville Warbler (*Vermivora ruficapilla*)	NAWA	T	T	23	116	17	236	nd	-1.8*	nd	-11.0*	-4.9*	-1.6*
Yellow Warbler (*Dendroica petechia*)	YWAR	B	B	268	114	141	30	-0.1	-2.4	-5.0	nd	-0.1	-0.1
Magnolia Warbler (*D. magnolia*)	MAWA	T	T	772	232	27	231	2.1	-2.2*	nd	-3.3	-6.4*	0.7
Yellow-rumped Warbler (*D. coronata*)	MYWA	T	B	183	4,446	377	935	1.4	-9.8*	10.8	-2.7	5.9*	-0.03
American Redstart (*Setophaga ruticilla*)	AMRE	B	B	921	1,047	70	112	-2.6	-5.5*	nd	-5.3	-0.9	-2.0*
Ovenbird (*Seiurus aurocapillus*)	OVEN	B	B	340	228	10	198	0.3	-1.7	nd	4.7	1.4*	-1.0*
Common Yellowthroat (*Geothlypis trichas*)	COYE	B	B	1,266	497	286	1,159	-1.3	-2.8*	-20.0*	-24.0*	-1.8*	-1.3*
Canada Warbler (*Wilsonia canadensis*)	CAWA	T	T	524	150	48	112	-3.5	-2.3	nd	-5.3	-1.2	-2.9*
Song Sparrow (*Melospiza melodia*)	SOSP	B	B	291	869	122	881	-1.9	-0.1	6.7*	-0.9	0.7	0.1
Swamp Sparrow (*M. georgiana*)	SWSP	T	B	314	257	31	206	0.7	3.0*	11.8*	5.9*	4.3	0.5
White-throated Sparrow (*Zonotrichia albicollis*)	WTSP	T	B	1,853	1,697	209	1,792	-3.6	-5.4	11.8*	19.4*	-2.2*	-1.7*
Dark-eyed Junco (*Junco hyemalis*)	DEJU	T	B	106	415	90	288	-3.3	-4.0*	nd	6.9*	-0.2	-3.0*
Purple Finch (*Carpodacus purpureus*)	PUFI	T	T	10	195	27	283	nd	-3.4	nd	6.3	-3.6	-5.3*

Note. "nd" denotes insufficient data for analysis.

[a] Status: T = strictly transient, B = regularly breeds within 25 km of banding site.

* denotes P = 0.05

banding stations, Manomet and the Vermont Institute of Natural Science (VINS). We use population indices based on migration captures to examine correlations between the two data sets, and we compare trends from banding data at each site with regional BBS trends to further assess congruence. We briefly examine age ratios and their correlation through time of fall migrants at both sites. Finally, we discuss the validity of comparing these two data sets in light of between-site differences.

METHODS

STUDY AREAS

Manomet, located on the western shore of Cape Cod Bay, Plymouth Co., Massachusetts (41°50'N, 70°30'W), lies about 250 km southeast of VINS, located in Woodstock, Windsor County, Vermont (43°36'N, 72°32'W). Both sites are characterized by heterogeneous second-growth deciduous shrub-woodland, consisting of brushy thickets interspersed with groves of largely mature trees. Hagan et al. (1992) described dominant vegetation on the 7-ha Manomet study plot. On the 3-ha study plot used for the VINS banding operation, dominant trees include sugar maple (*Acer saccharum*), bigtooth aspen (*Populus grandidentata*), black cherry (*Prunus serotina*), and white ash (*Fraxinus americana*); dominant shrubs include willow (*Salix* spp.), autumn olive (*Elaeagnus umbellata*), steeplebush (*Spiraea tomentosa*), hawthorne (*Crataegus* spp.), dwarf juniper (*Juniperus communis*), and common buckthorn (*Rhamnus cathartica*).

The rate of successional habitat change differed between Manomet and VINS, although vegetation data were not systematically collected at either site. Because of its coastal exposure, Manomet underwent little successional change during the 1981–1992 study period. Because of VINS's more sheltered, inland location, and the gradual maturation of its habitats from open farmland prior to 1970, relatively more rapid plant succession occurred at that site. Limited vegetation management at VINS during the study slowed the rate of habitat change, but vegetation height around some VINS nets likely increased by 50% or more over the 12-year period. Any effects of successional change on netting totals were probably more pronounced at VINS than at Manomet.

The two study sites occupy contrasting landscapes. Manomet is a 7-ha "oasis" in a coastal belt that is highly fragmented by suburban development, with an increasingly dense human population. VINS lies on a largely forested 32-ha preserve in a predominantly forested and unfragmented rural landscape, with little human population growth.

DATA COLLECTION

From 1969–1992, inclusive, Manomet annually operated 45–50 nylon mist nets (12 × 2.6 m, 4-panel, 36-mm extended mesh) at fixed locations. During the spring (15 April through 15 June) and fall (15 August through 15 November) migrations, nets remained open at least five days a week from 0.5 h before sunrise to 0.5 h after sunset. From 1981–1992, inclusive, VINS operated 15–20 mist nets (12 × 2.6 m, 4-panel, 36-mm extended mesh) each year, generally from 15 April to 15 June in spring, and 1 August to 15 November in fall. Standardization of the VINS operation was less uniform than at Manomet, and differed between 1981–1985 and 1986–1992. During the earlier period, nets were opened on an average of two to three days a week for three to five morning hours. Between 1986–1992, nets were opened five days a week for 6 h, beginning 0.5 h before sunrise. Although some net site locations at VINS shifted during the study period, nets were maintained at fixed locations after 1987. At both Manomet and VINS, nets were closed under adverse weather conditions, and records were kept of opening and closing times of nets.

Data Analysis

We analyzed data only for the period 1981–1992, when both banding stations were in operation. We compared both spring and fall data. We compared only those species for which ≥ 100 captures were obtained at each site, combined over both seasons and all years. To restrict our analyses to migrant birds, we eliminated all known or presumed breeding individuals, that is, those with enlarged cloacal protuberances or well-developed brood patches. For each species we calculated a site-specific temporal migration window, defined as those dates after the 1st percentile and before the 99th percentile of captures within each migration season, all years combined.

For each species we calculated a daily population index for each date within its migration window. This was derived by dividing the number of captured individuals of a species by the number of net hours for that date, multiplying that number by 1,000 and adding a constant of 1, then taking the natural log. We calculated an annual population index for each species at each site by computing the mean of the logged daily indices. This procedure smoothed out variation due to days with unusually large numbers of captures (Dunn and Hussell 1995). Population trends were then calculated as the slope of the annual indices regressed on year, producing an estimated annual percent rate of change. Because three species each had annual indices of zero in one year, we did not back-transform indices and remove the constant of one prior to calculating population trends, as log transformation of zero would have resulted in a negative index.

We examined population trends at Manomet and VINS by dividing the data into two time periods: the entire 12-year period from 1981–1992, and a 7-year subset from 1986–1992, during which time the VINS operation was relatively standardized. We suspected that the lack of uniform standards at VINS during 1981–1985 might have obscured or biased actual population trends at that site over the longer 1981–1992 study period. We thus compared trends over both 7 and 12 years.

We obtained BBS population trends for 1981–1992 from the U.S. Geological Survey's Patuxent Wildlife Research Center webpage (http://www.mbr-pwrc.usgs.gov/bbs/bbs.html). We compared trends from spring and fall migration capture data at both sites with trends from BBS data for three regions: Northern New England (physiographic strata 27), Northern Spruce-Hardwood (physiographic strata 28), and the province of Quebec. We believe that these three areas represent the most likely geographic source of migrants sampled at Manomet and VINS. We calculated Spearman rank correlations (one-tailed significance tests) between trends from VINS and Manomet banding totals and those from the BBS (SYSTAT 1998).

We compared age ratios in the migration window in those species with adequate sample sizes at both sites (see criteria above). We used only those species for which the proportion of unknown-age birds was less than 5% and less than the proportion of adults at each site. We used Manomet capture data from 1969 to 1992 and VINS data from 1981 to 1992. We excluded spring migrants from our analysis of age ratios due to generally small samples of known-age (second-year and after second-year) individuals at each site. We examined differences of age ratio differences using a t-test, and we compared annual changes in age ratios at both sites using a Pearson product-moment correlation (SAS Institute 1985).

RESULTS

Correlation Between Manomet and VINS Population Trends

The combined Manomet and VINS migration capture data set consisted of 22 species with sufficient sample sizes for between-site comparison (Table 1). Migration trends from 1981–1992 for all species combined for which there were data from both sites were uncorrelated both for fall ($r = -0.031$, $N = 21$ species, $P > 0.10$) and spring ($r = -0.238$, $N = 8$, $P > 0.10$; Fig. 1). For three species (American Robin, Common Yellowthroat, and White-throated Sparrow), VINS trends were biologically unrealistic (>15%/year increase or decrease), but excluding them did not improve the correlation among the remaining species in fall. Comparison of fall trends over the 7-year subset of data (1986–1992) revealed similarly poor correlation between the two sites ($r = 0.008$, $P > 0.10$).

Direction of Manomet and VINS Population Trends

Over the 12-year period, 13 species showed significant ($P \leq 0.05$) population trends in one or both seasons at Manomet, whereas populations of 10 species changed significantly at VINS (Table 1). During the

fall season, there was moderate agreement in the direction of trends between the two sites, with 13 (62%) species agreeing and eight (38%) disagreeing (Table 2). At Manomet, two species significantly increased in fall, whereas eight species experienced significant declines. VINS data showed significant increases in six species and significant declines in two. Swamp Sparrow was the only species to increase significantly at both sites in fall, whereas Nashville Warbler and Common Yellowthroat declined significantly at both. Only Dark-eyed Junco showed an opposite significant trend at the two sites, declining at Manomet and increasing at VINS (Table 1).

During the spring, there was little correspondence in trend direction between the two sites, with four species agreeing and four disagreeing (Table 2). At Manomet, three species showed significant population trends, all declines. Despite small sample sizes at VINS, which reduced the number of species included in spring analyses to eight, three species showed significant increases and one a significant decline (Table 1). No species showed the same significant trend at both sites, but Black-capped Chickadee declined significantly at Manomet while increasing significantly at VINS.

A comparison of population trends over both 12 and 7 years indicated that although most trends became non-significant over the shorter time period, three species showed significant population changes only during this period. Three species (Swamp Sparrow at Manomet, Common Yellowthroat and White-throated Sparrow at VINS) showed the same significant trend in the same season over both 12 and 7 years. Two species (American Redstart and Canada Warbler) at Manomet showed significant declines during both periods, but in different seasons. No species showed opposite significant trends at Manomet and VINS during 1986–1992.

Comparison of Banding Data with BBS Data

For neither site did trends correlate well with BBS trends from Quebec. Trends for all species from Manomet were significantly correlated with those from the Northern Spruce-Hardwood region when Black-capped Chickadee (an irruptive species) was excluded ($r = 0.424$, $N = 20$, $P < 0.05$) but not otherwise ($r = 0.312$, $N = 21$, $P > 0.05$; Fig. 2). The relationship between Manomet trends and BBS trends from Northern New England was weaker ($r = 0.112$, $P > 0.10$ for all species; and $r = 0.205$, $P > 0.10$ excluding Black-capped Chickadee).

TABLE 2. MEAN AGE RATIOS OF 21 SPECIES WITH ADEQUATE SAMPLE SIZES FROM FALL CAPTURES AT MANOMET (1969–1992) AND VINS (1981–1992)

Species	Mean age ratio (percent)			
	Manomet		VINS	
	After hatch year	Hatch year	After hatch year	Hatch year
Eastern Phoebe	10.99	89.01	7.43	92.57
Black-capped Chickadee	6.41	93.59	5.65	94.35
Ruby-crowned Kinglet	19.00	81.00	7.64	92.36
Veery	16.10	83.90	23.53	76.47
Swainson's Thrush *	5.57	94.43	36.47	63.53
Hermit Thrush	9.18	90.82	6.76	93.24
American Robin	4.86	95.14	9.51	90.49
Gray Catbird *	2.49	97.51	8.23	91.77
Red-eyed Vireo *	1.85	98.15	16.55	83.45
Nashville Warbler *	3.07	96.93	21.34	78.66
Magnolia Warbler *	5.08	94.92	33.57	66.43
Yellow-rumped Warbler	9.43	90.57	11.58	88.42
American Redstart *	2.86	97.14	18.32	81.68
Ovenbird *	2.69	97.31	17.49	82.51
Common Yellowthroat *	6.00	93.00	17.97	82.03
Canada Warbler *	3.18	96.82	21.45	78.55
Song Sparrow *	4.28	95.72	13.38	86.62
Swamp Sparrow *	1.87	98.13	28.50	71.50
White-throated Sparrow *	3.21	96.79	29.66	70.34
Dark-eyed Junco *	6.60	93.40	40.15	59.85
Purple Finch *	10.08	89.92	30.80	69.20

* denotes species with significantly different age ratios between sites (t-test, P < 0.05).

Similarly, trends from VINS were significantly correlated with those from Northern New England when White-throated Sparrow was excluded (r = 0.425, P < 0.05, n = 18), but not overall (r = 0.291, N = 19, P > 0.10; Fig. 3). Correlation with BBS from the Northern Spruce-Hardwood region was less strong (r = 0.083, P > 0.10).

Four specific examples, using fall data only from 1981–1992, illustrate the range of comparisons in population trends between the two sites and their congruence to regional BBS data:

Common Yellowthroat.—This species showed a highly significant decline in capture rate at both Manomet (r^2 = 0.410, P = 0.025) and VINS (r^2 = 0.851, P < 0.001; Fig. 4A). Both sites tracked a steady decline that was reflected in BBS data from both physiographic strata 27 and 28 (Table 1). However, the trend at VINS was so steep (24%/year) as to be biologically unrealistic.

Nashville Warbler.—Although population indices showed more variance over time for this species than for Common Yellowthroat, significant declines occurred at both Manomet (r^2 = 0.341, P = 0.046) and VINS (r^2 = 0.515, P = 0.009; Fig. 4B). These were also reflected in regional BBS data, as both strata 27 and 28 showed significant declines (Table 1).

Veery.—This species significantly increased at VINS (r^2 = 0.450, P = 0.017) and significantly decreased at Manomet (r^2 = 0.323, P = 0.054) during the study period (Fig. 4C). The population increase at VINS was due primarily to a pulse of migrants between 1989–1992. Regional BBS data indicated significant and nonsignificant declines in both strata. Veerys breed in the vicinity of the VINS banding station, and the increase at VINS may have reflected an increase in local breeding populations that masked a more widespread decline.

Red-eyed Vireo.—This species showed a significant decline at Manomet (r^2 = 0.482, P = 0.012), and a nonsignificant positive trend at VINS (r^2 = 0.287, P = 0.073; Fig. 4D). BBS data from the Northern Spruce-Hardwood region showed a significant increase in Red-eyed Vireos, whereas Northern New England BBS data showed a significant decline.

COMPARISON OF AGE RATIOS

Of the 21 fall migrant species for which we examined age ratios at the two sites, VINS captured a higher ratio of AHY (after hatching year) to HY (hatching year) birds for 17 (81%), whereas Manomet's ratio of AHY birds was higher for only

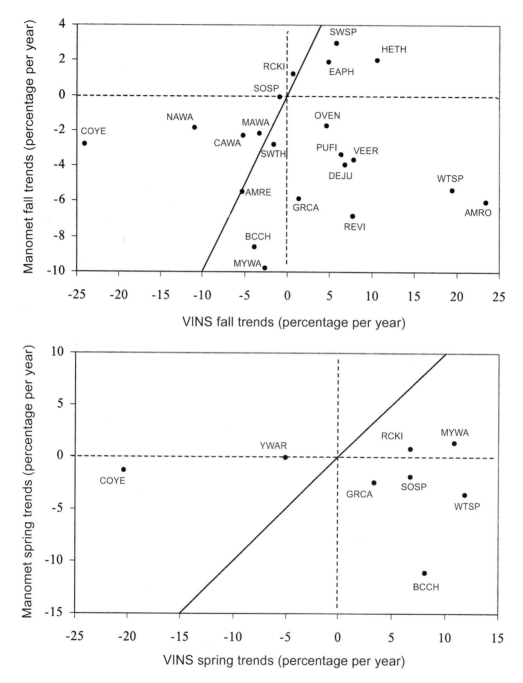

FIGURE 1. Rates of change (%/year) in fall (top) and spring (bottom) migration count indices at Manomet and VINS, 1981–1992. Solid line indicates one-to-one correspondence. See Table 1 for species codes.

four species (19%; Table 3). Fourteen of the 21 age ratio differences were significant (P < 0.05, t-test).

To assess the degree to which Manomet and VINS tracked changes in age ratios, we examined correlations among species over the 12-year period. We found no significant correlations; thus there appeared to be little year-to-year synchrony in age ratios at the two sites.

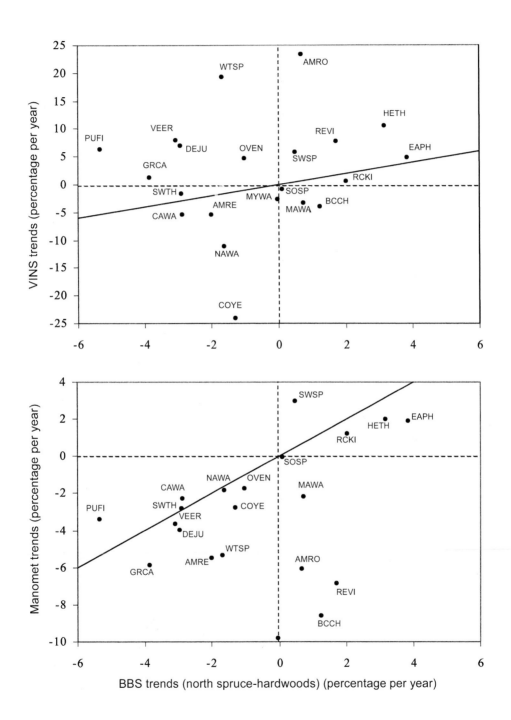

FIGURE 2. Rates of change (%/year) in fall migration capture indices at VINS (top) and Manomet (bottom) and BBS trends for Northern Spruce-Hardwoods physiographic stratum, 1981–1992. Solid line indicates one-to-one correspondence. See Table 1 for species codes.

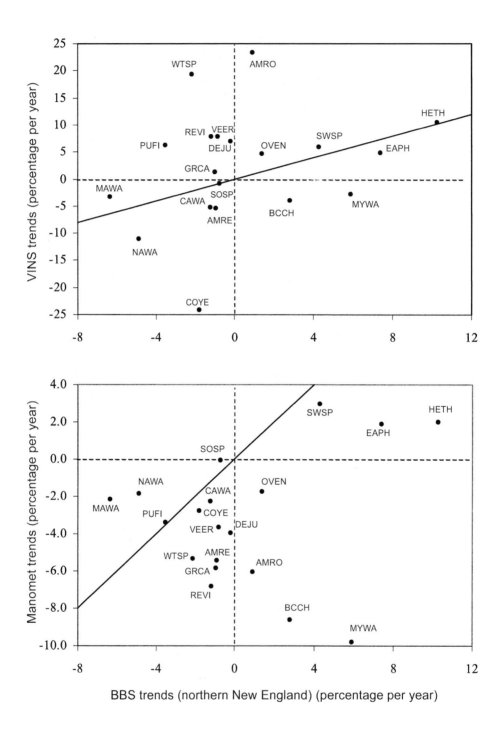

FIGURE 3. Rates of change (%/year) in fall migration capture indices at VINS (top) and Manomet (bottom) and BBS trends for Northern New England physiographic stratum, 1981–1992. Solid line indicates one-to-one correspondence. See Table 1 for species codes.

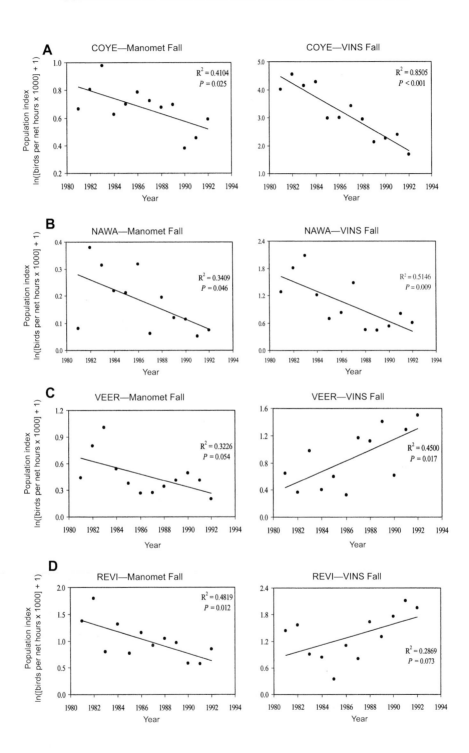

FIGURE 4. Linear regression of annual population indices from fall migration capture data for: (A) Common Yellowthroat; (B) Nashville Warbler; (C) Veery; and (D) Red-eyed Vireo during 1981–1992 at VINS and Manomet.

DISCUSSION

For three species, fall trends at VINS were biologically unrealistic (23.4% annual increase in American Robin, 24% annual decrease in Common Yellowthroat, and 19.4% annual increase in White-throated Sparrow). Even excluding these outliers, however, there was generally poor correlation between population trends calculated from Manomet and VINS migration capture data. Possible reasons include the following: (1) 7 or 12 years may be too short a period for detection of trends; (2) sample sizes at VINS, particularly during the 1981–1985 period, may have been inadequate for many species; (3) inconsistent standardization of methods at VINS during the study period may have obscured actual trends and reduced comparability of the two data sets; (4) changes in local breeding populations may have unduly biased VINS' data; (5) local or landscape-level habitat change may have biased population indices at either or both study sites, by differentially affecting the composition or abundance of species captured through time; and (6) different source populations may have been sampled by each station, such that population differences were real.

We suspect that the combination of small sample sizes (Table 1) and relative inconsistency of operating standards at VINS may have affected validity of many of the trend comparisons between VINS and Manomet. The minimum sample sizes we arbitrarily selected for analysis may have been too small, despite resulting in a number of significant trends for species captured in low numbers. For example, among species for which we obtained only 100–250 fall captures during 1981–1992, three of eight at Manomet and three of seven at VINS showed statistically significant population changes (Table 1). We can not be confident that trends based on such small samples are biologically meaningful. Inconsistent standardization of the VINS station, especially in 1981–1985 when fewer numbers of nets were used for shorter and more variable periods on fewer days each week than in 1986–1992, undoubtedly increased variance of the capture data in those early years. This unequal variance may in part explain the poor congruence of Manomet and VINS data. More rigorously standardized data collection at VINS would likely have resulted in more directly comparable data sets.

We suspect that the proportion of locally breeding and dispersing birds in the overall VINS sample was substantially higher than at Manomet. Among the VINS sample of 22 species, only six can be classified as true transients (regularly breeding >25 km from banding site), whereas 11 species captured at Manomet were wholly transient, or very nearly so (Table 1). Fluctuations in local breeding populations of migrants at and near VINS, as well as differing annual rates of dispersal onto and away from the site, may have obscured trends of transient populations at VINS, particularly in fall. However, of the six species that we judged to be strictly transient at both Manomet and VINS, five showed the same direction of trend in fall, whereas one species (Ruby-crowned Kinglet) with adequate capture data showed the same trend direction at both sites in spring (Table 1). Only Purple Finch showed opposite trends among fall transients, and this species is more of an irruptive than regular migrant at both sites (C. Rimmer and S. Faccio, unpubl. data; T. Lloyd-Evans, unpubl. data). Of the five transient species with similar fall trends at Manomet and VINS, 1982–1991 regional BBS data showed a corresponding trend for each (Table 1). This suggests that the two sites corresponded more closely in tracking population changes of fall transient species than of species with local breeding populations. Although we believe that the great majority of captures among all species at both Manomet and VINS were of migrant individuals rather than dispersing local breeders or fledglings, because of our migration window criteria, comparisons between sites could be strengthened if locally breeding species were excluded from trend analyses. Among the six transient species at both Manomet and VINS, the correspondence in trend directions (with the exception of Purple Finch) was not reflected in trend magnitudes, which correlated poorly ($r = -0.371$, $P > 0.10$).

Whereas the VINS site experienced greater vegetation succession than the Manomet site during the 12 years of study, Manomet may have been subject to greater landscape level habitat change, through increased suburbanization of coastal southeastern Massachusetts. Either type of change may have influenced the diversity and abundance of migrants using the two sites. The very large declines of some early to mid-successional species at VINS (e.g., Nashville Warbler, Common Yellowthroat) may have resulted in part from decreased habitat suitability of the maturing old field communities in the vicinity of the VINS banding station. Increased vegetation height around nets may also have reduced capture rates. At Manomet, increasing isolation of the 7-ha site as a habitat "fragment" in a predominantly suburban coastal landscape may have variably altered its use by stopover migrants over time. Local changes in vegetation at Manomet, while less pronounced than those at VINS, may also have contributed to changes in migrant bird populations using the site. Because no quantitative habitat assessment was conducted at either site, we were unable to evaluate the extent of such changes. We believe that regular, standardized measurements of habitat features on both local and landscape levels are needed to evaluate the context of changes in migrant bird populations within and between sites.

Trends from each of the two stations were most congruent with regional BBS data from different strata. Although the presumed southeasterly direction of many fall migrants in the northeastern United States (e.g., Ralph 1978) might well have carried some Vermont birds to coastal Massachusetts, this can not be assumed. BBS data suggest that Manomet migrants may have originated largely in northeastern areas of New England and maritime Canada, whereas VINS's migrant sample may have been composed largely of birds from northwestern New England, southern Quebec and southeastern Ontario. These results suggest that each station may have tracked largely independent population changes, as suggested by Hagan et al. (1992) in their comparison of data from Manomet and a station at Powdermill, Pennsylvania. Without knowledge of the source populations being sampled, and of possible annual variation in the geographic composition of migrant captures, population trends at different sites must be compared cautiously. We believe that careful, species-specific analyses of BBS data from appropriate physiographic strata or specific geographic regions may be a good means of inferring the extent to which different banding stations sample similar source populations.

POPULATION TRENDS

The preponderance of declining species at Manomet and of increasing species at VINS is difficult to explain, even in light of potential within- and between-site biases. The possibility that one or both sites failed to track population changes accurately can not be discounted. However, Hagan et al. (1992) demonstrated that Manomet migration capture data collected over a 19-year period accurately measured known population changes in several species in northeastern North America. The VINS data are less clear in this regard. Although several species (e.g., Nashville Warbler, Common Yellowthroat) showed corresponding trend directions at both sites and in regional BBS data, others (e.g., Veery, White-throated Sparrow, Dark-eyed Junco) showed

poor congruence between Manomet and VINS. That Manomet trend data more closely matched those of the BBS stratum directly to its north than did VINS, which correlated with BBS data within its own stratum, leads us to believe that Manomet more accurately measured actual population changes among migrants. Although a more detailed, species-by-species analysis of the two migration capture data sets and data from appropriate BBS strata might have enabled us to more fully evaluate this, such an analysis was beyond the scope of this paper.

PRODUCTIVITY INDICES

The significantly higher proportion of HY birds at Manomet and of AHY birds at VINS conforms to the coastal–inland ratio typical of most autumn passerine migrants (e.g., Drury and Keith 1962; Ralph 1971, 1978, 1981). The "coastal effect" results from most adults following overland routes in fall while immatures travel both inland and on the coast, or from differential behavior of the age classes upon reaching coastlines (Dunn and Nol 1980). Manomet migration capture data, which consisted largely of HY birds, may have been more strongly influenced, and thus potentially biased, by weather-related phenomena affecting their abundance and behavior at the coast (see Dunn et al. *this volume b* and Hussell *this volume* for evidence that weather affects age ratios). Further, age ratios at Manomet and VINS may have differed in part due to sampling different source populations, as discussed above. Finally, different trends in age ratios at the two sites may have masked agreement in the annual directions of change (Dunn et al. *this volume b*).

CONCLUSION

We recognize that our comparison of these two data sets is an imperfect one. We believe, however, that it reflects the realities of comparing migration capture data from geographically distant sites subject to different sources of variability. We further believe that migration capture data collected under standardized conditions (Ralph et al. *this volume a*) can provide a valid means of assessing avian population trends, and we encourage more comparisons of data among migration banding stations. Careful analyses of migration capture data from a network of long-term banding stations might yield valuable information on regional population trends and demographics of migrant birds. Comparisons among multiple sites could provide needed independent tests of results obtained from breeding season studies.

ACKNOWLEDGMENTS

We gratefully acknowledge the many volunteers, students and staff who have helped collect data at both banding sites over the years. We thank E. Dunn, K. McFarland, and C. J. Ralph for constructive comments on drafts of the manuscript. Financial support for banding studies at both Manomet and VINS has been provided from many sources, including the trustees and members of both organizations, the Malcolm Oakes Memorial Fund (Manomet), and the Plumsock Fund (VINS).

Studies in Avian Biology No. 29:135–143

MIST NETTING TRANS-GULF MIGRANTS AT COASTAL STOPOVER SITES: THE INFLUENCE OF SPATIAL AND TEMPORAL VARIABILITY ON CAPTURE DATA

Theodore R. Simons, Frank R. Moore, and Sidney A. Gauthreaux

Abstract. We used constant effort mist netting during spring migration to sample populations of trans-Gulf migrants at two coastal study sites from 1987 to 1992. Approximately 2,500 individuals of 70 species were netted each season with approximately 5,000 net-hours of effort. Although captures per net hour and total species captured were fairly consistent each year, the seasonal patterns of capture, arrival condition, stopover duration, diversity of species, and number of individuals showed considerable variation from year to year. Differences in seasonal and annual weather patterns, the arrival condition of migrants, and habitat quality at stopover sites all influenced the probability of capturing birds with mist nets at our coastal stopover sites. Mist-net capture rates from coastal stopover sites, migratory activity indicated by radar echoes, and counts of migrants from censuses at mainland sites were correlated within a geographic radius of 100–150 km.

Key Words: capture variability, migration, mist netting, stopover, trans-Gulf migrants.

Over 80% of North American birds are migratory to some extent, and about half of those species cross the Gulf of Mexico during migration (Lowery 1946, Rappole and Warner 1976, Moore and Kerlinger 1987). The trans-Gulf flight is a dangerous, energetically expensive phase of the annual cycle. A typical migrant like an Ovenbird (scientific names in Table 1) deposits 40–50% of its body weight in fat each spring before departing on a 15–20 h non-stop flight en route from its tropical wintering grounds to the breeding grounds in North America. Crossing a large ecological barrier like the Gulf of Mexico is a risky endeavor for migrants, exposing them to the unpredictable forces of spring cold fronts and thunderstorms (Buskirk 1980). For migrants, this unpredictability often means that they have little control over their precise migratory trajectories (Gauthreaux 1971, Rappole et al. 1979, Moore and Kerlinger 1991). The inherently unpredictable nature of migration may make it a limiting factor for some populations. The variability in migratory patterns that emerge each year have important implications for the interpretation of mist-netting data from migratory stopover sites along the northern Gulf coast.

The objectives of this paper are to examine how variability in seasonal patterns of capture, arrival condition, and stopover duration at stopover sites may confound estimates of larger scale population trends, and to compare mist-net capture data with indices of activity derived simultaneously from mainland censuses and weather surveillance radar.

METHODS

We worked at two study sites along the northern Gulf Coast from 1987 to 1992 (Fig. 1). Peveto Beach is a coastal woodland in southwestern Louisiana. East Ship and Horn islands are barrier islands in Mississippi Sound. The two stations are approximately 400 km apart. The vegetation and field methods have been described in detail elsewhere (Loria and Moore 1990, Moore and Kerlinger 1987, Moore et al. 1990, Kuenzi et al. 1991). Approximately 20, 12-m nets were run daily at each station from dawn to 1100 hours and from 1400 to 1800 hours. The field season ran from late March to early May each spring. Standard measurements were taken on all birds captured before they were banded and released. Levels of body fat were estimated according to the ordinal scale developed by Helms and Drury (1960). In 1992 we conducted 1-km strip transect censuses (Emlen 1977) in pine (N = 63) and deciduous forest (N = 63) habitats in coastal Mississippi (Simons et al. 2000). In that same year, we also analyzed the archived film record of the WSR-57 radar at Slidell, Louisiana from 23 March to 27 May (Gauthreaux 1971, 1992). To quantify the radar images we used a calibration curve that related the spatial extent of the migration echoes on the radar image (measured as the maximum radius in nautical miles) to the mean number of birds in the volume defined by the 1.75° conical radar beam (elevated 2.5°) sweeping 20° of azimuth at a range of 46.3 km (Gauthreaux 1994).

RESULTS

Trans-Gulf migration occurs in spring from mid-March to late May, although the peak of activity is concentrated in April. Approximately 70 species

TABLE 1. MEAN ANNUAL CAPTURES AT EAST SHIP ISLAND, 1987–1991

Species	Captures/1,000 net-h	CV
Yellow-billed Cuckoo (*Coccyzus americanus*)	2.33	1.42
EasternWood-Pewee (*Contopus virens*)	5.22	0.62
Yellow-bellied Flycatcher (*Empidonax flaviventris*)	1.05	1.16
Acadian Flycatcher (*E. virescens*)	4.76	0.23
Least Flycatcher (*E. minimus*)	0.57	0.93
Eastern Phoebe (*Sayornis phoebe*)	0.25	1.47
Great Crested Flycatcher (*Myiarchus crinitus*)	2.42	0.49
Eastern Kingbird (*Tyrannus tyrannus*)	1.26	0.76
White-eyed Vireo (*Vireo griseus*)	62.67	0.74
Yellow-throated Vireo (*V. flavifrons*)	10.48	0.35
Blue-headed Vireo (*V. solitarius*)	0.40	0.97
Warbling Vireo (*V. gilvus*)	0.07	2.24
Philadelphia Vireo (*V. philadelphicus*)	1.47	0.70
Red-eyed Vireo (*V. olivaceus*)	127.39	0.44
Black-whiskered Vireo (*V. altiloquus*)	0.12	1.38
Barn Swallow (*Hirundo rustica*)	0.13	2.24
Red-breasted Nuthatch (*Sitta canadensis*)	0.27	2.24
House Wren (*Troglodytes aedon*)	1.55	0.94
Ruby-crowned Kinglet (*Regulus calendula*)	1.44	1.40
Blue-gray Gnatcatcher (*Polioptila caerulea*)	0.69	1.43
Veery (*Catharus fuscescens*)	13.07	0.70
Gray-cheeked Thrush (*C. minimus*)	8.02	0.76
Swainson's Thrush (*C. ustulatus*)	12.24	0.93
Hermit Thrush (*C. guttatus*)	0.11	2.24
Wood Thrush (*Hylocichla mustelina*)	13.10	0.67
Cedar Waxwing (*Bombycilla cedrorum*)	0.07	2.24
Blue-winged Warbler (*Vermivora pinus*)	3.61	0.62
Golden-winged Warbler (*V. chrysoptera*)	0.42	0.90
Tennessee Warbler (*V. peregrina*)	9.31	0.55
Orange-crowned Warbler (*V. celata*)	0.07	2.24
Northern Parula (*Parula americana*)	4.39	0.39
Yellow Warbler (*Dendroica petechia*)	15.03	0.59
Magnolia Warbler (*D. magnolia*)	9.35	0.54
Cape May Warbler (*D. tigrina*)	4.79	1.40
Black-throated Blue Warbler (*D. caerulescens*)	1.16	0.68
Yellow-rumped Warbler (*D. coronata*)	2.25	1.60
Black-throated Green Warbler (*D. virens*)	2.95	0.79
Blackburnian Warbler (*D. fusca*)	1.31	0.92
Yellow-throated Warbler (*D. dominica*)	0.90	0.95
Prairie Warbler (*D. discolor*)	2.00	1.17
Palm Warbler (*D. palmarum*)	0.84	0.86
Bay-breasted Warbler (*D. castanea*)	4.84	0.67
Blackpoll Warbler (*D. striata*)	12.34	0.86
Cerulean Warbler (*D. cerulea*)	0.98	0.36
Black-and-white Warbler (*Mniotilta varia*)	16.17	0.27
American Redstart (*Setophaga ruticilla*)	8.50	0.34
Prothonotary Warbler (*Protonotaria citrea*)	9.41	0.67
Worm-eating Warbler (*Helmitheros vermivorus*)	9.64	0.53
Swainson's Warbler (*Limnothlypis swainsonii*)	1.13	0.92
Ovenbird (*Seiurus aurocapilla*)	13.53	0.66
Northern Waterthrush (*S. noveboracensis*)	6.75	0.56
Louisiana Waterthrush (*S. motacilla*)	0.56	0.77
Kentucky Warbler (*Oporornis formosus*)	8.15	0.74
Connecticut Warbler (*O. agilis*)	0.11	1.42
Common Yellowthroat (*Geothlypis trichas*)	14.29	0.66

TABLE 1.   CONTINUED

Species	Captures/1,000 net-h	CV
Hooded Warbler (*Wilsonia citrina*)	27.97	0.65
Wilson's Warbler (*W. pusilla*)	0.05	2.24
Yellow-breasted Chat (*Icteria virens*)	3.45	0.72
Chestnut-sided Warbler (*D. pensylvanica*)	2.41	0.67
Summer Tanager (*Piranga rubra*)	20.20	0.20
Scarlet Tanager (*P. olivacea*)	13.16	0.60
Dark-eyed Junco (*Junco hyemalis*)	0.05	2.24
Rose-breasted Grosbeak (*Pheucticus ludovicianus*)	18.47	0.68
Blue Grosbeak (*Guiraca caerulea*)	4.15	0.42
Indigo Bunting (*Passerina cyanea*)	43.85	0.54
Painted Bunting (*P. ciris*)	7.33	0.83
Dickcissel (*Spiza americana*)	0.38	1.56
Bobolink (*Dolichonyx oryzivorus*)	0.13	2.24
Orchard Oriole (*Icterus spurius*)	26.92	0.41
Baltimore Oriole (*I. galbula*)	4.49	0.49

were netted at each of our stations each year. Daily patterns of arrival at stopover sites varied considerably from year to year, as illustrated by five years of capture data from East Ship Island (Fig. 2). Numbers of individual birds captured/recaptured on East Ship Island each year were: 873/70 (1987), 2,327/385 (1988), 3,080/306 (1989), 2,585/437 (1990), and 2,151/240 (1991); and on Horn Island 2,022/419 (1992). The annual percent of birds recaptured one or more times ranged from 8.0–20.7% (mean = 13.05 ± 4.36%). Annual spring capture rates, first captures, and recaptures combined for all species, ranged from 0.35 to 0.70 birds per net hour.

The mean number of birds netted annually/1,000 net-h varied considerably within species (Table 1). Coefficients of variation (CV; Zar 1984) for annual mean rates from 1987 to 1991 on East Ship Island provide an index of annual within-station capture rate variability. For example, over all years, approximately 63 White-eyed Vireos were captured/1,000 net-h, but annual capture rates were highly variable (CV = 74%). In contrast, Black-and-white Warblers were caught less often (16/1,000 net-h), but annual capture rates were much less variable (CV = 27%).

Most of the birds captured at our study sites had low fat reserves. Overall, slightly over 50% were scored "0 fat," although there was some variation in the average condition of birds from year to year (Fig. 3).

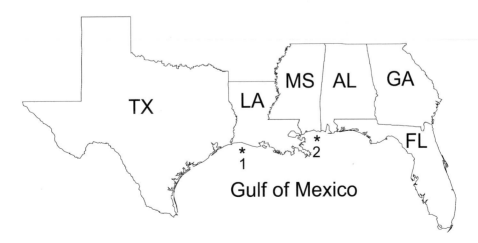

FIGURE 1. Study sites on the north shore of the Gulf of Mexico. Site 1 = Peveto Beach, Louisiana, Site 2 = Ship and Horn Islands, Mississippi.

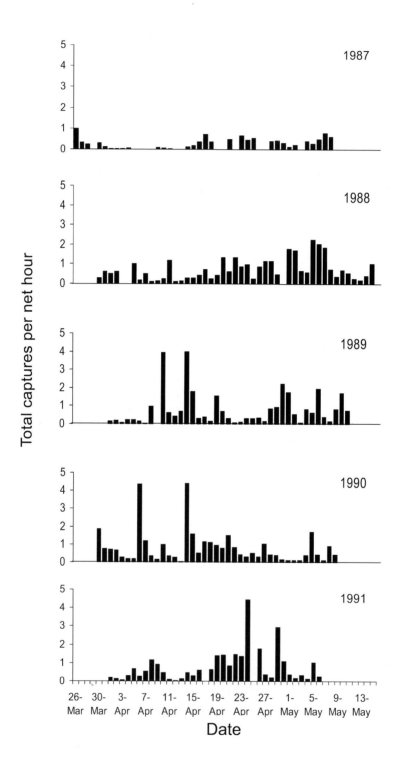

FIGURE 2. Capture rates of trans-Gulf migrants on East Ship Island, 1987–1991.

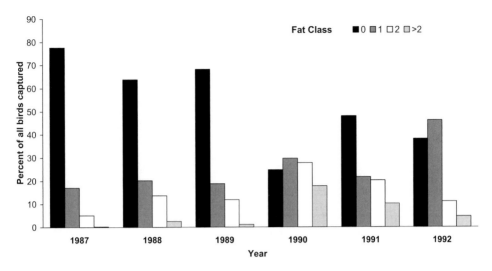

FIGURE 3. Distribution of arrival fat scores of trans-Gulf migrants netted at East Ship Island (1987–1991) and Horn Island (1992), Mississippi.

Birds with no fat reserves were more likely to remain at stopover sites and be recaptured than were birds with higher levels of body fat (Fig. 4). Examination of arrival weight and stopover length for six common species illustrates the pattern. In general, birds arrived at Peveto Beach in better condition (Table 2) and tended to depart sooner (Table 3) than birds at East Ship island. We previously found evidence of differences in habitat quality related to prey availability at the two stations (Moore and Simons 1992, Simons et al. 2000), which may explain why birds at Peveto Beach tended to gain weight more quickly than birds stopping over on East Ship Island (Table 4). Thus, the

capture probabilities for individual birds at these two stopover sites appeared to be a function both of the bird's arrival condition and the availability of food at the stopover sites.

We compared mist-netting data from Horn Island in Mississippi Sound with data collected simultaneously from a coastal weather radar site, and from field censuses on mainland habitats (Fig. 5), to evaluate the stopover habitat requirements of trans-Gulf migrants at broader geographic scales. Results provide some indication of the extent to which mist-net data from a single station reflect conditions at a broader scale (Fig. 6). Over the course of the entire

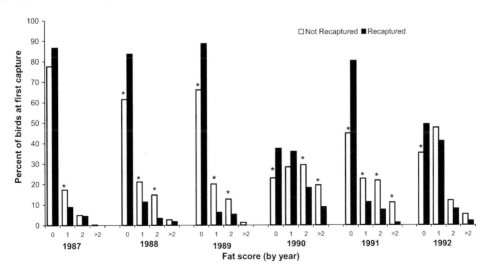

FIGURE 4. Fat score vs. recapture status of trans-Gulf migrants netted on East Ship Island (1987–1991) and Horn Island (1992), Mississippi. * indicates difference between percents (t-test, $P < 0.05$).

TABLE 2. AVERAGE ARRIVAL WEIGHT (GRAMS) OF TRANS-GULF MIGRANTS AT COASTAL STOPOVER SITES

Species	Site	1987	1988	1990	1991
Hooded Warbler	PEV	9.67 ± 0.86 (273) *	9.57 ± 0.90 (288)	9.84 ± 0.85 (134) **	9.62 ± 0.88 (58)
	ESI	9.40 ± 0.90 (31)	9.80 ± 0.90 (32)	9.30 ± 1.10 (152)	9.70 ± 1.00 (94)
Red-eyed Vireo	PEV	15.65 ± 0.16 (199) **	15.79 ± 1.59 (574) **	15.82 ± 1.53 (80)	16.26 ± 2.10 (25)
	ESI	15.00 ± 1.70 (170)	15.5 ± 1.60 (883)	15.70 ± 1.70 (280)	16.40 ± 1.90 (370)
Indigo Bunting	PEV	12.25 (1)	12.80 ± 1.38 (372) **	12.88 ± 1.21 (49)	13.08 ± 1.43 (85)
	ESI	12.70 ± 1.50 (50)	13.60 ± 1.80 (360)	12.80 ± 1.70 (101)	12.80 ± 1.40 (105)
Black-and-white Warbler	PEV	9.53 ± 0.89 (33)	9.56 ± 0.90 (147) **	9.62 ± 1.15 (31) **	9.30 ± 0.75 (27)
	ESI	9.30 ± 0.80 (29)	8.80 ± 1.00 (65)	8.60 ± 0.80 (62)	9.20 ± 0.90 (62)
Summer Tanager	PEV	27.17 ± 2.38 (56) *	27.63 ± 2.47 (154) **	28.60 ± 3.50 (73) *	27.77 ± 2.81 (37)
	ESI	26.10 ± 2.30 (45)	26.30 ± 2.30 (93)	27.30 ± 3.30 (73)	28.80 ± 3.10 (43)
White-eyed Vireo	PEV	11.15 ± 0.92 (41) **	11.42 ± 1.12 (138) **	11.27 ± 1.22 (81) **	11.27 ± 1.05 (17)
	ESI	10.60 ± 1.00 (73)	10.60 ± 0.90 (91)	10.60 ± 1.00 (536)	11.00 ± 1.20 (228)

Notes: PEV = Peveto Beach, Louisiana, ESI = East Ship Island, Mississippi. Data are reported as mean ± one SE (N). Two sample t-test for differences between sites, one-tailed P values reported as * (0.01 < P < 0.05), ** (P < 0.01).

TABLE 3. AVERAGE DAYS OF STOPOVER BY TRANS-GULF MIGRANTS AT COASTAL STOPOVER SITES (MOORE AND KERLINGER 1987)

Species	Site	1987	1988	1990	1991
Hooded Warbler	PEV	1.43 ± 0.74 (41)	3.15 ± 2.67 (106)	1.85 ± 1.66 (33) *	2.61 ± 1.75 (23)
	ESI	4.50 ± 4.95 (2)	1.00 (1)	2.97 ± 2.37 (30)	2.20 ± 1.48 (9)
Red-eyed Vireo	PEV	2.00 ± 1.00 (4)	2.00 ± 1.80 (36)	2.92 ± 2.23 (12)	2.00 (1)
	ESI	2.33 ± 1.53 (3)	1.97 ± 1.90 (29)	2.57 ± 1.90 (7)	1.80 ± 1.30 (5)
Indigo Bunting	PEV	—	3.10 ± 4.36 (11)	—	2.00 ± 2.00 (2)
	ESI	2.00 ± 1.00 (3)	3.52 ± 3.67 (31)	7.18 ± 9.81 (17)	2.20 ± 1.10 (5)
Black-and-white Warbler	PEV	1.33 ± 0.58 (3)	2.50 ± 2.00 (19) **	2.50 ± 2.12 (2)	2.00 ± 1.00 (3)
	ESI	1.50 ± 0.71 (2)	1.50 ± 0.65 (14)	3.41 ± 2.69 (17)	2.60 ± 3.72 (10)
Summer Tanager	PEV	1.75 ± 0.95 (4)	1.80 ± 0.87 (19)	2.22 ± 1.72 (9)	13.00 (1)
	ESI	3.00 ± 2.83 (2)	1.75 ± 1.49 (8)	3.80 ± 4.09 (5)	3.67 ± 3.06 (3)
White-eyed Vireo	PEV	1.83 ± 1.17 (6)	3.40 ± 3.45 (33)	2.18 ± 1.47 (11) **	2.00 ± 1.73 (3) **
	ESI	2.67 ± 1.63 (6)	2.90 ± 2.71 (30)	5.11 ± 5.71 (75)	4.84 ± 5.62 (37)

Notes: PEV = Peveto Beach, Louisiana, ESI = East Ship Island, Mississippi. Data are reported as mean ± one SE (N). Two sample t-test for differences between sites, one-tailed P values reported as * (0.01 < P < 0.05), ** (P < 0.01).

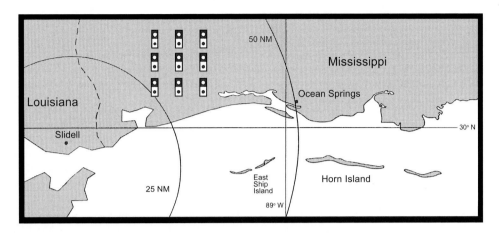

FIGURE 5. Study sites used for comparison of data on migratory bird activity collected using mist nets (Horn Island, Mississippi), field censuses (9 paired study sites in pine uplands and riparian habitats, coastal Mississippi; shown by paired squares with circles in them), and radar imagery (WSR-57 weather radar, Slidell, Louisiana).

season, mist-net capture rates, migratory activity indicated by radar echoes, and the number of migrants detected on field censuses were correlated within a geographic radius of 100 km. Peaks in coastal migratory bird activity evident in mist-net and radar data around 30 March, 7 April, 20 April, and 1 May were generally followed by peaks in number of passage migrants detected by field censuses on the mainland

(Fig 6; Kendall's rank correlation analysis, $W = 0.643$, $\chi^2 = 32.793$, $0.01 < P < 0.025$).

DISCUSSION

Data collected by netting birds at coastal stopover sites are useful for answering a variety of questions related to the ecology and habitat requirements of

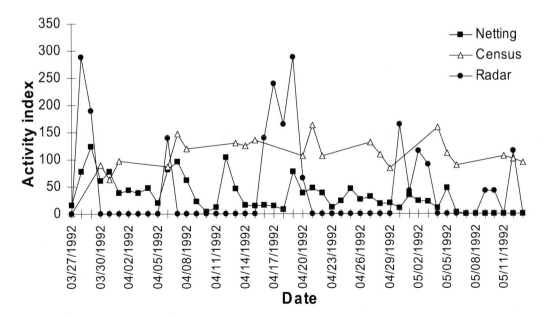

FIGURE 6. Comparison of migratory bird activity based on data from mist netting, field censuses, and WSR-57 radar imagery. Netting data (dark squares) are reported as number of birds captured/50 net-h. Census data (white triangles) are reported as total number of migrants counted in morning censuses. Radar data (dark circles) are reported as the mean number of flocks per 20^0 sector of the WSR-57 radar image (Gauthreaux 1994).

TABLE 4. AVERAGE MASS CHANGE (G/D, SEE KUENZI ET AL. 1991) OF TRANS-GULF MIGRANTS AT COASTAL STOPOVER SITES

Species	Site	1987	1988	1990	1991
Hooded Warbler	PEV	0.16 ± 0.69 (41)	0.18 ± 0.39 (106)	0.003 ± 0.43 (33)	0.22 ± 0.25 (23)
	ESI	0.38 ± 1.59 (2)	—	-0.42 ± 1.78 (30)	-0.25 ± 0.95 (9)
Red-eyed Vireo	PEV	0.10 ± 0.56 (11)	-0.19 ± 0.78 (36) **	0.18 ± 0.40 (12) **	0.18 (1)
	ESI	—	-1.25 ± 0.73 (29)	-1.23 ± 1.13 (7)	-0.23 ± 0.91 (5)
Indigo Bunting	PEV	—	0.12 ± 0.47 (29)	-0.21 ± 0.10 (2)	
	ESI	-0.17 ± 0.63 (3)	0.03 ± 0.95 (31)	0.48 ± 1.00 (17)	0.09 ± 0.65 (5)
Black-and-white Warbler	PEV	0.34 ± 0.26 (3)	0.15 ± 0.42 (33) *	0.19 ± 0.01 (2)	0.14 ± 0.60 (3)
	ESI	-0.50 ± 0.71 (2)	0.09 ± 1.24 (14)	0.21 ± 0.84 (17)	0.54 ± 0.71 (110)
Summer Tanager	PEV	0.60 ± 0.55 (4)	0.22 ± 2.27 (19) *	0.33 ± 1.00 (9) **	0.47 (1)
	ESI	1.25 ± 1.41 (2)	-1.64 ± 1.54 (8)	2.83 ± 1.47 (5)	0.72 ± 1.41 (3)
White-eyed Vireo	PEV	0.20 ± 0.65 (6)	0.33 ± 0.47 (33) *	0.16 ± 0.32 (11) **	0.27 ± 0.25 (3)
	ESI	-0.17 ± 0.70 (6)	0.08 ± 0.84 (30)	-0.43 ± 1.01 (75)	-0.07 ± 0.79 (37)

Notes: PEV = Peveto Beach, Louisiana, ESI = East Ship Island, Mississippi. Data are reported as mean ± one SE (N). Two sample t-test for differences between sites, one-tailed P values reported as * ($0.01 < P < 0.05$), ** ($P < 0.01$).

migratory birds. However, population indices, such as mist-net captures from stopover sites along the Gulf Coast, may not provide data suitable for monitoring population levels if capture probabilities vary over time or space (Pollock et al. 2002).

Analysis of the arrival condition of birds at stopover sites suggests that birds with sufficient energy reserves continue migration, or move to alternate habitats more quickly than lean birds, or that they may simply over-fly some coastal stopover sites entirely. Confirmation of this phenomena is provided during a typical bird "fallout," which occurs when birds encounter late cold fronts or local thunderstorms. Under these conditions, it is common to capture birds with large fat reserves that, under favorable weather conditions, would have simply over-flown these coastal sites (Moore et al. 1990). In 1990, when fallout conditions occurred on East Ship Island in early and mid-April (Fig. 2), birds were fatter on average than in years when fallout events were less common (Fig. 3).

Weather is clearly a dominant factor influencing the total number of birds captured per net-hour at an individual station (Buskirk 1980, Moore and Kerlinger 1987). Weather conditions favorable for migration will reduce the proportion of a population stopping at a migratory stopover site. Favorable weather also increases the likelihood that birds visiting stopover sites will be in better condition. We have shown that recapture rates are lower for migrants in better energetic condition. The average energetic condition of birds (determined by their condition on departure from the wintering grounds, distances flown, or wind conditions encountered enroute) will all influence capture probabilities at stopover sites. It is usually not possible to distinguish whether differences in capture rates at stopover sites reflect differences in the average energetic condition of migrants or actual differences in population levels. For long-term trends to be unbiased it has to be assumed that variation in mean annual energetic condition occurs randomly among years.

Finally, variability of habitat quality at stopover sites will also influence the likelihood and duration of stopover, and therefore capture probabilities. Both the yearly succession of vegetation and the temporary abundance of prey within years influence capture probabilities at stopover sites, which is why recommendations for migration monitoring emphasize the need for maintaining uniform habitat (Hussell and Ralph 1998). Thus, differences in seasonal and annual weather patterns, the arrival condition of migrants, and habitat quality at stopover sites all influence the probability of capturing birds with mist-nets at stopover sites along the northern Gulf coast.

Abundance estimates based on mist-net based count indices can be adjusted by modeling date, weather, moon phase and year as covariables (Dunn and Hussell 1995, Dunn et al. 1997, Hussell et al. 1992, Pyle et al. 1993). These approaches may be most suitable for inland sites adjacent to breeding areas where the energetic condition of migrants, habitat conditions, and migratory pathways are less variable. At sites with high daily turnover rates, modeling covariates may provide unbiased indices of population size if the assumption that only newly arrived birds are included in analyses can be met (Dunn and Hussell 1995). When recapture rates are low (<10%) this assumptions may be valid. Higher recapture rates (up to 20%) at our study sites along the Gulf Coast may make it difficult to meet the assumptions of this approach. Modeling covariables may not be sufficient to control for the variability in capture probabilities inherent to populations migrating across large ecological barriers such as the Gulf of Mexico.

Not surprisingly, differences in the factors affecting mist-net capture probabilities appear to increase with the distance between study sites. Differences in the arrival condition of birds at Peveto Beach and East Ship Island (400 km apart) suggest that these sites are sampling populations following different migratory routes. In contrast, local WSR 57 radar, field census results, and mist-net data were correlated on a scale of 50–100 km at our study sites in Mississippi. Williams et al. (2001) observed a similar local scale correspondence between observations of migrants in New Hampshire using portable marine radar, ceilometer, and ground census data.

Presumably, sampling at a fairly fine geographic scale across the northern Gulf would be necessary to understand population level patterns of trans-Gulf migration. Nevertheless, establishing a network of sampling sites along the Gulf Coast would probably prove to be an inefficient approach to population monitoring, because while migration can be viewed as a broad-front phenomena on decadal or longer time scales, annual patterns of arrival tend to be quite localized. In any single year only a small percentage of sites would be expected to collect data sufficient to assess population trends. Thus the sampling frame required to adequately track population trends would be very large and expensive.

Recent advances in the application of WSR-88D Doppler weather radar to bird migration hold the promise that it may one day be feasible to implement a sampling frame sufficient to monitor bird population trends through migration monitoring (Gauthreaux and Belser 1998, Gauthreaux and Russell 1998), although individual species can not be identified. On-going validation studies employing ground truthing of radar imagery with mist-net and census based field data will determine the potential of this new technology.

ACKNOWLEDGMENTS

Support of this research was provided by the U.S. Fish and Wildlife Service, the National Park Service, the U.S. Geological Survey, the University of Southern Mississippi Research Council, the National Geographic Society, and the State of Mississippi Natural Heritage Program. W. H. Buskirk, R. Chandler, P. Kerlinger, A. J. Kuenzi, C. J. Ralph, E. H. Dunn, and an anonymous reviewer made important contributions to this manuscript.

Studies in Avian Biology No. 29:144–150

BIRD POPULATION STUDIES IN PUERTO RICO USING MIST NETS: GENERAL PATTERNS AND COMPARISONS WITH POINT COUNTS

JOHN FAABORG, WAYNE J. ARENDT, AND KATIE M. DUGGER

Abstract. Mist nets have been used to monitor size, composition, and survival rates of bird populations in the Guanica Forest of Puerto Rico every winter since 1972. Each line of nets consists of 16, 12-m nets erected end-to-end in a straight line and operated from dawn to dark for three consecutive days. Here we examine features of the netting protocol that could affect quality of results for population studies, including species sampled, length and frequency of netting sessions, and numbers of captures and recaptures. Point counts and mist-net samples gave very different results for relative abundance of species. Number of birds captured for the first time within a sample declined rapidly over three days of netting, with few birds captured the third day, regardless of a species' abundance. Net avoidance was strong within 3-day samples, but not between different netting sessions (which were at least three months apart). We suggest these samples are indicative of avian populations resident within the area of net lines, and that three days is a sufficient length of time to capture the majority of birds using that area, at least in the low-statured vegetation of Guanica Forest. However, in more diverse or structurally complex habitats, mist nets may not sample as large a proportion of the species and individuals present.

Key Words: mist nets, net avoidance, population monitoring, survival.

Mist nets have been used to monitor bird populations in the Guanica Forest of Puerto Rico since 1972, first by J. Faaborg, and later in cooperation with all the authors. A variety of papers has resulted from this work (reviewed by Faaborg and Arendt 1990, Faaborg et al. 2000). Mist-net captures were used initially to compare population levels between islands (Terborgh and Faaborg 1973), and to look for patterns in the morphology of species making up island bird communities (Faaborg 1985). After a severe drought, monitoring was continued to assess the effect of drought on bird populations (Faaborg 1982, Faaborg et al. 1984, Faaborg and Arendt 1992a, Dugger et al. 2000). Captures of winter residents provided observations about site fidelity and territoriality (Faaborg and Winters 1979) and, after 15 years, a severe decline in captures of winter resident warblers was noted (Faaborg and Arendt 1989b, 1992b). With long-term recapture data, we were able to measure demographic traits of both resident and winter resident birds, looking first at longevity (Faaborg and Arendt 1989a) then, using advanced statistical models, survival rates (Faaborg and Arendt 1995). Our latest contribution (Dugger et al. 2000) examined relationships between rainfall patterns and both population and survival rate variation within the resident birds of the forest, using a 26-year data set from a netting site operated since 1973. Because hurricane Georges caused extensive damage to the forest in the fall of 1998, future work will have to incorporate the effects of this event on population and survival parameters.

In this paper, we evaluate our netting protocol. Although it is unlikely that we would change these after 30 years, it is important to understand strengths and weaknesses of our methods in order to better interpret our results, and to make recommendations to others.

METHODS

STUDY SITE

The Guanica Forest is managed by the Department of Natural Resources of the Commonwealth of Puerto Rico. It is a 4,000-ha reserve situated along the southwest coast, composed of approximately 50% natural subtropical deciduous forest and 50% regenerating forest. The relatively undisturbed parts of the forest are considered to be the best remaining examples of this forest type in the New World, and Guanica Forest is listed as a World Biosphere Reserve. Subtropical deciduous forest is short and thorny (see Terborgh and Faaborg 1973 for further descriptions and photographs). Mean canopy height in one study site was 5.2 m (Terborgh and Faaborg 1973), few trees exceeded 8 m, and vegetation height has remained fairly constant over the life of the study. Differences between species in vertical foraging behavior do not appear to be a major means of ecological separation among West Indian species (Faaborg 1985), especially in such a short forest, so nearly all birds found in the forest frequent the zone sampled by mist nets (<2.5 m).

NETTING PROTOCOL

The standard mist-netting protocol involves setting 16 nets, each 12 m long, as close to end-to-end as possible and in as straight a line as possible. From 1972 through 1996 we used 36-mm mesh nets (usually the Association of Field Ornithologists type ATX). Since 1996, we have used 30-mm mesh nets (from Spidertech) because these nets have a fuller bag, which we felt would increase captures of the smallest migrants while not reducing captures of the largest residents. No change in capture rate was apparent with the change in mesh sizes.

Most of the time we have only one netting session with each line annually, in January or early February, but on a few occasions we have operated a line again during the breeding season (June or July) or during early or late winter (October or March). The original net line, situated within undisturbed forest at an intermediate elevation (150 m), has been operated annually since 1973 (except 1977 and 1979). Eight new lines were added during 1989–1991, scattered throughout the central part of the forest to sample a range of locations and vegetation types, including lines in portions of the forest that were heavily disturbed over 60 years ago. All nine lines have been operated annually since 1991.

Two pairs of lines are 100 m apart (from the end of one line to first net of the next line), whereas other lines are at least 1 km from their nearest neighbor. Each line is operated for three consecutive days from dawn (as soon as bats stop flying) to dusk (just before bats start flying). In January, this is from approximately 0700 to 1800 hours. Lines are checked constantly during the first day when capture rates are high, and then regularly (at least every 20 min) after capture rate declines.

Point Count Methods

To determine the relative value of netting versus visual censusing for determining species composition and relative density, J. Faaborg and two colleagues (T. Donovan and B. Woodworth) conducted a series of point counts during 1993, following a modification of guidelines for winter censusing (Hutto et al. 1986). Five points were set up in alignment with each row of nets. The middle point was at the mid-point of the net line, one was at each end (100 m from the center), and the last ones were 100 m beyond the ends of the net line. These points are closer together than is usually recommended, but we felt this was necessary to ensure the points sampled the net line area. We conducted 10 min counts, recording birds both within a 25-m radius of the point and all birds recorded beyond this fixed radius. Each point was visited on three different mornings, when the nets were not in operation. Each visit was conducted by a different observer, each of whom was familiar with the calls and songs of Puerto Rican birds. Counts started 15 min before sunrise, and it took about one hour to complete sampling at each net line. For this paper, we computed average detections per point for unlimited distance for each species.

RESULTS

Species Composition

Guanica Forest supports a typical insular avifauna with relatively few species but high abundances among most of them. Over the course of 30 years, we have captured every bird that we have seen within the Guanica Forest (not counting swallows and similar species that we only see flying overhead). Large raptors and pigeons that are too big for the nets are captured only rarely, as are nocturnal species that generally have stopped moving by the time nets are opened.

We compared the relative frequency of birds detected on all of our point counts with those netted on all net lines during 1993 (Table 1). Although seven of the 10 most abundant species recorded by each technique were the same, their relative frequencies were often very different. For example, the Adelaide's Warbler (see Table 1 for scientific names) was by far the most detected bird on point counts. It is widespread throughout the forest, maintains territories and pair bonds, and sings frequently in the morning, even in January. We feel we caught most of those individuals whose territories occurred along the net lines, but this was often only four to five birds per line, which is a small segment of total captures (4.8%).

The most frequently netted bird, the Bananaquit (31% of captures in 1993), constituted only 10% of point count detections, perhaps, in part, because it sings infrequently at Guanica in mid-winter. High capture rate for this species probably reflected accurately a high density, rather than constant movement of transients, as nearly all cases of individuals caught in two different lines in the same year involved this species. The Puerto Rican Flycatcher is virtually silent in January, so it was rarely recorded on point counts (1.1% of detections) despite accounting for 5.6% of captures. In contrast, species that are large enough that they often get out of the nets but that have loud calls or songs, such as the Puerto Rican Woodpecker, Troupial, and Puerto Rican Lizard-cuckoo, were recorded on point counts more frequently than they were netted. Analyzing birds detected solely within 25 m of the count point would have reduced the number of detections for most species, but would have had little effect on the general relationship between the two inventory methods.

Perhaps the most striking difference in the results of the two techniques was for wintering warblers, which comprised 13% of captures in 1993 but which totaled only 0.2% of total detections on point counts (Table 1). Only two species were detected on point counts (American Redstart and Black-and-white Warbler), whereas nine species were netted. Wintering warblers are relatively quiet in the Guanica Forest in winter and were easily missed on point counts, especially if they foraged on the ground (such as the Ovenbird).

TABLE 1. Comparison of the ten most abundant species found by netting (percent of total captures on nine net lines) and by point counts (percent of all detections on all points)

	Relative frequency
Species	Percent captured
Netting results	
Bananaquit (*Coereba flaveola*)	31.2
Puerto Rican Bullfinch (*Loxigilla portoricensis*)	18.4
Caribbean Elaenia (*Elaenia martinica*)	11.2
Puerto Rican Flycatcher (*Myiarchus antillarum*)	5.6
Puerto Rican Tody (*Todus mexicanus*)	4.8
Adelaide's Warbler (*Dendroica adelaidae*)	4.8
Puerto Rican Vireo (*Vireo latimeri*)	4.8
Red-legged Thrush (*Turdus plumbeus*)	4.0
Pearly-eyed Thrasher (*Margarops fuscatus*)	4.0
Antillean Mango (*Anthracothorax dominicus*)	4.0
ALL WINTER RESIDENT SPECIES*	13.3

	Percent detected
Point count results	
Adelaide's Warbler	34.0
Caribbean Elaenia	16.6
Bananaquit	10.2
Puerto Rican Vireo	8.7
Puerto Rican Tody	7.1
Puerto Rican Bullfinch	6.5
Puerto Rican Woodpecker (*Melanerpes portoricensis*)	4.0
Troupial (*Icterus icterus*)	2.0
Puerto Rican Lizard-cuckoo (*Saurothera vielloti*)	1.9
Pearly-eyed Thrasher	1.3
ALL WINTER RESIDENT SPECIES**	0.2

* Black-and-white Warbler (*Mniotilta varia*), Swainson's Warbler (*Limnothlypis swainsonii*), Worm-eating Warbler (*Helmitheros vermivorum*), Northern Parula (*Parula americana*), Magnolia Warbler (*Dendroica magnolia*), Prairie Warbler (*D. discolor*), American Redstart (*Setophaga ruticilla*), Hooded Warbler (*Wilsonia citrina*), and Ovenbird (*Seiurus aurocapilla*).
** Black-and-white Warbler and American Redstart

CAPTURE RATES WITHIN THREE-DAY NETTING SESSIONS

The typical capture pattern through a three-day sampling period (all species pooled) was a steep linear decline in daily number of first captures (birds caught for the first time in a netting session). Some samples were very linear (e.g., 1973; Fig. 1), although a few were not (e.g., 1987; Fig. 1). In nearly all samples, however, fewer birds were caught during each subsequent day, and in all cases, capture rates declined over the entire three-day sample. We computed linear regressions of capture rate (number of daily first captures against day of sample for each year), and found similar slopes of capture rates, despite great variation in population levels. Capture rate by sample day, averaged across all years, also showed a strong decline (Fig. 2a), although SE was large due to large annual variation in total captures. When data were treated as percentages of total captures (to reduce variation resulting from varying

population sizes), SE was smaller, but the overall pattern remained the same (Fig. 2b). These results, based on 20 years of data from the original net line, were mirrored closely by data from over 60 other net lines during the period 1989–1993 (J. Faaborg, unpubl. data).

Samples with unusual capture patterns generally occurred only when population levels were low, or under exceptional weather conditions (especially high winds). With one exception, unusual patterns involved samples in which captures on the third day were higher than on the second, because of inclement conditions on the second day. In rare cases, we added a fourth day of netting under these circumstances. However, this always resulted in fewer captures than on the third day, suggesting that most of the birds using that area had already been caught in the first three days.

Most species showed daily declines in capture rates similar to the overall patterns illustrated above,

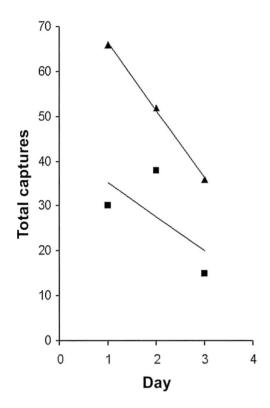

FIGURE 1. Daily capture rates of birds over three-day samples on the original Guanica net line, showing a particularly linear sample (triangles: 1973 sample, $r^2 = 0.99$) and a less linear sample (squares: 1987 sample, $r^2 = 0.41$).

but the pattern was most pronounced for abundant species (Fig. 3a). Less abundant species tended to show a similar trend (Fig. 3b), but when only four or five individuals are captured in three days, the slope of the capture rate will naturally be less steep than for abundant birds. Capture rates for these species are less likely to be linear, probably mainly by chance.

The group of species that migrate to Puerto Rico for the winter, nearly all of them warblers (Parulidae), was captured very rapidly (Fig. 3c). In general, the first two days of netting captured 85–90% of the three-day total of these species.

For species with large numbers of floaters in the population, we might expect captures to continue at a low level for more than three days and, depending upon the characteristics of the floaters, perhaps indefinitely. However, in our knowledge of more than 200 net lines operated throughout the West Indies, we are aware of only two records of an abundant species showing little or no decline in capture rate over a three-day sampling period. Neither was at Guanica

and both were on very small islands and apparently associated with extreme drought.

NET AVOIDANCE

Only 5–10% of birds were caught more than once in a three-day sample. Combined with a rapid decline in first captures, this indicates net avoidance. Otherwise, daily capture rates should have remained about constant, with only the proportion of first captures declining. We know that low recapture did not reflect movement out of the area, because we often saw banded birds nearby, and recaptured them in subsequent years. If net avoidance was specific to the exact location of capture, we might expect more than a 10% recapture rate, because birds could be recaptured further along the net line, but avoidance appeared to involve all nets along the nearly 200-m transect of a line. Due to net-avoidance, third day captures often involved 30 or fewer total individuals, compared to 150 or more birds on day one.

We do not know how long net avoidance continues in an individual bird. We occasionally ran net lines in June, between January samples, and saw no difference in expected capture rate in either sample (June or second January). Through more intensive studies of wintering ecology of migrants we have found that nets could be run in October, January, and March with no apparent carry-over of net avoidance (Latta and Faaborg 2001).

RATES OF CAPTURE THROUGH THE DAY

Morning (0700–0930 hours) was the best time to capture birds at Guanica, but there was another burst of activity in the evening (Fig. 4). The midday period (1200–1530 hours) was often slow and few captures occurred after noon on the third day. Because of the short, deciduous nature of the vegetation, many nets were exposed to full sunlight during mid-day, and nets had to be checked frequently at this time to protect birds from heat stress.

ANNUAL CAPTURE AND RECAPTURE RATES

Total annual captures of resident birds on the nine net lines varied from 550 to 1,142 individuals. Two species were caught at the rate of about 100 birds/year, three species at around 50 birds/year, and two species at around 30 birds/year. All the others generally are caught 20 times a year or less.

Most of the common species showed patterns of variation that suggested that we were tracking local populations. Annual numbers of the Bananaquit, for

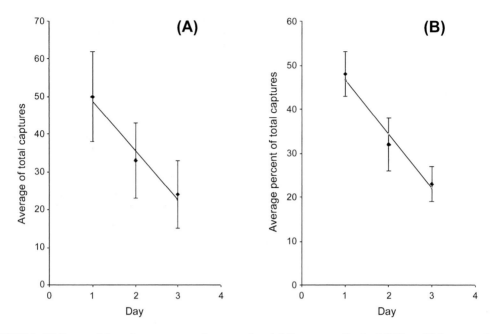

FIGURE 2. (A) Pattern of three-day capture rates by mean of total daily captures (A; r^2 = 0.972), or (B) by mean of the percent of total captures caught on each day of the sample (r^2 = 0.974) for 18 samples of the original Guanica net line run 1973–1993. Error bars show ±SE.

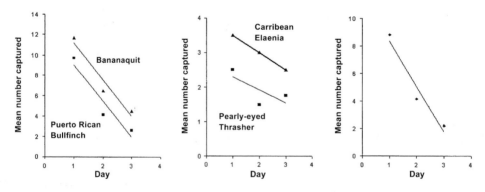

FIGURE 3. Capture rates of species and species groups during the three days of sampling, showing: (A) abundant species with steep declines in capture rates (Puerto Rican Bullfinch [r^2 = 0.906] and Bananaquit [r^2 = 0.945]); (B) species that have lower and more gradual capture rates (Caribbean Elaenia [r^2 = 0.998] and Pearly-eyed Thrasher [r^2 = 0.590]); and (C) winter resident species (primarily Parulidae [r^2 = 0.943]).

example, ranged from 124 to 485. However, in two ground feeding species, the Common Ground-dove (*Columbina passerina*) and Black-faced Grassquit (*Tiaris bicolor*), numbers varied so dramatically from year to year that dispersal into and out of the forest must have been a factor. For example, ground-doves increased from 5 to 59 to 115 captures in consecutive samples, which must have exceeded local reproductive rates, and they declined from 137 to 11 captures

in just a year. Both of these species also showed low rates of recapture of banded individuals.

Annual recapture rates were high enough to allow us to model survival rates for many species, using Cormack-Jolly-Seber mark-recapture models (Pollock et al. 1990, Lebreton et al. 1992) and Program MARK (White and Burnham 1999). As a by-product of survival rate estimation, we can estimate capture probability (the proportion of

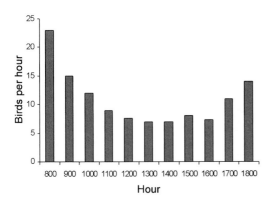

FIGURE 4. Capture rates of birds at the original Guanica net line through the day, averaged for 1990–1995 samples. Birds/hour was computed by counting total captures for the 60-min period ending on the hour (e.g., 0800 hours). First and last hourly periods may include a few birds caught before 0700 hours and after 1800 hours during the net opening and closing process.

previously banded birds present and alive each year that are recaptured). Our current analyses suggest that although recapture rates vary by species, they remain relatively constant from year to year within species and even within some guilds (Faaborg and Arendt 1995, Dugger et al. 2000). Because of this, the raw counts of mist-net capture totals can serve as relatively unbiased indices of population size for many of the species caught in mist nets in Guanica Forest. Estimates of annual recapture rates varied from 10% for some residents to over 35% for three of the common warbler species. Some individuals were extremely site faithful and long lived, including a 17-year-old Puerto Rican Flycatcher and an Ovenbird at least 7 years old.

About 1–2% of individuals were recaptured at a different net line (even when lines were >100 m apart), suggesting that there are some transient individuals in the Guanica samples. These occurred only in some years and almost always with the two most abundant species. Whereas mark–recapture models allow estimation of the proportion of transients in a population, it is sufficient for our purposes to note that population estimates may be misleading for species that show relatively equal capture rates throughout a three-day sample.

DISCUSSION

Results indicate that the netting protocol we use works well in meeting our study objectives. We catch a regular set of species that constitutes the vast majority of the avifauna of Guanica Forest. After three full days of netting, there are relatively few unmarked birds left to catch within a site. Because we rarely catch the same bird in the two net lines that are only 100 m apart, and because capture probability was relatively constant across years, we feel there is no great annual variation in territory or home range size or location. The relative constancy of recapture probability among years indicates that there are not important changes in territory or home range size among years. This stability results in recapture rates that are high enough to give good information on site faithfulness (Woodworth et al. 1999) and to allow estimation of survival rates for many species (Faaborg and Arendt 1995, Dugger et al. 2000), which is often not the case for mist-netting mark–recapture data sets.

In addition, since annual recapture rates appear to remain constant for most species and even across guilds, capture totals over our three-day sample can serve as an reliable index to population levels. Although our methods did not give actual densities, they appeared to give relative densities that could be compared in a meaningful way from year to year within a site or from site to site within the same forest type. For example, we have shown how Guanica bird population variation is highly correlated with certain rainfall characteristics (Faaborg and Arendt 1992a, Dugger et al. 2000), and we see regular variation in relative abundance of bird species in different net lines that seems to be related to variation in vegetation structure within the Guanica Forest.

Mist nets operated as in our protocol may be sufficient to monitor birds in low statured forests such as the Guanica Forest, given the nature of capture rates and the species involved. Recognizing that densities are relative, and noting that the forest here is too short for any sort of foraging stratification, removes the major complaints suggested for many mist-net studies by Remsen and Good (1996). Guanica is perhaps uniquely suited to monitoring with mist nets, because it consists of short, scrubby forest where few birds forage above the area of nets. It also supports a typically depauperate island avifauna with high abundance of most species and few species too large to be captured by a single size of net. Comparisons with sites where many individuals may forage above the nets must be done carefully, as the latter situation is undoubtedly one where only a subset of the overall bird community is being sampled effectively. In forests of tall stature, for example, one would expect that nets run at ground level would only capture the subset of the total bird community that forages and moves near the ground.

Point counts did not add much information on species composition to that of netting within this habitat during the non-breeding season, as no species was detected on point counts that was not netted at least once. This is not surprising, as neither residents nor winter residents are breeding during this, the peak of the dry season, so vocalizations are uncommon in most species. Flocking is also uncommon in this forest. This is not to say that use of point counts would not provide additional valuable information about population trends, particularly for large species that are not easily netted. However, only with detailed, long-term comparisons of the two techniques can we adequately determine the strengths and weaknesses of these two monitoring techniques in this forest.

After three days, capture rates had declined enough that continued netting was unproductive. The fact that for many resident species, third-day captures were very low relative to first day captures supports the idea that we captured a large proportion of the birds whose home ranges included the net line. Adding additional banding days would likely have added few new individuals to the totals. However, habitats with tall vegetation or with species that have much larger home ranges might require longer netting periods to catch as many birds as we get at Guanica in three days (Remsen and Good 1986).

Although it might be tempting to avoid the noontime lull in capture rates by operating nets only until noon or closing them for three to four hours at midday, this may not be an efficient use of time. Over a six-year period, an average of 43.9% of all captures were made in the second half of the day (after 1200 hours). This suggests that more than three mornings of netting would be needed to catch as many birds as three full days and, to the extent that some birds are active only during the afternoon, these individuals might be missed with morning-only netting.

Although capture rates are often expressed as birds/net-hour (DeSante et al. 1993), our results showed clearly that many more birds were captured on the first day of a sample than on day three. Until we understand more about the characteristics of net-avoidance in birds, we should be careful about comparing netted samples from sessions of different length. In addition, caution is needed in comparing data collected from frequent netting sessions. Running a net line once a year did not seem to have any effect on capture rates, and our data suggest that holding netting sessions as close as three months

apart also did not affect capture rates in any obvious way. Net lines operated again before net-avoidance disappeared would produce data that are not comparable to the original samples. Further work is needed to determine the time interval required for net avoidance to be lost. Frequent operation of nets may provide better data on survival rates, local movements, or the production of offspring than annual or infrequent netting does, but it does so at the expense of simple comparisons of short-term capture rates to estimate population sizes.

Any netting protocol that is replicated as precisely as possible on an annual basis will provide annual comparisons of capture rates and insights into population levels. The important rules for the use of mist nets to monitor bird populations involve consistency of effort from year to year within a location, care when comparing different netting regimes within a habitat type, and extreme care when comparing netting results from different habitat types.

ACKNOWLEDGMENTS

This research was done in cooperation with the University of Puerto Rico. Financial aid in recent years has been provided by the International Institute for Tropical Forestry, U.S. Department of Agriculture, Forest Service, with the help and support of A. Lugo, Director, and J. M. Wunderle, Jr., Wildlife Team Leader. The early years of our expanded effort were funded by the U.S. Fish and Wildlife Service through the National Museum of Natural History (with thanks to M. Foster) and the Cooperative Wildlife Unit Research Program (thanks to the late T. LaRoe, W. R. Goforth, and C. Rabeni). Even earlier work was supported by the Chapman Fund of the American Museum of Natural History, the National Science Foundation, the Graduate School of the University of Missouri-Columbia, and the U.S. Agency for International Development. A. Arendt has always been very gracious in allowing a group of north temperate migrants to descent on her home each January to prepare for fieldwork. The Puerto Rican Department of Natural Resources (D.N.R.) has provided permission for our work, and M. Canals of the D.N.R. has been extremely helpful with logistical concerns while we are at Guanica. Our list of field assistants is too long to print, but we thank all of you for suffering through netting in Puerto Rico in January and making the many nights around the picnic table delightful. Finally, the early version of this manuscript was improved by the comments of R. Holmes, M. Johnson, G. E. Wallace, and P. Porneluzi, while this draft has been aided by C. J. Ralph, E. H. Dunn, and the students of the M. U. Avian Ecology Laboratory.

Studies in Avian Biology No. 29:151–160

COPING WITH MIST-NET CAPTURE-RATE BIAS: CANOPY HEIGHT AND SEVERAL EXTRINSIC FACTORS

Elizabeth P. Mallory, Nicholas Brokaw, and Steven C. Hess

Abstract. Many factors other than a species' actual abundance can affect mist-net capture rates. We used ANCOVA models to quantify some potential biases and control their effects, producing adjusted estimates of capture rates that are more directly comparable among mist-net stations. Data came from 46 two-day mist-net sessions from September 1990 to May 1992 at six subtropical forest stations in the Rio Bravo Conservation and Management Area, northwest Belize. Factors evaluated included canopy height at net sites, long-term net shyness (days elapsed between first and last netting day of the entire study period), season (wet vs. dry), total rainfall during a netting session, and temperature. Number of individuals and species captured/10 net-h declined at each net with increasing canopy height above the net. Capture rates differed significantly among some of the stations. Elapsed days and rainfall caused significant bias in capture rates, which were statistically controlled within the ANCOVA, whereas season and temperature did not. Capture rates varied among sessions, but there was a slight and significant decline over the entire study period for all stations combined. Rainfall significantly depressed capture rates somewhat on a daily basis, but capture rates did not differ between wet and dry seasons. When we replaced the station variable in the ANCOVA with mean canopy height, the model was still highly significant, but did not explain as much of the variation in capture rates. Statistical analysis provides an objective means of interpreting data and estimating reliability, but only if statistical assumptions of the analyses are met. We discuss the need for including randomization in the experimental design, standardizing netting protocol, and quantifying sources of bias in the field, before ANCOVA or other parametric statistical techniques can be used to partition effects of biases.

Key Words: Belize, bias, birds, canopy height, capture rates, experimental design, mist net, multivariate statis-

In the tropics "a bird in the hand" may be worth more than "two in the bush" because bird vocalizations are relatively unknown, and observers require extensive experience with the bird community before becoming proficient at conducting point counts. For some cryptic or secretive and rarely vocal species in the understory, mist netting may be the best, or only, method of detection (Terborgh 1985, Remsen 1994). Thus, mist netting has several advantages over other kinds of counts and has often been used to describe bird species composition and relative abundances in tropical forests (Whitman *this volume*).

Nonetheless, mist netting is criticized as a technique for counting birds because susceptibility to capture depends on a bird's spatial and temporal activity, which varies according to species, age, sex, weather, season, time of day, experience with nets, and foraging stratum (Karr 1981a, Remsen and Parker 1983, Martin and Karr 1986, Rappole and Ramos 1995, Jenni et al. 1996, Remsen and Good 1996). Bird-community composition is often related to vegetation structure (Brokaw and Lent 1999), but differences in vegetation structure confound species-to-species, habitat-to-habitat, station-to-station, and even net-to-net capture-rate comparisons, because the proportion of individuals sampled of midstory, subcanopy, and

canopy species will likely decline as canopy height increases and the proportion of vegetation within net level decreases (Whitman et al. 1997).

Researchers using mist nets in the tropics have dealt with variable height-related capture probabilities, where some species seldom come down to mist-net level, in one of the following ways: (1) define the study species as only those species that occur at mist net level (the forest understory or low second growth); (2) limit analyses to only those species or guilds known to be vulnerable to capture; or (3) combine point counts and mist net results (e.g., Loiselle and Blake 1991, Petit et al. 1992, Stouffer and Bierregaard 1995, Gram and Faaborg 1997, Whitman et al. 1997). In principle, mark–recapture techniques can be used to estimate capture proportion and population size separately for each species caught (Kendall et al. *this volume*). However, mark–recapture cannot give good estimates for species rarely caught, and the method involves assumptions that cannot always be met. These four approaches may reduce, but not eliminate, height-related "species detectability" bias within forests of different height and vegetation structure.

Bias is "the difference between the actual population value and the mean of a sampling distribution"

(Dixon 1993:292). If the sample capture rate is centered on the true population mean and is not consistently too low or too high, then it is unbiased. If biases are strong and unaccounted for, the results of field studies will be erroneous. If a method does not detect individuals equally under all the conditions being compared, estimates of the true population differences among habitats and times will be biased, unless the counts are adjusted for the differing capture probability (Thompson 2002, Sauer and Link *this volume*). Part of the solution is to design studies to account for potential biases, quantifying them in the field when netting, and adding them as variables during analysis. In this way, the effect of each factor on capture rates can be determined. If bias is detected, and the data meet the statistical requirements, capture rates from netting samples can be statistically adjusted for the biases within a multifactor analysis (e.g., Ramsey et al. 1987, Boulinier et al. 1998). We use that approach in this paper, to investigate the effects of a selected set of potential biases on mist-net capture rates using data from our work on bird communities in several subtropical forest types in Belize.

METHODS

STUDY AREA

Data were collected from September 1990 to May 1992 in the Rio Bravo Conservation and Management Area (RBCMA), then a 92,000 ha preserve in northwest Belize (17°45'N, 89°00'W), managed by the Programme for Belize. The RBCMA is in the "subtropical moist" life zone, with a mean annual rainfall of about 1,500 mm, and a dry season that generally extends from February-March through May.

The six stations used in our analysis were established in relatively mature natural forest. The stations were named after the locally predominant vegetation: Mesic Upland Forest I and II (two stations), Dry Upland Forest (I and II), Riparian Forest, and Palm Forest. The nearctic migrants captured at stations in this study ranged from 16.7% of species and 15.7% of individuals at Mesic Upland Forest I to 25.6% of species at Riparian Forest and 24.7% of individuals at Dry Upland Forest I.

Each station consisted of a 1-km transect located near a road, but far enough from the road to avoid edge effects. The start of each transect was a random number between 100 and 350 m perpendicular into the forest from the first randomly selected point along the road that fell into the appropriate forest type. The direction each transect took from the starting point was also selected at random, from bearings not heading back toward the road. Transects were laid along a compass bearing and marked every 20 m with PVC pipe. The bearings of a few transects were adjusted at the 100-m point, or a gap was inserted, where the forest type changed appreciably or

there was some habitat anomaly. The distances separating transects ranged from 1.6 to 28 km.

MIST-NETTING PROCEDURES

On each transect we put up 13 36-mm mesh and two 30-mm mesh mist nets on collapsible tent poles. Nets were set up within a 500-m section of each 1-km transect, selected for ease of access and to avoid features that would not be comparable among transects. We stratified the 500-m section into 100-m segments, within each of which we established three net sites at randomly selected points for a total of 15 nets/transect. Placement of the two 30-mm mist nets was determined by chance at each netting session.

We netted at least seven times at each of the six stations, spanning two wet and two dry seasons. Each station was netted once during the first wet season, that is, in the third or fourth quarters of 1990 when transects were established. Afterwards, we netted each station once each quarter of the year during the study, for a minimum of two netting sessions from each of the wet and dry seasons per year. We ran additional sessions at two upland forest stations, to improve sampling with respect to migration.

We opened nets at first light each day, ran them hourly until dusk on the first day, and in most cases ended on the second day once we reached approximately 300 net-h for the session. We continually patrolled nets during light rain, brief showers, or during "rain drip" from the foliage after heavy rain, keeping nets open as long as we felt that captured birds were not in danger of becoming wet. We recorded the opening and closing of each net to the nearest 5 min, including closures for heavy rain or when an individual net was exposed to hot sun. There were several exceptions to the protocol of 300 net-h/session. The first session at stations ranged from 257 to 288 net-h due to our initial caution when netting on rainy days. Also, in January and February 1991, C. Robbins conducted 3-day sessions at these stations as part of his own survey work (Robbins et al. 1992). Only captures during the first 300 net-h in his sessions were used in our analyses. The actual mean net-hour/session was 335.1 ± 67.8 SD, but was reduced to 292.4 ± 18.47 SD when only captures during net hours up to and including 300 net-h were used. In total, 3,245 captures during 13,450 net-h were used in this analysis.

We aged and sexed wintering or transient nearctic migrants following Pyle's (1987) guide and our experience with birds in North America. For year-round residents and summer residents we based age and sex designations on plumage descriptions (Stiles and Skutch 1989, Howell and Webb 1995), presence of brood patch or cloacal protuberance, eye or gape color, feather condition, synchrony of growth bars on feathers, and, with caution, degree of skull pneumatization.

DEPENDENT VARIABLES

Capture rate (number of captures/10 net-h) were calculated for data pooled from the fifteen nets at each station for each 300 net-h session, the sample unit in most of our

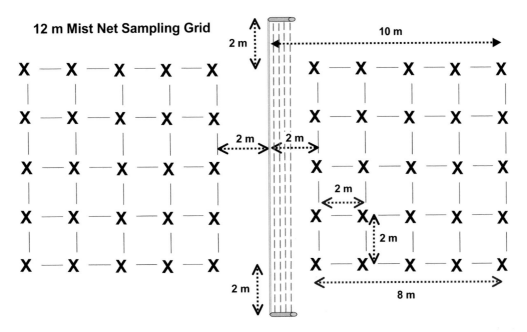

FIGURE 1. Layout of canopy height sample points (X's) at each net.

analyses (in all cases except the analysis of canopy height). Separate capture rates for each session provide repeated measure "snap-shots" of the local avifauna.

We examined six variations of capture rates, three involving total number of captures within a session (including recaptures), calculated separately for all species combined, for resident species alone, and for migrant species alone. Recaptures were included in these indices to give an index of overall bird activity. We also calculated rates for number of separate individuals captured (first captures within a session, including birds banded at any previous session), individuals recaptured (re-caught within a session and more than 2 h from the previous capture), and the number of species caught within each session. For evaluation of canopy height, we calculated capture rates as described above, but on a net-by-net basis rather than averaged for each of the six transects, because vegetation structure can vary widely among nets within a transect.

INDEPENDENT VARIABLES

Concurrent with our netting we recorded additional data to use as independent variables in our analyses of capture rates.

CANOPY was the mean maximum canopy height at each net, based on 50 sample points regularly distributed as shown in Figure 1. At each point we used a one-inch diameter, 2.5 m-long PVC pipe to sight an imaginary vertical line to the forest canopy, and then estimated the maximum canopy height along that line. Although the method requires estimating heights, we deemed it adequate for comparing vegetation height among stations because we regularly checked our estimates with a rangefinder.

STATION was a class variable for station.

DAYS was the number of days from start of the study, including days between netting sessions (values ranged from 0 to 571).

SEASON was a class variable describing dry season (mist-netting sessions from 9 January to 19 May 1991 and from 15 February to 21 April 1992) and wet season (sessions from 5 September to 25 November 1990 and 23 August to 9 November 1991).

RAIN indicated total rainfall during each netting session, taken from daily records of rainfall at Chan Chich Lodge, about 30 km from the stations. Given the local nature of tropical rainstorms, rainfall at Chan Chich may not have been directly related to rainfall at stations, but we felt that similarity was sufficient to justify inclusion of this factor.

TEMPERATURE was the maximum daily temperature recorded daily at Chan Chich during a netting session. Minimum temperatures were correlated with the maximums, so were not included in the analyses.

STATISTICAL ANALYSES

All numeric variables were tested for normality and homogeneity of variances among class levels, and converted to ranks if necessary for use in parametric or non-parametric statistics. We used a $\log_{10}$ transformation of the number of individuals/10 net-h and a square root transformation of the number of species/10 net-h to normalize distributions, and a $\log_{10}$ transformation to equalize variance of CANOPY.

We used a One-Way ANOVA to test for differences in CANOPY height at nets among STATIONs. For other factors, we used ANCOVA instead of a repeated-measures ANOVA, because our experimental design was unbalanced (three wet season versus four dry season sessions), and we had a combination of numerical and class variables we wished to examine simultaneously. ANCOVA combines numerical and class factors to (1) adjust for sources of bias to see whether class differences remain or become insignificant when adjusting a covariate (thus, we can adjust for the repeated-measures in a time series by incorporating a variable measuring time over the course of the sampling); (2) produce adjusted least-square means once sources of experimental error have been removed; or (3) study regressions in multiple groups to see if relationships between dependent and independent variables are the same within categories of the groups (Snedecor and Cochran 1967).

ANCOVA was used to test effects of CANOPY and STATION on capture rates for number of individuals and number of species, and to evaluate effects on capture rates of STATION, DAYS, SEASON, RAIN, and TEMPERATURE. The effects of these factors on capture rates were first tested in a full model ANCOVA. Non-significant factors and non-significant interactions among significant factors were then removed from the model before re-running ANCOVA again to produce final results. We then replaced the variable STATION with CANOPY in the final full-model ANCOVA to determine if this simple index of vegetation structure could explain a greater amount of variation. This variable substitution converted the six station classes to six ordinal measures. We used type III sums of squares to evaluate factor significance, type I sums of squares to investigate importance of interactions among independent variables, and adjusted least-square means (LSM) to produce probabilities for the hypothesis that one least square-estimated mean equals another.

We used SAS procedures PROC GLM, PROC UNIVARIATE, and PROC CORR for tests of significance (SAS Institute 1999). We calculated the Bartlett test scores and PROC REGRESSION to verify homogeneity of variances and slopes among class variables before using a parametric GLM.

RESULTS

Canopy Height (CANOPY)

Mean canopy height at nets differed significantly among stations (ANOVA, $r^2 = 0.704$, F = 40.04, P <

0.001; Table 1). Mesic Upland Forest II nets had higher CANOPY and Riparian Forest nets had lower CANOPY than nets at all other stations (P < 0.001). The only other difference among stations was that CANOPY at Palm Forest nets was higher than at Mesic Upland Forest I nets (P < 0.001).

On a net-by-net basis, the number of individuals captured/10 net-h declined significantly with increase in mean canopy height (r = -0.79, slope = -0.327/m, P < 0.001; Fig 2A). Both STATION (F = 13.36, P < 0.001) and CANOPY height (F = 5.4, P < 0.05) had significant independent effects, explaining 60.9% of the variation in capture rates (ANCOVA, F = 21.58, P < 0.001).

Similarly, the rate at which new species were caught at the nets declined with increasing canopy height (r = -0.78, slope = -0.316 species/m, P < 0.001; Fig 2B). The ANCOVA was significant ($r^2 = 0.623$, F = 22.87, P < 0.001), and both STATION (F = 13.52, P < 0.001) and CANOPY (F = 4.1, P < 0.05) affected species capture rates. Capture rates at Riparian nets, where CANOPY was lowest, were higher than capture rates at other stations (Fig. 2), but capture rates at other stations overlapped considerably despite a wide range of CANOPY heights.

Multifactorial Analyses

All species combined.—The full ANCOVA model was highly significant, explaining 89.7% of the variation in total capture rates of all species combined (Table 2). STATION and the two covariates DAYS and RAIN were significant factors, whereas SEASON and TEMPERATURE were not. There were no significant interactions among the independent variables, and no autocorrelation between the residuals of the significant variables, DAYS and RAIN (D = 2.318, > d_U = 1.622, N = 46, P < 0.05). Capture rates at Riparian Forest were significantly higher than at other stations (P < 0.001). Palm Forest capture rates were significantly higher than those at both Dry Upland stations (P < 0.05).

TABLE 1. MEAN CANOPY HEIGHT AT MIST NET STATIONS IN SIX TROPICAL FOREST STATIONS, RIO BRAVO CONSERVATION MANAGEMENT AREA, BELIZE

Station	Canopy height (m)				
	Mean	SE	SD	CV	N
Dry Upland Forest I	15.52	0.498	1.928	12.42	15
Dry Upland Forest II	15.22	0.882	3.416	22.44	15
Mesic Upland Forest I	14.95	0.821	3.179	21.26	15
Mesic Upland Forest II	20.96	0.800	3.099	14.79	15
Palm Forest	14.53	0.741	2.87	19.76	15
Riparian Forest	7.742	0.468	1.812	23.40	15

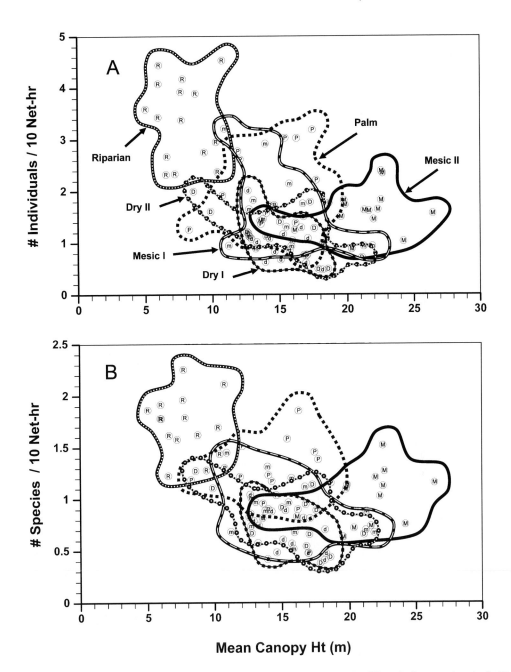

FIGURE 2. Capture rates versus mean canopy height (m) around each mist net (N = 90) at six forest stations in the Rio Bravo Conservation and Management Area, Belize (plotted on untransformed axes). (A) Total number of individuals from all species combined /10 net-h; (B) Total number of species/10 net-h. Each net is represented by a letter and the 15 nets at each station are delimited by polygons.

Capture rates clearly vary from session to session (Fig. 3). Nonetheless, there was a slight, yet significant, decline over the entire study period for all stations combined (slope = -0.017/10 day, t = 45, P ≤ 0.001), and at Dry Upland Forest I, Palm Forest,

and Riparian Forest separately. Riparian also had a significant positive interaction with RAINFALL.

Along with examination of the residual plots against DAYS, we found no evidence of autocorrelation in error terms within stations (D ranging

TABLE 2. ANALYSIS OF COVARIANCE (ANCOVA) OF CAPTURE RATES, COEFFICIENTS OF DETERMINATION (R^2), AND ADJUSTED LEAST SQUARE MEANS (LSM) (N = 46)

		Captures/10 net-h					Species/ session
		All species	Residents	Migrants	Individuals	Recaptures	
FULL MODEL	F^a	15.83***	12.43***	4.86***	9.24***	6.59***	7.38***
	r^2	0.897	0.873	0.728	0.836	0.784	0.803
	LSM	2.43	2.07	0.36	1.85	0.579	25.72
Class Effects							
STATION	F	43.53***	32.20***	11.91***	22.41***	15.56***	19.23***
Dry Upland I	LSM	1.30	1.05	0.255	1.04	0.262	18.94
Dry Upland II	LSM	1.56	1.38	0.176	1.15	0.403	21.45
Mesic Upland I	LSM	2.10	1.78	0.321	1.56	0.538	23.46
Mesic Upland II	LSM	2.05	1.82	0.231	1.73	0.324	23.73
Palm	LSM	2.70	2.3	0.408	2.05	0.641	28.82
Riparian	LSM	5.17	4.25	0.923	3.90	1.27	38.04
SEASON	F	0.40 ns	0.12 ns	0.72 ns	0.08 ns	0.63 ns	0.24 ns
Dry	LSM	2.42	2.10	0.324	0.018	0.630	26.16
Wet	LSM	2.54	2.09	0.447	0.020	0.516	25.32
Covariates							
DAYS	F	15.83***	16.62***	0.04 ns	24.44***	8.45**	0.89 ns
RAIN	F	9.06**	7.63**	1.19 ns	5.63*	1.51 ns	0.49 ns
TEMPERATURE	F	0.73 ns	2.96 ns	4.43	1.61 ns	1.23 ns	1.12 ns
Interactions							
STATION * SEASON	F	1.99 ns	1.79 ns	0.62 ns	1.38 ns	0.33 ns	1.52 ns
RAIN * SEASON	F	0.08 ns	0.03 ns	1.52 ns	0.02 ns	0.12 ns	0.07 ns
TEMPERATURE*SEASON	F	0.37 ns	0.12 ns	0.56 ns	0.06 ns	0.70 ns	0.27 ns

[a] F values for Type III Sums of Squares, probability of significance: $P < 0.05$ *, $P < 0.01$ **, $P < 0.001$ ***; ns = not significant.

from 1.81 at Mesic Upland Forest II to 3.05 at Dry Upland Forest I), except that at Dry Upland Forest II, D = 1.26, which is inconclusive. With seven to eight sessions at each station, we used the bounds for two independent variables for the smallest sample size available for the Durbin-Watson statistic (d_L = 0.95, d_U = 1.54, N = 15, $P \le 0.05$). Total capture rate for all species combined did not differ between wet and dry seasons, either before (F = 0.29, df = 45, ns) or after controlling for the effects of other factors (Table 2). However, capture rates were depressed with increasing rainfall during sessions (regardless of season), after adjusting for the other factors in the ANCOVA (slope = -0.811/10 day, $P < 0.001$). Riparian Forest was the only single station at which rainfall significantly affected overall capture rate (slope = -5.3, t = -5.47, $P < 0.01$; with significant interaction of DAYS).

A simple ANCOVA on overall capture rates (total captures, all species combined) for the 46 sessions with mean CANOPY as a class variable instead of STATION, and including DAYS, gave identical results as when class STATION was used (r^2 = 0.796, F = 25.43, $P < 0.001$; either STATION or CANOPY F = 29.65, $P < 0.001$; DAYS F = 8.42, $P <$ 0.01). When CANOPY was entered as a continuous variable, the model was still highly significant, but CANOPY did not explain the variation in capture rates as well as did STATION (r^2 = 0.451, F = 33.56, $P < 0.001$; DAYS F = 2.54, ns).

Other capture rates.—Separate multifactorial analyses were conducted for number of birds captured/10 net-h of resident species, migrant species, individuals of all species combined (excluding within-session recaptures), recaptured individuals of all species combined (within-session recaptures), and for the rate at which new species were detected within each session. Although there were differences in significance levels, patterns were similar to those described above for all species combined (Table 2). Migrant species stood out as having capture rates unaffected by DAYS, and this was the only group affected by TEMPERATURE, which probably reflects the seasonal difference in presence of these species in the study area. Rate at which new species were captured was significantly affected only by STATION. Numbers of species captured at the Riparian and Palm Forest stations were significantly higher than elsewhere, and were higher at both Mesic Upland Forest stations than at Dry Upland I.

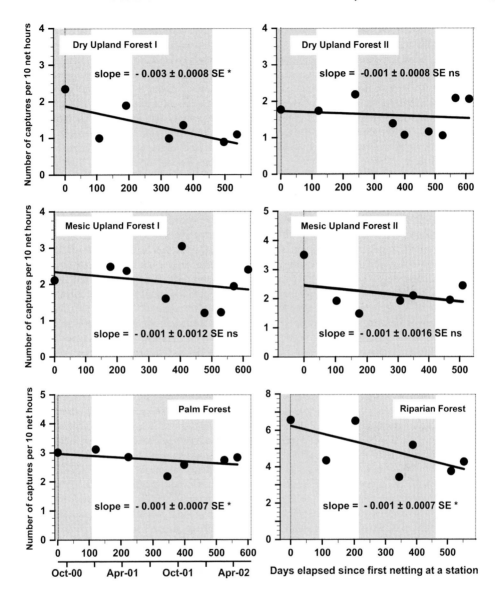

FIGURE 3. Mean capture rates (total captures, all species combined) for 46 sessions among six stations, in four forest types, netted from September 1990 to May 1992 in the Rio Bravo Conservation and Management Area, Belize. Sessions are in chronological order by the number of days elapsed since netting first began at each station, starting at zero along the horizontal axis. The *y*-axes are off-set in each plot to synchronize the *x*-axes by date (second axis on lower left). Wet seasons are shaded; dry seasons are unshaded. Slope of the regression ±SE is shown for each station, along with significance (asterisk indicating $P < 0.05$).

There was no autocorrelation among capture-rate residuals for resident species ($D = 2.072 > d_U = 1.622$, $N = 46$, $P < 0.05$), migrant species ($D = 1.879 > d_U = 1.622$, $N = 46$, $P < 0.05$), individuals ($D = 2.461 > d_U = 1.622$, $N = 46$, $P < 0.05$), recaptures ($D = 2.226 > d_U = 1.622$, $N = 46$, $P < 0.05$), or species ($D = 2.463 > d_U = 1.622$, $N = 46$, $P < 0.05$).

DISCUSSION

EFFECT OF CANOPY HEIGHT (CANOPY)

We chose canopy height as an index of vegetation structure because it is simple to measure and interpret, although structural complexity and density below the canopy will also influence the height distribution of birds and their probability of capture. The net-by-net decline in the number of individuals and number of species captured/10 net-h as canopy height increased demonstrates how capture rates may be biased by canopy height differences among habitats (see also Gram and Faaborg 1997, Whitman et al. 1997), but not all of the differences in capture rates among stations were explained by canopy height (Fig. 2.).

There are at least two reasons why relative capture rates among locations with vegetation of differing height would not reflect true relative abundance of some species. First, taller forests usually have more distinct vegetation layers than do shorter forests in the tropics, supporting midstory and subcanopy specialists, which rarely venture into the understory and get caught in mist nets. Some of these specialist species rarely occur in shorter forests, but many of them will shift their foraging lower as canopy height decreases, thereby increasing their probability of capture (Rappole and Ramos 1995, Remsen and Good 1996). Second, canopy and subcanopy species at times follow the foliage–air interface into shorter second-growth (Stiles 1983). In both cases, these specialists will be caught disproportionately more often in nets in shorter vegetation than in nets in taller forest, their primary habitat.

Unfortunately, measuring vegetation structure around nets cannot be used to adjust capture rates for canopy height bias unless the species-specific capture probabilities are known. Timed behavioral observations documenting the height distribution of many individuals of each species, in a variety of habitats, are needed to quantify these probabilities.

Multifactorial Analyses

The ANCOVA statistically isolated the effect of STATION on capture rate, and determined the significance of independent effects of SEASON, TEMPERATURE, RAINFALL, and DAYS elapsed since the first netting session at a station. Thus, potential biases that could affect comparisons of STATION were either statistically controlled or dismissed, using objective statistical tests, such that comparison of results among stations should be less biased by the factors we measured.

STATION.—ANCOVA results indicated that Riparian Forest capture rates (all measures) were significantly higher than at all other stations, and that there were also other station differences. However, it is important to remember that the GLM models do not indicate causes. Stations could differ for

ecologically meaningful reasons, because of biases not tested, or as a result of noise from random errors. Further analyses, for instance testing for capture-rate differences by taxon, guild, breeding status, flocking behavior, or foraging strata, could reveal why capture rates are different among stations.

DAYS.—Declining capture rates over time at a study location could be evidence of the development of long-term net shyness, caused by local birds learning to avoid net locations. Except for migrant captures and the number of species caught/10 net-h, the ANCOVAs detected significant declines in capture rates over 500–600 days since netting first began at stations. However, this represents a modest decline of about 1 fewer captures/100 net-h/60 days elapsed. Although unlikely given the length of our study, the decline could be a result of true decline in population size. This could be tested by simultaneous population monitoring with a method that does not involve capture.

We designed our protocol in part to reduce factors that could contribute to net shyness during set up and operation of nets by minimizing disturbance and net visibility. When we first established the net sites we cleared as little as needed to avoid net tangling and removed vegetation from sites. We did not cut net poles, but used tent poles. Following establishment, net sites needed little further maintenance. We used 15 nets, relatively few compared to some other studies, at randomized locations. Although it is currently unknown whether randomness of net site affects development of net shyness, it is certainly possible that linear net arrays or placement of nets in "good" sites for capture (where bird activity is high) would give birds a relatively high chance of gaining experience with specific net sites. The frequency of days between our netting sessions at stations was bimodal (modes = 41, 122 days; min = 38, max = 179). Usually nets were open on only two sequential days, an average of less than 3.4% of the days between first and last netting day at each station. Thus, any individual bird should have had few encounters with nets, and minimal visual cues for learning net sites.

Nonetheless, we have indirect evidence that some individuals might learn to avoid nets for several months after net establishment. A number of migrant warblers first banded in the fall 1990 and not recaptured during that over-wintering season, were recaptured the next year. Also, the proportion of migrants recaptured from the fall to following spring for each of the two over-wintering seasons were much higher during the second year than the first year, long after obvious visible cues to net site had disappeared.

SEASON.—In most tropical areas the distribution and behavior of animals changes with distinct wet and dry seasons (Karr 1976; Bell 1982a, b; Karr et al. 1982; Terborgh 1983; Levey 1988). In our study, capture rates were lower during rainy netting sessions, but did not differ between wet and dry seasons. This apparent contradiction could be a result of the fact that the dry seasons during our study were relatively wet (in fact, the two wettest sessions occurred in the dry season), and the wet seasons relatively dry. It can rain on any given day in either season, so capture rates on occasional netting days can, by chance, be unrepresentative of seasonal rainfall. Of note with respect to canopy height biases, Pearson (1971) suggested that foraging height in several species shifted seasonally.

On the other hand, we did not look at the effects on capture rates of several other factors that vary temporally, such as the breeding schedule of year-round residents, or timing of residency for nearctic migrants. Breeding in year-round residents is tied to the seasonality of food resources, and begins in February with a small pulse of young and immatures produced in March and a larger cohort produced starting in May, peaking in August and tapering off in December when hatching year plumages become undistinguishable. Nearctic migrants start arriving in August, and most depart by mid April. Migrant captures peak in November and April, likely the result of both passage-migrants wintering further south and local movements of winter residents settling in after arrival or becoming restless in preparation for their departure to the north. Riparian Forest had the most passage-migrant species of all stations, but transients are commonly observed in more open habitats in the RBCMA during migration (Mallory et al. 1998).

RAIN.—Except for migrants and species numbers, rain depressed capture rates. However, although significant, the effects were small relative to other variables in the ANCOVA. One might expect birds to be less active during rain and more active between rain showers. However, this was not borne out when capture rates from rainy and dry days are compared on the basis of time that nets were actually open. Flocks often continue moving or foraging during rain (Poulsen 1996; E. Mallory, pers. obs.). Elsewhere in the tropics with more rainfall or a harsher dry season, rain or the lack thereof may have larger effects on bird activity and capture rates. Also, if netting were repeated in the RBCMA during more typical wet or dry seasons than during this study, results could be different from what we report here.

CANOPY.—There are several reasons why average CANOPY height did not explain capture rates

better than STATION in the ANCOVA model. First, almost all the variation in canopy height among the nets was lost when reduced to the average values for the six stations (therefore reducing the power to adjust for this bias in capture rates). This indicates that single estimates of canopy height, even when based on data pooled from the exact net locations, are not adequate to statistically adjust for CANOPY height bias. Instead, statistical adjustments in capture rates would have to be calculated net-by-net, before averaging the results for a station. Second, the highest net canopies were at Mesic Upland II, but net capture rates there were not substantially different from those at other upland stations (Fig. 2), and the most productive nets there tended to be under the highest canopy. Third, true population differences in species richness and relative abundance exist among forests that are not directly related to canopy height. Fourth, other factors differing among stations, but not included in this model, could have had significant effects on capture rates and interacted with canopy height effects.

Tropical residents versus nearctic migrants.—Because 16–25% of captures were of migrants, which are absent from the study area for at least four months each year, our results were heavily influenced by the abundance and behavior of resident species. Migrant capture rates, and the number of migrant species captured, were significantly higher at Riparian Forest but showed no other differences. Migrants sample sizes may have to be enlarged to detect other effects.

CONCLUSIONS AND STATISTICAL CONSIDERATIONS

We have demonstrated the effects of several biases and how they can be controlled statistically. However, many other factors should be considered that may affect capture rates more than those we included in our study, such as sex, age, stage of molt, fat level, breeding condition, the successional stage of vegetation, distance of nets from a road, and habitat disturbance.

The goals of a mist-net study are usually a variant of the questions: how many birds of which species are present, where and when are they present, what they are doing, and why? Statistics provide an objective means of interpreting data, providing probabilities of reliability, as long as the data meet the assumptions of the models. Frequently, testing the assumptions of normality, independence, and homogeneity of variances among observations is ignored, invalidating the use of parametric statistics. For instance, it is rare that stations and their mist-net locations are randomized. We were able to control some bias in our analyses with multivariate techniques because our experimental design incorporated randomization of our station locations, we standardized our netting protocol, and we quantified the sources of bias in the field. We urge all mist-net operators to consider potential sources of bias, and design studies to incorporate measurements enabling statistical removal of these biases in the analysis stage.

ACKNOWLEDGMENTS

We thank A. Brown, J. Grant, and other staff at the Programme for Belize for helping us secure funding and Belizean trainees, and for logistical support. Also, we are grateful to the Belize Forest Department for research permits, and B. Bowen for permission to work on his land. D. Novelo, H. Bol, T. Rosado, P. Hererra, K. Ramnarace, C. Groutsche, R. Tillett, K. Thea, M. Schultz, A. Baker, B. Brown, and C. Robbins with his team helped with field work. T. and J. Harding provided us with food, lodging, and good cheer at Chan Chich. E. H. Dunn, C. J. Ralph, J. Brawn, J. Terborgh, C. Robbins, and an anonymous reviewer helped improve the analysis and writing. T. Lloyd-Evans provided a key reference. This study was partly funded by the Pew Charitable Trusts and the Island Foundation.

Studies in Avian Biology No. 29:161–167

USE OF MIST NETS FOR STUDY OF NEOTROPICAL BIRD COMMUNITIES

ANDREW A. WHITMAN

Abstract. I reviewed mist-netting protocols of 43 recent Neotropical bird inventory studies. Most studies had multiple objectives, which likely contributed to a broad range of protocols being used. Most studies used 36 mm mesh, 12 × 2.5 m nets set singly, ~25 m apart. Netting typically took place within the first 8 h of the day starting at sunrise, and was conducted for three consecutive days, but there was much protocol variation within and among studies. Tall forest and agricultural areas were the most frequently studied habitats. Number of captures is affected by effort, net type and distribution, number of net-hours per day, number of days netting at a station, and number of visits to a station within a season. Variation in protocols therefore makes it difficult to compare results among studies, although there are a few techniques for doing so. Inventory by mist nets of a large proportion of species may require an effort of 1,000 net-h, more than in most of the studies reviewed. Any inventory should include aural surveys as well.

Key Words: inventory methods, mist netting, Neotropical birds, Neotropical forest, survey methods.

Mist netting has been commonly used to study bird communities in the Neotropics (Karr 1981b). Because protocols often differ among studies, comparisons of results among mist-netting studies usually involve standardization of effort by expressing captures as birds per net-hour (1 net-h being one net open for 1 h; Ralph 1976). However, variation in other aspects of mist-netting protocols can also preclude direct comparison (e.g., Bierregaard 1990, Pardieck and Waide 1992, Ralph 1976, Remsen and Good 1996, Robbins et al. 1992). Here I review 43 Neotropical mist-netting studies that had species inventory as one of the objectives to illustrate the range of variation in mist-netting protocols and to indicate which factors influence capture rates.

METHODS

DATA SET

Studies reviewed here (Appendix) were selected from Keast and Morton (1980), Hagan and Johnston (1992), Gentry (1990), Wilson and Sader (1995), and from journals over the 16-year period 1986–2002 (including *Auk, Condor, Biotropica, Ecology, Ibis, Journal of Field Ornithology,* and *Wilson Bulletin*). I excluded studies with undefined mist-netting protocols, or that focused on migrating birds or food habits. The review included 43 Neotropical studies covering 194 sample locations. Studies resulting in multiple publications were included only once. When possible, I used data only from the period from December to March, because many Neotropical mist net studies take place in this period to survey residents and Neotropical migrants simultaneously. Most studies conducted surveys within one season or year. The seasonal restriction also reduced the ef-

fect of variation in capture rates caused by migration, or by seasonal shifts in the height strata used by different species (Karr 1981a,b).

For each study, I noted objectives, latitude, habitat (old field, scrub, secondary forest, tall forest, agricultural), canopy height (m), net mesh size (mm), net size (m), meters of mist net run per day, number of nets per net line (a net line being one or more adjacent nets set within 10 m of each other), distance between net lines (m), number of consecutive netting days, number of netting hours per day, use of other census techniques, total net-hours, number of species and of individuals caught, number of visits (periods of consecutive netting days), number of days between visits, and number of stations. "Stations," for the purposes of this paper, are defined as net arrays separated by habitat differences or >500 m. Habitats with canopy heights less than 15 m tall were classified as scrub habitat (including scrub forest).

ANALYSES

To determine which factors affected the number of species and of individuals captured in inventory studies, I used simple pairwise Pearson correlation of number of species and of individuals captured during the entire course of the study with the following as independent variables (Wilkinson 1990): distance between net lines, total net-hours, number of net lines surveyed, number of visits, latitude, number of consecutive days of mist netting during visits, canopy height (m), mesh size of net, meters of net per day, nets per net line, and hours of mist netting per day. I estimated correlations separately for forest stations (secondary and tall forest) and non-forest (old field, scrub, and agricultural) stations, because a preliminary analysis with habitat as a covariate indicated that capture rates may be differently affected by these variables in different habitats. Given the large number of tests (N = 52) and probable multi-collinearity of variables, it is likely that some significant results were spurious. Moreover, this statistical approach did not consider possible non-linear relationships. Nonetheless, results can be used as a preliminary indicator of the factors that affect numbers and kinds of species captured.

RESULTS

Study Characteristics and Protocols

Of the 43 studies reviewed (Appendix), 12 had the sole objective of inventory (i.e., characterization of a community by numbers of species or individuals, proportion of migrants, or relative abundance of individual species). About three-quarters (31 of 43) had one or more additional objectives, including habitat use (measuring relative abundance of several species in more than one habitat), mark–recapture (estimating site fidelity, survival, or population size), and population trends (change in abundance at the same location across years). In only about one-third of the papers (15 of 43) did authors discuss biases associated with mist netting. Only one study was based on a pilot study (Robbins et al. 1992), and only four papers cited methodological studies that verified whether mist netting was the best technique to achieve the stated research goals. About one-quarter of the studies (12 of 43) also included aural censuses.

In most studies, researchers used nets of with a mesh size of 36 mm (Fig. 1A) and used nets of only a single mesh size (Fig. 1B). Nets were typically 2.5 m tall × 12 m long (Figs. 1C, 1D). Nets were set in lines ranging from 1 to 30 nets (Fig. 1E). Lines of nets were spread widely (median = 25 to 50 m; Fig. 1F). In most studies researchers netted between 5 and 12 h/day starting at sunrise (Fig. 1G), and netted for one to three days at a location (Fig. 1H).

Tall forest and second growth forest were the most frequently surveyed habitats (Fig. 2A). Most stations were visited only once (Fig. 2B). Most stations were sampled for greater than 500 net-h (Fig. 2C), usually with over 100 m of mist net (Fig. 2D). At 47 inventory stations with net-hour data, however, only about 25% (11) were netted for >1,000 net-h. Inventory stations were netted for a mean of 2,012 net-h (SD = 3,268). Stations commonly captured between 20 and 39 species (Fig. 2E) and up to 400 individuals (Fig. 2F).

Factors Related to Number of Captures

The protocol parameters affecting number of species and number of individuals captured differed between habitats (Table 1). In non-forest habitats, there were only two significant correlations: number of species captured increased with greater distance between net lines, and number of individuals captured decreased with increasing latitude.

Number of species captured in forested habitats was significantly correlated with many parameters. These included effort variables (total net-hours), equipment (mesh size), sample area (distance between net lines and number of net lines surveyed), amount of continuous effort at a station (number of visits and number of consecutive days of netting at each visit), and habitat structure (canopy height). In forest habitats, the number of species captured was not correlated with latitude or with amount of daily netting effort (meters of net per day, number of nets per net line, or hours of netting per day).

In forested habitats, several parameters were also correlated with number of individuals captured. These included parameters related to effort (total net-hours), sample area (distance between net lines and number of net lines surveyed), and amount of continuous effort at a station (number of visits). The number of individuals captured in forest habitats was not correlated with number of consecutive days mist netting, vegetation structure (canopy height), mesh size, amount of daily mist netting (meters of net per day, number of nets per net line, or hours of mist netting per day), or latitude.

Protocol Variation

Sampling protocols varied significantly within individual inventory studies. Two-thirds (25 of 43) of the studies did not use the same sampling protocol at each station, and only 17% (7) used the same protocols for all locations sampled (variation in the protocols of the remaining 11 studies was not reported). Two-thirds of the studies sampled different sized areas at some stations (N = 12), or used different net densities (N = 10).

DISCUSSION

Results in this paper indicated a high variability of mist-netting methods in the Neotropics both among and within inventory studies. Variation of this magnitude makes it very difficult to directly compare results among studies (Magurran 1988). Here I discuss some of the effects of that variation on inventory results.

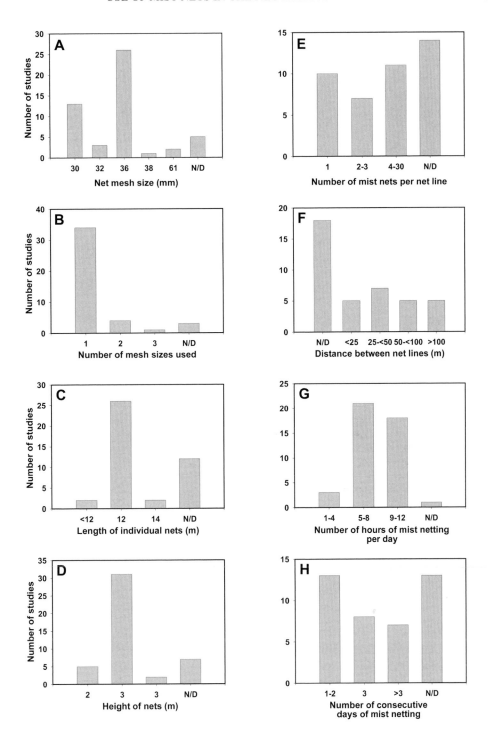

FIGURE 1. The frequency of studies (N = 43) using different: (A) net mesh sizes, (B) numbers of mesh sizes used, (C) length of individual mist nets, (D) height of individuals mist nets, (E) number of mist nets per net line, (F) distance between net lines, (G) number of hours of mist netting per day, and (H) number of consecutive days of mist netting at a visit. N/D = studies in which a variable was not described.

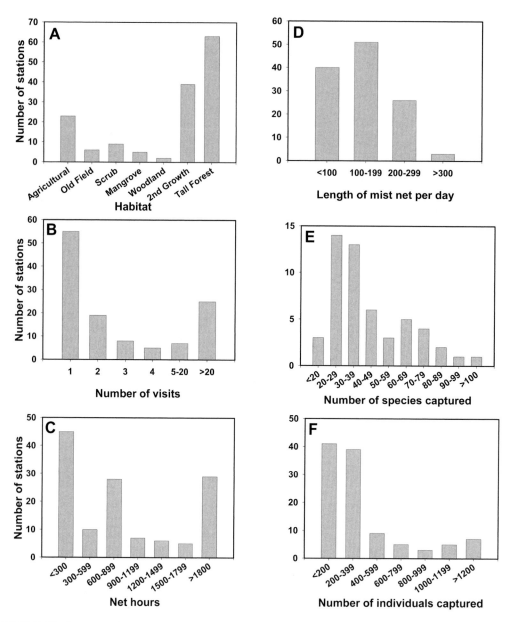

FIGURE 2. The frequency of stations (N = 194) with different: (A) habitats, (B) numbers of visits (netting sessions of one or more consecutive days), (C) net hours, (D) length of mist net operated per day, (E) numbers of species captured, and (F) number of individuals captured.

OVERALL EFFORT

Karr (1981a) concluded that for the purposes of species inventory, capture of 100 individuals was an adequate compromise between effort and quality of results. Most studies reviewed here met that objective (Fig. 2C). However, it should be recognized that such studies may not yield accurate assessment of species evenness (Bierregaard 1990), or reveal the

presence of uncommon species. In agricultural and shrub habitats, a sample of 700 net-h may be needed to detect most individuals and species (Petit et al. 1992, Borges and Stouffer 1999), whereas in forest habitats, a sample of 1,000 net-h may be needed (Blake and Loiselle 2001, Petit et al. 1992, Lopez de Casenave et al. 1998). Most studies in this review had <1,000 net-h (Fig. 2C).

Another way of evaluating the effort required

TABLE 1. PEARSON CORRELATION COEFFICIENTS BETWEEN THE NUMBER OF SPECIES OR OF INDIVIDUALS CAPTURED AND VARIOUS INVENTORY PROTOCOL PARAMETERS, IN NON-FOREST AND FOREST HABITATS

	Non-forest habitat			Forest habitat		
	Number of species	Number of individuals	Number of studies	Number of species	Number of individuals	Number of studies
Distance between net lines (m)	**0.598**	0.437	12	**0.918**	**0.990**	9
Total net-hours	0.337	0.325	22	**0.830**	**0.925**	13
Number of net lines surveyed	0.233	0.147	17	**0.717**	**0.801**	12
Number of visits	-0.007	0.364	25	**0.544**	**0.760**	17
Latitude (°)	-0.132	**-0.568**	26	-0.098	-0.396	18
Consecutive days of netting	-0.251	-0.127	25	**0.506**	0.442	14
Canopy height (m)	-0.190	-0.006	16	**0.574**	0.263	15
Mesh size of net (mm)	0.329	-0.275	26	**0.597**	0.221	15
Meters of net per day	0.241	0.022	17	0.433	0.385	12
Nets per net line	0.314	-0.007	26	0.302	0.480	15
Hours netted per day	-0.084	0.055	23	-0.013	0.172	16

Notes: Correlation coefficients in boldface were significant (P < 0.05).

for useful species inventory is to look at number of individuals captured. A high proportion of species was detected after capture of at least 500 individuals, whether in forest (Lynch 1989) or non-forest habitats (Borges and Stouffer 1999, Lynch 1989, Mallory and Brokaw 1993). However few studies included this many individuals (Fig. 2F), and an essentially complete survey in forest habitats may require a sample of 1,000 individuals (Blake and Loiselle 2001, Karr et al. 1990b). Although capture of more than 500 individuals usually does not detect many additional species, the new species will be ones that are rare. Thus, samples comprised of few captures will have low proportions of rare species and greater species evenness, as compared to samples with many captures.

Aural surveys detect many species better than mist netting (and hence more species and individuals; Blake and Loiselle 2001, Lynch 1989, Rappole et al. 1998, Wallace et al. 1996), but they are affected by observer bias (Faanes and Bystrak 1981, Levey 1988, Verner 1985). Mist netting, on the other hand, detects a few common bird species better than aural surveys, is not affected by observer bias, and may yield greater counts of individuals for some species (Blake and Loiselle 2001, Rappole et al. 1993, 1998, Wallace et al. 1996, Whitman et al. 1995). Therefore, thorough studies of Neotropical bird communities may require both aural surveys and mist netting.

NETTING PROTOCOL

Increasing mesh size correlates with increasing capture rates for larger species, so restriction of mesh-size biases inventory results (Heimerdinger and Leberman 1966, Pardieck and Waide 1992). In this review, 36-mm mesh nets were by far the most commonly used, and few studies used more than one size. Karr (1981a) suggested using 36-mm mesh nets as a good general mesh size for catching most species 8 to 100 g. However, 36-mm nets will catch up to 50% fewer individuals of small (<20g) species than will 30-mm mesh nets (Heimerdinger and Leberman 1966, Pardieck and Waide 1992).

Most researchers preferred distributing their nets uniformly within a study plot to eliminate observer bias in station selection. Some researchers argue for maximizing capture rates by placing nets at "good" locations that have many species, but this introduces observer bias, especially in the capture rates of individual species (Karr 1979, Whitacre et al. 1993), and may make statistical comparisons among stations inappropriate.

Spacing nets >50 m apart may maximize the numbers of unique individuals and species captured (e.g., Karr 1981a). However, for a fixed sample area, nets placed along a transect will cross more microhabitats and bird territories than nets placed in a grid, and therefore will capture more species and new individuals.

In Neotropical studies, number of sequential days of netting at a station has been shown to strongly influence capture rates (Robbins et al. 1992, Faaborg et al. *this volume*). The number of birds caught declines after the first day because the proportion of the population captured increases with each passing day, and captured birds avoid mist nets after being caught (Bierregaard 1990, Robbins et al. 1992, Terborgh and Faaborg 1973). Thus, a mist-netting study conducted on a single day may not be comparable to a study conducted on several days, unless the raw data are available and the analyses are restricted to data in common.

In tall forest, additional visits may increase the number of species and individuals captured as long as there are at least three weeks between visits. A three-week interval may sufficient to minimize net shyness (Bierregaard 1990), although other researchers suggests that much longer intervals may be necessary (J. Faaborg, pers. comm.).

ADDRESSING VARIATION IN PROTOCOLS

When mist nets are used to conduct inventories and accomplish other objectives as well, more than one sampling protocol may be necessary. For example, the chief goal of an inventory is to catch as many different species as possible, which includes minimizing effort spent on recapture. Mark–recapture studies have the opposite goal, that is, to maximize the number of recaptures. Simple comparisons of species richness among locations can be accomplished by using species accumulation curves from each station (Herzog et al. 2002) even when different protocols were used. If the original data are available and protocols do not differ significantly, bootstrap analysis can be an effective technique for eliminating the effect of unequal sampling effort on results (Karr et al. 1990b). However, use of standardized protocols whenever possible should help make results of mist netting studies more comparable.

ACKNOWLEDGMENTS

I thank G. R. Geupel, J. Faaborg, M. Kasprzyk, J. R. Karr, E. P. Mallory, C. J. Ralph, J. Hathaway, and E. H. Dunn for their generous comments.

APPENDIX. LOCATION, HABITAT, NUMBER OF SURVEY STATIONS, AND OBJECTIVES OF REVIEWED STUDIES

Study	Country(s)	Habitats[a]	Number of stations	Objectives[b]
Bierregaard 1990	Brazil	Tall forest	1	I, M, P
Blake 1989	Panama	Tall forest	3	I
Blake and Loiselle 1992	Costa Rica	Secondary and tall forest	5	H, I M
Borges and Stouffer 1999	Brazil	Old field	6	H, I
Lopez de Casenave et al. 1998	Argentina	Tall forest	1	H, I
Gonzalez-Alonso et al. 1992	Cuba	Shrub	1	I
Greenberg 1992	Mexico	Tall forest	5	H, I M
Karr 1990	Panama	Tall forest	1	I, M
Kricher and Davis 1992	Belize	Secondary and tall forest	3	H, I
	Belize	Old field	3	H, I
Lefebvre et al. 1992, 1994	Venezuela	Mangrove	1	I, M
Lopez de Casenave et al. 1998	Argentina	Tall forest	2	I
Lynch 1992	Mexico	Old field, scrub	2	H, I, P
Malizia 2001	Argentina	Tall forest	2	H, I
Mason 1996	Venezuela	Tall forest	14	H, I
Martin and Karr 1986	Panama	Secondary forest	1	I, M
Machado and Da Fonseca 2000	Brazil	Tall forest	4	I
Mills and Rogers 1992	Belize	Agricultural	5	I
Murphy et al. 1988	Bahamas	Low secondary forest	3	I
	Bahamas	Mangrove	2	I
	Bahamas	Old field, scrub	5	I
Poulin et al. 1993	Venezuela	Scrub, woodland	3	H, I
	Venezuela	Tall forest	3	H, I
Rappole et al. 1998	Mexico	Tall forest	10	H, I
	Mexico	Secondary forest	10	H, I
	Mexico	Agricultural/old field	10	H, I
Robbins et al. 1992	Puerto Rico	Agricultural	8	H, I
	Jamaica	Tall forest	8	H, I
	Belize	Tall forest	8	H, I
	Costa Rica	Tall forest	8	H, I
Robinson and Terborgh 1990	Peru	Tall forest	1	I, M, H
Stouffer and Bierregaard 1995	Brazil	Tall forest	9	I

APPENDIX.   CONTINUED

Study	Country(s)	Habitats[a]	Number of stations	Objectives[b]
Thiollay 1994	French Guiana	Tall forest	1	I
Waide 1980	Mexico	Old field, tall forest	5	H, I
Waide 1991	Puerto Rico	Tall forest	1	I, P
Wallace et al. 1996	Cuba	Secondary forest	6	H, I
		Low secondary forest	9	H, I
		Scrub	2	H, I
		Mangrove	1	H, I
Whitman et al. 1995	Belize	Tall forest	1	I, H
Will 1991	Nicaragua	Tall forest	1	I
Wunderle 1995	Puerto Rico	Tall forest	1	H, I, P
Young et al. 1998	Costa Rica	Tall forest	20	I

[a] Tree crops include citrus, coffee, cacao, mango.
[b] H = habitat use, I = inventory, M = mark–recapture, P = population monitoring.

Studies in Avian Biology No. 29:168–172

SOME CONSEQUENCES OF USING COUNTS OF BIRDS BANDED AS INDICES TO POPULATIONS

John R. Sauer and William A. Link

Abstract. In mist-net studies, it is often difficult to use capture–recapture methods to estimate number of birds present. Many investigators use number of birds captured as an index of population size. We investigate the consequences of using indices of bird abundance as surrogates for population size in hypothesis tests. Unless all of the birds present are captured, indices are biased estimates of local population size, and the amount of bias depends on the proportion of birds captured. We demonstrate the potential effects of bias on hypothesis tests based on indices. The bias generally causes type I error rates to be inflated. Investigators should either estimate the proportion of animals captured using capture–recapture methods or demonstrate that results of hypothesis tests based on indices are not consequences of bias in the indices.

Key Words: abundance estimation, banding, bias, capture–recapture, counts, index, population size

Banding data provide the only source of information regarding many interesting questions about bird populations. Data from mist-net studies are presently used to estimate population trends of passerine birds (Dawson 1990, Hussell et al. 1992), to examine survival and population sizes of birds (e.g., Faaborg and Arendt 1992b), and to evaluate productivity of passerines (DeSante 1992). Large-scale banding programs such as MAPS (DeSante 1992) and the British Constant Effort Sites (Peach 1993) provide the opportunity for monitoring trends and demographic characteristics at regional geographic scales.

Unfortunately, in mist-net studies, relatively few individuals of the target species are typically encountered. Because mist nets have a limited height, the probability of capturing a bird that does not forage in the understory is relatively small. Also, after being captured, birds may become aware of the location of nets, leading to low recapture rates (DeSante 1992). Consequently, most bird species are represented by small sample sizes from any study site.

Small sample sizes pose many challenges for analysts of mist-net data. The most important problem relates to use of capture-recapture methods with small samples. These methods provide many interesting opportunities for estimation of demographic parameters (Kendall et al. *this volume*), but small samples can preclude estimation from individual sites or greatly lower the power of tests for differences in parameters over time or between sites. Many investigators choose to avoid the problems inherent in small-sample capture–recapture analyses by using indices in their population analyses. For example, the total number of birds captured at a site is used as an index to total population size, trends are estimated based on changes in the total capture indices, total numbers of recaptures are used as an index of return (or survival) rates, and the ratio of number of young to adults captured is used as an index of productivity.

In this paper, we explore the consequences of using indices in analysis. We develop a conceptual framework for analyzing indices and relating them to possible changes in the underlying populations. Finally, we demonstrate how indices should be considered in terms of underlying capture–recapture models.

WHAT IS AN INDEX?

An index count is often defined as any kind of count that reflects the presence of animals, but not their absolute number. This definition is inadequate, in that it makes no statement about the relationship between the count C and the unknown population size N. To be an adequate reflection of N, C must have some consistent relationship with N. This relationship is sometimes defined by noting that C must be positively correlated with N. For an index C to be useful, however, C must be a reasonable surrogate for N, both in hypothesis tests and in its association with covariates.

Consider the count of birds captured (or recaptured) at a mist-netting site as a possible index to the population size. The relationship of captured birds at a mist-net site to the actual population size can be expressed as

$$\mathbf{E}(C|p,N) = pN$$

where $\mathbf{E}(C|p,N)$ denotes the expected value of C conditional on the actual population size N, and p is the proportion of animals encountered. In general, if p is not related to N, and is not 0, then C is a reasonable index of N. However, the correlation between C and N will depend on the variation of p, and any analysis of count data relies on some assumptions about either the magnitude of p or its consistency over any comparisons of populations that use counts. This has led to two major philosophical approaches to the analysis of index data.

Proponents of the first approach have said that "Using just the count of birds detected (per unit effort) as an index [of] abundance is neither scientifically sound or reliable" (Burnham 1981:324), and that "It is imperative in designing the preliminary survey to build in the capability…of testing homogeneity of the proportionality factor values…" (Skalski and Robson 1992:29). To apply this approach, an experimenter explicitly estimates p and tests for differences in p that can be confounded with the comparison of interest. For mist-nets, capture–recapture methods are used to estimate p (Kendall et al. *this volume*). If no differences in p are found, then the indices are used in analyses. However, without estimating p as a routine component of a study, these tests cannot be conducted, and the study will have little credibility (a point forcefully made by Anderson 2001).

In the second approach, indices are used in analyses without estimation of p. Instead, it is assumed that standardization and covariate analysis can be used to control variation in p that might invalidate hypothesis tests (e.g., differences in p might be confounded with treatments). Proponents of the second approach feel that it is impossible to design extensive studies to estimate p due to the practical constraints of low recapture rates and small sample sizes for most species in mist-net studies. In fact, many large-scale monitoring programs (such as the North American Breeding Bird Survey [BBS], Peterjohn and Sauer 1993) do not allow for estimation of p.

The first approach (in which p is estimated) should be considered in design of any field study, and the ornithological community increasingly attempts to estimate detectability in studies that count birds (e.g., Rosenstock et al. 2002). However, mist-netting samples are often too small to allow proper estimation, or the hypothesis tests based on the data have too low power to ever be able to test whether detection probabilities differ. In practice, many analyses are conducted on unadjusted counts of captured (or observed) birds.

ALTERNATIVE ESTIMATES OF POPULATION SIZE

Three distinct quantities are commonly referred to as the population size: first, N, the parameter (found only by censusing, which is almost never accomplished in bird monitoring); second, $\hat{N}$, the capture-recapture estimate, found by estimating p and defining

$$\hat{N}_i = \frac{C_i}{\hat{p}_i},$$

(Lancia et al. 1994); and third, C, the index. To investigators, it is not always clear how these quantities differ, and when it is appropriate to use $\hat{N}$ or C as a surrogate for N in hypothesis tests. To understand the consequences of this choice, we must consider two characteristics of the estimates, bias and precision.

BIAS

The bias of an estimate is the difference between the expected value of the estimate and the parameter. For the capture–recapture estimate, the expected value of $\hat{N}$ is $E(\hat{N}|N) \approx N$ (the estimator is slightly biased; Skalski and Robson 1992). In contrast, the bias of C is $E(C|N) - N = pN - N = N(p - 1)$; hence C is always biased unless $p \equiv 1$.

Bias can be an extremely serious deficiency in an estimator, if it is not taken into account in hypothesis tests. The possibility that bias can differ among treatments should be considered in any hypothesis test that uses counts, and obviously invalidates use of the index as an estimate of population size. An additional consequence of the bias in C is that comparative tests of population size based on the counts may also be invalid. For example, suppose that we have replicate counts from sites 1 and 2. We are interested in testing a null hypothesis:

$$H_0: N_1 = N_2,$$

by comparing mean counts. Counts should only be used in this analysis if $p_1 = p_2$. Of course, this condition of equal p's is also necessary for any comparative test (e.g., a ratio analysis of productivity, where groups 1 and 2 would denote different age classes).

Bias is therefore a critical consideration for any analysis of count data. Unfortunately, after counts are collected, most statistical tests do not directly include an assessment of possible bias, so investigators do not become aware of these difficulties in the analysis.

PRECISION

At a single site, sampling error is the variance of the estimate conditional on the population parameter. Sampling error for a population estimate $\hat{N}$ is denoted by $V(\hat{N}|N)$. In a capture–recapture study, $V(\hat{N}|N)$ is estimated by assuming N and p are unknown but fixed, and estimating p from observed counts of marked and unmarked animals (Skalski and Robson 1992). If multiple sites are sampled, an additional factor, the among-site variance $V(N)$, is also a component of error, and the variance calculated among site estimates i, $V(\hat{N})$, is

$$V(\hat{N}) = V(N) + \mathbf{E}(V(\hat{N}_i|N_i)),$$

where $\mathbf{E}(V(\hat{N}_i|N_i))$ is the expected value (average) of the within-site sampling errors. In most studies, $V(N)$ is the variance component of interest (Skalski and Robson 1992, Link and Nichols 1994).

If only counts are collected, this partitioning of sampling error and among-site variance cannot be conducted unless p is assumed fixed among sites, and known (Skalski and Robson 1992). Consequently, estimation of p is essential for studies in which estimation of variance components are of interest. Unfortunately, most studies of temporal variation in bird populations do not do this, and may provide incorrect results (Link and Nichols 1994).

Estimation of p still allows for use of C in hypothesis tests when p does not differ among populations to be compared. Skalski and Robson (1992) note that, unless $p = 1$, coefficients of variation of C will be smaller than coefficients of variation of $\hat{N}$ for a site. Hence, use of C in hypothesis tests will lead to higher power relative to tests based on $\hat{N}$, but only when p can be documented to be constant. Of course, if p is not constant the increased precision will only lead to an increased chance of a false rejection of the null hypothesis.

DEVELOPING A STRUCTURE FOR ANALYSIS OF COUNT DATA

The foregoing discussion provides a general view of the statistical properties of indices and capture–recapture-based estimates. However, investigators need specific methods for evaluation of the performance of indices and adjusted counts. Capture–recapture models provide a convenient framework for this evaluation. We can develop models for sampling the population, and see how counts and capture–recapture estimates differ in the context of the models. We provide an example of this based

on the Lincoln index, as defined by Skalski and Robson (1992:63–64).

In the model, banding occurs in two periods ($j = 1,2$) at a single site. We use this notation:

N = number of animals
n_j = number of animals captured in period j
p_j = probability of capture in period j
q_j = 1 - probability of capture in period j
m = number of marked animals from period 1 recaptured in period 2.
$C = n_1 + n_2 - m$ = number of distinct captures

Under this model, the estimates of population size are

$$\hat{N} = \frac{n_1 n_2}{m} \approx \frac{(n_1+1)(n_2+1)}{(m+1)} - 1,$$

with sampling variance

$$\hat{V}(\hat{N}|N) \approx \frac{N q_1 q_2}{p_1 p_2}.$$

The number of distinct animals counted is

$$C = n_1 + n_2 - m$$

with mean and variance

$$E(C|N) = N(1 - q_1 q_2)$$
$$V(C|N) = N q_1 q_2 (1 - q_1 q_2).$$

Under this model, we can directly estimate the bias and precision of counts and the capture–recapture population estimates.

Suppose that there are two sites, and a Lincoln experiment has been done on each. To test the null hypothesis that

$$H_0: N_1 = N_2,$$

two alternative statistics can be used. The first is based on the capture–recapture-based estimate, using the statistic

$$z_{\hat{N}} = \frac{\hat{N}_1 \bullet \hat{N}_2}{\sqrt{V(\hat{N}_1|N_1) + V(\hat{N}_2|N_2)}}$$

The second is based on the counts of animals captured, using the statistic

$$z_C = \frac{C_1 \bullet C_2}{\sqrt{V(C_1|N_1) + V(C_2|N_2)}}$$

Note that $z_{\hat{N}}$ and z_C do not test the same hypothesis. For $z_{\hat{N}}$, the null hypothesis is: H_o: $N_1 = N_2$, but for z_C it is: H_o: $\mu_{C1} = \mu_{C2}$ (where μ_{Ci} = mean count for i). These hypotheses are only the same when $p_1 \equiv p_2$.

To show the consequences of using z_C as a surrogate for $z_{\hat{N}}$, use the expected values given above in formulas for the z statistics, setting $N = N_1 = N_2$, $p_1 = p_{11} = p_{12}$, $p_2 = p_{21} = p_{22}$, and $p_1 \neq p_2$, to simplify the discussion. We can assess the differences in the tests for differing values of p_1 and p_2. For $z_{\hat{N}}$,

$$E(z_{\hat{N}}) = \frac{N - N(\pm \text{ small bias})}{\sqrt{N\left(\dfrac{q_1^2}{p_1^2} + \dfrac{q_2^2}{p_2^2}\right)}} \approx 0;$$

and for z_C,

$$\text{E}(z_C) = \frac{N(q_2^2 - q_1^2)}{\sqrt{N(q_1^2 + q_2^2 - q_1^4 - q_2^4)}}.$$

In other words, $\text{E}(z) \neq 0$ for a z statistic based on the C's, but $\text{E}(z) = 0$ for the statistic based on the N's, thus tests based on z_C will have an inflated probability of a type I error rate (α) level. Using the expected values, we can quantify the inflation for a fixed N, p_1, and p_2 as

$$\alpha_{N,p_1p_2} = \overline{\Phi}[z_{\alpha/2} - \text{E}(z_C)] + \Phi[-z_{\alpha/2} - \text{E}(z_C)]$$

where Φ signifies the cumulative normal probability, and $\overline{\Phi} = 1 - \Phi$. Calculating these as a function of N with $\alpha = 0.05$, it is evident that the inflation of α increases both as a function of N, p_1, and p_2 (Table 1). When the total population size is moderately large (e.g., $N > 100$), the inflation in α is quite large for even small (5%) changes in p.

We conclude that minor changes in p between treatments can lead to large increases in type I error rates. When hypothesis tests are based on counts, differences in detection rates are confounded with differences in the actual population sizes; significant differences found in the test of equality of counts between populations may be entirely due to differences in p. Changes in p do not appear anywhere in the count-based analysis, and would be interpreted as rejections of null hypotheses by the investigator.

The changes in detection probabilities affect all aspects of hypothesis testing. For example, power (the probability of rejecting a "false" null hypothesis) is a function of the difference between the estimate and a hypothesized value of the parameter, and increases as the variance of the estimate decreases. Because variances decrease as sample sizes increase, test power increases with sample size. Consequently, increasing the observed power of a test when the estimate is biased leads to greater probability of error. Standard sample allocation procedures are therefore invalid, and lead to higher than nominal type I error rates.

A MORE GENERAL CASE

Suppose we have a study that only collects count data from $j = 2$ treatments, where C_{i1}, $i = 1,...,I$, and C_{l2}, $l = 1,...,L$ represent the counts for I replicate sites in treatment 1 and L replicates in treatment 2. Further, assume that for each treatment the counts are indices to population size, and that $p_1 \neq p_2$ (i.e., the detection probability is constant within treatments but differs between treatments).

To test whether H_o: $N_1 = N_2$, we use

$$z_C = \frac{\overline{C}_1 - \overline{C}_2}{\sqrt{\hat{V}(\overline{C}_1) + \hat{V}(\overline{C}_2)}}$$

which actually tests H_o: $\mu_{C1} = \mu_{C2}$.

The numerator of the test has expected value

$$p_1 N_1 - p_2 N_2$$

which, when the null hypothesis is true, equals

$$N(p_1 - p_2).$$

TABLE 1. THE ACTUAL ALPHA (α') ASSOCIATED WITH HYPOTHESIS TESTS ON COUNT DATA WHEN THE PROPORTION OF ANIMALS DETECTED CHANGES, FOR A FIXED TOTAL POPULATION SIZE

N	$\alpha'(\Delta p = 0.5–0.55)$	$\alpha'(\Delta p = 0.5–0.6)$	$\alpha'(\Delta p = 0.4–0.6)$
10	0.0574	0.0793	0.1820
50	0.0878	0.2020	0.6486
100	0.1267	0.3545	0.9117
150	0.1663	0.4932	0.9819
200	0.2063	0.6116	0.9968

We can use the argument given above to demonstrate the effect of differences in p between treatments on the hypothesis tests. Specifically, for any observed difference in counts ($C_1 - C_2$), the numerator of the test, we can ask whether, given that the mean population is of size N at both sites, what differences in proportion detected between treatments (denoted by Δp) would be expected to produce the observed z value.

For fixed N between treatments, Δp is

$$\Delta p = \left(\frac{E(C_1)}{N} - \frac{E(C_2)}{N} \right)$$

If these Δp values are small, the tests have little credibility. For example, Hanowski et al. (1993) presented data on mean counts of Downy Woodpeckers (*Picoides pubescens*) on two treatments, each based on 40 point-count sites. The estimates for the two treatments were 0.35 ± 0.09 (SE) and 0.17 ± 0.08. For fixed values of N, we calculate values of Δp that would produce the observed difference in means, given that both treatments have the same N ($N_1 = N_2 = N$). For example, if N equals 1.0 in both treatments, a Δp of 0.18 would be needed to produce the observed difference in counts, but if $N = 2.0$, a Δp of 0.09 will produce the observed difference in counts. If the counts are similar in magnitude to the actual population size (e.g., p is close to 1.0), then it is unlikely that changes in p are causing the observed differences in counts. However, if the p_m is much less than 1.0 (i.e., N is much greater than C), then relatively small differences in proportions detected between treatments will explain the differences between the observed counts. In this case, and in any analysis involving counts as surrogates for population size, it is informative to play "what if" games to evaluate whether the analysis is likely to be affected by differences in detection probabilities between treatments. To do this, postulate the detection probabilities and evaluate the consequences for the analysis. A similar procedure can be developed for any hypothesis test based on counts, such as testing for change over time or for ratios of counts.

CONCLUSIONS

In this paper, we have provided a framework for the analysis of count data, and identified some of the fundamental attributes of counts of birds captured as surrogates of population parameters.

• Counts are always biased unless $p = 1$. This means that counts do not estimate population size, but estimate population size times p.

• Counts are always more precise than adjusted population estimates. This is due to the bias in the estimate ($p < 1$), and the additional error associated with estimating p that occurs in the adjusted estimates. Counts are most precise when $p = 0$, which demonstrates that the increased precision of counts is not useful for hypothesis testing unless differences in p are accommodated in the analysis.

• Sample allocations based on C are not appropriate, because increased samples lead to more precise estimates of $E(C)$ rather than of N. This amplifies the bias in statistical tests.

• Simple analyses of C omit discussion of bias. Hypothesis tests do not accommodate the possibility of differences in p, and will produce inflated α levels with even moderate differences in p.

• We can use mark–recapture structure to incorporate bias into the analysis, and simulate the effects of changes in p between treatments. If no estimate of p is available, we can model possible effects of variation in p on analysis.

• It is wrong to eliminate p from analyses of count data. The best way of incorporating p in the analysis is to estimate p for each treatment, test for differences in p between treatments, and if necessary incorporate the ps in the hypothesis tests (e.g., Skalski and Robson 1992). If p cannot be estimated, then it must be demonstrated that the hypothesis test is likely to be valid for moderate differences in p between treatments. However, ignoring the possibility of differences in p will lead to analyses with low credibility.

Studies in Avian Biology No. 29:173–181

ON THE USE OF CAPTURE–RECAPTURE MODELS IN MIST-NET STUDIES

WILLIAM L. KENDALL, JOHN R. SAUER, JAMES D. NICHOLS, ROGER PRADEL, AND JAMES E. HINES

Abstract. Capture–recapture models provide a statistical framework for estimating population parameters from mist-net data. Although Cormack-Jolly-Seber and related models have recently been used to estimate survival rates of birds sampled with mist nets, we believe that the full potential for use of capture–recapture models has not been realized by many researchers involved in mist-net studies. We present a brief discussion of the overall framework for estimation using capture–recapture methods, and review several areas in which recent statistical methods can be, but generally have not yet been, applied to mist-net studies. These areas include estimation of (1) rates of movement among areas; (2) survival rates in the presence of transients; (3) population sizes of migrating birds; (4) proportion of birds alive but not present at a breeding site (one definition of proportion of nonbreeding birds in a population); (5) population change and recruitment; and (6) species richness. Using these models will avoid the possible bias associated with use of indices, and provide statistically valid variance estimates and inference.

Key Words: Capture–recapture, estimation, population size, species richness, survival rate, statistics, transients.

Recent publications that document population changes in migratory birds (Robbins et al. 1989, Hagen and Johnston 1992) have led to great public interest in the population status of birds. Partners in Flight and conservation organizations have attempted to focus this interest into programs for monitoring the status of bird populations and conducting research into the causes of population change in birds. Several monitoring programs, such as Monitoring Avian Productivity and Survival (MAPS; DeSante 1992), use banding data to address questions about population change at both local and regional scales. We believe that banding studies provide the only realistic way of addressing many questions of interest to population ecologists, and careful design of programs will allow estimation of many relevant parameters.

Monitoring and research programs frequently share a common goal: estimation of some demographic parameter for some pre-defined population. Clearly, the initial step in any banding program is definition of the parameter to be estimated and specification of a goal for precision of the estimate. Parameters of interest for both monitoring and research programs include population size, survival, recruitment, species richness, and movement probabilities among multiple study locations. Historically, monitoring programs tended to emphasize estimation of changes in these parameters over time, whereas research programs tended to evaluate differences in these parameters among pre-defined treatments. However, modern approaches to

management require that information from monitoring be nested within a modeling framework, in which the monitoring is used to evaluate the validity of predictions (from models) of the consequences of management actions. The additional rigor associated with adaptive management and modeling exercises provides a strong impetus for designing monitoring programs that can be used to evaluate population responses to management.

There has recently been a great deal of statistical research regarding estimation of demographic parameters from banding studies (Seber 1982; Brownie et al. 1985; Burnham et al. 1987; Pollock et al. 1990; Lebreton et al. 1992; Nichols 1992, 1994; Schwarz and Seber 1999; Williams et al. 2002). Application of these procedures to mist-netting studies will greatly enhance the validity and credibility of the results. In this paper, we discuss methods and designs for estimating population parameters from banding studies. We emphasize capture–recapture methods because they are commonly used for passerine birds.

WHY NOT USE INDICES?

Naïve users of data from mist-net studies often draw inferences about the parameters mentioned above using capture indices. For example, the total number of animals captured is an index to total population size, and the return rate of birds to a location between years is an index to survival rate. The expected values of these indices differ from the actual population values by some unknown proportion, and any hypothesis test must make assumptions about the constancy of the proportions. In general, these constancy assumptions are not tested, and the proportions of animals detected may differ among treatments or over time, invalidating hypothesis tests.

This difficulty with the use of indices is easily documented in any hypothesis test. If the differences between group means can be explained by differences in detection probabilities, then the rejection of the null hypothesis cannot be attributed to the treatment (Sauer and Link *this volume*). For example, if mean captures from two treatments are 11.5 and 14.0, it cannot be established that the 2.5 more birds in one treatment are due to higher capture rates or a larger population in the treatment. In fact, a "better" study in terms of a larger number of replicates will lead to a higher chance of a false result, if the difference in counts is due to differences in capture rates (Barker and Sauer 1995).

We will not discuss the statistical properties of these indices (see Sauer and Link *this volume*), but we note that the methods we discuss here provide a means for testing the assumptions implicit in the use of indices for comparative purposes (Skalski and Robson 1992, MacKenzie and Kendall 2002, Sauer and Link *this volume*). Capture–recapture methods allow us to estimate the proportions of animals detected and test whether the proportions are constant over time or treatments. If the assumption of constancy is concluded to be reasonable, then inferences may be based on the index statistics in some cases (Skalski and Robson 1992, MacKenzie and Kendall 2002). However, if the hypothesis of constant sampling proportions is rejected, then inferences should be based on the capture–recapture model estimates. Interestingly, the use of indices relative to detectability-adjusted estimates continues to be a topic of discussion in the literature. However, we believe that it is time to move past this topic, and we agree with Anderson et al. (2003) that index-based designs are limiting the value of wildlife studies.

A SIMPLE INTRODUCTION TO CAPTURE–RECAPTURE PROCEDURES

All capture–recapture methods require that there are trapping occasions in which animals are captured, previously marked animals are recorded as recaptures, new animals are marked, and animals are released. If there are k of these occasions, we can define a capture history for each animal in which a 1 indicates a capture in occasion i and a 0 represents no

capture of the individual in occasion i, as

Animal number	Trapping occasion (i)				
	1	2	3	4	.. k
9999	0	1	1	0	.. 1

The capture history of animal 9999 reflects that it was not captured in occasions 1 and 4 but was captured in occasions 2, 3, and k. The capture history is a fundamental format used in capture–recapture estimation and modeling.

There are two major categories of capture–recapture models (e.g., Seber 1982, White et al. 1982, Pollock et al. 1990, Nichols 1992, Williams et al. 2002). The population is "open" when sufficient time exists between capture occasions to allow animals to leave (via death or movement) or enter (via birth or movement) the population, and open-population estimation procedures estimate parameters such as survival between occasions and population size at trapping occasions. On the other hand, the population is "closed" when little time occurs between capture occasions, and it is assumed that population size is not changing among the occasions. Closed-population estimation procedures are used to estimate population size or density during the trapping occasions. Finally, some studies employ a "robust design" (Pollock 1982, Pollock et al. 1990, Kendall et al. 1995, Schwarz and Stobo 1997, Kendall and Bjorkland 2001), in which an investigator will conduct several trapping occasions during a short period of time, and then repeat the sampling at a future time. The data from the short period of time are usually used with closed-population models to estimate detection probability and population size, and data from the repeated samples are used with open-population models to estimate survival and movement in and out of the study area (Kendall et al. 1997). In addition, the robust design can permit (1) estimation of population size, survival, and recruitment for more periods than standard open population analyses; (2) estimation of components of recruitment; and (3) estimation that is robust to unequal catchability. This design is quite similar to the design employed by MAPS and other constant-effort programs.

Statistical procedures for all of these designs share a common approach. Parameters are defined and used to model the events giving rise to specific capture histories. These parameters are typically defined as probabilities, and are associated with both sampling (e.g., detection probability) and demographic (e.g., survival probability) processes. The events giving rise to a particular capture history are thus used to develop a probability model for that history. The probability models for the different capture histories, together with the numbers of animals observed to exhibit each history (the data), are used to obtain estimates of the model parameters and their variances.

As with all statistical procedures, there are assumptions that must be met for the estimates to be completely valid. There are several basic assumptions, such as the banded sample must be representative of the population and bands must not be lost or misread, that apply to all models (Seber 1982). Then, each model has a specific set of assumptions about how the parameters of interest are defined. For example, survival might be time specific, requiring a separate estimate for each year, or constant over time, requiring only a single estimate. Generally, tests and model selection statistics are available to allow users to assess the validity of the assumptions and determine whether models with different sets of parameters might be more appropriate for the data.

STATISTICAL METHODS AND MODELS

OPEN POPULATION CAPTURE–RECAPTURE MODELS

For open populations, the basic model, called the Cormack-Jolly-Seber (CJS) model after the individuals who first developed it, considers capture histories in terms of two sets of parameters:

ϕ_i: Probability(survive from trapping occasion i to $i+1$ | alive and present at time i)

p_i: Probability(captured at trapping occasion i | alive and present at time i)

Note that the vertical bar indicates that the probabilities are conditional, and reflect the probabilities of the event described before the vertical bar given that the event described after the bar occurred. Capture histories can be described in terms of products of these parameters. For example, for animals captured in period 1 and subsequently released, a capture history of 1 0 1 would have associated probability $\phi_1(1 - p_2) \phi_2 p_3$. Of course, there will be many different capture histories in any study, and each history can be written in terms of the underlying probabilities. These probabilities form cells in a multinomial distribution, and this multinomial model can be used as a basis for estimating ϕ_i, p_i, and their variances. Due to technical issues of estimation, some of the parameters cannot be separately estimated, and therefore we cannot always estimate survival and capture probabilities for all periods. See Lebreton et al. (1992) for an excellent explanation of the estimation procedure.

This modeling structure, in conjunction with appropriate software such as Program MARK (White and Burnham 1999; www.cnr.colostate.edu/~gwhite/software.html) is extraordinarily flexible. Beginning with the basic CJS model, any number of variations can be implemented. For example, survival or detection probabilities can be modeled as time dependent or constant. Age dependence in parameters can be implemented. In addition, data for groups of animals (e.g., males vs. females or birds found in mature vs. early successional woodlands) can be separately but simultaneously analyzed, to permit comparison of parameters (e.g., Peach 1993, Hilton and Miller 2003, Miller et al. 2003, Peach et al. *this volume*). Finally, survival and capture probabilities can be modeled as functions of covariates. For example, if winter temperature is thought to influence survival, it can be incorporated into the analysis by modeling survival as a function of temperature.

Estimation of population size from capture–recapture data requires a more stringent assumption than is required to estimate survival rate, because both marked and unmarked birds must have similar capture probabilities. Although population size can be estimated directly using program MARK, the Jolly-Seber population size estimation feature in the program is subject to numerical problems. Programs JOLLY (www.mbr-pwrc.usgs.gov/software.html) and POPAN (www.cs.umanitoba.ca/~popan/) provide direct estimates of population size. Alternatively, one could estimate population size indirectly from the number of birds caught in a given time period (n_t) and the estimate of detection probability ($\hat{p}_i$) as $n_i/\hat{p}_i$ (e.g., Williams et al. 2002).

The flexibility of the model structure and the relatively user-friendly nature of software such as MARK can lead to "data snooping," as it is tempting to model parameters as a function of an inordinate number of factors. Given the limited sample sizes that often result from mist-net studies, consideration of too many factors increases the risk of spurious results (i.e., good fit but not repeatable and with little predictive ability). Therefore one is better off taking the time *a priori* to formulate hypotheses about the key causal factors that drive the survival process.

Once an *a priori* set of models (e.g., constant survival, time-dependent survival, survival that is age-dependent and influenced by temperature) is chosen, the significance of these factors (relative to the amount of data available) can be evaluated for certain cases through direct tests (i.e., likelihood-ratio tests when models are nested). Alternatively, information theory criteria like AIC (Burnham and Anderson 1998) can be used to choose the most appropriate of the candidate models, or to average parameter estimates across all candidate models, using relative model selection metrics as weights (Burnham and Anderson 1998).

Closed Population Capture–recapture Models

In closed population studies, the goal is to estimate population size (N). Because the population size, although unknown, is assumed to be constant over the trapping occasions, the modeling procedure fits alternative models that differ with regard to assumptions about temporal, behavioral, and individual heterogeneity in capture probabilities. Otis et al. (1978) and White et al. (1982) reviewed models for closed populations and developed program CAPTURE (Otis et al. 1978, Rexstad and Burnham 1991) to fit four models: (1) M_0: Probabilities of capture are the same for all individuals at all capture occasions; (2) M_h: Probabilities of capture differ among individuals, but do not change over capture occasions; (3) M_t: Probabilities of capture differ over capture occasions, but not among individuals; (4) M_b: Probabilities of capture do not change over capture occasions or individuals, but change the first time an animal is captured (behavioral response), so all unmarked animals have one capture probability and all marked animals a different probability. An extreme case of the latter occurs when individuals are only seen once, then they are never seen again (a "removal" model). Models combining these assumptions also exist, including M_{tb}, M_{th}, M_{bh}, and M_{tbh}. Population size can be estimated under all of these models (Chao 2001). In general, individual heterogeneity in detection probability causes difficulties, unless that heterogeneity is small or can be described completely in terms of covariates. Program CAPTURE can be accessed within program MARK. In addition, MARK itself provides the ability to model closed population data for models M_0, M_t, M_b, and M_{tb}, and model M_h, where heterogeneity consists of two unspecified groups with different capture probabilities between them, but homogeneity within group (Pledger 2000).

For those models where program MARK can be used directly, model selection can be conducted using likelihood-ratio tests or AIC, as described above. Program CAPTURE uses a different model selection procedure based on multivariate statistics, which is not always considered reliable. Stanley and Burnham (1998) were unable to develop a satisfactory model selection algorithm and recommended use of an estimator averaging approach.

TOPICS IN CAPTURE–RECAPTURE ANALYSIS

Developments in capture–recapture analysis over the last decade provide some interesting possibilities for analysis of mist-net data. In this section, we briefly discuss some of these developments and their relevance to mist-net studies of passerine birds.

Estimation of Movement Rates

Large-scale banding projects tend to have multiple netting stations scattered over large areas. Sometimes, it is of interest to estimate probabilities of moving among stations. The movement can be seasonal, as occurs when moving from breeding to wintering ranges, or can be between years among locations located on the breeding or wintering grounds, or among stopover sites. In fact, many interesting hypotheses about age-specific site fidelity of passerine birds can be phrased in terms of a movement probability study. Models for estimating movement probabilities have been developed by Arnason (1972, 1973), Hestbeck et al. (1991), Nichols et al. (1993), Schwarz (1993), Schwarz et al. (1993), and Brownie et al. (1993).

Movement probabilities have been estimated for birds using resighting data (e.g., Hestbeck et al. 1991, Nichols et al. 1993), band recovery data (Schwarz 1993), and recapture data (Spendelow et al. 1995, Blums et al. 2003). These models have been used with passerines (Senar et al. 2002), but such uses are relatively rare. The almost complete absence of recapture information of birds banded as juveniles poses a particular challenge for capture–recapture studies of passerine birds.

To estimate movement probabilities among locations, the experimental design requires multiple capture stations, and multiple capture occasions at each station. This design yields data on the locations of captured animals at the various sampling periods at the different stations (c.f. Hestbeck et al. 1991). From these fates, we can define capture histories in which stations are indexed by characters (A = at station A, B = at station B) and these characters replace the "1" in the capture history. For example, a capture history for six periods at two stations could be 0A0BBA. Probabilistic models are developed for such data using the following parameters:

ϕ_i^{rs} = transition probability that an animal alive and at station r at time i is alive and at station s at time $i + 1$.

p_i^s = probability of capture for an animal at station s at time i.

The parameters ϕ^{rs} and p_i^s can be estimated from these data using the multinomial-based statistical models. Because ϕ_i^{rs} is a parameter that includes two interesting events, survival and movement, it is sometimes useful to decompose the transition probabilities. If survival from i to $i + 1$ depends only on location at i, and not on location at $i + 1$, then we can write the transition probabilities as:

$$\phi_i^{rs} = S_i^r \, \psi_i^{rs}$$

where S_i^r = probability that an animal in location r at time i survives until $i + 1$, and $\psi0_i^{rs}$ = conditional probability that an animal in location r at time i, is present in location s at $i + 1$, given that it is alive at $i + 1$.

Many interesting ecological hypotheses can be tested using these models (Nichols and Kendall 1995). One elaboration is that sometimes these movement probabilities are not simply a consequence of the location of animals at the most recent time period. Instead, animals may retain memories of where they were in earlier periods and the memories can modify their movements. We can develop a test to see whether transition probabilities depend only on location at time i (a Markovian model), or are influenced by location from earlier time periods (a memory model; see Hestbeck et al. 1991, Brownie et al. 1993). To do this, we add additional parameter subscripts, conditioning on releases at i for which locations at time i-1 are known.

Markovian models can be implemented using programs MARK (White and Burnham 1999) and MSSURVIV (Hines 1994). These programs provide estimates (and associated variances) of location-specific survival, capture, and movement probabilities. Memory models can be implemented in program MSSURVIV. It has been difficult to assess fit of multistate models, but a new goodness-of-fit test has been developed by Pradel et al. (2003) for this purpose.

An example of multistate modeling is provided in Hestbeck et al. (1991) using an extensive mark–resighting study of Canada Geese (*Branta canadensis*). Geese were neck-collared at several locations in eastern North America, and resighted in winter for several years in the Mid-Atlantic states, the Chesapeake Bay region, and the Carolinas. The goal of the study was to look at location changes between years in wintering populations. Estimates of mean annual movement probabilities (Table 1) showed that probability of remaining in the same wintering area was lowest for the Carolina population, and that movement probabilities differed among study areas.

ACCOUNTING FOR TRANSIENTS

One enduring problem in the analysis of capture–recapture data from mist-net studies has been the separation of resident birds from transients in analysis. Because migration periods are difficult to define, and because they may change yearly, many breeding-season banding programs experience transients early and late in the season, and the presence of these birds can greatly influence the results of the capture–recapture analysis. Several approaches have been taken to minimize the effects of transients in the analysis, such as only analyzing data from the period of greatest population stability, eliminating birds from the analysis if they are never recaptured, and eliminating initial captures of all birds. Unfortunately, these approaches either bias survival rate estimates (if all birds seen only once are eliminated from the analysis) or use data inefficiently (if all initial captures are eliminated). Pradel et al. (1997) have developed a model that avoids these problems by incorporating the proportion of transients among newly released birds as a parameter in the model. Let γ_i = proportion of transients in the sample of unmarked birds at period i. In the model, the survival probability for first-captured animals is a sum of survival rates for transients (ϕ_i^t) and residents (ϕ_i^r), each weighted by its proportion, or:

$$\gamma_i \phi_i^t + (1 - \gamma_i) \phi_i^r$$

The "survival" rate (that is, the chance of surviving and returning to the study location) of transients is 0 by definition. Information exists on the survival rate of residents from previously marked animals in the population. This survival probability (ϕ_i^r) can be estimated from animals seen in at least one previous period, permitting estimation of γ_i in the standard multinomial framework. Pradel et al. (1997) illustrate this method with data from Lazuli Buntings (*Passerina amoena*). Their estimates of resident survival rates are substantially higher with this model than with the standard CJS model. This model is implemented in program TMSURVIV (www.mbr-pwrc.usgs.gov/software.html) and can be implemented in MARK (White and Burnham 1999) as a model with trap response in survival.

Peach (1993) describes two alternative procedures for eliminating transient birds from survival analysis of resident birds, and suggests that defining a group of birds recaptured at least 10 days after initial marking will provide sufficient information for separating the cohort into transients and residents. Hines et al. (2003) formalized the suggestion of

TABLE 1. Mean annual movement probabilities with associated standard errors for Canada Geese in three wintering locations in the eastern United States (Hestbeck et al. 1991)

Location year i	Location year $i+1$		
	Mid-Atlantic	Chesapeake	Carolinas
Mid-Atlantic	0.71 (0.02)	0.29 (0.02)	0.009 (0.001)
Chesapeake	0.10 (0.01)	0.89 (0.01)	0.02 (0.002)
Carolinas	0.07 (0.01)	0.37 (0.02)	0.56 (0.03)

Peach (1993) as an extension of the model of Pradel et al. (1997). A bird first captured in period i, which would normally be assigned to the release cohort of unknown resident status, is instead reassigned to the cohort of known residents if it is recaptured at least x days after initial release in the season of release. Nott and DeSante (2002) applied this approach to data for several species from the MAPS program.

ESTIMATING THE PROPORTION OF BIRDS ALIVE BUT NOT BREEDING (PRESENT) AT A STUDY LOCATION

The proportion of animals in a population that are active breeders is an important demographic parameter, but is extremely difficult to estimate. However, there are several possible approaches to estimation of this proportion, if we are willing to assume that presence of a breeding-age animal in a breeding area is evidence of breeding. This assumption, although not generally appropriate, may be acceptable for some bird species. The expected value of the capture probability estimate from an open population model can be written as $E(\hat{p}_i) = \alpha_i p_i^*$, where α_i = probability that the animal is in the sample area (equivalent to breeding probability), p_i^* = conditional probability that the animal is caught, given that it is in the sample area. Recently, two approaches have been developed to estimate the parameter α_i. Both approaches depend on the ability to estimate p_i^*.

Clobert et al. (1990, 1993, 1994) suggested that if we assume that $\alpha_i = 1$ for adult birds, then $E(\hat{p}_i) = p_i^*$ for all i for adults. Thus, we can estimate α_i for other age classes based on the ratio of $\hat{p}_i$ for the class of interest to $\hat{p}_i$ for adults. Pradel and Lebreton (1999) suggest using a multi-state approach to the same model, which permits the use of program MARK or MSSURVIV for maximum-likelihood estimation (Spendelow et al. 2002, Lebreton et al. 2003).

Alternatively, we can use the robust design to estimate α_i (Kendall et al. 1997). Within a season, closed population models can be used to directly estimate p_i^*. Between seasons, CJS models are used to estimate p_i. The ratio of these estimates can be used as an estimate of α_i in cases where all birds at time i have the same probability of being a breeder. Kendall et al. (1997) also consider a more complicated model in which the probability of an individual breeding at time i depends on whether it bred at time $i - 1$. Programs MARK and RDSURVIV permit estimation of α_i for robust design data. Fujiwara and Caswell (2002), and Kendall and Nichols (2002) consider the estimation of α_i when robust design data are not available or possible, but their results confirm that the robust design should be used if at all possible.

ESTIMATION OF RECRUITMENT AND POPULATION CHANGE

One of the most interesting new developments in capture–recapture methods is the possibility that the Jolly-Seber approach can be reparameterized to directly estimate the demographic parameters of recruitment rate and finite rate of population change. In the original J-S model, survival and capture probabilities are the primary parameters to be estimated. Population size and recruitment do not appear as model parameters, but can only be estimated as functions of capture and survival rates. However, Pradel (1996) has shown that the model can be reformulated to include any one of these parameters:

$1 - \gamma_i$ = proportion of birds in the population at i that are new (i.e., that entered the population between periods $i - 1$ and i; this can be viewed as a turnover statistic).

f_i = number of new animals present at $i + 1$, per animal present at i (this can be viewed as a per capita recruitment rate).

λ_i = finite rate of population increase (N_{i+1}/N_i).

Under some circumstances, γ_i and $1 - \gamma_i$ represent the proportional contributions of survival and recruitment to population growth, an interpretation analogous to elasticities for asymptotic population projection modeling (Nichols et al. 2000).

Uses of the new parameterizations include (1) direct modeling of γ_i or f_i as functions of other study data (e.g., estimates of nest success) or of environmental covariates, which can help provide a mechanistic understanding of the recruitment process; (2) direct incorporation of recruitment rate estimates into population projection models; and (3) use of the λ-parameterization to provide a canonical framework for estimation of population change from capture–recapture and other sources of data. Under situation 3, if another formal estimation method (e.g., variable circular plot, line transect) is used on the mist-net study site, then a joint likelihood can be constructed and λ_i estimated using both data sources. If count data (e.g., point counts) are obtained on the study area, then λ_i can be modeled as a function of these data permitting (1) a test of the hypothesis that the count data really do provide a good "index" of population change and, if they do, (2) use of these data as covariates to obtain a better estimate of λ (Nichols and Hines 2002).

This modeling is relatively recent (Pradel 1996), and few examples exist of its application to mist-net studies (but see Nichols et al. in press). However, we believe the approach of a canonical framework permitting direct estimation of rate of population change using all relevant data (e.g., capture–recapture and point-count) simultaneously, should be preferable to the approach of obtaining separate estimates of λ_i from different data sources and then attempting to combine them or reconcile differences among them.

CAPTURE–RECAPTURE AND MIGRATION BANDING

Banding of birds during migration occurs at many capture stations throughout North America, and data from these stations provide a sometimes controversial view of population changes in birds that breed in the northern regions of North America. Most investigators who attempt to estimate trends in migrating birds use indices to number of birds passing through a banding station (e.g., total number of individual birds captured), but this index is clearly influenced by many environmental variables (Dawson 1990). Though data can be adjusted for some of these variables (e.g., effects of date, weather, and moon phase; Dunn and Hussell 1995, Dunn et al. 1997, Hussell *this volume*), capture probability may be influenced by other factors not measured or accounted for. Capture–recapture methods provide a reasonable alternative to these index approaches, and use of open-population models permits estimation of both the total number of birds passing through a station and residence times of birds at migration stations (Nichols 1996).

Although not commonly done (but see Brownie and Robson 1983, Pollock et al. 1990), it is possible

to estimate residence times ("survival") at migration banding stations using standard CJS models. These analyses would use recapture data from the stations to estimate the proportion of animals missed by the sampling, and "survival" rates (primarily the probability of remaining at the station) of marked birds at the station. From these rates an average residence time can be estimated as $-1/\ln(\hat{\phi})$, where $\hat{\phi}$ is the estimate of average survival rate between sample intervals. The total population passing through the station can be estimated as the sum of the CJS estimates of B_i, the number of new animals entering the population between sampling periods (e.g., Shealer and Kress 1994).

Schaub et al. (2001) further generalized the above approach for estimating total stopover duration. They use the method of Pradel (1996) to estimate stopover duration before or after capture, using "recruitment" and "survival" analyses, respectively. They then combine them into total stopover time. They implement this approach in Program SODA (www.cefe.cnrs-mop.fr/wwwbiom/Dyn-Populations/biom-ftp.htm).

The superpopulation modeling approach of Crosbie and Manly (1985) and Schwarz and Arnason (1996) provides an alternative approach to analyzing migration banding data. Under this approach, parameters reflecting entry of new animals into the population are incorporated directly into the model, and total number of individual birds using the station during the entire sampling period (between the first and last samples) can be estimated. If migration banding as described above is conducted for a series of years, the within- and between-year information can be combined to estimate survival rate, as well as the probability that an individual used that particular stopover site in a given year (Schwarz and Stobo 1997, Kendall and Bjorkland 2001).

Of course, these analyses require recapture or resighting data for survival rate estimation, and hence they will only work well when "sufficient" recaptures or observations exist. Even though limited recapture information exists for most species, we feel that these methods have great potential to improve estimation associated with migration banding programs as they provide a means for investigators to directly evaluate the critical assumption of consistency in proportions of animals captured. Innovative applications of methods to increase the number of recaptures (e.g., through resighting procedures) may increase the feasibility of applying capture–recapture methods to a larger number of species, and provide a means for generally estimating the proportion of birds "missed" in capture indices during migration.

SPECIES RICHNESS ESTIMATION

Information on biodiversity has become of increasing importance to conservation, and surveys of species richness are frequently conducted in the Neotropics. Often, the total number of species captured in mist nets, or identified through other sampling procedures, is used as the estimate of species richness. Unfortunately, this estimate is clearly biased, and the extent of the underestimate is a function of both the probabilities of encountering species and the sampling effort. Capture–recapture methods can be used with replicated species list data to directly estimate the total numbers of species present from mist-net and other samples (Dawson et al. 1995, Nichols and Conroy 1996, Boulinier et al. 1998).

To do this, species are treated as individuals, and capture histories can be developed for each species by (1) observing presence–absence of the species at multiple trapping occasions at a single station; (2) observing presence–absence over multiple stations at a single occasion; or (3) recording number of individuals per species at a single station and occasion. The data from approaches (1) and (2) can be analyzed using the closed population models of Otis et al. (1978); models that allow heterogeneity in capture probabilities among species (such as model M_h) are likely to be most useful. In these models, total number of species is estimated, allowing each species to have a different chance of capture.

If data from only a single trapping period are available (scenario 3), a version of the Burnham and Overton (1979) model, M_h, can still be used to estimate total species richness. For this estimator, data are summarized as number of species for which one bird was caught or seen, the number of species for which two individuals were caught or seen, etc., up to the number of species for which five individuals were seen. J. E. Hines has written a program to estimate species richness using the limiting form of model M_h with capture frequency data (Hines et al. 1999). Application of this approach to mist-net data is shown in Karr et al. (1990b).

We view these species-richness estimation methods as providing a useful way of resolving some of the sampling problems that occur in tropical mist-net studies, in which the mist nets do not sample species with equal probability, and counts encounter a different (but not necessarily independent) subset of the bird species present in an area. For these areas, data can be combined from mist-net captures and point counts to get a composite species richness estimate that is free of the bias associated with total number of species captured (Dawson et al. 1995). These methods also permit estimation of parameters associated with community dynamics, such as rate of change in species richness, local extinction rate, and local colonization or immigration rate (Nichols et al. 1998a,b).

CONCLUSIONS

In this paper we have tried to provide some insights into how capture–recapture estimation can be useful in mist-net studies, and describe some new procedures that should be of use to biologists. We emphasize that capture–recapture models form an appropriate structure for thinking about mist-netting studies, and should be considered in the design of any mist-net study. Indices that are not adjusted for the proportion of birds missed by the sampling procedure involve untested assumptions, and capture–recapture provides a way to test these assumptions (Skalski and Robson 1992, MacKenzie and Kendall 2002).

All of the statistical models discussed in this paper are defined in terms of a series of parameters that are assumed to be of importance. Investigators must collect data and use evidence from the data (such as goodness-of-fit tests) to evaluate whether the set of parameters is reasonable for their data sets. Estimation of some parameters, such as number of transients in the population, requires more restrictive assumptions (equal capture probabilities of transients and residents in the transient model) than does estimation of other parameters (e.g., proportion of transients in the sample of unmarked birds does not require this assumption). Before using these models, investigators should evaluate the underlying biological and statistical assumptions implicit in each model. However, we emphasize that these methods will often be preferable to index-based methods, as the latter frequently require much more restrictive assumptions, although these are often left unspecified.

There have been many exciting advances in capture–recapture work over the last decade, and we have discussed advances in the estimation of movement probabilities, survival rates in the presence of transients, populations at migration stopover sites, temporary emigration (breeding proportions), rate of population change, and species richness. User-friendly computer programs exist for application of most of these procedures. Understanding these methods will allow investigators to (1) define the parameters that they want to estimate using a banding study; (2) develop study designs that will allow them to estimate the parameters; and (3) define needed sample sizes, in terms of capture probabilities and number of animals captured and recaptured, that will be needed to achieve prespecified goals of estimate precision and test power. Studies designed with such a focus should permit stronger inferences about avian population dynamics than have been possible previously.

Studies in Avian Biology No. 29:182–186

EFFECTIVENESS OF INFORMAL BANDING TRAINING AT THREE WESTERN CANADIAN BANDING STATIONS

Brenda C. Dale

Abstract. Skills of trainee banders from three western Canadian banding stations were assessed in 1993, using minimum performance standards in use at that time. Each trainer–trainee combination independently examined the same birds. Quantitative skills appeared to be learned quickly, but there were few passing scores on aging, sexing, skulling, and fat assessment, and none on overall achievement using the test standards. However, many trainee errors were of a non-critical nature, which was not well reflected in the scoring system. Several individuals did score well if the nature of their errors was taken into account. Time spent with a trainer, experience, and personality may all play a role in trainee performance. Results demonstrate the need for trainers to meet an established standard, and for continued spot-checking of skills after training has been completed.

Key Words: banding techniques, banding test standards, bander training.

Use of data collected at banding stations for such important international programs as Monitoring Avian Productivity and Survival (MAPS) and migration monitoring is predicated on the belief that data are collected accurately. However, standards for obtaining banding permits vary greatly throughout the world. In a few cases, a formal test is administered, but in North America permits are awarded on the basis of letters of recommendation from banders who already have permits.

Recently, the North American Banding Council (NABC) developed detailed guides on banding techniques, a guide for trainers, and specialized manuals for the banding of landbirds, hummingbirds, and raptors (Hull et al. 2001; North American Banding Council 2001a, b, c; Russell et al. 2001). Intensive training courses are increasingly available, and a bander can now undergo testing to earn formal certification. In the last few years the Canadian Bird Banding Office and the U.S. Bird Banding Lab have begun to accept certification as proof of sufficient skill, knowledge, and experience to warrant a permit.

Despite the growth of opportunities for formal training, many North American banders gain their initial skills, knowledge, and experience through informal training, defined here as working in the presence of a trainer until the latter is satisfied with the consistency and correctness of data collection techniques and procedures. The purpose of this study was to investigate the outcomes of informal training, by comparing results to the minimum performance standards in use at the time of the study (1993), prior to development of NABC materials. Although these criteria are now largely outdated, the study demonstrates the importance of both training

and evaluation procedures in ensuring accurate and consistent results.

METHODS

Research took place in 1993 at Beaverhill Bird Observatory in Alberta, Last Mountain Bird Observatory in Saskatchewan, and Delta Marsh Bird Observatory in Manitoba. Informal training varied among these stations, but in all cases the trainer did not allow the trainee to collect data alone until the trainee had achieved a high degree of agreement with the trainer. Quantifying length of the training period was often difficult, because checking diminished gradually in most cases. For each trainee, we obtained an estimate of total experience, and an estimate (from the trainer) of the time the trainee had access to the trainer. I chose to define training period as time spent in proximity to the trainer, because this could be most readily quantified.

Each trainer–trainee combination independently examined and collected data on the same birds. Number of birds measured by each trainer–trainee combination varied from 37 to 171. All data were collected in August and September, so participants were not usually able to use cloacal protuberance and brood patches as an indication of the sex or age of the birds. All stations used a five-point fat scale. Two stations used a three-class and one a six-class skull ossification scale. All participants recorded data without input from others (usually out of sight from one another). No discussion of birds being handled was allowed for the entire length of the experiment. For the purposes of this study, it was assumed that the trainer had correctly classified, assessed, and measured the bird.

For measurements, I calculated the average of the absolute deviations of trainee data from those of the trainer, and divided deviation by the average value achieved by the trainer. For categorical scores (fat and skull), I determined the proportions of cases in which a trainee scored the bird the same as the trainer (agreement), differed by one class, or differed by two classes. For age and sex I calculated the

182

proportion of cases in which a trainee scored the bird exactly the same as the trainer (agreement).

Scores were assessed by comparison to minimum performance standards suggested by C. J. Ralph (pers. comm.), which were developed in 1993 for a one-week training course to teach banding skills. These criteria are shown in Table 1. However, some errors are less important than others, and thus I also determined whether errors were "critical" or "non-critical." A trainee classifying a bird as "unknown age" (or sex) when the trainer felt able to classify to an age or sex category was a non-critical error, whereas errors when trainer and trainee assign opposing age or sex classes were critical. For skulling, a class error within the hatch year categories was considered non-critical.

RESULTS

QUANTITATIVE MEASURES

Analysis of quantitative measurement differences were limited to wing chord. One trainee was in the "top" category, using the standards in Table 1, and the rest were comfortably within the "pass" category (Table 2). The bulk of the birds measured were small passerines with wing chords less than 100 mm, so any error was almost sure to put the trainee in the pass rather than top category. Most errors were similar in magnitude to the amount of variation typical of an individual repeatedly measuring the same bird. There was no relationship to the amount of time the trainee had spent in proximity to the trainer or to overall length of experience. Wing measurement appears to be a skill that is learned quickly, and the skill is retained well after contact with the trainer is over.

QUALITATIVE MEASURES

Species

Correct identification of species ranged from 98 to 100%. Two of the four errors committed were

transcription errors, with the trainee writing the name of the previous species instead of the species being processed. The other two errors involved confusion between Least (*Empidonax minimus*) and Alder (*E. alnorum*) flycatchers. Examination of measurements collected by the trainer and application of formulas showed that the trainees made the wrong decisions because they did not collect all the necessary data. Using the Table 1 standard of 100% to pass, there were two passing and three failing individuals.

Age

Using 100% as the pass score (Table 1), no trainee achieved a passing score for assigning age (Table 3). One trainer–trainee combination did agree on the age of 99% of the birds. The only disagreement was a bird classed as unknown age by the trainee. Of the remaining four banders, three achieved scores in excess of 80% and one failed by a wide margin. Most errors by these four banders were of a critical nature (an adult bird called hatch year or vice versa), rather than non-critical (an adult or hatching year called unknown age).

Sex

No trainee achieved a perfect score on assigning sex (Table 3), so all failed according to the standards in Table 1. One trainee achieved a score of 98%, three more achieved scores above 80%, and one failed by a wide margin. Most errors were of a non-critical nature, in which the trainee classed the bird as unknown sex while the trainer classified it as known sex. However, every trainee made at least one critical error.

Skull

No individual attained a top score for correct skull classification (Table 4) according to the standards in

TABLE 1. MINIMUM PERFORMANCE STANDARDS FOR BANDERS EXPRESSED AS ACCEPTABLE PERCENT ERRORS OR CONCURRENCE BETWEEN TRAINEE AND TRAINER

	Measurement	Species, age, sex	Qualitative (skull, fat)	
	% error	% agree	% agree	% differ by one class
Top	< 1	100	> 95	< 5
Pass	> 1 to 3	100	80–95	< 20
Marginal/ fail	> 3 to < 5	n/a[a]	50–80	20–40
Definite fail	> 5	< 100	< 50	> 50

Notes: Standards are those suggested by C. J. Ralph (pers. comm.) in 1993. All rates of agreement or error are in reference to answer as determined by the trainer.

[a] Anything less than 100% agreement for these categories was considered a failure so there is no marginal score for these skills.

TABLE 2. TRAINEE SCORES FOR WING MEASUREMENT AND SPECIES IDENTIFICATION

Trainer/Trainee (N)	Wing measurement % deviation	Species identification % agreement[a]
A / B (171)[b]	1.77	**99**
B / C (169)	1.62	**98**
D / E (100)	0.72	**99**
F / G (86)	1.90	100
F / H (37)	1.40	100

[a] Bold marks are failures by standards in Table 1.

[b] Sample size for these two skills for each pairing of personnel appears in parentheses.

Table 1. One passed, two achieved marginal scores, and two failed. With the exception of bander H, most errors were of a non-critical nature (differed in class within bird of the year categories), and these birds would have been aged correctly on the basis of skull. Using critical and non-critical classification for errors produces somewhat different results than does "differences of one class." Judging on the basis of Table 1, the number of serious errors made by G and H would have been underestimated, and the number of serious errors made by B would have been overestimated (Table 4).

Observer H had a high number of errors in skulling (Table 4). According to F (the trainer), H appeared to be skulling well at the end of the training period but had not subsequently asked for confirmation on many birds when trainer and trainee were in proximity. There was some parallel between scores on age and skull for H. This did not hold true for B, C, and E who seemed to have acceptable skulling ability (at least 85% agreement or non-critical errors), but did not assess ossification on some birds, and this is where most of their aging errors occurred. Skulling every bird would probably have improved their age classification performance.

Fat

There was one pass and three marginal scores (Table 5). Almost all errors, even by the failing individual H, were within a class of the trainer's determination.

Training levels

All the trainees had achieved a high degree of agreement with their trainers after initial training

TABLE 3. TRAINEE SCORES FOR AGE AND SEX DETERMINATION

Trainer/ Trainee (N)	Age			Sex		
	% agree	% non-critical error	% critical error	% agree	% non-critical error	% critical error
A / B (171)[a]	**84**[b]	1	15	**70**	29	1
B / C (169)	**92**	0	8	**98**	0	2
D / E (100)	**99**	1	0	**85**	11	4
F / G (86)	**93**	1	6	**86**	9	5
F / H (37)	**65**	0	35	**84**	8	8

Notes: Values are expressed as percent of agreement, non-critical, and critical error.

[a] Sample size for these two skills for each pairing of personnel appears in parentheses.

[b] Bold marks are failures by standards in Table 1.

TABLE 4. TRAINEE SCORES FOR SKULL OSSIFICATION

Trainer/Trainee (N)	% agree	% non-critical error	% critical error	% differ by one class	% differ by two classes
A / B (52)[a]	**48**[b]	40	12	37	15
B / C (51)	63	33	4	33	4
D / E (87)	74	26	0	26	0
F / G (76)	80	13	7	19	1
F / H (37)	**46**	24	30	49	5

Notes: Values are expressed as percent agreement and percent by error type.

[a] Sample size for this skill for each pairing of personnel appears in parentheses.

[b] Bold marks are failures by standards in Table 1.

TABLE 5. TRAINEE SCORES FOR FAT ASSESSMENT

Trainer/Trainee (N)	% Agree	% Differ by one class	% Differ by two classes
A/B (171)[a]	79	19	2
B/C (169)	87	12	1
D/E (100)	61	31	8
F/G (86)	56	41	3
F/H ((37)	**40**[b]	49	11

Notes: Values are expressed as percent agreement and percent by error type.
[a] Sample size for this skill for each pairing of personnel appears in parentheses.
[b] Bold marks are failures by standards in Table 1.

(prior to this experiment). Experience gained subsequent to training (as measured by number of birds banded), and the period of long term access to the trainer following training, differed among those tested (Table 6). There was only one trainee (B) who was given a defined period of training and then banded alone thereafter.

It was recognized from the onset that it would be difficult to separate the influences of training and experience, because both are often acquired together and quantifying them in a meaningful way is difficult. The small sample size precludes quantitative analysis. Although data for the first three individuals in Table 6 suggest that access to a trainer beyond the first intensive period may be a factor in long term performance, this was not consistent. For example, bander H had a very long period of access to a trainer, but the worst score.

Results from bander B suggest that practice alone does not increase performance (Table 6). DeSante et al. (*this volume*) also presented data indicating that experience of banders does not necessarily ensure a higher degree of accuracy.

Discussions with F, the trainer of G and H, revealed that personality or temperament may be an important factor in training effectiveness. For example, trainee G was trained for a short time but was extremely cautious. Trainee G frequently asked questions of the trainer and spent a lot of time reading source and reference materials. Trainee H did well in initial training and testing, but rarely asked

TABLE 6. ACCESS TO TRAINER, EXPERIENCE AND PERFORMANCE OF BANDING TRAINEES

Bander	Access to trainer (days)	Experience (birds banded)	Cumulative score (out of 600)
B	10	>3,000	478
C	65	~1,000	536
E	55	~2,000	518
G	29	~2,000	513
H	60	~2,000	433

questions during the extensive period following training when the trainer F was accessible but not actively probing and testing H.

DISCUSSION

No individual attained a fully satisfactory performance level based on the standards in Table 1. Several individuals had mainly errors of a non-critical nature, which was not reflected in the Table 1 scoring system that was in use at the time of the study. Current standards for performance assessment are quite different. The NABC does not treat all errors as equal, and although the council sets a high standard, it does not expect performance of 100% in aging and sexing birds. NABC standards also penalize critical errors more harshly than non-critical errors, because classing a bird as unknown age or sex is preferable to categorizing it incorrectly. Determination of age and sex is often based on subtle plumage characteristics, and it is to be expected that trainees will record a greater number of unknowns than trainers. Indeed, a trainee who rarely uses the "unknown" category may be overconfident, and probably should be rechecked for errors (M. McNicholl, pers. comm.). Nonetheless, the NABC does impose some penalty for non-critical errors made during testing, to encourage precision when a true determination is possible.

Despite the improvement of training guides and development of performance standards for certification, results in this paper indicate that individual differences among banders can readily arise and be promulgated. A good example of this is the case of banders B and C in this study. Bander B was given a short period of intensive training and then banded for a summer. The next year, B trained C, and the two worked together for the summer. It appears that because C had constant access to B prior to testing in this study, there was a high degree of agreement with B during the test. In fact, C was the only individual who came close to achieving a passing score. It appears B had done a very good job of passing on information to C, which was the testing criterion in this study. However, B's score indicates that the information passed on to C was incomplete or incorrect.

Results of this study indicate that trainers should achieve a common standard before we rely on agreement of trainer and trainee results as the test of competency for new banders. Without this initial standardization, we will be perpetuating high variability in standards, because trainees reflect their trainer's skills. Moreover, it is important to recognize that learning and evaluation must not cease at the end of the training period. Recommendations to address these issues include the following:

1. More banding stations should undertake evaluations of their training effectiveness. This may clarify which factors most influence performance, and identify weaknesses in training programs. Especially needed is development of a schedule for follow-up spot checking after initial training has been completed.

2. Trainers should attend regional or national workshops so that all trainers teach from a similar standard. Contact and verification among trainers in a region should take place at least annually to maintain consistency.

3. Station personnel (regardless of experience) should periodically compare results, and immediately discuss sources of variation to iron out any problems revealed. For example, as a result of this study, F gave H a refresher course and they began regular comparisons, which showed a much higher level of agreement.

4. The role of trainer and trainee temperament should be given consideration in designing and carrying out training and assessment.

ACKNOWLEDGMENTS

The cooperation of the Beaverhill Bird Observatory, Last Mountain Bird Observatory, and Delta Marsh Bird Observatory is greatly appreciated. They are to be commended for permitting this experiment and for their positive attitude in using the results to improve their programs. I especially thank the anonymous trainers and trainees. R. D. Dickson, E. H. Dunn, E. Hayakawa, M. K. McNicholl, and C. J. Ralph offered helpful comments on the manuscript.

Studies in Avian Biology No. 29:187–196

RECOMMENDATIONS FOR THE USE OF MIST NETS FOR INVENTORY AND MONITORING OF BIRD POPULATIONS

C. John Ralph, Erica H. Dunn, Will J. Peach, and Colleen M. Handel

Abstract. We provide recommendations on the best practices for mist netting for the purposes of monitoring population parameters such as abundance and demography. Studies should be carefully thought out before nets are set up, to ensure that sampling design and estimated sample size will allow study objectives to be met. Station location, number of nets, type of nets, net placement, and schedule of operation should be determined by the goals of the particular project, and we provide guidelines for typical mist-net studies. In the absence of study-specific requirements for novel protocols, commonly used protocols should be used to enable comparison of results among studies. Regardless of the equipment, net layout, or netting schedule selected, it is important for all studies that operations be strictly standardized, and a well-written operation protocol will help in attaining this goal. We provide recommendations for data to be collected on captured birds, and emphasize the need for good training of project personnel.

Key Words: mist net, monitoring, recommendations, standards, technique.

Mist netting is a valuable tool for monitoring bird populations (Dunn and Ralph *this volume*). Since becoming widely available over the last half of the 20th century, mist nets have been employed in a wide variety of studies, often using very different protocols. Information has gradually accumulated about the effects on capture rates of netting equipment, spatial arrangement of nets, and netting protocol. We are now in a position to make recommendations on the best practices. It is important to use methods that are effective and efficient, because mist netting requires specialized training and intense effort. Standardization is crucial to preventing spurious variation in capture rates. Finally, using widely accepted and tested protocols whenever possible will facilitate comparison of results across studies, and pooling of data for common analysis.

This paper contains recommendations for mist netting that are appropriate for a wide variety of inventory and monitoring purposes, taking into consideration the welfare of captured birds. The paper integrates the latest information contained in this volume and prior literature, and represents a general consensus of the authors contributing to this volume and of other participants in the workshop giving rise to it (see Preface). All recommendations apply to all seasons, unless specifically noted otherwise, and are summarized in Table 1.

PRIOR TO SETTING UP A NETTING STATION

Study Design

The number and type of nets used, their placement, target levels of netting effort, and data to be collected, all should be chosen to address the study objectives most effectively. Therefore, prior to selecting station locations and setting up nets, it is important to clearly define goals for population parameters to be measured, geographic scope, temporal frames of interest, and targets for species and sample size. For example, species inventory projects may require netting in a wide variety of habitats, as opposed to a study whose objective is to compare population parameters among particular habitats. Long-term monitoring will require a location that is likely to remain accessible over the life of the study, and for some purposes it will be important that habitat also remain relatively unchanged. A desire to capture particular target species will influence the habitats and vegetation structure where netting should take place, and may require use of special net types or capture techniques (such as canopy nets, or lures such as water drip traps or tape recordings; e.g., Whitaker 1972, Wilson and Allan 1996, Sogge et al. 2001). For some habitats or species (including certain grassland birds), netting may not be the best means of obtaining population data, and other methods should be considered.

Objectives of the study should consider the most appropriate geographic scale, which in turn affects the number of netting stations to be established. Is the intention to compare results among several stations to contrast distinct habitats or management practices, or are data to be pooled from multiple stations and habitats to represent a region as a whole? Adding effort at a single station can enlarge sample size, which is particularly important for estimation of survivorship (Nur et al. 2000, *this volume*; Ballard

TABLE 1. SUMMARY OF RECOMMENDED PROCEDURES FOR MIST-NETTING STUDIES

Parameter	Season	Recommendations
Station location(s)	All	Stations likely to be accessible for life of study
		Study-specific requirements are addressed
		Capture rates are sufficient to meet study objectives
Number of nets	All	Sufficient for sample size objectives to be met
		Matched to number of personnel available, at effort level sustainable for life of study
Mesh size of nets	All	Most suitable size for target species, or use range of sizes for species inventory
Net placement	All	Convenient and fast to check
	Breeding and wintering	Study-specific criteria are met (nets placed to sample target species or habitats, or systematically sample several habitats)
		Grid arrays to maximize territorial individuals captured and increase recapture probability, although lines may be better for sampling territorial birds when size of individual ranges are unknown or are variable among target species
Net density	All	1–5 nets/ha to sample as many territories or home ranges as possible
		>1–5 nets/ha, if desired, when birds are not territorial
Distribution of sampling periods[a]	All	Equal sampling periods throughout season
Number of sampling periods	Breeding	Demography: 10 to 12 consecutive 10-day periods, covering whole breeding season
		Abundance/site fidelity: minimum of 3 sampling periods per season, but more is better
	Wintering	1–3 sampling periods per season is a common protocol, but more frequent sampling is likely to provide better information
	Migration	Annual abundance indices and long-term trends: near-daily sampling, either at a single station or spread among a cluster of stations[b]
		Comparison of abundance among stations within years: 5–10 sampling periods (with simultaneous netting sessions)
Length of netting session[c]	Breeding	One day/10-day period (multiple stations pooling data), or up to 7/10-day period (single station studies where greater sample sizes are required, capture rates remain high enough for continued netting to be efficient, or sampling periods are relatively few)
	Wintering	1–2 days, or longer if capture rates remain high enough for continued netting to be efficient
	Migration	Annual indices of abundance or age ratio: near-daily netting through season
		Comparison of abundance among stations within a year: one or more days per netting session (preferably with simultaneous sampling at stations to be compared)
Hours of operation	All	At least 4 h, starting at dawn (unless peak activity of target species occurs at a different time)
		Effort level should be sustainable over life of study
Standardization	All	Standardize all equipment, net placement, and effort parameters within stations
		Standard protocol can differ among stations if direction and magnitude of temporal changes is being studied, but not if capture rates are being directly compared
	Breeding and wintering	Maintain stable vegetation height and density at net sites at net sites at sites to extent possible.
		Mark–recapture studies require less strict adherence to constant effort than studies relying on indices, but equipment, net placement, and vegetation at net sites should still be standardized
Training	All	Ensure that all participants are trained to standards of the North American Banding Council
		Train all participants to follow a standard protocol that is detailed in a written document
Data	All	Develop field recording and data management procedures to ensure uniformity in collection of all relevant data, and to enable rapid analysis
		Collect metadata relevant to station (including protocols and at least basic habitat description)
		Record daily effort data

[a] Period within which a netting session of 1+ consecutive days will take place.
[b] Effect on results of pooling less than daily data from each of several stations has not been tested (Dunn and Ralph *this volume*).
[c] Period of consecutive days of netting within a sampling period.

et al. *this volume*). However, increased netting within a site can sometimes lead to net avoidance, and may not sample a directly proportional increased number of territories. Increasing number of stations may often enlarge sample size more than increasing effort within a site, and sampling at multiple stations allows estimation of sample variance at the same time that overall sample size is increased (Burton and DeSante *this volume*). Sometimes, the sample size needed for a good measure of annual survival can often be obtained only by combining results from a network of stations (Hilton and Miller 2003). Single stations are poor at tracking annual changes in regional productivity for at least some species (Nur et al. 2000), but as few as 3–10 stations may be sufficient to produce representative regional results (Bart et al. 1999, Ralph et al. *this volume b*). Of course, pooling data among stations can obscure important differences among sites.

Once a decision has been made to establish multiple stations, further decisions are needed on how many, how far apart, and in what habitats they should be placed. The number of stations to be established should be based on target sample size (see below), as well as on availability of funding and personnel. If there is a likelihood of high turnover in the set of stations contributing data for pooled analysis, the effect of such turnover on quality of results also should be considered. Optimal spacing of stations will depend on study objectives (e.g., study of juvenile dispersal or adult emigration may require stations to be clustered). For the greatest power to represent an entire region, stations should be distributed according to geographic or habitat strata.

Before beginning the study, an investigator should decide upon the desired precision of an estimate or the effect size to be detected, which will help determine the minimum sample size required (number of mist-net stations and nets, number of birds captured and recaptured, or both). For survival analyses, the minimum sample size will be determined primarily by the number of birds recaptured. For comparisons of productivity, the number of mist-net stations and number of birds captured will be considerations. A preliminary estimate of sample size required to meet study objectives can be made through review of published papers on similar studies, or consultation with a statistical expert. Because of variability of capture rates among species, plans should be made for a pilot study and power analysis of preliminary data to allow for adjustment of effort.

Researchers should be well aware that mist-net captures are indices of the population being monitored, and that the proportion of the true population that is captured is unknown and variable (Nur et al. *this volume*). Much variation in capture proportion can be avoided through good study design and standardizing protocols, but capture proportion is not necessarily constant over time or space, thereby introducing potential bias into comparisons among indices (Sauer and Link *this volume*). Whenever feasible, the parameter of interest (e.g., adult population size) should be studied using mark–recapture techniques or other means of estimating capture probability (Dunn and Ralph *this volume*, Peach and Baillie *this volume*, Nur et al. *this volume*, Kendall et al. *this volume*).

Monitoring of population size and demography nearly always benefits from standardized netting. It is therefore recommended that alternative net placements be tested in a pilot study, such that a standardized array can be maintained without further change throughout the actual study period. Pilot work should also test the most appropriate distribution and length of sampling periods for a particular study. Careful thought should be given to the likelihood that the proposed netting schedule (daily hours of operation as well as duration and frequency of netting sessions) can be sustained over the intended life of the project, after station operators' initial flush of enthusiasm has waned.

TRAINING

All personnel should be well trained before beginning a study that involves use of mist nets. Such training should include the operation and care of nets, safe and ethical handling of birds, procedures for obtaining permits, and record keeping. Hands-on training should be done under the tutelage of a bander experienced in the use of mist nets and adept at training, and can be arranged by contacting a certified trainer, a local bird banding organization, or bird observatory. Such resources can be found by searching the Internet or by contacting the U.S. or Canadian banding offices.

All prospective participants in a mist-netting study should follow the guidelines in the appropriate North American Banding Council training guide (Hull et al. 2001; North American Banding Council 2001a, b; Russell et al. 2001). These guides are very detailed, so here we need only to emphasize the importance of appropriately training all project personnel. Joint training sessions for all participants in a particular study, regardless of experience level, is particularly desirable to ensure uniformity of technique (Dale *this volume*) and familiarity with the specific study protocols.

NETS

SELECTING A STATION LOCATION

Locations for mist-netting stations should be selected in accordance with the geographic scope of the study and question being addressed, but the choice should be tempered by accessibility, security from disturbance, and availability of personnel and support facilities. Often, station locations will be chosen to sample a pre-selected group of locations or habitats, perhaps employing a stratified or other sampling design. Depending on the study objective, it may also be very important to select specific locations with high capture probabilities (e.g., for studies involving mark–recapture). Capture rates are usually higher in riparian and shrubby habitats than in forest, in part because many birds fly above net level when vegetation is taller than the nets. If multiple stations are being established and study of dispersal is not a research objective, stations should be at least 1–5 km apart to ensure that most individuals will not be caught at more than one location (Ralph et al. *this volume b*).

For migrating birds, the most suitable study locations for long-term trend monitoring are ones from which birds are likely to move on as quickly as possible (i.e., locations that are not especially attractive for stopover), because some current methods for trend analysis assume that each day's count is an independent sample of the population (Dunn and Hussell 1995). By contrast, if the monitoring questions involve interest in stopover ecology, suitability of habitat, resident birds, and similar questions, then it may be preferable to find locations that have large populations of birds overall, including migrants with more lengthy stopovers. Locations for abundance monitoring during migration should be selected where overall habitat change will be minimal (Kaiser and Berthold *this volume*). Otherwise, change in use of the area by migrants could be interpreted as a change in the size of the breeding population in the region from which the migrants came (Ballard et al. 2003). Suitable locations with relatively stable habitat include those kept at an early successional stage by natural processes (such as regular flooding), or locations where the station operator has permission to cut vegetation regularly throughout the study area to maintain habitat structure and vegetation height at relatively stable levels.

NUMBER OF NETS

The number of nets used at each station should be defined both by the target sample size (related to the study questions) and by the ability of available personnel to handle the normal rate of capture. The North American Banding Council (2001a) gives detailed guidelines on the balance between bird numbers and the number of personnel. In general, most well-trained people can handle 5 birds/h. We suggest that if capture rates at a two-person station regularly exceed 50 birds in a 5-h period, consideration should be given to adding personnel, or reducing the number of nets. If the capture rate is consistently less than 3 birds/person-h, consideration should be given to increasing the number of nets (if higher numbers are needed to meet study objectives), or to having a single person operate the station and sending other personnel to operate additional stations.

Sometimes the number of nets that can safely be operated varies widely from day to day, for example, during migration seasons, or at locations where high winds often make certain nets unusable. In such cases, a core group of nets can be designated that includes nets opened on essentially all days that netting takes place. One or two additional groups can then be defined, of nets that will be closed first (as a unit) when some nets must be closed. A variable representing the net groups opened each day can then be added to analyses to model the effect of variable effort.

NET PLACEMENT

Several factors should be considered in deciding how to place nets within the study area.

Ease of checking nets.—A person should be able to complete a net round within about 15 min or less, if no birds are captured. Rounds can be longer if one person can patrol nets constantly and someone else processes the birds, as long as birds are never left in a net for much more than 30 min (North American Banding Council 2001a). If the study design allows, it is efficient to place nets in an array that brings the observer back to the starting point at the end of the net round (e.g., circular or grid array, rather than linear).

Habitat.—Many studies require sampling of particular habitats, species, or locations. If there are no such constraints, nets should be placed where (a) capture rates will be reasonably high, (b) nets are sheltered from prevailing winds, and (c) vegetation at net sites can be manipulated to maintain it at a relatively constant stage for the duration of the study. For relatively random sampling, making no prior assumptions about movements of birds or relative use of habitat, nets should be placed systematically across a study area or with some element of randomization in placement and orientation.

Net density.—The optimal distance between nets varies widely with research question. Number of species inventoried will increase with low net density and sampling of a large area. For studies of adult population size and survival rates, obtaining large sample sizes and having high capture and recapture probabilities will increase precision of estimates (Pollock et al. 1990). As net density is increased, capture probability of individual adults will increase but effective population size sampled will decrease to a certain threshold, which will be related to size of home range or territory.

If territorial birds are being captured, then nets should be spaced at distances appropriate to sampling as many territories as possible (DeSante et al. *this volume*). Nur et al. (*this volume*) and Ballard et al. (*this volume*) found that resident birds >200 m from nets had a very low probability of capture, and Remsen and Good (1996) indicated that species with typically short flight distance would be captured with lower probability than species making longer flights. DeSante et al. (*this volume*) suggested a net density of 1–1.5 nets/ha as a good starting point for breeding season studies for studies of North American breeding birds, whereas 5 nets/ha is the recommendation of the French STOC monitoring program (Suivi Temporel des Oiseaux Communs; C. Vansteenwegen, pers. comm.).

Faaborg et al. (*this volume*) used linear arrays of nets set end to end for winter sampling in the Neotropics. This design is less efficient for sampling many territories (either breeding or wintering) than is a more dispersed array of nets, because several nets may fall within the territory of a single bird when they are set end to end. Moreover, relatively small shifts in territory location between years can have a large effect on recapture probability. However, this design should increase capture probability for birds whose territories are being sampled, which could be important if netting effort at a station is very limited. Moreover, a linear array of nets should sample species with a wide range of territory sizes, whereas dispersed nets could be less efficient in this circumstance.

For capture of migrating birds, nets can be placed much closer together than if territorial birds are the target.

TYPE OF NETS

Mesh size should be appropriate to the target species (Heimerdinger and Leberman 1966, Pardieck and Waide 1992, Jenni et al. 1996). Small birds become unduly tangled in large-mesh nets, whereas large birds often bounce out of small-mesh nets. Capture rate and ease of using nets also depends on net material and fullness. For most passerines, capture rates are highest using 30- or 36-mm-mesh nets (as measured by the maximum stretch), but certain study objectives (e.g., species inventory) might well require use of a variety of mesh sizes. Nets of standard dimension (12 m long, with four panels) are recommended because they are easier to handle than very long or very high nets, and non-standard nets or novel placements should be used only if especially needed (e.g., Whitaker 1972, Wilson and Allan 1996). See North American Banding Council (2001a) for additional information on net types.

SCHEDULE OF OPERATION

CHOICE OF SEASONS

Netting across seasons can provide valuable data on within- and between-season movements that could be missed by more limited efforts (e.g., Ralph and Hollinger 2003). However, limiting netting to specific seasons may be important for certain studies. Species-specific migration seasons can be defined as the period in which 95% of the individuals of the target species pass through a particular area, as in Hussell et al. (1992). It can be useful to define species-specific breeding seasons in a similar way, as the period in which 95% of individuals in an area confine their breeding activities, from territorial establishment until post-breeding dispersal of juveniles. Using these definitions, post-breeding dispersal is that period between the breeding season and fall migration, and "wintering" season is the period between fall and spring migration. Because the timing of these seasons, particularly the periods of dispersal and migration, can vary markedly with species, age, sex, location, and year, the best dates for study will have to be determined individually for each locale.

For some studies, netting across the boundaries of seasons can cause problems for analyses because of misclassification of transients. For example, inclusion of late migrants in a study of survival rates of local breeders may bias results because one cannot distinguish mortality from emigration through netting alone (Pollock et al. 1990). Even though transients can be dealt with to some degree with mark–recapture analyses (Brownie and Robson 1983; Pradel et al. 1997; Nur et al. 2000, *this volume*), it may be best for survival studies to avoid such complications to the extent possible, through judicious choice of netting dates (DeSante et al. *this volume*).

It has been suggested that capture of local residents during the migration season could lower the chances of recapturing those individuals during the breeding season due to net avoidance. This, in turn, could bias certain kinds of population studies, although statistical methods exist for reducing such bias. No reduction in capture probability across seasons was found by Nur et al. (*this volume*), but only one species has been investigated. If studies are being carried out both in the migration and the breeding season, consideration can be given to using a different study area for each season. On the other hand, if capture of late-migrating individuals will not bias results of a particular breeding season study, it will be most efficient to use a single study area, and to define the breeding season as beginning when the first summer residents arrive, even though migrants may still be passing through.

NUMBER AND LENGTH OF SAMPLING PERIODS

The number and length of sampling periods (each containing a netting session of one to several consecutive days) should be selected on the basis of study objectives, tempered by availability of personnel and accessibility of the station. Multiple and evenly spaced sampling periods are important, both to increase sample size and to ensure that annual samples are not biased by within- and between-year variation in abundance or capture probability of age and sex groups. Optimum length of sampling periods will depend upon the selected length of netting sessions within these periods (see below), and the desired length of gaps between netting sessions.

The MAPS protocol calls for dividing the breeding season into 10-day sampling periods, which we recommend as the standard unless there is need for more frequent sampling. Wintering season studies frequently sample only 1-3 times/season (e.g., Faaborg et al. *this volume*). Although this may be sufficient for detecting site fidelity and long-term changes in use of a location (e.g., Latta and Faaborg 2002), monthly or more frequent sampling should offer better opportunities for detecting intra-seasonal variation in movements of age and sex classes, and for greatly increasing precision of population parameter estimates.

For monitoring population change of migrating populations, it is best if sampling is conducted daily or near daily, to allow modeling of the effects of date and weather on number of migrants present, and to increase precision of parameter estimates (Dunn et al. *this volume a*, Hussell *this volume*, Thomas et al. *this volume*).

LENGTH OF NETTING SESSIONS

Depending on the length of the gaps between successive netting sessions, personnel may be able to rotate among stations and sample several locations within a single sampling period. Moreover, gaps allow birds to lose net shyness between sampling periods (see below), and can decrease the chance of recapturing transients within seasons, making it easier to identify transients in mark–recapture models (Pradel et al. 1997). Regardless of the number of days in each netting session, we recommend that nets be operated for the same number of days in each session so that capture effort will be the same in each sampling period.

The MAPS protocol calls for 1 day of netting per 10-day sampling period, which produces a sufficient sample size when data are pooled among many stations. In other studies, especially where stations are visited infrequently and may be quite inaccessible, or when larger sample sizes are needed to determine local (rather than regional) metrics, it may be desirable to net for two, three, or more days in a row to catch the maximum number of birds possible. It is often found that netting for more than 3 days in a row becomes unproductive because of net avoidance, so that few naïve birds remain to be captured (Burton and DeSante *this volume*, Faaborg *this volume*). Even birds stopping over during migration may show net avoidance after first capture (Dorsch 1998). Some evidence suggests that recapture probability may be depressed for as much as a month after capture or even longer, based on tropical wintering birds (Faaborg et al. *this volume*; J. Faaborg, pers. comm.). However, DeSante et al. (*this volume*) suggested that in temperate breeding birds, net avoidance may last only a week or less, and in some species there is no evidence of any net avoidance (Nur and Geupel 1993a, Ballard et al. *this volume*). Whenever feasible, the presence and duration of net avoidance should be studied for each target species to determine the most efficient netting schedule for a particular study (Burton and DeSante *this volume*).

Despite the possibility of net avoidance, near-daily netting effort may be necessary during the breeding season to capture representative numbers of breeding adults or locally produced young birds, which may be present on the study plot for only a few days after fledging (Ballard et al. *this volume*). Optimal length of netting sessions therefore varies with study species and objectives.

During seasons when birds are relatively resident, abundance is assumed not to vary systematically from day to day, such that samples collected from a variety of locations on different days will give the same results as if all samples had been collected simultaneously. However, temporal change can be rapid, even during the breeding season, and species differ in the timing of breeding activities (Ralph and Hollinger 2003, Ballard et al. *this volume*). For within-year comparisons among locations, therefore, netting sessions should be paired temporally to the extent possible.

During migration, abundance and species composition of migrants present at any given station are very likely to differ from day to day, depending largely on weather and date in the season. Studies aimed at comparing habitat use by species or age classes during migration should therefore sample all stations on the same days, especially if relatively few netting sessions can be undertaken. Over a period of years, however, a network of stations operated on different days should provide similar information, although with greater variance.

DAILY TIMING OF OPERATIONS

Netting normally should take place early in the morning, because capture rates are usually highest in the first 4-6 h after dawn when birds are most active. To obtain a good sample of the birds present, nets should be open for at least 4 h (weather permitting), as is the norm at the vast majority of stations. Depending on objectives of the study, and on predictable availability of personnel, nets can be run for a longer period, even for the entire day (e.g., Kaiser and Berthold *this volume*). This may be the preferred option in situations where birds are known to be active throughout the day (Faaborg et al. *this volume*; E. Mallory, unpubl. data), or when logistics make it more efficient to increase effort within a netting session than to add visits to the station. Whatever the choice of daily hours of operation, that level should be sustainable throughout the expected life of the study to maintain standardization of data collection (see below).

DATA TO BE COLLECTED

BIRD DATA

There is broad agreement on basic data that should be collected for every bird captured, but ongoing discussion on how much extra data should be taken that banders have no plans to use in their own analyses (e.g., time of day that a bird was weighed, fat score, or molt). However, these data can be of great value when pooled with those from other study locations (e.g., Dunn 2002), and in some cases only pooled data can provide samples large enough for analysis. As long as the data can be collected without stress to birds (i.e., holding and handling times are not too great), we recommend that banders collect all data listed in Table 2. Physical samples, such as blood for genetic study or feather samples for genetic or isotopic analysis, should only be collected as part of a specifically designed project for which necessary permits have been obtained.

Methods used for taking measurements and for recording skull pneumatization should follow the recommendations of the North American Banding Council (2001a, b). Pyle (1997) provided detail on aging and sexing birds by plumage characteristics.

We recommend that a camera be kept on hand at every netting station to document characteristics of birds that are unusual (as well as to document habitat at net sites; see below).

OTHER DATA

We recommend that information on station operation be recorded at a level of detail that would allow others to reconstruct the study if desired. These metadata should include at the minimum: definition of the boundaries of the study area, number and type of nets, individual net locations (carefully mapped with compass orientation and preferably GPS documented), and schedule of operation.

Depending on the goal of the study, it may be necessary to collect detailed data on vegetation in and around the study area, including the type, density, and height of each vegetation type at each net site. Even if not part of the study, we recommend that a simple, broad habitat classification be done each year, as described in Ralph et al. (1993). Annual photographs of net sites can also aid in documenting habitat. This material will provide important evidence for interpreting the factors responsible for capture rates at each net site over the course of the study. A brief description of the landscape in which the study area is embedded can also help in interpreting results, and can be helpful when comparing results among different projects. Plotting net locations onto a topographic map or aerial photograph is a good way to document landscape and land use characteristics of the surrounding area.

In addition, banders should record daily effort data, including date, hours of opening and closing nets, which nets were open (if not all), and names of personnel participating. We recommend also that a daily narrative be written, covering any events that may have affected results (e.g., presence of

TABLE 2. RECOMMENDATIONS FOR COLLECTION OF DATA ON CAPTURED BIRDS.

Data type	Comments
Mandatory	
Data required by Banding Offices	Date, location, band number, auxiliary marking status, species, age, sex
	Age, sex, or both should be recorded as "unknown" unless designation is at least 95% certain
Retrap status	First capture vs. retrap
Recommended	
Subspecies	If difficult to distinguish or unusual, record characters used to identify
Tail length	If needed to identify subspecies
Bill dimensions	If needed to identify subspecies
Tarsus length	If needed to identify subspecies
Skull pneumatization	Record score in appropriate season, and use routinely in combination with plumage characters that are not known to be at least 95% accurate
Breeding condition	Record condition code in appropriate season
How aged and sexed	Record codes for how aged and sexed (e.g., codes used by MAPS; http://www.birdpop.org/DownloadDocuments/manual/ Newband.PDF), recording presence of brood patch or cloacal protuberance, eye color, molt limits, tail shape, or other criteria on which aging and sexing is based
Wing length	Banders in the Western Hemisphere are advised to measure unflattened wing chord (the norm in North America), which is thought by some to be most reproducible and which allows most opportunity for direct comparison and pooling of data; Europeans usually measure flattened wing chord (or length, or both, of the eighth primary; Kaiser and Berthold *this volume*)
Weight	Specify weighing equipment in station protocol
Fat score	Ralph et al. (1993) is widely used in North America, but use of Kaiser (1993a) may lead to less variation in scoring among observers (Dunn 2003)
Time of handling	Select time of start or end of net round, or time of weighing (for standard use; record time to nearest 10 min)
Net of capture	Useful in assessing factors affecting capture rates (habitat, distance from nest); some people also record side of net and net panel in which individuals are captured
Molt	In appropriate season, record details or, at a minimum, the presence or absence of wing and body molt
Notes	E.g., on aberrant plumage, disease or parasites, deformities, or to note that photos were taken; record extent of juvenile plumage; record probable age and sex if designation was <95% certain

predators, windstorm, or other disturbance). Records should be kept as well of factors that could affect year-to-year results (such as insect epidemics or presence of heavy fruit crops in the study area). If weather variables are to be used in analyses, it often may be easier to obtain computerized data from a nearby weather station than to record it in great detail at the netting station. Nonetheless, weather conditions on site may differ from weather office records (particularly wind speed and occurrence of local showers), so keeping simple local records can be worthwhile, and will aid in interpretation of daily capture rates. Automated weather stations can be purchased relatively inexpensively.

STANDARDIZATION

Most monitoring studies are intended to detect temporal and spatial variation in bird abundance or demographic parameters. It is therefore crucial that capture operations be standardized as much as possible over time and space. Without standardization, ascribing variation in capture rates to test variables can be criticized, because it always can be argued that the variation may have resulted from changes in capture protocol. Standardization will help minimize variation in capture probability and allow use of more powerful yet parsimonious statistical models in estimation of survival and population size (Peach and Baillie *this volume*, Sauer and Link *this volume*). If a change in protocol is required (such as new net locations or different hours of operation), we recommend that the old and new protocols be used on alternate dates for a year or two so that the effect of the change can be appropriately modeled in analysis. This approach, however, is cumbersome and expensive in time and effort. It is far preferable to conduct a pilot study to determine the optimal equipment, net placement, and operation protocol, and then follow that protocol strictly throughout the life of the project.

Nets

We strongly recommend that net number and placement be held constant when abundance monitoring is a study objective. It is often tempting to open more nets when extra personnel are available or to add or alter net sites during the course of a study. However, this can bias results, because net sites are not equal in the number and types (species, age, sex) of birds captured. For example, birds captured per net-hour could differ between years simply because in one year nets were placed where they were particularly efficient at catching the target species.

Type of net (length, height, and mesh size) also should remain constant if at all possible, and if several types of net are used, the different types either should be placed always at the same location, or rotated frequently and on a regular schedule among all possible locations. Net characteristics such as the relative fullness of nets between trammel lines, whether or not nets are tethered, and material of construction (nylon vs. polyester) also may affect capture rates (North American Banding Council 2001a), but their effects have not been rigorously tested. The rule of thumb is to use exactly the same type of net (from the same maker if possible) in each location throughout the life of the study.

Finally, height of the net affects capture rates. Nets should be set such that a bird captured in the lowest panel just clears the ground (North American Banding Council 2001a), unless the study goals require otherwise (e.g., inventory studies in which ground-hugging species could be missed using normal settings). Some netting stations mark poles with tape showing where each net loop should go to ensure uniformity among personnel in the way nets are set each day. Thibodeau (1999) felt this unnecessary because he found that most birds were captured in middle panels of nets at his station. However, Jenni et al. (1996) found a higher capture rate in upper panels, suggesting that variation in the height of the top of the net could indeed affect overall capture rate.

Any use of lures (bait, water drip traps, tape recordings) should normally be avoided, because it difficult to use them in a standardized manner. In some monitoring studies, however, their use is important (e.g., Sogge et al. 2001; or for nocturnal netting of owls, Erdman and Brinker 1997). Lures should be used on a regular schedule and either should be placed in the same location at each use or rotated regularly among placements. Sound lures should use the same recordings throughout the study and should be broadcast on standard equipment at a specified volume. Digital recordings (solid state or CD) are less subject to degrading than are tape recordings.

Schedule of Operation

Just as net locations are not equal in number and kinds of birds (species, age, sex) that are captured per net-hour, neither are time periods equal (hour in day, day in season). If the schedule of operation changes in a systematic way during the study (e.g., running nets in the morning in one year, but all day in another), then birds captured per net-hour will likely differ between temporal samples solely because of the change in schedule. If nets are operated longer on some days than others, we recommend that analysis be limited to the time period in which nets are always open, as with MAPS (see DeSante et al. *this volume*). Capturing a bird during non-standard hours, however, may result in net avoidance during subsequent standard netting hours, such that excluding data from these non-standard periods from analysis might result in biased estimates of population parameters. Although the likelihood of this happening probably varies seasonally, it may be advisable to avoid non-standard netting within study areas where standardized protocols are in place and net avoidance is suspected to occur.

It is not critical that dates of netting sessions within each sampling period be exactly the same year after year, but they should be paired as closely as practicable. Length of the netting session (consecutive netting days) also should be standardized to the extent possible, to ensure that effects of net-avoidance are the same in every sampling period.

HABITAT

Even if netting is completely standardized, changes in vegetation around nets can cause changes in the numbers and kinds of birds captured, independently of changes in local bird populations (Ballard et al. 2003). More birds fly over nets as vegetation becomes taller and fuller, and more (or fewer, depending upon the species) may be captured if understory vegetation fills in gaps next to net lanes. It is therefore important either to choose net sites at which vegetation is likely to remain relatively unchanged for the life of the study, to control vegetation at the net site through regular trimming and thinning, or to use mark–recapture methods to track changes in capture probability over time (Kendall et al. *this volume*). As noted above, we recommend that photography and vegetation assessment be undertaken each year at each net site to document vegetation height and density, and to serve as a reference for vegetation management.

WRITTEN PROTOCOL

An important aspect of maintaining standardization is to prepare a formal operating protocol for the project. This requires clearly defining the standards, serves as a reference for future personnel, and also serves as a record of metadata that are relevant to the use and interpretation of results. The protocol should describe the exact net locations, type of net to be used at each net site (with full detail on maker, material, mesh size, dimensions, etc.), schedule of operation, instructions on keeping habitat around nets at a clearly defined constant height, methods used for measuring birds or taking fat scores, and all other operational details. The protocol should be sufficiently detailed so that a person experienced in mist netting, but without experience of the study or study location, could continue the study without any guidance beyond the written protocol. While ensuring standardization of operations and quality of data, a protocol also will contribute to safety of birds (e.g., by providing instructions on frequency of net checks and procedures to use in case of bad weather).

CONCLUSION

All people using mist nets should use methods that are ethical and ensure safety of birds that are captured. Beyond that, it is important to select netting methods that will best meet the specific objectives of each study. Whenever possible, however, researchers should use the recommended and commonly used protocols described here, to provide the most opportunity for direct comparison of results among independent studies.

ACKNOWLEDGMENTS

This paper benefited from discussion among all workshop participants and authors (see list in Preface). We especially appreciated reviews contributed by G. Ballard, D. F. DeSante, G. R. Geupel, D. J. T. Hussell, J. Faaborg, N. Nur, C. M. Francis, P. Pyle, and A. A. Whitman.

LITERATURE CITED

AKAIKE, H. 1973. Information theory and an extension of the maximum likelihood principle. Pp. 267–281 in B. N. Petran, and F. Csaki (editors). International Symposium on Information Theory. Akademiai Kiadi, Budapest, Hungary.

AMERICAN ORNITHOLOGISTS' UNION. 1983. Checklist of North American birds, 6th ed. American Ornithologists' Union, Washington, D.C.

ANDERS, A. D., J. FAABORG, AND F. R. THOMPSON, III. 1998. Post-fledging dispersal, habitat use, and home-range size of juvenile Wood Thrushes. Auk 115:349–358.

ANDERSON, D. R. 2001. The need to get the basics right in wildlife field studies. Wildlife Society Bulletin 29:1294–1297.

ANDERSON, D. R., E. G. COOCH, R. J. GUTIÉRREZ, C. J. KREBS, M. S. LINDBERG, K. H. POLLOCK, C. R. RIBIC, AND T. M. SHENK. 2003. Rigorous science: Suggestions on how to raise the bar. Wildlife Society Bulletin 31:296–305.

ARNASON, A. N. 1972. Parameter estimates from experiments on two populations subject to migration and death. Researches in Population Ecology 13:97–113.

ARNASON, A. N. 1973. The estimation of population size, migration rates and survival in a stratified population. Researches in Population Ecology 15:1–8.

BAILLIE, S. R. 1990. Integrated population monitoring of breeding birds in Britain and Ireland. Ibis 132:151–166.

BAILLIE, S. R., H. Q. P. CRICK, D. E. BALMER, L. P. BEAVEN, I. S. DOWNIE, S. N. FREEMAN, D. I. LEECH, J. H. MARCHANT, D. G. NOBLE, M. J. RAVEN, A. P. SIMPKIN, R. M. THEWLIS, AND C. V. WERNHAM. 2002. Breeding birds in the wider countryside: Their conservation status 2001. BTO Research Report No. 278. BTO, Thetford, U.K. <http://www.bto.org/birdtrends/> (29 September 2003).

BAILLIE, S. R., R. E. GREEN, M. BODDY, AND S. T. BUCKLAND. 1986. An evaluation of the Constant Effort Sites Scheme. BTO Research Report No. 21, British Trust for Ornithology, Thetford, U.K.

BAILLIE, S. R., AND J. H. MARCHANT. 1992. The use of breeding bird censuses to monitor common birds in Britain and Ireland: Current practices and future prospects. Vogelwelt 113:172–182.

BAILLIE, S. R., AND N. MCCULLOCH. 1993. Modelling the survival rates of passerines ringed during the breeding season from national ringing and recovery data. Pp. 123–140 in J.-D. Lebreton and P. M. North (editors). Marked individuals in the study of bird populations. Birkhäuser Verlag, Basel, Switzerland.

BAILLIE, S. R., AND P. M. NORTH. 1999. Large-scale studies of marked birds. Proceedings of the EURING97 Conference. Bird Study 46 (supplement):1–308.

BAILLIE, S. R., AND W. J. PEACH. 1992. Population limitation in migrants. Ibis 134 (supplement 1):120–132.

BAIRLEIN, F. 1981. Ökosystemanalyse der Rastplätze von Zugvögeln: Beschreibung und Deutung der Verteilungsmuster von ziehenden Kleinvögeln in verschiedenen Biotopen der Stationen des "Mettnau-Reit-Illmitz-Programmes." Ökologie der Vögel 3:7–137.

BAIRLEIN, F. 1998. The European-African songbird migration network: New challenges for large-scale study of bird migration. Biologia e Conservazione della Fauna 102:13–27.

BAIRLEIN, F., AND B. GIESSING. 1997. Spatio-temporal course, ecology and energetics of western Palearctic-African songbird migration. Summary Report 1994–96. Institut für Vogelforschung, Wilhelmshaven, Germany.

BAIRLEIN, F., L. JENNI, A. KAISER, A. KARLSSON, A. VAN NOORDWIJK, W. PEACH, A. PILASTRO, AND F. SPINA. 1994. European-African Bird Migration Network. Manual of field methods. Institut für Vogelforschung, Wilhelmshaven, Germany.

BAKER, M., N. NUR, AND G. R. GEUPEL. 1995. Correcting biased estimates of dispersal and survival due to limited study area: Theory and an application using Wrentits. Condor 97:663–674.

BALLARD, G., G. R. GEUPEL, AND N. NUR. 2004 (this volume). Influence of mist-netting intensity on investigations of avian populations. Studies in Avian Biology 29:21–27.

BALLARD, G., G. R. GEUPEL, N. NUR, AND T. GARDALI. 2003. Long-term declines and decadal patterns in population trends of songbirds in western North America. Condor 105:737–755.

BALMER, D., AND L. MILNE. 2002. CES comes of age. BTO News 239:14–15.

BARKER, R. J., AND J. R. SAUER. 1995. Statistical aspects of point count sampling. Pp. 125–130 in C. J. Ralph, J. R. Sauer, and S. Droege (editors). Monitoring bird populations by point counts. USDA Forest Service Gen. Tech. Rep. PSW-GTR-149. USDA Forest Service Pacific Southwest Research Station, Albany, CA.

BART, J., AND S. EARNST. 2002. Double-sampling to estimate density and population trends in birds. Auk 199:36–45.

BART, J., C. KEPLER, P. SYKES, AND C. BOCETTI. 1999. Evaluation of mist-net sampling as an index to productivity in Kirtland's Warblers. Auk 116:1147–1151.

BASTIAN, A. 1992. Mobilität von Kleinvögeln in einem süddeutschen Rastgebiet während der Wegzugperiode. Ökologie der Vögel 14:121–163.

BAUCHAU, V., AND A. J. VAN NOORDWIJK. 1995. Comparison of survival estimates obtained from three different methods of recapture in the same population of the Great Tit. Journal of Applied Statistics 22:1031–1037.

BAUER, H.-G., AND P. BERTHOLD. 1997. Die Brutvögel Mitteleuropas. Bestand und Gefährdung. 2. Auflage. Aula-Verlag, Wiesbaden, Germany.

BELL, B. D. 1969. Some thoughts on the apparent ecological expansion of the Reed Bunting. British Birds 62:209–218.

BELL, B. D., C. K. CATCHPOLE, AND K. J. CORBETT. 1968. Problems of censusing Reed Buntings, Sedge Warblers and Reed Warblers. Bird Study 15:16–21.

BELL, H. L. 1982a. A bird community of New Guinean lowland rainforest. 2. Seasonality. Emu 82:24–41.

BELL, H. L. 1982b. A bird community of New Guinean lowland rainforest. 3. Vertical distribution of the avifauna. Emu 82:143–162.

BERTHOLD, P. 1974. Die gegenwärtige Bestandsentwicklung der Dorngrasmücke (Sylvia communis) und anderer Singvogelarten im westlichen Europa bis 1973. Vogelwelt 95:170–183.

BERTHOLD, P. 1996. Control of bird migration. Chapman and Hall, London, U.K.

BERTHOLD, P. 2001. Bird migration. A general survey. Oxford University Press, Oxford, U.K.

BERTHOLD, P. 2004 (this volume). Use of mist nets for monitoring landbird autumn population trends, and comparison with other methods. Studies in Avian Biology 29:112–115.

BERTHOLD, P., W. FIEDLER, R. SCHLENKER, AND U. QUERNER. 1998. 25-year study of the population development of Central European songbirds: A general decline, most evident in long-distance migrants. Naturwissenschaften 85:350–353.

BERTHOLD, P., G. FLIEGE, G. HEINE, U. QUERNER, AND R. SCHLENKER. 1991. Wegzug, Rastverhalten, Biometrie und Mauser von Kleinvögeln in Mitteleuropa. Eine kurze Darstellung nach Fangdaten aus dem Mettnau-Reit-Illmitz-Programm der Vogelwarte Radolfzell. Vogelwarte 36 (Sonderheft):1–224.

BERTHOLD, P., G. FLIEGE, U. QUERNER, AND H. WINKLER. 1986. Die Bestandsentwicklung von Kleinvögeln in Mitteleuropa: Analyse von Fangzahlen. Journal für Ornithologie 127:397–437.

BERTHOLD, P., AND W. FRIEDRICH. 1979. Die Federlänge: Ein neues nützliches Flügelmaß. Vogelwarte 30:11–21.

BERTHOLD, P., E. GWINNER, AND H. KLEIN. 1970. Vergleichende Untersuchung der Jugendentwicklung eines ausgeprägten Zugvogels, Sylvia borin, und eines weniger ausgeprägten Zugvogels, S. atricapilla. Vogelwarte 25:297–331.

BERTHOLD, P., A. KAISER, U. QUERNER, AND R. SCHLENKER. 1993. Analyse von Fangzahlen im Hinblick auf die Bestandsentwicklung von Kleinstvögeln nach 20-jährigem Betrieb der Station Mettnau, Süddeutschland. Journal für Ornithologie 134:283–299.

BERTHOLD, P., AND U. QUERNER. 1978. Über Bestandsentwicklung und Fluktuationsrate von Kleinvogelpopulationen: Fünfjährige Untersuchungen in Mitteleuropa. Ornis Fennica 56:110–123.

BERTHOLD, P., AND R. SCHLENKER. 1975. Das "Mettnau-Reit-Illmitz-Programm": ein langfristiges Vogelfangprogramm der Vogelwarte Radolfzell mit vielfältiger Fragestellung. Vogelwarte 28:97–123.

BEZZEL, E., H.-W. HELB, AND K. WITT. 1992. Vogel des Jahres 1992: Das Rotkehlchen (Erithacus rubecula). Pp. 128–139 in Ornithologen-Kalender 1992. Aula-Verlag, Wiesbaden, Germany.

BIBBY, C. J., N. D. BURGESS, AND D. A. HILL. 1992. Bird census techniques. Academic Press, London, U.K.

BIERREGAARD, R. O., JR. 1990. Species composition and trophic organization of the understory bird community in a central Amazonian Terra Firme forest. Pp. 217–236 in A. H. Gentry (editor). Four Neotropical forests. Yale University Press, New Haven, CT.

BLAKE, J. G. 1989. Birds of primary forest undergrowth in western San Blas, Panama. Journal of Field Ornithology 60:178–189.

BLAKE, J. G., AND B. A. LOISELLE. 1992. Habitat use by Neotropical migrants at La Selva Biological Station and Braulio Carrillo National Park, Costa Rica. Pp. 257–272 in J. M. Hagan, III, and D. W. Johnston (editors). Ecology and conservation of Neotropical migratory landbirds. Smithsonian Institution Press, Washington, D.C.

BLAKE, J. G., AND B. A. LOISELLE. 2001. Bird assemblages in second growth and old-growth forests, Costa Rica: Perspectives from mist nets and point counts. Auk 118: 304–326.

BLUMS, P., J. D. NICHOLS, M. S. LINDBERG, J. E. HINES, AND A. MEDNIS. 2003. Estimating breeding dispersal movement rates of adult female European ducks with multistate modeling. Journal of Animal Ecology 72: 292–307.

BODDY, M. 1992. Timing of Whitethroat arrival, breeding and moult at a coastal site in Lincolnshire. Ringing and Migration 13:65–72.

BÖHNING-GAESE, K. 1995. Dynamik von Zugvogelgemeinschaften in verschiedenen Gebieten und Zeiträumen. Journal für Ornithologie 136:149–158.

BOHONAK, A. J. 2002. RMA software for reduced major axis regression v.1.12. San Diego State University, Department of Biology, San Diego, CA. <http://www.bio.sdsu.edu/pub/andy/RMA.html> (29 September 2003).

BORGES, S. H., AND P. C. STOUFFER. 1999. Bird communities in two types of anthropogenic successional vegetation in central Amazonia. Condor 101:529–536.

BOULINIER, T., J. D. NICHOLS, J. R. SAUER, J. E. HINES, AND K. H. POLLOCK. 1998. Estimating species richness: The importance of heterogeneity in species detectability. Ecology 79:1018–1028.

BRADLEY, M., R. JOHNSTONE, G. COURT, AND T. DUNCAN. 1997. Influence of weather on breeding success in Peregrine Falcons in the Arctic. Auk 114:786–791.

BRENSING, D. 1977. Nahrungsökologische Untersuchungen an Zugvögeln in einem südwestdeutschen Durchzugsgebiet während des Wegzuges. Vogelwarte 29:44–56.

BRENSING, D. 1989. Ökophysiologische Untersuchungen der Tagesperiodik von Singvögeln. Beschreibung und Deutung der tageszeitlichen Fangmuster der Fänglinge des "Mettnau-Reit-Illmitz-Programmes" und von Versuchsvögeln. Ökologie der Vögel 11:1–148.

BREWER, A. D., A. W. DIAMOND, E. J. WOODSWORTH, B. T. COLLINS, AND E. H. DUNN. 2000. The Atlas of Canadian Bird Banding, 1921–1995. Volume 1: Doves, Cuckoos and Hummingbirds through Passerines. Canadian Wildlife Service Special Publication, Ottawa, Canada.

BROKAW, N. V. L., AND R. A. LENT. 1999. Vertical structure. Pp. 373–399 *in* M. L. Hunter, Jr. (editor). Maintaining biodiversity in forest ecosystems. Cambridge University Press, Cambridge, U.K.

BROWNIE, C., D. R. ANDERSON, K. P. BURNHAM, AND D. S. ROBSON. 1985. Statistical inference from band recovery data: A handbook, 2nd ed. U.S. Fish and Wildlife Service Resource Publication 156, Washington, D.C.

BROWNIE, C., J. E. HINES, J. D. NICHOLS, K. H. POLLOCK, AND J. B. HESTBECK. 1993. Capture–recapture studies for multiple strata including non-Markovian transition probabilities. Biometrics 49:1173–1187.

BROWNIE, C., AND D. S. ROBSON. 1983. Estimation of time-specific survival rates from tag–resighting samples: A generalization of the Jolly-Seber model. Biometrics 39: 437–453.

BUCKLAND, S. T. 1982. A mark–recapture survival analysis. Journal of Animal Ecology 51:833–847.

BUCKLAND, S. T., D. R. ANDERSON, K. P. BURNHAM, J. L. LAAKE, D. L. BORCHERS, AND L. THOMAS. 2001. Introduction to distance sampling: Estimating abundance of animal populations. Oxford University Press, New York, NY.

BUCKLAND, S. T., AND S. R. BAILLIE. 1987. Estimating survival rates from organized mist-netting programmes. Acta Ornithologica 23:89–100.

BUCKLAND, S. T., AND A. C. HEREWARD. 1982. Trap-shyness of Yellow Wagtails *Motacilla flava flavissima* at a pre-migratory roost. Ringing and Migration 4:15–23.

BURNHAM, K. P. 1981. Summarizing remarks: Environmental influences. Studies in Avian Biology 6:324–325.

BURNHAM, K. P., AND D. R. ANDERSON. 1998. Model selection and inference: a practical information theoretic approach. Springer-Verlag, New York, NY.

BURNHAM, K. P., D. R. ANDERSON, G. C. WHITE, C. BROWNIE, AND K. H. POLLOCK. 1987. Design and analysis methods for fish survival experiments based on release–recapture. American Fisheries Society Monograph No. 5, Bethesda, MD.

BURNHAM, K. P., AND W. S. OVERTON. 1979. Robust estimation of population size when capture probabilities vary among animals. Ecology 60:579–604.

BURTON, K. M., AND D. F. DESANTE. 2004 (*this volume*). Effects of mist-netting frequency on capture rates at Monitoring Avian Productivity and Survival (MAPS) stations. Studies in Avian Biology 29:7–11.

BUSKIRK, W. H. 1980. Influence of meteorological patterns and trans-Gulf migration on the calendars of latitudinal migrants. Pp. 485–491 *in* A. Keast and E. S. Morton (editors). Migrant birds in the Neotropics: Ecology, behavior, distribution, and conservation. Smithsonian Institution Press, Washington, D.C.

BUTCHER, G. S. 1992. Needs assessment: Monitoring Neotropical migratory birds. Partners in Flight Monitoring Working Group, Virginia, September 4–5, 1992. Neotropical Migratory Bird Conservation Program, Cornell Lab of Ornithology, Ithaca, NY.

BUTCHER, G. S., B. G. PETERJOHN, AND C. J. RALPH. 1993. Overview of national bird population monitoring programs and databases. Pp. 192–203 *in* D. M. Finch, and P. W. Stangel (editors). Status and management of Neotropical migratory birds. USDA Forest Service Gen. Tech. Rept. RM-229. USDA Forest Service Rocky Mountain Research Station, Ft. Collins, CO.

CAROTHERS, A. D. 1973. The effects of unequal catchability on Jolly-Seber estimates. Biometrics 29:79–100.

CAROTHERS, A. D. 1979. Quantifying unequal catchability and its effects on survival estimates in an actual population. Journal of Animal Ecology 48:863–869.

CHAO, A. 2001. An overview of closed capture–recapture models. Journal of Agricultural, Biological, and Environmental Statistics 6:158–175.

CHASE, M. K., N. NUR, AND G. R. GEUPEL. 1997. Survival, productivity, and abundance in a Wilson's Warbler population. Auk 114:354–366.

CILIMBURG, A. B., M. S. LINDBERG, J. J. TEWKSBURY, AND S. J. HEJL. 2002. Effects of dispersal on survival probability of adult Yellow Warblers (*Dendroica petechia*). Auk 119: 778–789.

CLOBERT, J., R. JULLIARD, AND R. H. MCCLEERY. 1993. The components of local recruitment. Pp. 281–294 *in* J.-D. Lebreton and P. M. North (editors). Marked individuals in the study of bird populations. Birkhäuser Verlag, Berlin, Germany.

CLOBERT, J., J.-D. LEBRETON, AND D. ALLAINE. 1987. A general approach to survival rate estimation by recaptures or resightings of marked birds. Ardea 75:133–142.

CLOBERT, J., J.-D. LEBRETON, D. ALLAINE, AND J.-M. GAILLARD. 1994. The estimation of age-specific breeding probabilities from recaptures or resightings in vertebrate populations: II. Longitudinal models. Biometrics 50: 375–387.

CLOBERT, J., J.-D. LEBRETON, AND G. MARZOLIN. 1990. The estimation of local immature survival rate and age-specific proportions of breeders in bird populations. Pp. 199–213 *in* J. Blondel, A. Gosler, J.-D. Lebreton, and R. McCleery (editors). Population biology of passerine birds: An integrated approach. Springer-Verlag, Berlin, Germany.

COCHRAN, W. G. 1963. Sampling techniques, 2nd ed. John Wiley and Sons, Inc., New York, NY.

COCHRAN, W. G. 1977. Sampling techniques, 3rd ed. John Wiley and Sons, Inc., New York, NY.

COHEN, J. 1988. Statistical power analysis for the behavioral sciences, 2nd ed. Lawrence Erlbaum Associates, Inc., Hillsdale, NJ.

COKER, D. (EDITOR). 1993. The B-RING user guide. British Trust for Ornithology, Thetford, U.K.

COLLISTER, D. M., AND R. G. FISHER. 1995. Trapping techniques for Loggerhead Shrikes. Wildlife Society Bulletin 23:88–91.

COOCH, E., R. PRADEL, AND N. NUR. 1996. A practical guide to capture–recapture analysis using SURGE. Centre d'Ecologie Fonctionelle et Evolutive: CNRS, Montpellier, France.

CORMACK, R. M. 1964. Estimates of survival from sightings of marked animals. Biometrika 51:429–438.

CRAMP, S., AND K. E. L. SIMMONS (EDITORS). 1977. The Birds of the Western Palearctic, Vol. 1. Oxford University Press, Oxford, U.K.

CRICK, H. Q. P. 1992. A bird-habitat coding system for use in Britain and Ireland incorporating aspects of land-management and human activity. Bird Study 39:1–12.

CROSBIE, S. F., AND B. F. J. MANLY. 1985. Parsimonious modeling of capture–mark–recapture studies. Biometrics. 41:385–398.

CUBITT, M. 2002. Integrated population monitoring reporter general overview, Version 2. British Trust for Ornithology, Thetford, U.K.

DALE, B. C. 2004 (this volume). Effectiveness of informal banding training at three western Canadian banding stations. Studies in Avian Biology 29:182–186.

DAWSON, D. K. 1990. Migration banding data: A source of information on bird population trends? Pp. 37–40 in J. R. Sauer, and S. Droege (editors). Survey designs and statistical methods for the estimation of avian population trends. Biological Report 90(1). U.S. Fish and Wildlife Service, Washington, D.C.

DAWSON, D. K., J. R. SAUER, P. A. WOOD, M. BERLANGA, M. H. WILSON, AND C. S. ROBBINS. 1995. Estimating bird species richness from capture and count data. Journal of Applied Statistics 22:1063–1068.

DESANTE, D. F. 1981. A field test of the variable circular-plot censusing technique in a California coastal scrub breeding bird community. Studies in Avian Biology 6:177–185.

DESANTE, D. F. 1991a. An avian biomonitoring program for the National Parks and other natural areas to detect large-scale, long-term changes in the productivity and survivorship of land birds. Pp. 285–296 in J. Edelbrock and S. Carpenter (editors). Natural areas and Yosemite: Prospects for the future. Yosemite Centennial Symposium Proceedings. U.S. National Park Service, Denver Service Center, Denver, CO.

DESANTE, D. F. 1991b. The Monitoring Avian Productivity and Survivorship (MAPS) program: First annual report. The Institute for Bird Populations, Inverness, CA.

DESANTE, D. F. 1992. Monitoring Avian Productivity and Survivorship (MAPS): A sharp, rather than blunt, tool for monitoring and assessing landbird populations. Pp. 511–521 in D. R. McCullough and R. H. Barrett (editors). Wildlife 2001: Populations. Elsevier Applied Science, London, U.K.

DESANTE, D. F. 1995. Suggestions for future directions for studies of marked migratory landbirds from the perspective of a practitioner in population management and conservation. Journal of Applied Statistics 22:949–965.

DESANTE, D. F. 1997. General evaluation of the Monitoring Avian Productivity and Survivorship (MAPS) Program. The Institute for Bird Populations, Point Reyes Station, CA.

DESANTE, D. F. 2000. Patterns of productivity and survivorship from the MAPS Program. Pp. 166–177 in R. Bonney, D. N. Pashley, R. J. Cooper, and L. Niles (editors). Strategies for bird conservation: The Partners in Flight planning process. USDA Forest Service Gen. Tech. Rep. RMRS-P-16. USDA Forest Service Rocky Mountain Research Station, Ogden, UT.

DESANTE, D. F., AND K. M. BURTON. 1994. The Monitoring Avian Productivity and Survivorship (MAPS) program third annual report (1992). Bird Populations 2:62–89.

DESANTE, D. F., K. M. BURTON, AND D. R. O'GRADY. 1996. The Monitoring Avian Productivity and Survivorship (MAPS) Program fourth and fifth annual report (1993 and 1994). Bird Populations 3:67–120.

DESANTE, D. F., K. M. BURTON, J. F. SARACCO, AND B. L. WALKER. 1995. Productivity indices and survival rate estimates from MAPS, a continent-wide programme of constant-effort mist netting in North America. Journal of Applied Statistics 22:935–947.

DESANTE, D. F., K. M. BURTON, P. VELEZ, AND D. FROEHLICH. 2002. MAPS Manual: 2002 Protocol. The Institute for Bird Populations, Point Reyes Station, CA.

DESANTE, D. F., K. M. BURTON, AND O. E. WILLIAMS. 1993a. The Monitoring Avian Productivity and Survivorship (MAPS) program second annual report (1990–1991). Bird Populations 1:68–97.

DESANTE, D. F., AND G. R. GEUPEL. 1987. Landbird productivity in central coastal California: The relationship to annual rainfall, and a reproductive failure in 1986. Condor 86:636–653.

DESANTE, D. F., M. P. NOTT, AND D. R. O'GRADY. 2001. Identifying the proximate demographic cause(s) of population change by modeling spatial variation in productivity, survivorship, and population trends. Ardea 89 (special issue):185–207.

DESANTE, D. F., D. R. O'GRADY, K. M. BURTON, P. VELEZ, D. FROEHLICH, E. E. FEUSS, H. SMITH, AND E. D. RUHLEN. 1998. The Monitoring Avian Productivity and Survivorship (MAPS) Program Sixth and Seventh Annual Report (1995 and 1996). Bird Populations 4: 69–122.

DESANTE, D. F., D. R. O'GRADY, AND P. PYLE. 1999. Measures of productivity and survival derived from standardized mist netting are consistent with observed population changes. Bird Study 46 (Supplement):178–188.

DESANTE, D. F., J. F. SARACCO, D. R. O'GRADY, K. M. BURTON, AND B. L. WALKER. 2004 (this volume). Methodological considerations of the Monitoring Avian Productivity and Survivorship (MAPS) Program. Studies in Avian Biology 29:28–45.

DESANTE, D. F., O. E. WILLIAMS, AND K. M. BURTON. 1993b. The Monitoring Avian Productivity and Survivorship (MAPS) Program: Overview and progress. Pp. 208–222 in D. M. Finch, and P. W. Stangel (editors). Status and management of Neotropical migratory birds. USDA Forest Service Gen. Tech. Rep. RM-229. USDA Forest Service Rocky Mountain Research Station, Ft. Collins, CO.

DIXON, P. M. 1993. The bootstrap and the jackknife: Describing the precision of ecological indices. Pp. 290–318 in S. M. Scheiner and J. Gurevitch (editors). Design and analysis of ecological experiments. Chapman and Hall, New York, NY.

DORSCH, H. 1998. Faktoren, die den Fang von Kleinvögeln mit Spannnetzen beeinflussen. Vogelwelt 119:91–104.

DRURY, W. H., AND J. A. KEITH. 1962. Radar studies of songbird migration in coastal New England. Ibis 104: 449–489.

DU FEU, C. R., AND J. M. MCMEEKING. 1991. Does constant effort netting measure juvenile abundance? Ringing and Migration 12:118–123.

DU FEU, C. R., AND J. M. MCMEEKING. 2004 (*this volume*). Relationship of juveniles captured in constant-effort netting with local abundance. Studies in Avian Biology 29: 57–62.

DUGGER, K. M., J. FAABORG, AND W. J. ARENDT. 2000. Rainfall correlates of bird populations and survival rates in a Puerto Rican dry forest. Bird Populations 5:11–27.

DUNN, E. H. 2002. A cross-Canada comparison of mass change in birds during migration stopover. Wilson Bulletin 114:368–379.

DUNN, E. H. 2003. Recommendations for fat scoring. North American Bird Bander 28:58–63.

DUNN, E. H. In press. Counting migrants to monitor bird populations: State of the art. *In* C. J. Ralph and T. D. Rich (editors). Bird conservation implementation and integration in the Americas: Proceedings of the third international Partners in Flight conference 2002. USDA Forest Service Gen. Tech. Rep. PSW-191. USDA Forest Service Pacific Southwest Research Station, Albany, CA.

DUNN, E. H., AND D. J. T. HUSSELL. 1995. Using migration counts to monitor landbird populations: Review and evaluation of current status. Current Ornithology 12: 43–88.

DUNN, E. H., D. J. T. HUSSELL, AND R. J. ADAMS. 1997. Monitoring songbird population change with autumn mist netting. Journal of Wildlife Management 61: 389–396.

DUNN, E. H., D. J. T. HUSSELL, AND R. J. ADAMS. 2004b (*this volume*). An investigation of productivity indices derived from banding of fall migrants. Studies in Avian Biology 29:92–96.

DUNN, E. H., D. J. T. HUSSELL, C. M. FRANCIS, AND J. D. MCCRACKEN. 2004a (*this volume*). A comparison of three count methods for monitoring songbird abundance during spring migration: Capture, census, and estimated totals. Studies in Avian Biology 29:116–122.

DUNN, E. H., AND E. NOL. 1980. Age-related migratory behavior of warblers. Journal of Field Ornithology 51: 254–269.

DUNN, E. H., AND C. J. RALPH. 2004 (*this volume*). Use of mist nets as a tool for bird population monitoring. Studies in Avian Biology 29:1–6.

EMLEN, J. T. 1977. Estimating breeding season bird densities from transect counts. Auk 94:455–468.

ERDMAN, T. C., AND D. F. BRINKER. 1997. Increasing mist net captures of migrant Northern Saw-whet Owls (*Aegolius acadius*) with an audiolure. Pp. 533–544 *in* J. R. Duncan, D. H. Johnson, and T. H. Nicholls (editors). Biology and conservation of owls of the Northern Hemisphere. USDA Forest Service Gen. Tech. Rep. NC-190. USDA Forest Service North Central Research Station, St. Paul, MN.

ERICKSON, M. M. 1938. Territory, annual cycle, and numbers in a population of Wrentits *Chamaea fasciata*. University of California Publications in Zoology 42:247–333.

FAABORG, J. 1982. Avian population fluctuations during drought conditions in Puerto Rico. Wilson Bulletin 94: 20–30.

FAABORG, J. 1985. Ecological constraints on West Indian bird distributions. Ornithological Monographs 36:621–653.

FAABORG, J., AND W. J. ARENDT. 1989a. Longevity estimates of Puerto Rican birds. North American Bird Bander 14: 11–13.

FAABORG, J., AND W. J. ARENDT. 1989b. Long-term declines in winter resident warblers in a Puerto Rican dry forest. American Birds 43:1226–1230.

FAABORG, J., AND W. J. ARENDT. 1990. Long-term studies of Guanica Forest Birds. Acta Científica 4:69–90.

FAABORG, J., AND W. J. ARENDT. 1992a. Rainfall correlates of bird population fluctuations in a Puerto Rican dry forest: A 15-year study. Ornitología Caribeña 3:10–19.

FAABORG, J., AND W. J. ARENDT. 1992b. Long-term declines of winter resident warblers in a Puerto Rican dry forest: Which species are in trouble? Pp. 57–63 *in* J. M. Hagan, III, and D. W. Johnston (editors). Ecology and conservation of Neotropical migrant landbirds. Smithsonian Institution Press, Washington, D.C.

FAABORG, J., AND W. J. ARENDT. 1995. Survival rates of Puerto Rican birds: Are islands really that different? Auk 112:503–507.

FAABORG, J., W. J. ARENDT, AND K. M. DUGGER. 2000. The Guanica, Puerto Rico, bird monitoring project. Bird Populations 5:102–111.

FAABORG, J., W. J. ARENDT, AND K. M. DUGGER. 2004 (*this volume*). Bird population studies in Puerto Rico using mist nets: General patterns and comparisons with point counts. Studies in Avian Biology 29:144–150.

FAABORG, J., W. J. ARENDT, AND M. S. KAISER. 1984. Rainfall correlates of bird population fluctuations in a Puerto Rican dry forest: A nine year study. Wilson Bulletin 96: 557–595.

FAABORG, J., AND J. E. WINTERS. 1979. Winter resident returns and resident longevity and weights of Puerto Rican birds. Bird-Banding 50:216–223.

FAANES, C. A., AND D. BYSTRAK. 1981. The role of observer bias in the North American Breeding Bird Survey. Studies in Avian Biology 6:353–359.

FINCH, D. M., AND P. W. STANGEL (EDITORS). 1993. Status and management of Neotropical migrant birds. USDA Forest Service Gen. Tech. Rep. RM-GTR-229. USDA Forest Service Rocky Mountain Research Station, Ft. Collins, CO.

FOWLER, J., AND L. COHEN. 1986. Statistics for ornithologists, 2nd ed. British Trust for Ornithology, Thetford, U.K.

FRANCIS, C. M., AND D. J. T. HUSSELL. 1998. Changes in numbers of land birds counted in migration at Long Point Bird Observatory, 1961–1997. Bird Populations 4:37–66.

FUJIWARA, M, AND H. CASWELL. 2002. A general approach to temporary emigration in mark–recapture analysis. Ecology 83:3266–3275.

FULLER, R. J. 1987. Comparison and structure of bird communities in Britain. Ph.D. dissertation. University of London, London, U.K.

FULLER, R. J. 1995. Bird life of woodland and forest. Cambridge University Press, Cambridge, U.K.

FULLER, R. M., G. B. GROOM, A. R. JONES, AND A. G. THOMSON. 1993. Countryside Survey 1990. Mapping the land cover of Great Britain using Landsat imagery: A demonstrator project in remote sensing. Institute for Terrestrial Ecology, Abbots Ripton, Huntingdon, U.K.

FULLER, R. J., AND J. H. MARCHANT. 1985. Species-specific problems of cluster analysis in British mapping censuses. Pp. 83–86 in K. Taylor, R. J. Fuller, and P. C. Lack (editors). Bird census and atlas studies. Proceedings VIII international conference on bird census and atlas work. British Trust for Ornithology, Tring, U.K.

FULLER, R. M., G. M. SMITH, J. M. SANDERSON, R. A. HILL, A. G. THOMSON, R. COX, N. J. BROWN, R. T. CLARKE, P. ROTHERY, AND F. F. GERARD. 2002. Land cover map 2000. Final Report. Centre for Ecology and Hydrology, Abbots Ripton, Huntingdon, U.K.

GANTNER, B., AND J. MADSEN. 2001. An examination of methods to estimate population size in wintering geese. Bird Study 48:90–101.

GARDALI, T., G. BALLARD, N. NUR, AND G. R. GEUPEL. 2000. Demography of a declining population of Warbling Vireos in Coastal California. Condor 102:601–609.

GATES, J. E., AND L. W. GYSEL. 1978. Avian nest dispersion and fledgling success in field-forest ecotones. Ecology 59:871–883.

GAUTHREAUX, S. A., JR. 1971. A radar and direct visual study of passerine spring migration in southern Louisiana. Auk 88:343–365.

GAUTHREAUX, S. A., JR. 1992. The use of weather radar to monitor long-term patterns of trans-Gulf migration in spring. Pp. 96–100 in J. M. Hagan, III, and D. W. Johnston (editors). Ecology and conservation of Neotropical migrant landbirds. Smithsonian Institution Press, Washington, D.C.

GAUTHREAUX, S. A., JR. 1994. Remote sensing of spatio-temporal patterns in bird migration. Journal für Ornithologie 135:504.

GAUTHREAUX, S. A., JR., AND C. G. BELSER. 1998. Displays of bird movements on the WSR-88D: Patterns and quantification. Weather and Forecasting 13:453–464.

GAUTHREAUX, S. A., JR., AND K. R. RUSSELL. 1998. Weather surveillance radar quantification of roosting Purple Martins in South Carolina. Wildlife Society Bulletin. 26:5–16.

GEISSLER, P. H. 1997. Review of The Monitoring Productivity and Survivorship (MAPS) Program. The Institute for Bird Populations, Point Reyes, CA.

GEISSLER, P. H., AND J. R. SAUER. 1990. Topics in route-regression analysis. Pp. 54–57 in J. R. Sauer, and S. Droege (editors). Survey designs and statistical methods for the estimation of avian population trends. U.S. Fish and Wildlife Service Biological Report, 90(1). U.S. Fish and Wildlife Service, Washington D.C.

GENTRY, A. H. 1990. Four Neotropical rainforests. Yale University Press, New Haven, CT.

GERRODETTE, T. 1987. A power analysis for detecting trends. Ecology 68:1364–1372,

GEUPEL, G. R., AND G. BALLARD. 2002. Wrentit (Chamaea fasciata). In A. Poole and F. Gill (editors). The Birds of North America, No. 654. The Birds of North America, Inc., Philadelphia, PA.

GEUPEL, G. R., AND D. F. DESANTE. 1990. Incidence and determinants of double brooding in Wrentits. Condor 92:67–75.

GIBBONS, D. W., J. B. REID, AND R. A. CHAPMAN. 1993. The new atlas of breeding birds in Britain and Ireland: 1988–91. T. and A. D. Poyser, London, U.K.

GONZALEZ-ALONSO, H., M. K. MCNICHOLL, P. B. HAMEL, M. ACOSTA, E. GODINEZ, J. HERNANDEZ, D. RODRIGUEZ, J. A. JACKSON, C. M. GREGO, R. D. MCRAE, AND J. SIROIS. 1992. A cooperative bird-banding project in Peninsula de Zapata, Cuba, 1988–1989. Pp. 131–142 in J. M. Hagan, III, and D. W. Johnston (editors). Ecology and conservation of Neotropical migratory landbirds. Smithsonian Institution Press, Washington, D.C.

GORDON, M. 1972. Reed Buntings on an Oxfordshire farm. Bird Study 19:81–90.

GRAM, W. K., AND J. FAABORG. 1997. Distribution of Neotropical migrant birds wintering in the El Cielo Biosphere Reserve, Tamaulipas, Mexico. Condor 99: 658–670.

GREEN, R. E. 1999. Diagnosing the causes of bird population declines using comparative methods: The value of data from ringing. Ringing and Migration 19 (supplement):S47–S56.

GREENBERG, R. 1992. Forest migrants in non-forest habitats on the Yucatan Peninsula. Pp. 273–286 in J. M. Hagan, III, and D. W. Johnston (editors). Ecology and conservation of Neotropical migratory landbirds. Smithsonian Institution Press, Washington, D.C.

GREENWOOD, J. J. D., S. R. BAILLIE, H. Q. P. CRICK, J. H. MARCHANT, AND W. J. PEACH. 1993. Integrated population monitoring: Detecting the effects of diverse changes. Pp. 267–342 in R. W. Furness and J. J. D. Greenwood (editors). Birds as monitors of environmental change. Chapman and Hall, London, U.K.

GREENWOOD, P. J. 1980. Mating systems, philopatry and dispersal in birds and mammals. Animal Behaviour 28: 1140–1160.

GROSCH, K. 1995. Die Nahrungszusammensetzung rastender Kleinvögel auf der Halbinsel Mettnau. M.S. thesis. University of Bayreuth, Bayreuth, Germany.

HAGAN, J. M., III, AND D. W. JOHNSTON (EDITORS). 1992. Ecology and conservation of Neotropical migratory landbirds. Smithsonian Institution Press, Washington, D.C.

HAGAN, J. M., III, T. L. LLOYD-EVANS, J. L. ATWOOD, AND D. S. WOOD. 1992. Long-term changes in migratory landbirds in the northeastern United States: Evidence from migration capture data. Pp. 115–130 in J. M. Hagan, III, and D. W. Johnston (editors). Ecology and conservation of Neotropical migrant landbirds. Smithsonian Institution Press, Washington, D.C.

HALL, G. A. 1981. Fall migration patterns of wood warblers in the southern Appalachians. Journal of Field Ornithology 52:43–49.

HANOWSKI, J. M., J. G. BLAKE, G. J. NIEMI, AND P. T. COLLINS.

1993. Effects of extremely low frequency electromagnetic fields on breeding and migrating birds. American Midland Naturalist 129:96–115.

HARRISON, N. M., M. J. WHITEHOUSE, P. A. PRINCE, AND N. HUIN. 2000. What problems do local habitat change represent for the Constant Effort Site ringing scheme? Ringing and Migration 20:1–8.

HEIMERDINGER, M. A., AND R. C. LEBERMAN 1966. The comparative efficiency of 30 and 36 mm mesh in mist nets. Bird-Banding 37:280–286.

HELMS, C. W, AND W. H. DRURY. 1960. Winter and migratory weight and fat: Field studies on some North American buntings. Bird-Banding 31:1–40.

HERZOG, S. K., M. KESSLER, AND T. M. CAHILL. 2002. Estimating species richness of tropical bird communities from rapid assessment data. Auk 119:49–769.

HESTBECK, J. B., J. D. NICHOLS, AND K. A. MALECKI. 1991. Estimate of movement and site fidelity using mark–resight data of wintering Canada Geese. Ecology 72:523–533.

HILDÉN, O., AND J. SHARROCK. 1982. Recent changes in the status of European birds. Lintumies 17:150–160.

HILTON, B., JR., AND M. W. MILLER. 2003. Annual survival and recruitment in a Ruby-throated Hummingbird population, excluding the effect of transient individuals. Condor 105:54–62.

HINES, J. E. 1994. MSSURVIV user's manual. USGS Patuxent Wildlife Research Center, Laurel, MD.

HINES, J. E., T. BOULINIER, J. D. NICHOLS, J. R. SAUER, AND K. H. POLLOCK. 1999. COMDYN: Software to study the dynamics of animal communities using a capture–recapture approach. Bird Study 46 (Supplement):209–217.

HINES, J. E., W. L. KENDALL, AND J. D. NICHOLS. 2003. On the use of the robust design with transient capture–recapture models. Auk 120:1151–1158.

HOSMER, D. W., AND S. LEMESHOW. 2000. Applied logistic regression, 2nd ed. John Wiley, New York, NY.

HOWELL, S. N. G., AND S. WEBB. 1995. A guide to the birds of Mexico and northern Central America. Oxford University Press, Oxford, U.K.

HULL, B., P. BLOOM, AND THE NORTH AMERICAN BANDING COUNCIL. 2001. The North American banders' manual for raptor banding techniques. North American Banding Council Publications Committee, Point Reyes Station, CA. Available through <http://www.nabanding.net/nabanding/pubs.html> (29 September 2003).

HUMPLE, D., AND G. R. GEUPEL. 2002. Autumn populations of birds in riparian habitat of California's Central Valley. Western Birds 33:35–50.

HUSSELL, D. J. T. 1981. The use of migration counts for monitoring bird population levels. Studies in Avian Biology 6:92–102.

HUSSELL, D. J. T. 1982. Migrations of the Yellow-bellied Flycatcher in southern Ontario. Journal of Field Ornithology 53:223–234.

HUSSELL, D. J. T. 1991. Fall migrations of Alder and Willow flycatchers in southern Ontario. Journal of Field Ornithology 62:260–270.

HUSSELL, D. J. T. 2004 (this volume). Determining productivity indices from age composition of migrants captured for banding: Problems and possible solutions. Studies in Avian Biology 29:82–91.

HUSSELL, D. J. T., M. H. MATHER, AND P. H. SINCLAIR. 1992. Trends in numbers of tropical- and temperate-wintering migrant landbirds in migration at Long Point, Ontario, 1961–88. Pp. 101–114 in J. M. Hagan, III, and D. W. Johnston (editors). Ecology and conservation of Neotropical migrant landbirds. Smithsonian Institution Press, Washington, D.C.

HUSSELL, D. J. T., AND C. J. RALPH. 1998. Recommended methods for monitoring bird populations by counting and capture of migrants. <http://www.fs.fed.us/psw/topics/wildlife/birdmon/pif/migmon.html> (29 September 2003).

HUTTO, R. L., S. M. PLETSCHET, AND P. HENDRICKS. 1986. A fixed-radius point count method for non-breeding and breeding season use. Auk 103:593–602.

JENNI, L., M. LEUENBERGER, AND F. RAMPAZZI. 1996. Capture efficiency of mist nets with comments on their role in the assessment of passerine habitat use. Journal of Field Ornithology 67:263–274.

JENNI, L., AND R. WINKLER. 1994. Moult and ageing of European passerines. Academic Press, London, U.K.

JOHNSON, M. D., AND G. R. GEUPEL. 1996. The importance of productivity to the dynamics of a Swainson's Thrush population. Condor 98:133–141.

JOHNSON, N. K. 1972. Origin and differentiation of the avifauna of the Channel Islands, California. Condor 74:295–315.

JOLLY, G. M. 1965. Explicit estimates from capture–recapture data with both death and immigration: Stochastic model. Biometrika 52:225–247.

KAISER, A. 1992. Fat deposition and theoretical flight range of small autumn migrants in southern Germany. Bird Study 39:96–110.

KAISER, A. 1993a. A new multi-category classification of subcutaneous fat deposits of songbirds. Journal of Field Ornithology 64:246–255.

KAISER, A. 1993b. Rast- und Durchzugsstrategien mitteleuropäischer Singvögel. Analysen von Fang- und Wiederfangdaten von Fangstationen zur Beschreibung der Ökophysiologie und Verhaltens rastender Populationen. Ph.D dissertation. University of Konstanz, Konstanz, Germany.

KAISER, A. 1995. Estimating turnover, movements and capture parameters of resting passerines in standardized capture–recapture studies. Journal of Applied Statistics 22:1039–1047.

KAISER, A. 1996. Zugdisposition mitteleuropäischer Kleinvögel: Mauser, Körpermasse, Fettdeposition und Verweildauer. Journal für Ornithologie 137:141–180.

KAISER, A., AND H.-G. BAUER. 1994. Zur Bestimmung der Populationsgröße von Brutvögeln mit der Fang-Wiederfang-Methode und gängigen Kartierungsmethoden. Vogelwarte 37:206–231.

KAISER, A., AND P. BERTHOLD. 1995. Population trends of resting migratory passerines at the Mettnau Peninsula, Germany: First annual report of the MRI-program (1992 and 1993). Bird Populations 2:127–135.

KAISER, A., AND P. BERTHOLD. 2004 (*this volume*). A European example of standardized mist netting in population studies of birds. Studies in Avian Biology 29:75–81.

KANYAMIBWA, S., A. SCHIERER, R. PRADEL, AND J.-D. LEBRETON. 1990. Changes in adult annual survival rates in a western European population of the White Stork *Ciconia ciconia*. Ibis 132:27–35.

KARR, J. R. 1976. Seasonality, resource availability, and community diversity in tropical bird communities. American Naturalist 110:973–994.

KARR, J. R. 1979. On the use of mist nets in the study of bird communities. Inland Bird Banding 51:1–10.

KARR, J. R. 1981a. Surveying birds with mist nets. Studies in Avian Biology 6:62–67.

KARR, J. R. 1981b. Surveying birds in the tropics. Studies in Avian Biology 6:548–553.

KARR, J. R. 1990. The avifauna of Barro Colorado Island and the Pipeline Road, Panama. Pp. 183–198 *in* A. H. Gentry (editor). Four Neotropical forests. Yale University Press, New Haven, CT.

KARR, J. R., J. D. NICHOLS, M. K. KLIMKIEWICZ, AND J. D. BRAWN. 1990a. Survival rates of birds of tropical and temperate forests: Will the dogma survive? American Naturalist 136:277–291.

KARR, J. R., S. K. ROBINSON, J. G. BLAKE, AND R. O. BIERREGAARD, JR. 1990b. The birds of four Neotropical forests. Pp. 237–272 *in* A. H. Gentry (editor). Four Neotropical forests. Yale University Press, New Haven, CT.

KARR. J. R., D. W. SCHEMSKE, AND N. V. L. BROKAW. 1982. Temporal variation in the understory bird community of a tropical forest. Pp. 441–453 *in* E. G. Leigh, A. S. Rand, and D. M. Windsor (editors). The ecology of a tropical forest: Seasonal rhythms and longer-term changes. Smithsonian Institution Press, Washington, D.C.

KASPAREK, M. 1981. Die Mauser der Singvögel Europas: ein Feldführer. Dachverband Deutscher Avifaunisten, Lengede, Germany.

KEAST, A., AND E. S. MORTON (EDITORS). 1980. Migrant birds in the Neotropics: Ecology, behavior, distribution, and conservation. Smithsonian Institution Press, Washington, D.C.

KENDALL, W. L., AND R. BJORKLAND. 2001. Using open robust design models to estimate temporary emigration from capture–recapture data. Biometrics 57:1113–1122.

KENDALL, W. L., AND J. D. NICHOLS. 2002. Estimating state-transition probabilities for unobservable states using capture–recapture–resighting data. Ecology 83:3276–3284.

KENDALL, W. L., J. D. NICHOLS, AND J. E. HINES. 1997. Estimating temporary emigration and breeding proportions using capture–recapture data with Pollock's robust design. Ecology 78:563–578.

KENDALL, W. L., K. H. POLLOCK, AND C. BROWNIE. 1995. A likelihood-based approach to capture–recapture estimation of demographic parameters under the robust design. Biometrics 51:293–308.

KENDALL, W. L., J. R. SAUER, J. D. NICHOLS, R. PRADEL, AND J. E. HINES. 2004 (*this volume*). On the use of capture–recapture models in mist-net studies. Studies in Avian Biology 29:173–181.

KRICHER, J. C., AND W. E. DAVIS. 1992. Patterns of avian species richness in disturbed and undisturbed habitats in Belize. Pp. 24–246 *in* J. M. Hagan, III, and D. W. Johnston (editors). Ecology and conservation of Neotropical migratory landbirds. Smithsonian Institution Press, Washington, D.C.

KUENZI, A. J., F. R. MOORE, AND T. R. SIMONS. 1991. Stopover of Neotropical landbird migrants on East Ship Island following trans-Gulf migration. Condor 93: 869–883.

LACK, D. 1966. Population studies of birds. Oxford University Press, Oxford, U.K.

LANCIA, R. A., J. D. NICHOLS, AND K. H. POLLOCK. 1994. Estimating the number of animals in wildlife populations. Pp. 215–253 *in* T. A. Bookhout (editor). Research and management techniques for wildlife and habitats. The Wildlife Society, Bethesda, MD.

LATTA, S. C., AND J. FAABORG. 2001. Winter site fidelity of Prairie Warblers in the Dominican Republic. Condor 103:455–468.

LATTA, S. T., AND J. FAABORG. 2002. Demographic and population responses of Cape May Warblers wintering in multiple habitats. Ecology 83:2502–2515.

LEBRETON, J.-D., K. P. BURNHAM, J. CLOBERT, AND D. R. ANDERSON. 1992. Modeling survival and testing biological hypotheses using marked animals: A unified approach with case studies. Ecological Monographs 62:67–118.

LEBRETON, J.-D., J. E. HINES, R. PRADEL, J. D. NICHOLS, AND J. A. SPENDELOW. 2003. The simultaneous estimation by capture–recapture of accession to reproduction and dispersal-fidelity in a multisite system. Oikos 101: 253–264.

LEFEBVRE, G., B. POULIN, AND R. MCNEIL. 1992. Abundance, feeding behavior, and body condition of nearctic warblers wintering in Venezuelan mangroves. Auk 104:400–412.

LEFEBVRE, G., B. POULIN, AND R. MCNEIL. 1994. Temporal dynamics of mangrove bird communities in Venezuela with special reference to migrant warblers. Auk 111: 405–415.

LEVEY, D. J. 1988. Tropical wet forest treefall gaps and distributions of understory birds and plants. Ecology 69: 1076–1089.

LINK, W. A., R. J. BARKER, J. R. SAUER, AND S. DROEGE. 1994. Within-site variability in surveys of wildlife populations. Ecology 75:1097–1108.

LINK, W. A., AND J. D. NICHOLS. 1994. On the importance of sampling variance to investigations of temporal variation in animal population size. Oikos 69:539–544.

LINK, W. A., AND J. R. SAUER. 1994. Estimating equation estimates of trends. Bird Populations 2:23–32.

LITTELL, R. C., G. A. MILLIKEN, W. W. STROUP, AND R. D. WOLFINGER. 1996. SAS system for mixed models. SAS Institute Inc., Cary, NC.

LOERY, G., K. H. POLLOCK, J. D. NICHOLS, AND J. E. HINES. 1987. Age-specificity of avian survival rates: An analysis of capture–recapture data for a Black-capped Chickadee population, 1958–1983. Ecology 68:1038–1044.

LOISELLE, B. A., AND J. G. BLAKE. 1991. Temporal variation in birds and fruits along an elevational gradient in Costa Rica. Ecology 72:180–193.

LOPEZ DE CASENAVE, J., J. P. PELOTTO, S. M. CAZIANI, M. MERMOZ, AND J. PROTOMASTRO. 1998. Responses of avian assemblages to a natural edge in a Chaco semiarid forest in Argentina. Auk 115:425–435.

LORIA, D. E., AND F. R. MOORE. 1990. Energy demands of migration on Red-eyed Vireos, *Vireo olivaceus*. Behavioral Ecology 1:24–35.

LOWERY, G. H. 1946. Evidence of trans-Gulf migration. Auk 63:175–211.

LYNCH, J. F. 1989. Distribution of over wintering nearctic migrants in the Yucatan Peninsula, I: General patterns of occurrence. Condor 91:515–544.

LYNCH, J. F. 1992. Distribution of over wintering nearctic migrants in the Yucatan Peninsula, II: Use of native and human-modified vegetation. Pp. 178–196 *in* J. M. Hagan, III, and D. W. Johnston (editors). Ecology and conservation of Neotropical migratory landbirds. Smithsonian Institution Press, Washington, D.C.

MACHADO, R. B., AND G. A. B. DA FONSECA. 2000. The avifauna of Rio Doce Valley, southeastern Brazil, a highly fragmented area. Biotropica 32:914–924.

MACKENZIE, D. I., AND W. L. KENDALL. 2002. How should detection probability be incorporated into estimates of relative abundance? Ecology 83:2387–2393.

MÄDLOW, W. 1994. Die Habitatwahl auf dem Wegzug rastender Kleinvögel in einer norddeutschen Uferzone. Acta Ornithoecologica 3:57–72.

MAGURRAN, A. E. 1988. Ecological diversity and its measurement. Princeton University Press, Princeton, NJ.

MALIZIA, L. R. 2001. Seasonal fluctuations of birds, fruits, and flowers in a subtropical forest of Argentina. Condor 103:45–61.

MALLORY, E. P., AND N. V. L. BROKAW. 1993. Birds of Rio Bravo Conservation and Management Area, Belize. Manomet Bird Observatory, Manomet, MA.

MALLORY, E. P., N. BROKAW, AND S. C. HESS. 2004 (*this volume*). Coping with mist-net capture-rate bias: Canopy height and several extrinsic factors. Studies in Avian Biology 29:151–160.

MALLORY, E. P., A. C. VALLELY, AND N. V. L. BROKAW. 1998. Rapid Bird Assessment of the Rio Bravo Conservation and Management Area, Belize. A project of Wings of the Americas. The Nature Conservancy, Arlington, VA.

MANLEY, P. 1993. U.S. Forest Service goals and programs for monitoring Neotropical migratory birds. Pp. 252–257 *in* D. M. Finch and P. W. Stangel (editors). Status and management of Neotropical migratory birds. USDA Forest Service Gen. Tech. Rep. RM-229. USDA Forest Service Rocky Mountain Research Station, Ft. Collins, CO.

MARCHANT, J. H. 1992. Recent trends in breeding populations of some common trans-Saharan migrant birds in northern Europe. Ibis 134 (supplement 1):113–119.

MARCHANT, J. H., R. HUDSON, S. P. CARTER, AND P. WHITTINGTON. 1990. Population trends in British Breeding Birds. Maund and Irvine, Ltd., and British Trust for Ornithology, Tring, U.K.

MARTIN, T. E., AND G. R. GEUPEL. 1993. Nest-monitoring plots: Methods for locating nests and monitoring success. Journal of Field Ornithology 64:507–519.

MARTIN, T. E., AND KARR, J. R. 1986. Temporal dynamics of Neotropical birds with special reference to frugivores in second-growth woodlands. Wilson Bulletin 98:38–60.

MASON, D. 1996. Responses of Venezuelan understory birds to selective logging, enrichment strips, and vine cutting. Biotropica 28:296–309.

MAWSON, P. 2000. Sex bias or sampling bias? What you see isn't necessarily what you get. Eclectus 8:12–14.

MILLER, M. W., A. ARADIS, AND G. LANDUCCI. 2003. Effects of fat reserves on annual apparent survival of blackbirds *Turdus merula*. Journal of Animal Ecology 73:127–132.

MILLS, E. D., AND D. T. ROGERS. 1992. Ratios of Neotropical migrant and Neotropical resident birds in winter in a citrus plantation in central Belize. Journal of Field Ornithology 63:109–240.

MOORE, F. R., AND P. KERLINGER. 1987. Stopover and fat deposition by North American wood-warblers (Parulinae) following spring migration over the Gulf of Mexico. Oecologia 74:47–54.

MOORE, F. R., AND P. KERLINGER. 1991. Nocturnality, long distance migration, and ecological barriers. Acta XX Congressus Internationalis Ornithologici:1122–1129.

MOORE, F. R., P. KERLINGER, AND T. R. SIMONS. 1990. Stopover on a Gulf coast barrier island by spring trans-Gulf migrants. Wilson Bulletin. 102:487–500.

MOORE, F. R., AND T. R. SIMONS. 1992. Habitat suitability and the stopover ecology of Neotropical passerine migrants. Pp. 345–355 *in* J. M. Hagan, III, and D. W. Johnston (editors). Ecology and conservation of Neotropical migrant landbirds. Smithsonian Institution Press, Washington, D.C.

MURPHY, M. T., K. L. CORNELL, AND K. L. MURPHY. 1998. Winter bird communities on San Salvador, Bahamas. Journal of Field Ornithology 69:402–414.

MURRAY, B. G., JR. 1966. Migration of age and sex classes of passerines on the Atlantic coast in autumn. Auk 83:352–360.

NAYLOR, A., AND R. GREEN. 1976. Timing of fledging and passage of juvenile Reed Warblers. Wicken Fen Group Report 8:15–18.

NEMAC, A. F. L. 1991. Power analysis handbook for the design and analysis of forestry trials. W. A. Bergerud (editor). Biometrics information handbook, 2. British Columbia Ministry of Forests, Victoria, BC.

NETER, J., AND W. WASSERMAN. 1974. Applied linear statistical models. Richard D. Irwin, Inc., Homewood, IL.

NETER, J., W. WASSERMAN, AND M. H. KUTNER. 1990. Applied linear statistical models: Regression, analysis of variance, and experimental designs, 3rd ed. Richard D. Irwin, Inc., Homewood, IL.

NICE, M. M. 1937. Studies in the life history of the Song Sparrow. Volume I. Transactions of the Linnean Society of New York 4:1–247.

NICHOLS, J. D. 1992. Capture–recapture models: Using marked animals to study population dynamics. BioScience 42:94–102.

NICHOLS, J. D. 1994. Capture–recapture methods for bird population studies. Proceedings of the Italian Ornithological Congress 6:31–51.

NICHOLS, J. D. 1996. Sources of variation in migratory movements of animal populations: Statistical inference and a selective review of empirical results for birds. Pp. 147–197 in O. E. Rhodes, R. K. Chesser, and M. H. Smith (editors). Spatial and temporal aspects of population processes. University of Chicago Press, Chicago, IL.

NICHOLS, J. D., T. BOULINIER, J. E. HINES, K. H. POLLOCK, AND J. R. SAUER. 1998a. Estimating rates of local extinction, colonization and turnover in animal communities. Ecological Applications 8:1213–1225.

NICHOLS, J. D., T. BOULINIER, J. E. HINES, K. H. POLLOCK, AND J. R. SAUER. 1998b. Inference methods for spatial variation in species richness and community composition when not all species are detected. Conservation Biology 12:1390–1398.

NICHOLS, J. D., C. BROWNIE, J. E. HINES, K. H. POLLOCK, AND J. B. HESTBECK. 1993. The estimation of exchanges among populations or subpopulations. Pp. 265–279 in J.-D. Lebreton and P. N. North (editors). Marked individuals in the study of bird populations. Birkhäuser Verlag, Berlin, Germany.

NICHOLS, J. D., AND M. J. CONROY. 1996. Estimation of species richness. Pp. 226–234 in D. E. Wilson, J. D. Nichols, R. Rudran, F. R. Cole, and M. S. Foster (editors). Measuring and monitoring biodiversity: Standard methods for mammals. Smithsonian Institution Press, Washington, D. C.

NICHOLS, J. D., AND J. E. HINES. 2002. Approaches for the direct estimation of lambda, and demographic contributions to lambda, using capture–recapture data. Journal of Applied Statistics 29:539–568.

NICHOLS, J. D., J. E. HINES, J.-D. LEBRETON, AND R. PRADEL. 2000. Estimation of contributions to population growth: A reverse-time capture–recapture approach. Ecology 81: 3362–3376.

NICHOLS, J. D., AND W. L. KENDALL. 1995. The use of multistate capture–recapture models to address questions in evolutionary ecology. Journal of Applied Statistics 22: 835–846.

NICHOLS, J. D., T. S. SILLETT, J. E. HINES, AND R. T. HOLMES. In press. Approaches for the direct estimation of rate of increase in population size using capture–recapture data. In C. J. Ralph and T. D. Rich (editors). Bird conservation implementation and integration in the Americas. Proceedings of the third international Partners in Flight conference 2002. USDA Forest Service Gen. Tech. Rep. PSW-191. USDA Forest Service Pacific Southwest Research Station, Albany, CA.

NORTH AMERICAN BANDING COUNCIL. 2001a. The North American banders' study guide. North American Banding Council Publications Committee, Point Reyes Station, CA. Available through <http://www.nabanding.net/nabanding/pubs.html> (29 September 2003).

NORTH AMERICAN BANDING COUNCIL. 2001b. The North American banders' manual for banding passerines and near passerines (excluding hummingbirds and owls). North American Banding Council Publications Committee. Point Reyes Station, CA. Available through <http://www.nabanding.net/nabanding/pubs.html> (29 September 2003).

NORTH AMERICAN BANDING COUNCIL. 2001c. The instructor's guide to training passerine bird banders in North America. North American Banding Council Publications Committee. Point Reyes Station, CA. Available through <http://www.nabanding.net/nabanding/pubs.html> (29 September 2003).

NOTT, M. P., AND D. F. DESANTE. 2002. Demographic monitoring and the identification of transients in mark–recapture models. Pp. 727–736 in J. M. Scott, P. J. Heglund, M. L. Morrison, J. B. Haufler, M. G. Rafael, W. A. Wall, and F. B. Samson (editors). Predicting species occurrences: Issues of accuracy and scale. Island Press, Covello, CA.

NOTT, M. P., D. F. DESANTE, R. B. SIEGEL, AND P. PYLE. 2002. Influences of the El Niño/Southern Oscillation and the North Atlantic Oscillation on avian productivity in forests of the Pacific Northwest of North America. Global Ecology and Biogeography 11:333–342.

NUR, N., AND G. R. GEUPEL. 1993a. Validating the use of constant effort mist-netting to monitor avian populations. Report of the Point Reyes Bird Observatory to Office of Migratory Bird Management, U.S. Fish and Wildlife Service, Laurel, MD. (Available from PRBO, Stinson Beach, CA 94970.)

NUR, N., AND G. R. GEUPEL. 1993b. Evaluating mist-netting, nest-searching and other methods of monitoring demographic processes in landbird populations. Pp. 237–244 in D. M. Finch, and P. W. Stangel (editors). Status and management of Neotropical migratory birds. USDA Forest Service Gen. Tech. Rep. RM-229. USDA Forest Service Rocky Mountain Research Station, Ft. Collins, CO.

NUR, N., G. R. GEUPEL, AND G. BALLARD. 1995. Validating the use of constant effort mist-netting to monitor avian populations. II: Studies of Song Sparrows, Wrentits and other species. Report by Point Reyes Bird Observatory to U.S. Fish and Wildlife Service, Office of Migratory Bird Management. (Available from PRBO, 4990 Shoreline Highway, Stinson Beach, CA 94970).

NUR, N., G. R. GEUPEL, AND G. BALLARD. 2000. The use of constant-effort mist-netting to monitor demographic processes in passerines: Annual variation in survival, productivity, and floaters. Pp. 185–194 in R. Bonney, D. N. Pashley, R. J. Cooper, and L. Niles (editors). Strategies for bird conservation: The Partners in Flight planning process. USDA Forest Service Proceedings RMRS-P-16. USDA Forest Service Rocky Mountain Research Station, Ogden, UT.

NUR, N., G. R. GEUPEL, AND G. BALLARD. 2004 (this volume). Estimates of adult survival, capture probability, and recapture probability: Evaluating and validating constant-effort mist netting. Studies in Avian Biology 29:63–70.

NUR, N., S. L. JONES, AND G. R. GEUPEL. 1999. A statistical guide to data analysis of avian monitoring programs. U.S.

Fish and Wildlife Service Biol. Tech. Publ. BTP-R6001-1999. Department of the Interior, Washington, D.C.

O'CONNOR, R. J., AND R. J. FULLER. 1984. A re-evaluation of the aims and methods of the Common Birds Census. BTO Research Report No. 15. British Trust for Ornithology, Thetford, U.K.

O'CONNOR, R. J., AND J. H. MARCHANT. 1981. A field validation of some Common Birds Census techniques. BTO Research Report No. 4. British Trust for Ornithology, Thetford, U.K.

OTIS, D. L., K. P. BURNHAM, G. C. WHITE, AND D. R. ANDERSON. 1978. Statistical inference from capture data on closed animal populations. Wildlife Monographs, No. 62.

PAGEN, R. W., F. R. THOMPSON, III, AND D. E. BURHANS. 2002. A comparison of point-count and mist-net detections of songbirds by habitat and time-of-season. Journal of Field Ornithology 73:53–59.

PARDIECK, K., AND R. B. WAIDE. 1992. Mesh size as a factor in avian community studies using mist nets. Journal of Field Ornithology 63:250–255.

PEACH, W. J. 1993. Combining mark–recapture data sets for small passerines. Pp. 107–122 in J.-D. Lebreton, and P. M. North (editors). Marked individuals in the study of bird populations. Birkhäuser Verlag, Basel, Switzerland.

PEACH, W. J., AND S. R. BAILLIE. 1990. Population changes on constant effort sites, 1988–1989. BTO News 167:6–7.

PEACH, W. J., AND S. R. BAILLIE. 1993. Population changes on Constant Effort Sites 1991–92. BTO News 186:10–12.

PEACH, W. J., AND S. R. BAILLIE. 1994. Implementation of the Mountford indexing method for the Common Birds Census. Pp. 653–662 in W. Hagemeijer and T. Verstrael (editors). Bird numbers 1992: Distribution, monitoring and ecological aspects. Proceedings of 12th international conference of the International Bird Census Committee and European Ornithological Atlas Committee. SOVON, Beek-Ubbergen, The Netherlands.

PEACH, W. J., AND S. R. BAILLIE. 2004 (this volume). Estimating adult survival rates from between-year recaptures in the British Trust for Ornithology Constant Effort Sites scheme. Studies in Avian Biology 29:71–74.

PEACH, W. J., S. R. BAILLIE, AND D. E. BALMER. 1998. Long-term changes in the abundance of passerines in Britain and Ireland as measured by constant effort mist-netting. Bird Study 45:257–275.

PEACH, W. J., S. R. BAILLIE, AND S. T. BUCKLAND. 2004 (this volume). Current practices in the British Trust for Ornithology Constant Effort Sites scheme and comparisons of temporal changes in mist-net captures with changes in spot-mapping counts at the extensive scale. Studies in Avian Biology 29:46–56.

PEACH, W. J., S. R. BAILLIE, AND L. UNDERHILL. 1991. Survival of British Sedge Warblers Acrocephalus schoenobaenus in relation to west African rainfall. Ibis 133:300–305.

PEACH, W. J., S. T. BUCKLAND, AND S. R. BAILLIE. 1990. Estimating survival rates using mark–recapture data from multiple ringing sites. Ring 13:87–102.

PEACH, W. J., S. T. BUCKLAND, AND S. R. BAILLIE. 1996. The use of constant effort mist-netting to measure between-year changes in the abundance and productivity of common passerines. Bird Study 43:142–156.

PEACH, W. J., H. Q. P. CRICK, AND J. H. MARCHANT. 1995. The demography of the decline in the British Willow Warbler population. Journal of Applied Statistics 22:905–922.

PEACH, W. J., C. R. DU FEU, AND J. M. MCMEEKING. 1995. Site tenacity and survival rates of wrens and treecreepers in a Nottinghamshire wood. Ibis 137:497–507.

PEACH, W. J., G. M. SIRIWARDENA, AND R. D. GREGORY. 1999. Long-term changes in over-winter survival rates explain the decline of Reed Buntings in Britain. Journal of Applied Ecology 36:798–811.

PEARSON, D. L. 1971. Vertical stratification in birds in a tropical dry forest. Condor 73:46–55.

PERRINS, C. 1979. British tits. New Naturalist, Collins, London, U.K.

PETERJOHN, B. G., AND J. R. SAUER. 1993. North American Breeding Bird Survey annual summary 1990–1991. Bird Populations 1:1–15.

PETIT, D. R., L. J. PETIT, AND K. G. SMITH. 1992. Habitat associations of migratory birds overwintering in Belize, Central America. Pp. 247–256 in J. M. Hagan, III, and D. W. Johnston (editors). Ecology and conservation of Neotropical migrant landbirds. Smithsonian Institution Press, Washington, D.C.

PLEDGER, S. 2000. Unified maximum likelihood estimates for closed capture–recapture models using mixtures. Biometrics 56:434–442.

POLLOCK, K. H. 1982. A capture–recapture design robust to unequal probability of capture. Journal of Wildlife Management 46:757–760.

POLLOCK, K. H., J. D. NICHOLS, C. BROWNIE, AND J. E. HINES. 1990. Statistical inference for capture–recapture experiments. Wildlife Monographs, No. 107.

POLLOCK, K. H., J. D. NICHOLS, T. R. SIMONS, G. L. FARNSWORTH, L. L. BAILEY, AND J. R. SAUER. 2002. The design of large scale wildlife monitoring studies. Envirometrics 13:1–15.

POULIN, B., G. LEFEBVRE, AND R. MCNEIL. 1993. Variations in bird abundance in tropical arid and semi-arid habitats. Ibis 135:432–441.

POULSEN, B. O. 1996. Relationships between frequency of mixed-species flocks, weather and insect activity in a montane cloud forest in Ecuador. Ibis 138:466–470.

PRADEL, R. 1993. Flexibility in survival analysis from recapture data: Handling trap-dependence. Pp. 29–37 in J.-D. Lebreton, and P. M. North (editors). Marked individuals in the study of bird populations. Birkhäuser Verlag, Basel, Switzerland.

PRADEL, R. 1996. Utilization of capture–mark–recapture for the study of recruitment and population growth rate. Biometrics 52:703–709.

PRADEL, R., J. CLOBERT, AND J.-D. LEBRETON. 1990. Recent developments for the analysis of capture–recapture multiple data sets. Ring 13:193–204.

PRADEL, R., J. E. HINES, J.-D. LEBRETON, J. D. NICHOLS, AND A. VIALLEFONT. 1997. Capture–recapture survival models taking account of transients. Biometrics 53:60–72.

PRADEL, R., AND J.-D. LEBRETON. 1999. Comparison of different approaches to the study of local recruitment of breeders. Bird Study 46 (Supplement):74–81.

PRADEL, R., C. M. A. WINTREBERT, AND O. GIMINEZ. 2003. A proposal for a goodness-of-fit test to the Arnason-Schwarz multisite capture–recapture model. Biometrics 59:43–53.

PRATT, A. M., AND W. J. PEACH. 1991. Site tenacity and annual survival of a Willow Warbler *Phylloscopus trochilus* population in southern England. Ringing and Migration 12:128–134.

PYLE, P. 1997. Identification guide to North American birds, Part 1, Columbidae to Ploceidae. Slate Creek Press, Bolinas, CA.

PYLE, P., N. NUR, AND D. F. DESANTE. 1994. Trends in nocturnal migrant landbird populations at southeast Farallon Island, California, 1968–1992. Studies in Avian Biology 15:58–74.

PYLE, P., N. NUR, R. P. HENDERSON, AND D. F. DESANTE. 1993. The effects of weather and lunar cycle on nocturnal migration of landbirds at Southeast Farallon Island, California. Condor 95:343–361.

PYLE, P., S. N. G. HOWELL, R. P. YUNICK, AND D. F. DESANTE. 1987. Identification guide to North American passerines. Slate Creek Press, Bolinas, CA.

RALPH, C. J. 1971. An age differential of migrants in coastal California. Condor 73:243–246.

RALPH, C. J. 1976. Standardization of mist net captures for quantification of avian migration. Bird-Banding 47:44–47.

RALPH, C. J. 1978. The disorientation and possible fate of young passerine coastal migrants. Bird-Banding 49:237–247.

RALPH, C. J. 1981. Age ratios and their possible use in determining autumn routes of passerine migrants. Wilson Bulletin 93:164–188.

RALPH, C. J., E. H. DUNN, W. J. PEACH, AND C. M. HANDEL. 2004a (*this volume*). Recommendations for the use of mist nets for inventory and monitoring of bird populations. Studies in Avian Biology 29:187–196.

RALPH, C. J., G. R. GEUPEL, P. PYLE, T. E. MARTIN, AND D. F. DESANTE. 1993. Handbook of field methods for monitoring landbirds. USDA Forest Service Gen. Tech. Rep. PSW-144. USDA Forest Service, Pacific Southwest Research Station, Albany, CA. <http://www.fs.fed.us/psw/publications/gtrs.shtml≥ (29 September 2003).

RALPH, C. J., AND K. HOLLINGER. 2003. The status of the Willow and Pacific-slope flycatchers in northwestern California and southern Oregon. Studies in Avian Biology 26:104–117.

RALPH, C. J., K. HOLLINGER, AND S. L. MILLER. 2004b (*this volume*). Monitoring productivity with multiple mist-net stations. Studies in Avian Biology 29:12–20.

RALPH, C. J., J. R. SAUER, AND S. DROEGE (EDITORS). 1995. Monitoring bird populations by point counts. USDA Forest Service Gen. Tech. Rep. PSW-GTR-149. USDA Forest Service Pacific Southwest Research Station, Albany, CA.

RAMSEY, F. L., V. WILDMAN, AND J. ENGBRING. 1987. Covariate adjustments to effective area in variable-area wildlife surveys. Biometrics 43:1–11.

RAPPOLE, J. H., W. J. MCSHEA, AND J. VEGA RIVERA. 1993. Evaluation of two survey methods in upland avian breeding communities. Journal of Field Ornithology 64:55–70.

RAPPOLE, J. H., AND M. A. RAMOS. 1995. Determination of habitat requirements for migratory birds. Pp. 235–241 in M. H. Wilson, and S. A. Sader (editors). Conservation of Neotropical migratory birds in Mexico. Maine Agricultural and Forest Experiment Station, Miscellaneous Publication 727. Orono, ME.

RAPPOLE, J. H., M. A. RAMOS, R. J. OEHLENSCHLAGER, D. W. WARNER, AND C. P. BARKAN. 1979. Timing of migration and route selection in North American songbirds. Pp. 199–214 in D. L. Drawe (editor). Proceedings first Welder Wildlife Foundation symposium. Welder Wildlife Foundation, Sinton, TX.

RAPPOLE, J. H., AND D. W. WARNER. 1976. Relationships between behavior, physiology and weather in avian transients at a migration stopover site. Oecologia 26:193–212.

RAPPOLE, J. H., K. WINKER, AND G. V. N. POWELL. 1998. Migratory bird habitat use in southern Mexico: Mist nets versus point counts. Journal of Field Ornithology 69:635–643.

REMSEN, J. V., JR. 1994. Use and misuse of bird lists in community ecology and conservation. Auk 111:225–227.

REMSEN, J. V., JR., AND D. A. GOOD. 1996. Misuse of data from mist-net captures to assess relative abundance in bird populations. Auk 113:381–398.

REMSEN, J. V., JR., AND T. A. PARKER, III. 1983. Contribution of river-created habitats to bird species richness in Amazonia. Biotropica 15:223–231.

REXSTAD, E., AND K. P. BURNHAM. 1991. User's guide to interactive program CAPTURE. Department of Biology and Wildlife, University of Alaska, Fairbanks, AK.

RICHARDSON, W. J. 1978. Timing and amount of bird migration in relation to weather: A review. Oikos 30:224–272.

RIMMER, C. C., S. D. FACCIO, T. L. LLOYD-EVANS, AND J. M. HAGAN, III. 2004 (*this volume*). A comparison of constant-effort mist netting results at a coastal and inland New England site during migration. Studies in Avian Biology 29:123–134.

ROBBINS, C. S., B. A. DOWELL, D. K. DAWSON, J. A. COLÓN, R. ESTRADA, A. SUTTON, R. SUTTON, AND D. WEYER. 1992. Comparison of Neotropical migrant landbird populations wintering in tropical forest, isolated forest fragments, and agricultural habitats. Pp. 207–220 in J. M. Hagan, III, and D. W. Johnston (editors). Ecology and conservation of Neotropical migrant landbirds. Smithsonian Institution Press, Washington, D.C.

ROBBINS, C. S., J. R. SAUER, R. S. GREENBERG, AND S. DROEGE. 1989. Population declines in North American birds that migrate to the Neotropics. Proceedings of the National Academy of Sciences (USA) 86:7658–7662.

ROBINSON, S. K., AND J. TERBORGH. 1990. Bird communities of the Cocha Cashu Biological Station in Amazonian Peru. Pp. 199–216 in A. H. Gentry (editor). Four Neotropical forests. Yale University Press, New Haven, CT.

ROSENBERG, D. K. 1997. Evaluation of the statistical properties of the Monitoring Avian Productivity and Survivorship (MAPS) Program. The Institute for Bird Populations, Point Reyes Station, CA.

ROSENBERG, D. K., D. F. DeSANTE, AND J. E. HINES. 2000. Monitoring survival rates of landbirds at varying spatial scales: an application of the MAPS program. Pp. 178–184 in R. Bonney, D. N. Pashley, R. J. Cooper, and L. Niles (editors). Strategies for bird conservation: the Partners in Flight planning process. USDA Forest Service Gen. Tech. Rep. RMRS-P-16. USDA Forest Service Rocky Mountain Research Station, Ogden, UT.

ROSENBERG, D. K., D. F. DeSANTE, K. S. McKELVEY, AND J. E. HINES. 1999. Monitoring survival rates of Swainson's Thrush Catharus ustulatus at multiple spatial scales. Bird Study 46 (Supplement):198–208.

ROSENSTOCK, S. S., D. R. ANDERSON, K. G. KIESEN, T. LEUKERING, AND M. F. CARTER. 2002. Landbird counting techniques: Current practices and an alternative. Auk 119:46–53.

ROTH, R. R., AND R. K. JOHNSON. 1993. Long-term dynamics of a Wood Thrush population breeding in a forest fragment. Auk 110:37–48

RUSSELL, S. M., R. O. RUSSELL, AND THE NORTH AMERICAN BANDING COUNCIL. 2001. The North American banders' manual for banding hummingbirds. North American Banding Council Publications Committee, Point Reyes Station, CA. Available through <http://www.nabanding.net/nabanding/pubs.html> (29 September 2003).

SAS INSTITUTE. 1985. SAS user's guide: Statistics, Version 5. SAS Institute Inc., Cary, NC.

SAS INSTITUTE. 1988. SAS user's guide: Statistics, 5th ed. SAS Institute Inc., Carey, NC.

SAS INSTITUTE. 1993. SAS companion for the OS/2 environment, Version 6, 2nd ed. SAS Institute Inc., Cary, NC.

SAS INSTITUTE. 1996. SAS/STAT user's guide (Release 6.03). SAS Institute Inc.

SAS INSTITUTE. 1999. SAS statistical software (Release 8.0). SAS Institute Inc., Cary, NC.

SAUER, J. R., J. E. HINES, I. THOMAS, J. FALLON, AND G. GOUGH. 2000. The North American Breeding Bird Survey, results and analysis 1966–1999. Version 98.1. USGS Patuxent Wildlife Research Center, Laurel, MD.

SAUER, J. R., AND W. A. LINK. 2004 (this volume). Some consequences of using counts of birds banded as indices to populations. Studies in Avian Biology 29:168–172.

SCHAUB, M., R. PRADEL, L. JENNI, AND J.-D. LEBRETON. 2001. Migrating birds stop over longer than usually thought: An improved capture–recapture analysis. Ecology 82:852–859.

SCHWARZ, C. J. 1993. Estimating migration rates using tag recovery data. Pp. 255–264 in J.-D. Lebreton and P. M. North (editors). Marked individuals in the study of bird populations. Birkhäuser Verlag, Berlin, Germany.

SCHWARZ, C. J., AND A. N. ARNASON. 1996. A general methodology for the analysis of capture–recapture experiments in open populations. Biometrics 52:860–873

SCHWARZ, C. J., J. F. SCHWEIGERT, AND A. N. ARNASON. 1993. Estimating migration rates using tag-recovery data. Biometrics 49:177–193

SCHWARZ, C. J., AND G. A. F. SEBER. 1999. Estimating animal abundance: Review III. Statistical Science 14:427–456.

SCHWARZ, C. J., AND W. T. STOBO. 1997. Estimating temporary migration using the robust design. Biometrics 53:178–194.

SEBER, G. A. F. 1965. A note on the multiple-recapture census. Biometrika 52:249–259.

SEBER, G. A. F. 1982. The estimation of animal abundance and related parameters. Macmillan, New York, NY.

SENAR, J. C., M. J. CONROY, AND A. BORRAS. 2002. Asymmetric exchange between populations differing in habitat quality: A metapopulation study on the Citril Finch. Journal of Applied Statistics 29:425–441.

SENAR, J. C., J. DOMÈNECH, AND M. J. CONROY. 1999. Funnel traps capture a higher proportion of juvenile Great Tits Parus major than automatic traps. Ringing and Migration 19:257–259.

SHEALER, D. A., AND S. W. KRESS. 1994. Post-breeding movements and prey selection of Roseate Terns at Stratton Island, Maine. Journal of Field Ornithology. 65:349–362.

SILKEY, M., N. NUR, AND G. R. GEUPEL. 1999. The use of mist-net capture rates to monitor annual variation in abundance: A validation study. Condor 101:288–298.

SIMONS, T. R., F. R. MOORE, AND S. A. GAUTHREAUX. 2004 (this volume). Mist netting trans-Gulf migrants at coastal stopover sites: The influence of spatial and temporal variability on capture data. Studies in Avian Biology 29:135–143.

SIMONS, T. R., S. A. PEARSON, AND F. R. MOORE. 2000. Application of spatial models to the stopover ecology of trans-Gulf migrants. Studies in Avian Biology 20:4–14.

SIRIWARDENA, G. M., S. R. BAILLIE, S. T. BUCKLAND, R. M. FEWSTER, J. H. MARCHANT, AND J. D. WILSON. 1998. Trends in the abundance of farmland birds: A quantitative comparison of smoothed Common Birds Census indices. Journal of Applied Ecology 35:24–43.

SKALSKI, J. R., AND D. S. ROBSON. 1992. Techniques for wildlife investigation: Design and analysis of capture data. Academic Press, Inc., New York, NY

SNEDECOR, G. W., AND W. G. COCHRAN. 1967. Statistical methods, 6th ed. Iowa State University Press, Ames, IA.

SOGGE, M. K., J. C. OWEN, E. H. PAXTON, S. M. LANGRIDGE, AND T. J. KORONKIEWICZ. 2001. A targeted mist net capture technique for the Willow Flycatcher. Western Birds 32:167–172.

SPENDELOW, J. A., J. D. NICHOLS, J. E. HINES, J.-D. LEBRETON, AND R. PRADEL. 2002. Modeling post-fledging survival and age-specific breeding probabilities in species with delayed maturity: A case study of Roseate Terns at Falkner Island, Connecticut. Journal of Applied Statistics 29:385–405

SPENDELOW, J. A., J. D. NICHOLS, I. C. T. NISBET, H. HAYS, G. D. CORMONS, J. BURGER, C. SAFINA, J. E. HINES, AND M. GOCHFELD. 1995. Estimating annual survival and movement rates within a metapopulation of Roseate Terns. Ecology 76:2415–2428.

STAMM, D. D., D. E. DAVIS, AND C. S. ROBBINS. 1960. A

method of studying wild bird populations by mist-netting and banding. Bird-Banding 31:115–130.

STANLEY, T. R., AND K. P. BURNHAM. 1998. Estimator selection for closed-population capture–recapture. Journal of Agricultural, Biological, and Environmental Statistics 3: 31–150.

STATACORP. 1997. Stata statistical software: Release 5.0. Stata Corporation, College Station, TX.

STEIDL, R. J., AND L. THOMAS. 2001. Power analysis and experimental design. Pp. 14–26 in Scheiner, S. and J. Gurevitch (editors). Design and analysis of ecological experiments, 2nd ed. Oxford University Press, Oxford, U.K.

STILES, F. G. 1983. Chapter 10. Birds. Introduction. Pp. 502–530 in D. H. Janzen (editor). Costa Rican natural history. University of Chicago Press, Chicago, IL.

STILES, F. G., AND A. F. SKUTCH. 1989. A guide to the birds of Costa Rica. Cornell University Press, Ithaca, NY.

STOUFFER, P. C., AND R. O. BIERREGAARD. 1995. Use of Amazonian forest fragments by understory insectivorous birds. Ecology 76:2429–2445.

STREIF, M. 1991. Analyse der Biotopppräferenzen auf dem Wegzug in Süddeutschland rastender Kleinvögel. Ornithologische Jahreshefte für Baden-Württemberg 7: 1–132.

STUTCHBURY, B., AND S. ZACK. 1992. Delayed breeding in avian social systems: The role of territory quality and floater tactics. Behaviour 123:194–219.

SVENSSON, L. 1992. Identification guide to European passerines. Lars Svensson, Stockholm, Sweden.

SWINEBROAD, J. 1964. Net-shyness and Wood Thrush populations. Bird-Banding 35:196–202.

SYSTAT. 1998. SYSTAT 8.0 statistics. SPSS Inc., Chicago, IL.

TEMPLE, S. A., AND J. A. WIENS. 1989. Bird populations and environmental changes: Can birds be bio-indicators? American Birds 43:260–270.

TERBORGH, J. 1983. Five New World primates: A study in comparative ecology. Princeton University Press, Princeton, NJ.

TERBORGH, J. 1985. The role of ecotones in the distribution of Andean birds. Ecology 66:1237–1246.

TERBORGH, J. 1989. Where have all the birds gone? Essays on the biology and conservation of birds that migrate to the American tropics. Princeton University Press, Princeton, NJ.

TERBORGH, J., AND J. FAABORG. 1973. Turnover and ecological release in the avifauna of Mona Island, Puerto Rico. Auk 90:759–779.

THIBODEAU, M. D. 1999. Analysis of mist net tier capture frequencies in a coastal California riparian habitat. North American Bird Bander 24:3–5.

THIOLLAY, J.-M. 1994. Structure, density, and rarity in an Amazonia rainforest bird community. Journal of Tropical Ecology 10:449–481.

THOMAS, L. 1997. Evaluation of statistical methods for estimating long-term population change from extensive wildlife surveys. Ph.D. dissertation. University of British Columbia, Vancouver, BC.

THOMAS, L., G. R. GEUPEL, N. NUR, AND G. BALLARD. 2004

(this volume). Optimizing the allocation of count days in a migration monitoring program. Studies in Avian Biology 29:97–111.

THOMAS, L., AND K. MARTIN. 1996. The importance of analysis method for Breeding Bird Survey population trend estimates. Conservation Biology 10:479–490.

THOMPSON, W. L. 2002. Towards reliable bird surveys: Accounting for individuals present but not detected. Auk 119:18–25.

THOMSON, D. L., S. R. BAILLIE, AND W. J. PEACH. 1997. The demography and age-specific annual survival of Song Thrushes during periods of population stability and decline. Journal of Animal Ecology 66:414–424.

THOMSON, D. L., S. R. BAILLIE, AND W. J. PEACH. 1999. A method for studying post-fledging survival rates using data from ringing recoveries. Bird Study 46 (supplement):104–111.

TUCKER, G. M. AND M. F. HEATH. 1994. Birds in Europe: Their conservation status. BirdLife International (BirdLife Conservation Series 3), Cambridge, U.K.

VANSTEENWEGAN, C., G. HÉMERY, AND E. PASQUET. 1990. Une réflexion sur le programme français du suivi temporel du niveau d'abondance des populations d'oiseaux terrestres communs (S.T.O.C.). Alauda 58:36–44.

VEGA RIVERA, J. H., J. H. RAPPOLE, W. J. MCSHEA AND C. A. HAAS. 1998. Wood Thrush postfledging movements and habitat use in northern Virginia. Condor 100:69–78.

VERNER, J. 1985. Assessment of counting techniques. Current Ornithology 2:247–302.

WAIDE, R. B. 1980. Resource partitioning between migrant and resident birds: The use of irregular resources. Pp. 337–352 in A. Keast and E. S. Morton (editors). Migrant birds in the Neotropics: Ecology, behavior, distribution, and conservation, Smithsonian Institution Press, Washington, D.C.

WAIDE, R. B. 1991. The effect of Hurricane Hugo on bird populations in the Luquillo Experimental Forest Puerto Rico. Biotropica. 23(4 Part A):475–480.

WALLACE, G. E., H. G. ALONZO, M. K. MCNICHOLL, D. R. BATISTA, R. O. PRIETO, A. L. SOSA, B. S. ORIA, AND E. A. H. WALLACE. 1996. Winter surveys of forest-dwelling Neotropical migrant and resident birds in three regions of Cuba. Condor 98:745–768.

WANG, Y., AND D. M. FINCH. 2002. Consistency of mist netting and point counts in assessing landbird species richness and relative abundance during migration. Condor 104:59–72.

WASSENAAR, L., AND K. A. HOBSON. 2001. A stable-isotope approach to delineate geographical catchment areas of avian migration monitoring stations in North America. Environmental Science and Technology 35: 1845–1850.

WHITACRE, D. F., J. MADRID M., C. MARROQUIN, M. SCHULTZE, L. JONES, J. SUTTER, AND A. J. BAKER. 1993. Migrant songbirds, habitat change, and conservation prospects in northern Peten, Guatemala: Some initial results. Pp. 339–345 in D. M. Finch, and P. W. Stangel (editors). Status and management of migratory birds. USDA Forest Service Gen. Tech. Rept. RM-229. USDA Forest

Service Rocky Mountain Forest and Range Experimental Station, Ft. Collins, CO.

WHITAKER, A. H. 1972. An improved mist net rig for use in forests. Bird-Banding 43:1–8.

WHITE, G. C., D. R. ANDERSON, K. P. BURNHAM, AND D. L. OTIS. 1982. Capture–recapture and removal methods for sampling closed populations. LA-8787-NERP, Los Alamos National Laboratory, Los Alamos, NM.

WHITE, G. C., AND K. P. BURNHAM. 1999. Program MARK: Survival estimation from populations of marked animals. Bird Study 46 (supplement):120–139.

WHITMAN, A. A. 2004 (this volume). Use of mist nets for study of Neotropical bird communities. Studies in Avian Biology 29:161–167.

WHITMAN, A. A., J. H. HAGAN, III, AND N. V. L. BROKAW. 1995. A comparison of two bird survey techniques in a sub-tropical forest. Manomet Bird Observatory, Manomet, MA.

WHITMAN, A. A., J. M. HAGAN, III, AND N. V. L. BROKAW. 1997. A comparison of two bird survey techniques used in a subtropical forest. Condor 99:955–965.

WILKINSON, L. 1990. SYSTAT: The system for statistics. SYSTAT, Inc., Evanston, IL.

WILL, T. 1991. Birds of a severely hurricane-damaged Atlantic coast rain forest in Nicaragua. Biotropica. 23(4 Part A):497–507.

WILLIAMS, B. K., J. D. NICHOLS, AND M. J. CONROY. 2002. Analysis and management of animal populations. Academic Press, New York, NY.

WILLIAMS, T. C., J. M. WILLIAMS, P. G. WILLIAMS, AND P.

STOKSTAD. 2001. Bird migration through a mountain pass studied with high resolution radar, ceilometers, and census. Auk 118:389–403.

WILSON, M. S., AND S. A. SADER (EDITORS). 1995. Conservation of Neotropical migratory birds in Mexico. Maine Agricultural and Forest Experimental Station, Miscellaneous Publication 727. Orono, ME.

WILSON, R. R., AND R. S. ALLAN. 1996. Mist netting from a boat in forested wetlands. Journal of Field Ornithology 67:82–85.

WINSTANLEY, D., R. SPENCER, AND K. WILLIAMSON. 1974. Where have all the Whitethroats gone? Bird Study 21: 1–14.

WOODFORD, J., AND D. J. T. HUSSELL. 1961. The use of a Heligoland trap and mist-nets at Long Point, Ontario. Bird-Banding 32:115–125.

WOODWORTH, B. L., J. FAABORG, AND W. J. ARENDT. 1999. Survival and longevity of the Puerto Rican Vireo. Wilson Bulletin 111:376–380.

WUNDERLE, J. M., JR. 1995. Responses of bird populations in a Puerto Rico forest to Hurricane Hugo: The first 18 months. Condor 97:879–896.

YOUNG, B. E., D. DEROISER, AND G. V. N. POWELL. 1998. Diversity and conservation of understory birds in the Tilaran Mountains, Costa Rica. Auk 115:998–1016.

ZAR, J. H. 1984. Biostatistical analysis, 2nd ed. Prentice-Hall, Englewood Cliffs, NJ.

ZINK, G. 1973–1985. Der Zug europäischer Singvögel. Ein Atlas der Wiederfunde beringter Vögel. Vol. 1–4. Vogelzug Verlag, Möggingen, Germany.